Informational Writing Mini-Lessons

Your Go-To Guide for Flexible, High-Impact Instruction

170+ Lessons

by Erik Lepis, Michelle Stone, and Kirsten Widmer

Contents

Why We Wrote This Book

We developed this book because we've been there—we are former classroom teachers who have felt that thirst to dip into a deep well of lessons for teaching informational writing. That's why we went with a "more is more" approach, providing 171 lessons so you have options for a wide range of students.

The lessons in this book address various genres of informational writing, one of the most important text types your students will learn to write. They also support students at a range of developmental stages, from Kindergarten through sixth grade. Each lesson is designed with your busy schedule in mind, and includes these features among others:

- the ideal genre(s) for the strategy presented
- suggested developmental stage(s)
- concise and explicit teaching language
- cross-references to other augmenting lessons
- tips for making the learning stick

Michelle

Kirsten

In each lesson, we took a flexible approach to teaching, prioritizing one of four different methods while still offering alternative approaches for instruction. This feature is critical to our vision because so many of the teachers with whom we work have conveyed frustration with ready-made lessons that didn't differentiate for students—or for teachers. So you will discover, in most lessons, recommendations and alternative options for:

Demonstration when you sense that students need explicit modeling

Explain with Examples when you want students to learn from experts

Guided Practice when you think your students are ready to join in

Inquiry when students have enough background knowledge to construct their own meaning

These four options help you scaffold instruction so you can be responsive to the needs of your unique class. The options also help you forge a path between the complexity of a particular strategy and students' current writing abilities.

And last but not least, the resource is also built on a deep trust in you—in your desire to bring each lesson to life with your own style, language, personal anecdotes, favorite mentor texts, and anchor charts. We hope it helps you build learning that is both personal and grounded in common understandings of the informational genre.

Sincerely,

Erik, Michelle, and Kirsten

LLN, The Living Literacy Network

www.thelivingliteracynetwork.com

How This Book Works

This book of lessons is organized by tabbed sections: **Engagement & Habits, Foundations & Conventions, Generate & Experiment, Choose & Refine, Plan & Develop, Draft & Revise, Edit & Proofread,** and **Present & Reflect.** Each section includes an At-a-Glance Guide of lesson topics that are generally ordered by complexity and loosely grouped by genre when possible. With each lesson, the At-a-Glance Guide indicates the genres and developmental stage(s) that are most appropriate for that lesson. The developmental stages of writers are generalized into three broad categories: Emergent, Transitional, and Fluent. See the chart below.

Developmental Stage	Descriptors	Typical Grade Levels
Emergent	• Use detailed illustrations with labels, phrases, or simple sentences to convey meaning.	Kindergarten, Early First Grade
Transitional	• Use sketches and multiple sentences to write with detail. • Use a variety of strategies to approximate words and spell many words correctly.	Late First, Second, Early Third Grade
Fluent	• Write with many details easily across paragraphs. • Use a large repertoire of strategies and spelling patterns to spell words with ease.	Late Third, Fourth, Fifth, Sixth Grade

Figure 1: Tab Template with Explanations

Engagement & Habits

Engagement & Habits

The series of lessons in this section address habits of writing that go beyond just informational writing. The lessons:

- can be used in any unit of study and can be dispersed throughout the unit;
- are especially useful in the beginning of the year, while getting a writing workshop up and running; and
- can be revisited throughout the year to ensure that engagement and good habits remain central to nurturing student growth.

Descriptors for High Levels of Engagement and Good Habits

Emergent Writers	Fluent Writers
• Keep writing in a 2-pocket folder—one side is designated for work in progress, while the other is for booklets that are finished "for now." • Use tools to support independence: alphabet, blend, and digraph charts; banks of high-frequency words; and small copies of anchor charts. • Build stamina for writing, beginning at 5 minutes and increasing to 30 minutes by year's end. • Increase the volume of writing, beginning with a single sheet of paper that includes an illustration and quickly moving to stapled booklets of 3 pages or more. • Write a simple sentence or two per day, moving toward 2 or more pages with 8-plus lines per day.	• Keep prewriting in a composition notebook and draft on loose-leaf paper stored in a folder or on a laptop. • Use tools to support independence: word banks, dictionaries, thesauruses, and small copies of anchor charts. • Build stamina for writing, beginning at 25 minutes and increasing to 45 minutes per sitting. • Aim for 1–2 full notebook or loose-leaf pages per day as the volume of writing.

 | 17

The first two sections: **Engagement & Habits** and **Foundations & Conventions** comprise lessons that can and should be taught throughout the writing process. The rest of the sections are dedicated to a phase in the writing process, offering lessons and also some nuances that might be present at certain grade levels.

At the front of each tab, we included indicators for emergent and fluent writers to provide you with a quick reference point for expectations in student performance.

Flexible Use

You can utilize this book for several different purposes:

- to create genre-based writing units
- to enhance current units
- to differentiate instruction
- to support other writing tasks

Create Genre-Based Writing Units

If you are using this book to create your own genre-based writing units or to enhance your current curriculum, the book works under the assumption that the writing process is the driving force of the unit. The writing process looks slightly different across the grades *(Figure 2)*. The primary writing process (K–2) is meant to be cyclical in nature, giving students multiple exposures to writing in a genre, building their stamina as writers, and most importantly, producing a high volume of writing. This means that emergent writers will have illustrated and written numerous booklets/texts before choosing one that moves on to the final stages of the writing process.

In the intermediate grades (3–5), the writing process is more linear in nature. The volume of writing will appear differently in each stage of the writing process. In the early phases, volume refers to notebook entries. Typically, in Grade 3, writers are able to fill one notebook page in a sitting; fifth graders may fill 2–3 pages per sitting. For drafting, volume refers to the number of sentences on a page, paragraphs written, or even time-on-task if a student is particularly engaged. However, it is important to note that a student should not produce only one piece of writing after a five week unit. Rather, a student could produce multiple drafts within a unit to allow for increased independence and improved skill at writing in a genre before choosing one to publish.

Figure 2: Writing Process

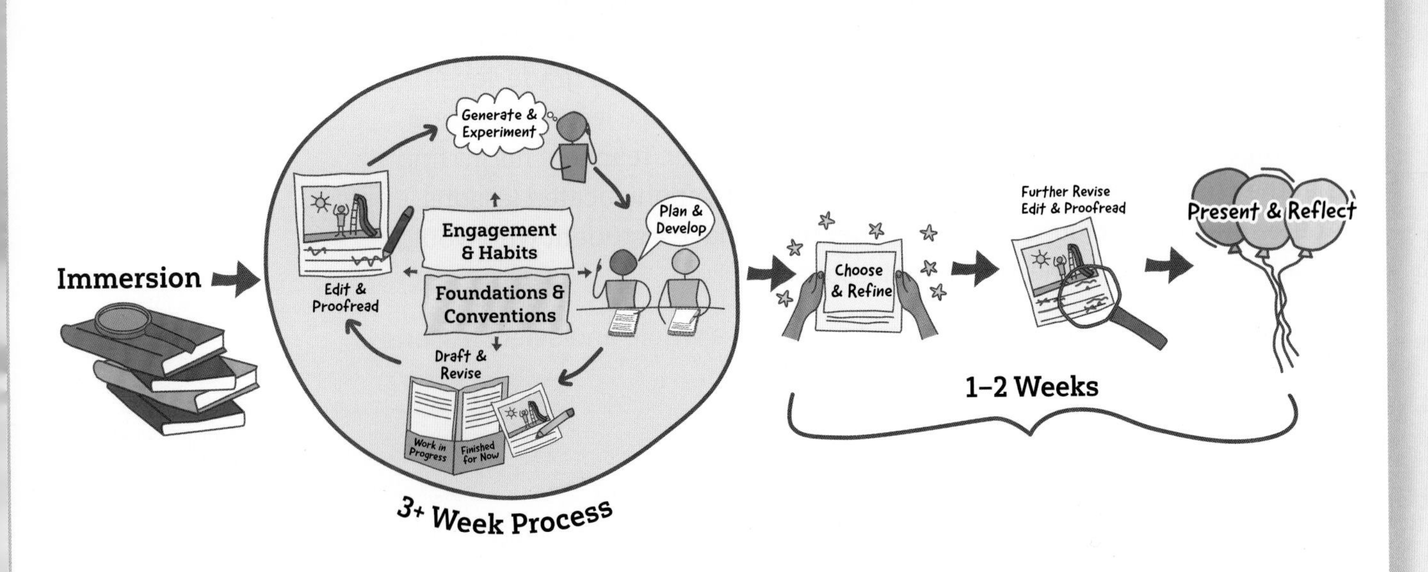

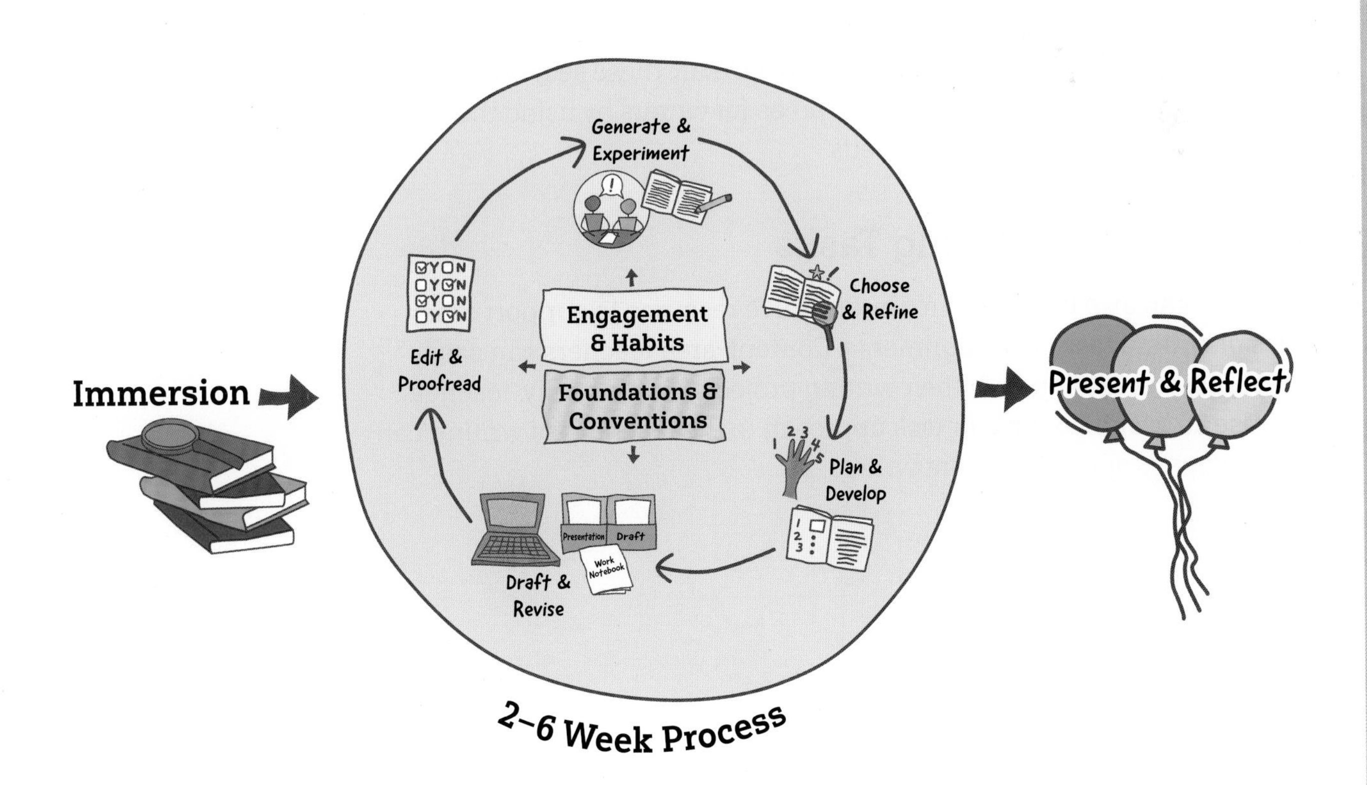

Enhance Current Units

In each tabbed section, you will find a series of lessons. Generally, the lessons move from least complex to most complex. Most of the time, if you are looking for a lesson for emergent writers, those lessons can be found toward the beginning of the section. There is an indicator that alerts you to the developmental stage of that lesson. There are no grade-level indicators because it's highly likely that teachers will use lessons ranging in complexity to meet the needs of individual writers. Teachers might find that they have a first grader who is ready for more sophisticated lessons. At the same time, a fourth-grade teacher might have a student who would benefit from some of the emergent lessons.

The vision is for teachers to look at their units as a whole and select lessons as needed to fill in any instructional gaps.

The four parts of the mini-lesson are separated into columns, with teaching moves at the top of each column, written in bold, and lesson language for teaching below. The gist of the lesson in bold allows for independent planning, whereas the plain text provides a sample lesson plan if needed.

Differentiate Instruction

The tabbed sections make it easy to find lessons that address needs in 1:1 conferences or in small groups because each section is organized by skill. Again, because the lessons generally progress from Emergent to Fluent, you will know where in the section to look to find relevant teaching points. For instance, you might have a specific group of students who need help planning with focus. In that case, the "Plan & Develop" section will have an array of lessons to choose from to map out a series of small-group lessons. If some students struggle to find ideas, you could go to the "Generate & Experiment" tabbed section to find support. Overall, these sections help you create a game plan that targets specific areas for writers by using the lessons you think will meet the students' needs.

Support Other Writing Tasks

This book can also be used as a dip-and-dive resource to support other types of writing tasks or assignments. Content-area teachers can easily access lessons to align with their writing projects. Additionally, teachers who use an assigned topic or task approach to the teaching of writing can find lessons to support student writers.

Figure 3: Lesson Template with Labels and Explanations

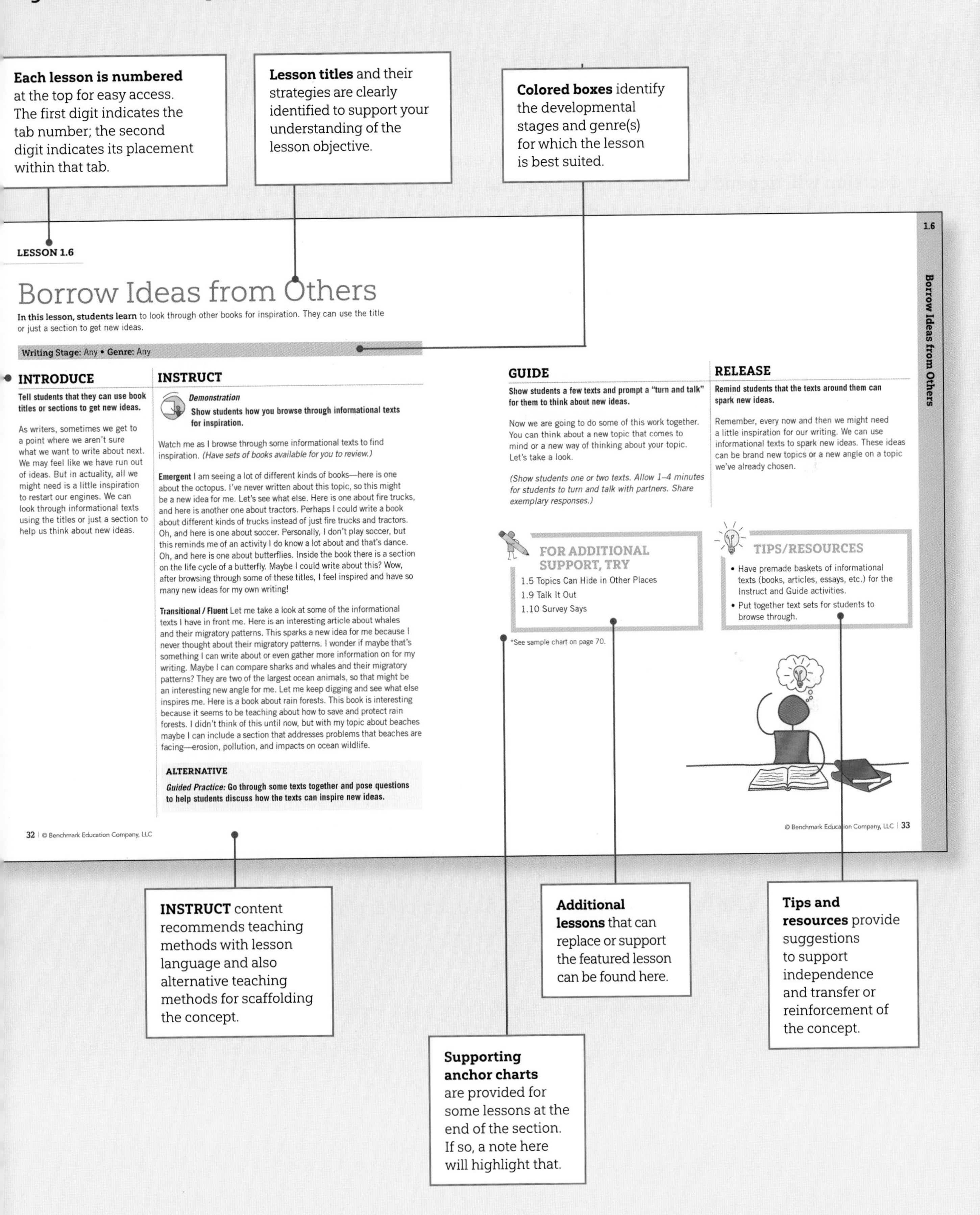

Intentional Teaching Methods

You might consider a variety of ways to teach each lesson. Making the decision will depend on the complexity of the strategy or concept, the level of scaffolding and support needed, and the method that will be most timely. These considerations make lessons effective and efficient. Each lesson offers suggestions using these teaching methods.

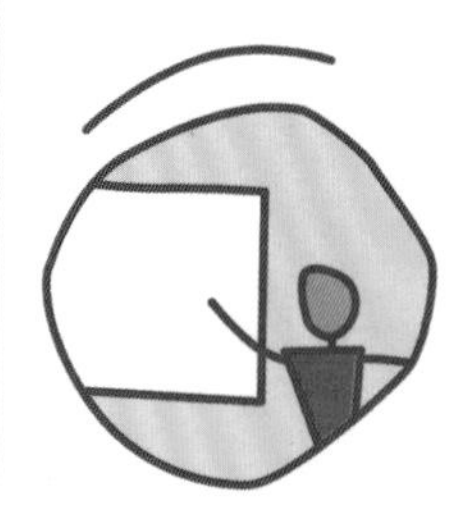

Demonstration

"Watch me as I show you how I do it in my writing" is a common refrain for your demonstration. *Demonstration* shows students how you utilize a strategy or technique while exposing your thought process as you go about your writing. Through "thinking out loud," you show your decision-making as you consider multiple possibilities before landing on the best choice. It also allows you to anticipate and front-load support for the struggles and challenges that your students will likely face when approaching their own writing.
(See Lesson 1.1 on pages 22–23 for a sample Demonstration lesson.)

Explain with Examples

"Let's take a look at a few examples." With this refrain, you display examples of writing and discuss the effect that a particular technique might have on the writing or on the reader. Examples can be pulled from a teacher model, writing produced by fellow classmates, or the writing of published authors. These examples are complete and ready to share before instruction, which saves time when models are too lengthy to write while students are watching. It is particularly powerful when a classmate's work is presented as a way to learn from peers.
(See Lesson 1.2 on pages 24–25 for a sample Explain with Examples lesson.)

Guided Practice

"Let's try it together," you might exclaim when guiding students through the steps of a strategy. Collaborating helps students brainstorm possibilities and make decisions collectively. When students coauthor in this way, the level of engagement is particularly high, as all students are participating while you synthesize responses. This method is beneficial if the strategy is relatively easy or familiar. With guided practice, you will have students brainstorm, then do some shared writing, interactive writing, or interactive editing. The three approaches are briefly described below:

Shared Writing

In shared writing, you write with the students and act as the scribe. Many or all of the ideas will come from the students as you guide, offer suggestions, combine ideas, and ask questions to provoke elaboration. Shared writing works in all forms, purposes, and genres of writing. However, in order for the students to contribute in meaningful ways, the topic must be based on shared experiences or content knowledge. Because you act as scribe, the students are able to focus their attention toward idea development, language, style, and other key features of the writing.

Interactive Writing

Interactive writing, much like shared writing, provides students with the opportunity to write with you. However, in this instructional approach you share the pen with the students. The act of "passing the pen" invites students to come to the front of the class and write parts of the composition. The rest of the class observes or participates on dry-erase boards. Most often, interactive writing focuses on conventions. With younger students, you might focus on listening for sounds in words, using appropriate capitalization, or including punctuation. With older students, interactive writing can be used for spelling patterns, using conjunctions and connectors, and punctuation.

Interactive Editing

Interactive editing also involves sharing the pen with students. However, here the focus is on editing rather than composing. Instead of facing a blank page, as is the case with interactive writing, in interactive editing the text is already written. The focus is on checking for errors and making corrections. Depending on the grade level, you might also decide to teach students proofreading marks in order for them to transfer that work to peer editing and proofreading each other's work. *(See Lesson 7.3 on pages 366–367 for a sample Guided Practice lesson.)*

Inquiry

"What do you notice the writer has done here?" A teacher will often ask this question during a guided inquiry while presenting a text. Students will uncover the techniques that an author has used and also how and why they are being used in a text. Inquiry is powerful because it allows students to investigate, draw conclusions, and discover for themselves how writers can learn from other writers. Inquiry is best for studying author's craft, complex sentence structures, and the appropriate use of conventions. *(See Lesson 1.21 on pages 62–63 for a sample Inquiry lesson.)*

Structuring the Lesson

Once you determine the teaching method that is best for students, organize your plan for the day. In this book, the lessons are structured using a mini-lesson format. A mini-lesson is a brief presentation to provide instruction in whole-class and small-group settings. You remind students of where they are in the writing process and offer a tip with some guidance on how to move forward. This tip is not an assignment but an offering of a helpful strategy, tool, or technique that students might try in their own writing when applicable. Since students are working with a variety of topics, are at different points in their writing projects, and above all, are developmentally different, every strategy or technique that you teach may not be applicable or useful to every student on a particular day. (Note: Forcing immediate application of the day's mini-lesson strategy may lead to confusion, frustration, or superficial technique application.)

Four-Part Structure

We recommend this four-part mini-lesson structure:

1. **Introduce**
2. **Instruct**
3. **Guide**
4. **Release**

INTRODUCE

(1–2 Minutes)

In the first part of the mini-lesson, you contextualize the new day's learning.

Then you directly state the day's lesson objective and discuss why a writer would use that particular technique and how it affects the development of the writing piece or its impact on the reader.

INSTRUCT

(3–5 Minutes)

In the second part of the mini-lesson, you apply one of four teaching methods—*Demonstration, Explain with Examples, Guided Practice, or Inquiry*—depending on the level of scaffolding needed, student engagement, and allotted time.

GUIDE

(2–4 Minutes)

In the third part of the mini-lesson, you guide students through a quick opportunity to process or attempt the technique together with you. During this time, students can: help add to your writing; contribute ideas for a shared writing; notice how a writer uses the strategy in a mentor text; try it on a dry-erase board or in their own writing; or, most often, name with a partner where they might attempt this strategy in their own writing. This is a crucial step to set students up for transfer, to assess understanding, and to provide time to work on speaking and listening skills.

RELEASE

(1 Minute)

In the final part of the mini-lesson, you reiterate the lesson focus and remind students of how this new learning fits into the writing process. Remind students that the day's lesson is also transferable to other writing projects throughout the unit and beyond. Then students go off to work independently on their own writing while you confer.

Pathways to Teaching Genre

Immerse students in a particular genre at the start of a unit of study. Immersion allows for students to see the "big picture" before the unit starts and to get a sense of how this kind of writing typically looks. To do this, gather a variety of texts and place them in specific areas in the classroom where they are accessible—bins or baskets, labeled bookshelves, or displayed on top of bookcases. Typically, immersion happens during reading, but it can also happen in writing during the first few days of a unit. You read aloud to students, first to enjoy the text, and then to notice specific aspects of the writing, including the features, structures, craft, and style. You can create genre bulletin boards and chart students' noticings to serve as a reference throughout the unit.

Immersion increases students' domain-specific vocabulary because they are exposed to terms related to writing and writing techniques, such as: expository writing, headings, compare and contrast structure, facts, statistics, onomatopoeia, etc.

Informational Genres

Information writing encompasses any genre of writing whose primary purpose is to inform the reader or convey information about a topic. Within any text type, whether it be narrative, informational, or opinion/argument, there exist many different genres and subgenres. The genre is the vehicle for presenting information. Although a genre cannot be reduced to a simple formula, it has common features that can be named and described. Many lessons in this book can be used across genres due to these similar features. However, some lessons are better suited to teaching particular genres rather than others. In the chart on page 15, the genres we highlight in this text are listed and described.

Helpful Terms

Text structure: how the overall text, or a section of a text, is organized (compare/contrast, cause/effect, etc.)

Text feature: components of a text that are generally not part of the main body (bold words, diagrams, sidebars, etc.)

Highlighted Genres

Genre	Description	Examples	Sample Titles
List Book	Descriptive list structure Title is the topic Broad or narrow in focus Pages name or describe an aspect of the topic Can grow with child's development: wordless, label, list, sentences	Wordless books Concept books (colors, numbers, shapes) Label books List books	*Exactly the Opposite* by T. Hoban (Greenwillow, 1997) *My First Library: Boxset of 10 Board Books for Kids* (Wonder House, 2018) *Freight Train* by D. Crews (Greenwillow, 2003) *National Geographic Readers: Go, Cub!* by S. B. Neuman (National Geographic Kids, 2014)
Pattern Book	Uses the same sentence pattern on most pages; 1–2 sentences per page About a single topic Uses many high-frequency words	Repeating Pattern See-Saw Pattern Question and Answer	*Reading Partners* by M. Dufresne (Pioneer Valley, 2004) *I Can Fly* by M. Dufresne (Pioneer Valley, 2014) *What Do You Do With a Tail Like This?* by S. Jenkins & R. Page (Clarion Books, 2008)
How-To Book	Follows a procedural structure Sequential steps to complete a task OR A descriptive list structure for ideas where the order is less important	Recipes Game instruction Routines Chores Hobbies Movements Construction	*Making Pancakes* by P. Sloan & S. Sloan (Sundance, 2000) *Making a Bug Habitat* by N. Lunis (Benchmark, 2002) *Wash Your Hands* by M. Sokoloff, S. Spellman, & T. Fuller (Wright Group, 2001) *Making Tortillas* by M. Freeman (National Geographic Society, 2003) *How to Read a Story* by K. Messner & M. Siegel (Chronicle, 2016)
All-About Book	Single topic with descriptive chapters Topics can be broad or focused, concrete or abstract Utilizes informational text features Derived from student expertise rather than research	Concrete and broad topics (e.g., school) Concrete and specific (e.g., soccer goalies) Abstract and broad (e.g., kindness) Abstract and specific (e.g., being a good friend)	*Apples* by G. Gibbons (Holiday House, 2001) *Penguins!* by A. Schreiber (National Geographic Kids, 2009) *My Soccer Book* by G. Gibbons (Collins, 2000) *Our Solar System* by S. Simon (Collins, 2014) *Sharks* by S. Simon (Collins, 2006)
Feature Article	Can use various informational text structures and features Explores a specific angle of a topic in-depth May include interviews, polling information, surveys	Behind-the-scenes accounts Profiles (historical or current day people, authors) Historical or cultural events Geographical areas or locations Scientific processes and concepts	*National Geographic for Kids* Magazine *Sports Illustrated Kids* Magazine *Time for Kids* (Time USA) *Scholastic News* (Scholastic) *Cobblestone* Magazine (Carus) *Faces* Magazine (Cricket Media) *OWL* Magazine (Bayard Canada)
Research Report	Research is divided into chapters, categories, or subcategories Can feel similar to a Feature Article or All-About Book	Informational reports (categories of information related to a topic) Analytical reports (attempts to solve problems or answer a question)	*Just the Facts: Writing Your Own Research Report* (Picture Window, 2009)
Biography	Teaches about a person's full life or a meaningful moment Organized sequentially Can take the form of biographical sketch, paragraph, or essay	Historical Current day Subject has had an impact or made a difference in the world or community	*Abe Lincoln: The Boy Who Loved Books* by K. Winters and N. Carpenter (Aladdin, 2003) *Can You Fly High, Wright Brothers?* by M. & G. Berger (Scholastic, 2006) *My First Biography ...* Series by M. D. Bauer (Scholastic) *Who Was? ...* Series by Various (Penguin Workshop)
Literary Nonfiction	Uses techniques typically associated with narrative or poetry writing Language and word choice create mood that is often absent in more traditional information writing Point of view can be first-, second-, or third-person	Life cycles Day in the life of ... Aspect of life (motherhood)	*Are You a Butterfly?* by J. Allen & T. Humphries (Kingfisher, 2000) *Read and Wonder ...* Series by Various (Candlewick Press) *Waiting for Ice* by S. Markle & A. Marks (Charlesbridge, 2012) *Over and Under the Pond* by K. Messner (Chronicle, 2017) *Creature Features: Twenty-Five Animals Explain Why They Look the Way They Do* by S. Jenkins (HMH Books, 2014)
Expository Nonfiction	Similar to All-About Book Utilizes different text structures Narrow in focus Often relies on research to elaborate or to provide statistics Writers strive to explain facts clearly rather than creatively	One aspect of a larger topic A more detailed, sophisticated, or comprehensive take on a larger topic	*Secrets of the Mummies* by H. Griffey (DK, 1998) *The Phases of the Moon* by G. Pendergast (Gareth Stevens, 2015) *Oh, Rats! The Story of Rats and People* by A. Marrin & C. B. Mordan (Penguin Group, 2006) *Shh! We're Writing the Constitution* by G. Fritz (Puffin, 1997) *If You Lived ...* Series by Various (Scholastic Paperbacks)
Expository Essay	Uses an essay structure Groups ideas logically, explaining ideas using evidence	Writing about reading Content-area writing Personal essays	*Surprising Sharks* by N. Davies (Candlewick Press, 2003)
Hybrid	Single, focused topic Mixes two or more genres from above in a single piece of writing	Literary Nonfiction including How-To Feature article with a Biography (biographical profile) Expository Nonfiction that includes a Literary Nonfiction story	*Pop! The Invention of Bubble Gum* by M. McCarthy (Simon and Schuster, 2010) *Magic School Bus ...* Series by J. Cole & B. Degen (Scholastic) *Grand Canyon* by J. Chin (Roaring Book Press, 2017) *Fry Bread* by K. N. Maillard (Roaring Book Press, 2019)

Tips for Making Every Lesson Great

1. **Chart your instruction.** Anytime your lesson has steps, strategic questioning, or rules, make an anchor chart that can act as a co-teacher. Color-code it, add visuals, and display it. You might even consider providing students with small copies of the charts to glue into their writer's notebooks, keep in their writing folders, or to add to a new folder exclusively for resources.

2. **Use the entire school day.** Reading, math, science, and social studies can all present opportunities to reinforce a skill or concept taught. Weave them in naturally to give students many at-bats to gain mastery. Content-area subjects are an ideal place to utilize shared writing and interactive writing practice.

3. **Engage in shared writing and interactive writing.** Both activities provide a wealth of opportunities to reinforce skills. Shared writing is helpful for idea development—from considering a text's structure to elaborating with details. Interactive writing is essential for reinforcing conventions, including capitalization, spelling, and punctuation.

4. **Make sure every child can see.** Write down definitions, descriptions, and examples. Use large, bold print so information is visible to children in the back of the classroom or off to the side. Be mindful of students with visual impairments, and of emergent readers, by keeping text in plain fonts without excessive use of colors or designs. Add visuals to serve as instant reminders.

5. **Coach through voice-overs.** As children turn and talk to practice during the Guide portion, listen carefully and voice over to steer students in the right direction when needed. Provide concise prompts, pose questions, and share exemplary responses to facilitate the conversations.

6. **Share exemplary responses.** Share out only the best answers (or mistakes that you feel children can learn from). Refrain from randomly calling on students without previewing their responses. Irrelevant or incorrect comments can confuse students. We want to send students off with correct information before they go off to work independently.

7. **Model with developmentally appropriate work.** Help students shoot for the stars yet keep expectations attainable. When you model, have your volume of writing match what your students can do developmentally—though it never hurts to nudge them a bit further. The same holds true for topics, vocabulary, and craft elements.

8. **Balance spelling expectations.** Balance wanting students to spell words correctly with knowing what is acceptable at different stages of development. While students are developing phonological awareness, it is best to encourage them to use what they know about letters and sounds. This may mean that some words are not perfectly spelled and that's okay. Furthermore, when students are choosing topics, drafting, and revising, let them focus on content. When publishing is close, focus on writing words correctly.

Engagement & Habits

The series of lessons in this section address habits of writing that go beyond just informational writing. The lessons:

- can be used in any unit of study and can be dispersed throughout the unit;
- are especially useful in the beginning of the year, while getting a writing workshop up and running; and
- can be revisited throughout the year to ensure that engagement and good habits remain central to nurturing student growth.

Descriptors for High Levels of Engagement and Good Habits

Emergent Writers	Fluent Writers
• Keep writing in a 2-pocket folder—one side is designated for work in progress, while the other is for booklets that are finished "for now." • Use tools to support independence: alphabet, blend, and digraph charts; banks of high-frequency words; and small copies of anchor charts. • Build stamina for writing, beginning at 5 minutes and increasing to 30 minutes by year's end. • Increase the volume of writing, beginning with a single sheet of paper that includes an illustration and quickly moving to stapled booklets of 3 pages or more. • Write a simple sentence or two per day, moving toward 2 or more pages with 8-plus lines per day.	• Keep prewriting in a composition notebook and draft on loose-leaf paper stored in a folder or on a laptop. • Use tools to support independence: word banks, dictionaries, thesauruses, and small copies of anchor charts. • Build stamina for writing, beginning at 25 minutes and increasing to 45 minutes per sitting. • Aim for 1–2 full notebook or loose-leaf pages per day as the volume of writing.

At-a-Glance Guide

Engagement & Habits

Title		Lesson
1.1	**Dream a Little Dream**	Make book covers with titles and illustrations to represent possible topics.
1.2	**All About Me**	Create an interest collage in a notebook or folder with images of interests and hobbies.
1.3	**Artifacts Can Give You Ideas**	Use artifacts as tools to generate ideas.
1.4	**Something Old, Something New**	Look in old writing for ideas that "pop" or patterns that reveal a topic of interest.
1.5	**Topics Can Hide in Other Places**	Try on a new genre to find ideas for writing.
1.6	**Borrow Ideas from Others**	Look through other books for inspiration.
1.7	**Try It On for Size**	Create a table of contents to see if a topic is viable.
1.8	**Give a Synopsis**	Try on an idea by writing a summary blurb for the inside jacket or back of the book.
1.9	**Talk It Out**	Talk with a partner to share information on a topic.
1.10	**Survey Says**	Interview curious individuals to find a focus and an audience.
1.11	**Just Get Started**	Think about a topic by talking, touching, drawing, and writing.
1.12	**Writers Are Never Done**	Return to previous writing to revise, quick edit, start a new piece, or practice a technique.
1.13	**Keep It Together**	Manage writing projects in a folder.

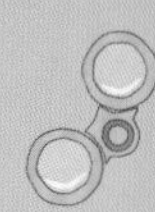

Writing Stage	Genre	
Emergent Transitional	List Pattern	How-To All-About
Any	Any	
Any	Any	
Any	Any	
Any	Any	
Any	Any	
Transitional Fluent	All-About Feature Article Literary Nonfiction Expository Nonfiction	Biography Research Report Expository Essay
Transitional Fluent	All-About Feature Article Literary Nonfiction Expository Nonfiction	Biography Research Report Expository Essay
Any	Any	
Any	Any	
Emergent Transitional	List Pattern	How-To All-About
Any	Any	
Emergent Transitional	List Pattern	How-To All-About

Engagement & Habits continued

Title		Lesson
1.14	**See Where It Takes You**	"Brain-dump" ideas on a topic with a fast and furious quick write.
1.15	**A Picture Is Worth a Thousand Words**	Write off of a picture, photo, or sketch to create detailed explanations.
1.16	**Be a Writer**	Develop independent writing lives by trying a second topic or starting an independent project.
1.17	**Be a Copycat**	Study a mentor text for content, structure, and author's craft.
1.18	**Go with the Flow**	Don't get slowed down by spelling concerns.
1.19	**Stronger Than Yesterday**	Set goals for writing by reflecting on how much and how long you typically write.
1.20	**Word Collectors**	Keep a bank of new and interesting words to draw on when needed.
1.21	**Be Resourceful!**	Consult resources to help when you feel stuck.
1.22	**Partners Are Resources, Too!**	Partners can generate ideas, rehearse how writing will go, share their writing, relieve writer's block, and more.
1.23	**Writers Take a Pause**	Pause to read writing out loud—to listen for errors and for places where more information is needed.
1.24	**On Your Mark, Get Set, Go!**	Quickly draft a piece in one sitting.

Writing Stage	Genre
Transitional Fluent	All-About Feature Article Literary Nonfiction Expository Nonfiction Biography Research Report Expository Essay
Any	Any
Any	Any
Any	Any
Any	Any
Any	Any
Transitional Fluent	All-About Feature Article Literary Nonfiction Expository Nonfiction Biography Research Report Expository Essay
Any	Any
Any	Any
Any	Any
Fluent	Expository Essay

Dream a Little Dream

In this lesson, students learn to make book covers with titles and illustrations to represent all the different topics they could write about.

Writing Stage: Emergent, Transitional • **Genre:** List, Pattern, How-To Book, All-About Book

INTRODUCE

Tell students that writers get "warmed up" by making multiple book covers for all the different topics they can write about.

Sometimes writers need some time to think, plan, and sort through their ideas for their books. In physical education class, we call this a warm-up. It gets your body moving and your blood pumping, and you practice some movements you might do in the real game. Similarly, writers need to warm up and get their ideas flowing to help them get ready to write. We can do this by making multiple book covers with titles and illustrations to represent all the different topics we can teach others through writing. Once we have a bunch of covers made, we can use them to help us remember our ideas and write about each one!

INSTRUCT

Demonstration

Model for students how you create a book cover for your ideas and then share the other covers you have created.

Watch me as I make multiple book covers for all my ideas, each with a title and an illustration.

One idea that I want to write about is sharks. I can draw a picture of a shark on the cover and then write a title for my book. In the picture, I can include the ocean. Then I could draw some other sea animals and make the shark big and in the center. Maybe a title for my book could be *Sharks, Sharks, Sharks. (Quickly make the book cover.)*

What other book covers can I make? I was thinking about writing a book about gardening and maybe another book about cats. Oh, and another one about dancing, and another about ice cream! I have so many ideas that I can make book covers for. (*Show the class book covers you have made.)* For the sake of time, I have already made the rest to show you. Look at all these covers! I have *Gardening Fun, All You Need to Know About Cats, All About Dance,* and *We All Scream for Ice Cream.* I will keep all these book covers in my folder so that I can refer to them and use them when I am ready.

Did you see how I thought about my ideas and made a cover for each one? I drew a picture to represent my idea and thought of a title for each topic. Then I placed the book cover in my folder to use when I need some ideas.

 |

GUIDE

Ask students to think about possible book cover ideas and then prompt them to turn and talk.

Now it's your turn to try. Think about your ideas. What will you draw on the covers to represent your ideas? What will the titles of your books be? We can always change a title later if we want to, but try to think about ones for now. Once you have your ideas, turn and tell your partner some book covers that you can create to represent those ideas.

(Allow 1–4 minutes for students to turn and talk with partners. Share exemplary responses.)

RELEASE

Remind students to make multiple book covers to represent their ideas.

Remember that sometimes when you sit down to write, you might need to warm up your brain first. Just like you warm up in gym class—get that writing energy flowing! We can make multiple book covers with illustrations and titles that represent our different topics. Then we can keep those covers in our folders to use when we are ready to write.

FOR ADDITIONAL SUPPORT, TRY

1.2 All About Me

1.6 Borrow Ideas from Others

1.11 Just Get Started

TIPS/RESOURCES

- Prepare multiple book covers to show students during Instruct.
- Provide paper choices for book covers.

All About Me

In this lesson, students learn to create an interest collage in or on their notebooks or folders, with photos or sketches of interests and hobbies that reflect them.

Writing Stage: Any • **Genre:** Any

INTRODUCE

Tell students that they will create a collage that reflects their interests.

One of the cool things about our class is that even though we are all in the same grade, learning the same things, we are also all different. Each of you has different interests, hobbies, experiences, friends, and more. Therefore, no one can share their ideas exactly like you can—because you are unique. To help you explore your own uniqueness, you can make an interest collage, with photos, sketches, and magazine cutouts of all the things that you are interested in and that reflect who you are as a person and a writer.

INSTRUCT

Explain with Examples

Explain to students what a collage is and how you went about making your own.

A collage is a collection of pictures, cutouts, drawings, stickers, and other items that represent ideas. People make collages for all sorts of reasons. As writers, we will make a collage that represents us.

Before I show you my interest collage, let me share some of the things I thought about to help me create it. I thought about some of my favorite activities, hobbies, games, and toys. I thought about what makes me super interested and piques my curiosity. I considered the special people in my life and the places that are meaningful to me.

I realized I am interested in cats, the beach, bike riding, gardening, and exercising. For simple things that I love, I thought about pizza, coffee, fancy shoes, and flowers. I knew all of these had to be included in my collage. I also knew that if I couldn't find these pictures, I could either draw them or find pictures that represented these ideas. (*Show the interest collage you made. Discuss why you included certain things and how you represented your ideas. Make sure you've included similar media to what the students will have access to so they feel it's replicable.)*

Collages like these can help you create a visual for the many interests that make you unique. Keep in mind you don't have to include everything you thought of. Sometimes it can be hard to fit everything.

 |

GUIDE

Prompt students to think about their ideas and how they will represent them in a collage.

Before you get started on creating your own collage, let's think about some of the things you plan on including in it. What do you envision it looking like? Turn and talk to share your ideas with your partner. Discuss what and how you plan on representing your interests—a picture, drawing, a magazine cutout, stickers, etc.

(Allow 1–4 minutes for students to turn and talk with partners. Share exemplary responses.)

RELEASE

Remind students that interest collages can be helpful writing tools.

Today is a different kind of writing day. We are going to get started on our interest collages. These collages will represent us as writers, showing things we are interested in and things we love. The collage will be a great source of ideas for us as we write, and it can be a tool we revisit again and again while writing.

FOR ADDITIONAL SUPPORT, TRY

1.3 Artifacts Can Give You Ideas
1.15 A Picture Is Worth a Thousand Words
3.2 Think with Your Heart

TIPS/RESOURCES

- Have your collage done ahead of time to show students.
- Gather magazines, stickers, and other art supplies for students.
- Ask parents to send in pictures ahead of time.

Artifacts Can Give You Ideas

In this lesson, students learn to use artifacts as tools to generate ideas. They can collect ticket stubs, brochures, menus, manuals, maps, and more!

Writing Stage: Any • **Genre:** Any

INTRODUCE

Tell students that they will use artifacts to generate ideas.

Sometimes when we see something—have it right in front of us and in our hands—it helps us think about possible ideas for our nonfiction writing. These things are sometimes referred to as artifacts or objects connected to a specific moment or purpose. Artifacts can be tickets, photographs, brochures, menus, manuals, maps, collectibles, and more. We can use artifacts to help us generate ideas and write about them, too. When we use an artifact to help us get started, we have the object right in front of us to remind us of everything we know about it.

INSTRUCT

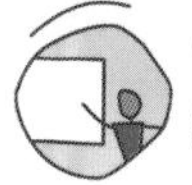

Demonstration

Show students how you use your artifacts to spark different writing ideas.

Let me look at some of my artifacts and think about what ideas come to mind that I can write about.

Here I have a photograph of my cats when they were kittens. I have been taking care of these two since they were kittens and therefore have a lot of information on how to take care of them. I also have this menu from the ice cream shop. This reminds me that I love ice cream so much I could teach others about it. I could teach about the origin of ice cream, the different flavors, how it's made—even delicious recipes!

Let me continue to look at some of my other artifacts. Here I have an old dance program from long ago, when I took dance classes. This sparks some different ideas for me. I could write all about dance and share my expertise, including different types of dances and dance moves. I could also write about the discipline of ballet, because, when I think back, I recall the dedication, effort, and pain that was involved in the training. I'm even remembering famous ballerinas whom I admired. I could write about one of them. I have so many ideas from just looking at these artifacts! I am definitely ready to get to work and start writing.

Did you notice how I used my artifacts to spark ideas for writing topics? Having the artifact right in front of me sparked more memories than I ever imagined.

ALTERNATIVE

Guided Practice: **Use artifacts that relate to the whole class (picture from a school-related event; assembly flyer; band, chorus, orchestra concert program; etc.) and brainstorm possible writing ideas.**

GUIDE

Prompt students to look at one of their artifacts and consider the possible writing ideas it might spark. Have them share their ideas with a partner.

Now it's your turn. You each have a few artifacts that you brought to class. Choose one artifact that you want to share with your partner and explore the ideas that come up. Try to push your thinking to see how many ideas you can come up with from just one artifact.

(Allow 1–4 minutes for students to turn and talk with partners. Share exemplary responses.)

RELEASE

Remind students about the importance of using writing tools, such as artifacts, to think of ideas.

Today you learned about the importance of using artifacts as a writing tool. Writers sometimes need tools to help them get started, say more, focus, and feel connected to their topics. Artifacts, like the ones we discussed, are perfect tools to spark ideas.

FOR ADDITIONAL SUPPORT, TRY

1.2 All About Me

1.4 Something Old, Something New

1.5 Topics Can Hide in Other Places

1.15 A Picture Is Worth a Thousand Words

TIPS/RESOURCES

- Write a parent/caregiver letter requesting permission for students to bring artifacts into class in advance of the lesson (and be specific about what is allowed).
- Give a mini-lesson on artifacts to build background knowledge in advance of the lesson.

Something Old, Something New

In this lesson, students learn to look for new ideas in old writing, scanning for ideas that "pop" or for patterns that reveal a topic of high interest.

Writing Stage: Any • **Genre:** Any

INTRODUCE

Tell students that they are going to look back through their older writing to discover new ideas.

Have you ever rediscovered an old toy, book, or sweatshirt and realized how much you loved it? I recently found an old charm from when I was little—a silly little plastic charm I loved. I decided to repurpose it and put it on the zipper of my work bag. Now it has a whole new function for me. We can do this with our old writing, too. We can look back for topics and ideas within those pieces. Sometimes we even find patterns in our writing that we can develop to teach others.

INSTRUCT

Demonstration

Show students how you go through your writing to search for new ideas. Show them how patterns can emerge from ideas that you wrote about again and again.

I am going to put my detective lenses on to see if I come across any ideas or patterns in my old writing that I can turn into their own topic.

Emergent In this book, I listed all different kinds of sports—soccer, baseball, basketball, hockey, and tennis. Maybe I can write a book about just one of these sports, perhaps soccer. I can create a whole book on how you play, the rules of the game, the equipment you need, etc. Let me keep looking. Here I have a book about different types of dances, costumes, dance shoes, and more! I also wrote a story about my first dance recital. Dance seems to be a pattern in my writing. Maybe a new idea that I can write about is just ballet or my dance teacher. Now I have all of these new ideas and they came from my own writing!

Transitional / Fluent Let me look back at some of my older writing entries to see if I can discover some new ideas. Here I have a story about the time I went to the aquarium and I was so fascinated by the octopus that I stared at the tank for what felt like hours. There could be something here. Let me keep sifting through some old writing. Here I have a story about a time when I was at the beach and a big storm came. Then I have this sketch I drew of the beach and another entry describing beaches. This feels like a pattern emerging. The beach is obviously a topic I like to think and write about. Maybe I could write about the importance of beaches as an ecosystem, or perhaps I can write about how beaches are disappearing due to erosion. Wow, so many ideas are now racing through my head!

Did you see how I read through my old writing, paying attention to the ideas that emerged? And how I also looked for patterns?

 |

GUIDE

Prompt students to look through their writing for new ideas.

Let's start this work together. I want you to take a minute or two to go through your old writing in search of a new topic. Look for patterns or ideas that pop.

(Allow students 1–2 minutes to skim through their old writing and then prompt them to turn and talk. Ask them to share out some of their new ideas.)

RELEASE

Remind students of the importance of looking back at old writing to get new ideas.

Today we talked about the importance of using your old writing to come up with new ideas. Sometimes we also come across a pattern that signals a topic that we can explore again.

We can end up with more ideas than ever!

FOR ADDITIONAL SUPPORT, TRY

1.5 Topics Can Hide in Other Places

1.7 Try It On for Size

1.9 Talk It Out

1.16 Be a Writer

TIPS/RESOURCES

- Gather previous writing pieces, as needed, if folders or notebooks are limited to current booklets/entries.

Topics Can Hide in Other Places

In this lesson, students learn to try on a new genre to find ideas for their writing. They explore a story, poem, comic, song, or any other genre to look for the topics that "hide" inside of them.

Writing Stage: Any • **Genre:** Any

INTRODUCE

Tell students that they will write in another genre to help them discover new writing ideas.

Sometimes I need to give my brain a break and switch gears to help me think of topics and connect to new ideas. Today we are going to pause our informational writing and try on another genre—a story, poem, comic, or song—to help us think about new ideas. Some of our best informational writing ideas are waiting to be discovered!

INSTRUCT

Demonstration

Show students how you write in a different genre to pull out new ideas for your writing.

Watch me as I write in a different genre to help me discover new ideas.

Emergent This past weekend I went for a bike ride with some friends and we saw so many birds! We saw seagulls, geese, ducks, and even some swans. The geese were so cute because there was a whole family of them. So I can write that story and then think about whether I can discover any new ideas for my informational writing. To save time, I have my story right here to show you. *(Quickly read your story aloud.)* Now that I think about it, another topic that I just discovered is geese! I loved watching them, and the baby geese were so fuzzy and looked so different from the adult geese. Maybe I could write an informational book about geese. Another idea that popped out to me is bikes. I love riding my bike and I think I could probably help someone learn how to ride a bike, so that could be another informational topic I found from my story.

Transitional / Fluent Last weekend I went for a bike ride with some friends, and I was thinking of writing a poem about it. It might go like this:

> "Pedal, pedal, pedal. I push and steer my bike along. Sun shining. People coming and going. Dogs walking. Geese waddling along. Pedal, pedal, pedal. I push and steer my bike along. Fresh air. Wind on my face. Nature all around."

As I read aloud my poem, some other ideas come to mind. I could write about bike riding and how it helps the environment. I could also write about exercise because bike riding is a form of exercise. I also can't stop thinking about the cute little baby geese I saw and how they were all in a single file marching along. It made me curious about them so that might be another topic.

Do you see how I took a few moments to write in a new genre? This helped me come up with new ideas for my informational writing.

GUIDE

Prompt students to think about the genre they will try and how they can mine it for new ideas.

Now you are going to start this work with a partner. Pause your informational writing and think about a different genre you can write in today—any other type that you feel inclined to write. Once you have your idea, turn and talk to your partner. While you are sharing your idea, think about what new informational topics pop out to you.

(Allow 1–4 minutes for students to turn and talk with partners. Share exemplary responses.)

RELEASE

Remind students that they can write in a different genre to help them discover new ideas.

Today we took a moment and paused our informational writing. This helped us think about some new informational writing ideas. You will continue this work during writing time today to see what new informational topics you can discover. I hope you'll remember that when you feel stuck, or feel like you need more ideas for informational writing, you can switch to a different genre, then look back at that writing to see if a new idea comes up.

FOR ADDITIONAL SUPPORT, TRY

1.3 Artifacts Can Give You Ideas
1.4 Something Old, Something New
1.6 Borrow Ideas from Others

TIPS/RESOURCES

- Have pages of texts from a variety of genres for students to review.

Borrow Ideas from Others

In this lesson, students learn to look through other books for inspiration. They can use the title or just a section to get new ideas.

Writing Stage: Any • **Genre:** Any

INTRODUCE

Tell students that they can use book titles or sections to get new ideas.

As writers, sometimes we get to a point where we aren't sure what we want to write about next. We may feel like we have run out of ideas. But in actuality, all we might need is a little inspiration to restart our engines. We can look through informational texts using the titles or just a section to help us think about new ideas.

INSTRUCT

Demonstration

Show students how you browse through informational texts for inspiration.

Watch me as I browse through some informational texts to find inspiration. *(Have sets of books available for you to review.)*

Emergent I am seeing a lot of different kinds of books—here is one about the octopus. I've never written about this topic, so this might be a new idea for me. Let's see what else. Here is one about fire trucks, and here is another one about tractors. Perhaps I could write a book about different kinds of trucks instead of just fire trucks and tractors. Oh, and here is one about soccer. Personally, I don't play soccer, but this reminds me of an activity I do know a lot about and that's dance. Oh, and here is one about butterflies. Inside the book there is a section on the life cycle of a butterfly. Maybe I could write about this? Wow, after browsing through some of these titles, I feel inspired and have so many new ideas for my own writing!

Transitional / Fluent Let me take a look at some of the informational texts I have in front me. Here is an interesting article about whales and their migratory patterns. This sparks a new idea for me because I never thought about their migratory patterns. I wonder if maybe that's something I can write about or even gather more information on for my writing. Maybe I can compare sharks and whales and their migratory patterns? They are two of the largest ocean animals, so that might be an interesting new angle for me. Let me keep digging and see what else inspires me. Here is a book about rain forests. This book is interesting because it seems to be teaching about how to save and protect rain forests. I didn't think of this until now, but with my topic about beaches maybe I can include a section that addresses problems that beaches are facing—erosion, pollution, and impacts on ocean wildlife.

ALTERNATIVE

Guided Practice: **Go through some texts together and pose questions to help students discuss how the texts can inspire new ideas.**

 |

GUIDE

Show students a few texts and prompt a "turn and talk" for them to think about new ideas.

Now we are going to do some of this work together. You can think about a new topic that comes to mind or a new way of thinking about your topic. Let's take a look.

(Show students one or two texts. Allow 1–4 minutes for students to turn and talk with partners. Share exemplary responses.)

RELEASE

Remind students that the texts around them can spark new ideas.

Remember, every now and then we might need a little inspiration for our writing. We can use informational texts to spark new ideas. These ideas can be brand new topics or a new angle on a topic we've already chosen.

FOR ADDITIONAL SUPPORT, TRY

1.5 Topics Can Hide in Other Places

1.9 Talk It Out

1.10 Survey Says

TIPS/RESOURCES

- Have premade baskets of informational texts (books, articles, essays, etc.) for the Instruct and Guide activities.
- Put together text sets for students to browse through.

Try It On for Size

In this lesson, students learn to see if they have enough to say by creating a table of contents.

Writing Stage: Transitional, Fluent

Genre: All-About Book, Feature Article, Literary Nonfiction, Expository Nonfiction, Biography, Research Report, Expository Essay

INTRODUCE

Tell students that they will create tables of contents to get a feel for their topics.

Have you ever bought something without trying it on first, only to find that it doesn't fit? If you had taken the time to try it on quickly, you could have made adjustments, tried another size, or decided not to buy it at all. As writers, we, too, can try on our ideas before we move forward with our writing to see if an idea fits. To do this, we can create a possible table of contents and think about how much we have to say about our topic.

INSTRUCT

Demonstration

Show students how you think about your idea and jot down a possible table of contents. Show students how it feels when an idea is and isn't a good fit.

Watch me as I create a table of contents for my idea—to see if it feels like a good fit.

I have been thinking of writing about gardening. Let me think about a table of contents. *(You can have the table of contents already made or quickly jot it down.)* I could have a part where I write about the different types of gardens—a flower garden, vegetable garden, or a fruit garden. I could also include a part about how to plant a garden. So my table of contents would look like this: "Different Types of Gardens, Planning a Garden"... I don't know. This doesn't seem like the best fit for me. I know I have some things to say, but I feel like I ran out of ideas.

Let me try on another idea—octopuses, how they hide and escape, their babies, what they eat, cool facts. Wow, I could keep going! This feels like a better fit already—I have so much to say. Let me jot this down on a table of contents: *(You can have the table of contents made in advance or quickly jot it down.)* I wrote: "About the Octopus, Different Types, Hiding and Escaping, Octopus Babies, What They Eat, Cool Facts."

Did you notice how with my first idea I had some things to say but then I realized it wasn't the best fit for me? And then, when I tried on my second idea it felt like a better fit? That is important because we want to make sure we have enough to say about our ideas before we start writing.

 |

GUIDE

Prompt students to think about their ideas and what they would include in a table of contents. Ask them to share their ideas with a partner.

Now it's your turn to try. You will start this work with your partner. Think about an idea for your writing. What are some things you could include in your table of contents? Turn and talk to share your thinking with your partner. If you have time, you can try on a few different ideas.

(Allow 1–4 minutes for students to turn and talk with partners. Encourage them to try on a few different ideas. Share exemplary responses.)

RELEASE

Remind students to create a table of contents to help them determine if they have enough to say about their topics.

Today we focused on the importance of trying on an idea before we start writing about it. We thought about a table of contents for our ideas and how that helps us realize whether our ideas are a good fit or not. Remember, when the fit feels right, it's usually because we have a lot to say about our topic and we feel connected to our idea.

FOR ADDITIONAL SUPPORT, TRY

1.8 Give a Synopsis

1.14 See Where It Takes You

1.17 Be a Copycat

TIPS/RESOURCES

- Have table of contents templates available.
- Save time by making your table of contents in advance, prior to the Instruct demonstration.

Give a Synopsis

In this lesson, students learn to try on an idea by writing a blurb for the inside jacket or back of the book that captures the main idea(s) for what they will teach.

Writing Stage: Transitional, Fluent

Genre: All-About Book, Feature Article, Literary Nonfiction, Expository Nonfiction, Biography, Research Report, Expository Essay

INTRODUCE

Tell students that they can determine the focus of their books by writing a synopsis first.

As readers, we know that one important habit is to take a peek at the inside jacket or the back of the book for a summary blurb to help us get our minds ready to read. Authors usually include a little synopsis telling the reader what the book is mainly about. Writers can also use this as a tool to help think about what they might teach in their writing. We can try on an idea by writing the blurb first.

INSTRUCT

Demonstration

Show students how you think about your topic and try writing a synopsis that captures the main idea.

Watch me as I try on this idea.

I have been thinking and writing about sharks, but I haven't really thought about what the main idea is. I have written about how long they have existed, their features, how fierce they are, and how they are at the top of the food chain. So let me try writing a synopsis about sharks and see if it captures my main idea. (*Quickly read aloud your synopsis.*)

> "Sharks are incredibly fascinating creatures. They have lived on Earth longer than humans and have been around since dinosaurs roamed the earth. Sharks have features that make them one of the fiercest animals on the planet. From their rows of sharp teeth to their aerodynamically shaped bodies, they continue to dominate the oceans and remain an apex predator."

It sounds to me that while my topic is sharks, I also have a more narrowed focus on how sharks are fierce creatures with features that have allowed them to dominate the oceans. That really helped me to clarify the focus for my writing. Now as I write, I can be sure to stay aligned with the main idea I just stated.

Did you see how after writing my synopsis, it became clear to me what the focus is for my writing?

ALTERNATIVE

Explain with Examples: **Using mentor texts, show how authors include a back or inside cover blurb that reveals the main idea of their writing.**

 |

GUIDE

Prompt students to think about a shared topic and what they would include in a synopsis about that topic.

Let's try this together. One of the topics we have been learning about is the importance of "going green" to help the environment. What have we learned about ways we can go green? What are some of the impacts?

(Allow 1–4 minutes for students to turn and talk with partners. Using their ideas, write a brief synopsis that captures the main idea.)

RELEASE

Remind students that writing a brief synopsis helps capture the main idea of a topic.

Today we talked about important work that authors do in real life—writing a synopsis! We can each think about our topic and try writing a synopsis for the inside jacket or the back cover that helps capture our main idea. This is a good habit because it helps us think about what we really want to teach others.

FOR ADDITIONAL SUPPORT, TRY

1.7 Try It On for Size

1.9 Talk It Out

1.14 See Where It Takes You

TIPS/RESOURCES

- Have a variety of book jackets and back cover blurbs of mentor texts to share with students.

Talk It Out

In this lesson, students learn to get ideas going by talking with a partner to share what they know.

Writing Stage: Any • **Genre:** Any

INTRODUCE

Tell students that writers often get started by talking about their ideas.

Writers often get started either by talking to a partner or to themselves about their topics—to get ideas flowing. When explaining to a partner, writers recall what they know, which helps them elaborate and say more.

INSTRUCT

Demonstration

Model for students how you begin by talking out loud about your topic. Start with the broad topic then get more granular.

When I get started in my writing, I often sit and talk through my ideas—either with myself or with others. Once I have talked it out, I transcribe that information onto the page. This is often helpful when I struggle to get started with the first sentences.

Let me show you. For example, let's say I am planning to write about ice cream. I can say out loud to you, my partners, everything I know:

> "Ice cream is a sweet and delicious treat. It can be enjoyed on a hot summer's day—or any day of the year—as a dessert or special snack. Many people enjoy ice cream because it comes in so many flavors that virtually anyone can find the flavor for them. People enjoy it in many ways—in a cup, on a cone, in a sundae, on a stick, in a sandwich, or as a cake."

Now I can start to think about the sections of my book. I might have a chapter or section on when people typically eat ice cream or a section on ice cream flavors. I can even have a section on the different ways to eat it!

Let's say I wanted to focus on when people eat ice cream. First, I say everything I know about this aspect:

> "Ice cream can be enjoyed at so many different times. It is a perfect treat to help you cool off on a hot summer's day. It can even be eaten throughout the year as a dessert or special treat. Sometimes, people use ice cream for celebrations. People eat ice cream at birthdays and other special occasions, like concerts, recitals, and graduations. Ice cream is also a special reward. Sometimes, people eat ice cream to celebrate an accomplishment like getting a good report card."

Do you see how I first began talking about my whole topic? Then I could elaborate to say more about one specific part.

 |

GUIDE

Encourage students to ask you questions about your topic.

When I talk out loud with others, I often let them ask questions because it encourages me to include more information. When I am talking to myself, I sometimes imagine the kinds of questions that others would ask. Partners, will you help me say even more? Do you have any questions about my topic or parts of my topic that might help me include more parts or say more about a part I already have? Who has some questions?

(Either allow 1–2 minutes for students to turn and share questions with partners, or call on students directly to ask you questions about your topic. Share how relevant questions help you plan or say more.)

RELEASE

Remind students that talking is a great way to get ideas going.

So, writers, remember that when you are getting ready to write, talking about your topic to yourself or others is a great way to get your ideas going. This works whether you are trying out a topic to see if you want to write about it, if you are planning how your writing could go, or if you are ready to write just one part. Don't forget to anticipate or ask questions to say even more!

FOR ADDITIONAL SUPPORT, TRY

1.2 All About Me

1.3 Artifacts Can Give You Ideas

TIPS/RESOURCES:

- Have students use photos, artifacts, or video clips to stimulate ideas.
- Transcribe a partnership conversation about a topic and share it with the class.

Survey Says

In this lesson, students learn to interview curious individuals to help them find a focus and audience for their writing.

Writing Stage: Any • **Genre:** Any

INTRODUCE

Tell students that nonfiction writers consider what people are curious about to help them plan their writing.

Nonfiction writers are experts in their subject areas, yet they are aware that everyone does not have their same passion or knowledge. In order to find a focus and get an audience for their writing, they question and survey others to see what aspects of the topic might be intriguing and exciting.

INSTRUCT

Demonstration

Explain to students that writers give readers background information on their topics and then solicit questions from them. Model by providing background on a topic.

When I write, I always think about what would interest or benefit my audience. I question people to get a sense of what information would interest or help them. I make sure to survey people with varying interests and backgrounds to get more complete feedback. Then I write to respond to some or many of the questions.

To survey my audience, I first give them a bit of background about my topic. Then I help by giving them question starters that usually begin with *who*, *what*, *when*, *where*, *why*, *how*, or *do*.

Let's try it out! I am an expert on skyscrapers. Skyscrapers are fascinating. Skyscrapers are tall buildings found in cities. The first skyscrapers were only 10 or 20 stories, or floors. Now those buildings are commonplace and not nearly as big or impressive as today's skyscrapers. Today a skyscraper is a building that has more than 40–50 floors!

Did you see how I gave you a little bit of interesting information about my topic to get you all curious? I provided a definition, a description, and some fascinating facts to get you thinking.

ALTERNATIVE

***Guided Practice:* Coach students to pose questions on a topic from another content area that they have some experience with but are still curious about.**

GUIDE

Use sentence starters to gather questions about the topic.

Now I want to know if you have any questions. I will give you a question starter and you and your partner will think about a question you might have. *(Guide students to brainstorm and share questions one prompt at a time. Record their questions on an anchor chart. See examples below.)*

- Do you have any "who" questions? *(Example: Who designed the first skyscraper?)*
- Do you have any "what" questions? *(Example: What is the tallest skyscraper?)*
- Do you have any "when" questions? *(Example: When was the first skyscraper built?)*
- Do you have any "where" questions? *(Example: Where in the world do skyscrapers exist?)*
- Do you have any "why" questions? *(Example: Why were skyscrapers designed?)*
- Do you have any "how" questions? *(Example: How are skyscrapers built?)*
- Do you have any "do" questions? *(Example: Do skyscrapers ever get torn down?)*

Now that you asked me so many questions, I have many more ideas of where I can go with my topic. I could provide some historical background to include who designed the first skyscraper and when it was built. I could write about skyscrapers in cities around the world and include information about the tallest ones on each continent. I could even write technical information about how they are constructed or demolished!

RELEASE

Remind students that an audience's interest can help them find a focus.

So, writers, remember that when you are writing about topics you care about, it's important to find out what your audience is interested to learn. This can help you determine what kind of information you might include.

FOR ADDITIONAL SUPPORT, TRY

1.3 Artifacts Can Give You ideas

1.8 Give a Synopsis

1.9 Talk It Out

TIPS/RESOURCES

- Give students time to conduct interviews with a range of peers in and out of class.
- Have students consider a few different topics and ask which ones interest readers most.

LESSON 1.11

Just Get Started

In this lesson, students learn to think about what they want to write about by talking, touching, drawing, and writing.

Writing Stage: Emergent, Transitional • **Genre:** List, Pattern, How-To Book*, All-About Book*

INTRODUCE

Tell students that writers begin on their own by thinking, talking, and writing.

As writers, we can get started quickly and easily by thinking, talking, and writing. We think about a topic we know about, we touch a page, and we say something about that topic. We draw a picture to match. Then we do it again!

INSTRUCT

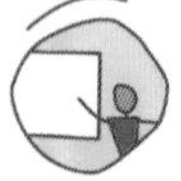

Demonstration

Model in your own book by naming a topic and relevant fact, touching the page and saying out loud what you will write, then drawing and writing what you've said.

Watch me get started by thinking and talking. Today I was thinking about smartphones. Now, I am not going to just start drawing and writing. First, I think, "What is something I know about smartphones?" I know that smartphones can take pictures. I will touch the first page of my book and say it out loud. *(Touch a blank page of a booklet and say your fact out loud.)* "Smartphones take pictures." Now I am ready to draw a picture with matching words! I will draw a picture of myself holding a smartphone in front of my eyes, taking a picture of a pretty tree. I will write "Smartphones take pictures." at the bottom of the page. Did you see how I thought about something I knew about and then touched the page to say what I was going to write? Now I do it again on the next page. *(Turn to the next page of your stapled booklet.)*

What else do I know about smartphones? I know they send messages. Should I draw and write? No! I have to touch the page and say it out loud, "Smartphones send messages." Now I am ready to draw a picture and write the words that match. I am going to draw a smartphone very big with two thumbs pressing the letter buttons and a message that says, "I love you." I write the words "Smartphones send messages." at the bottom of the page. Now I do it again on the next page. *(Turn to the next page and repeat. Emphasize how you aren't ready to draw and write until you think, touch the page, and say what you will write.)*

**Note: If teaching this lesson for How-To Books, demonstrate with just one feature of the smartphone and tell it step-by-step. For All-About Books, use the same examples as above, but explain with multiple sentences depending on the levels of your writers. For example:*

Smartphones can take pictures. When taking pictures, you can choose between live photos or still photos. A live photo shows movement. A still photo doesn't. When taking still photos, you can choose portrait mode, which makes the background blurry and the main object crystal clear.

GUIDE

Ask students to help you add to the next part of your book.

Can you think of something else I can say about smartphones? Close your eyes and picture a smartphone.

(Allow 1–4 minutes for students to turn and talk with partners. Share exemplary responses.)

RELEASE

Remind students about the importance of rehearsing before they draw and write.

So remember, you don't begin writing until you plan first. Think, touch the page, say it out loud, and then draw a picture with words to match! Repeat it, page after page, until you feel you have shared everything you know about your topic.

FOR ADDITIONAL SUPPORT, TRY

1.9 Talk It Out

TIPS/RESOURCES:

- Post an anchor chart in your classroom outlining the steps to getting started.*
- Let students work together and tell what they plan to write by touching the page and saying their facts.

*See sample chart, "Just Get Started," on page 70.

Writers Are Never Done

In this lesson, students learn that when they think they're done, they can always go back to revise, quick edit, start a new piece, or practice a technique.

Writing Stage: Any • **Genre:** Any

INTRODUCE

Tell students that writing is a practice and writers use their full writing time to be productive.

Writing is a daily practice, where writers use their time wisely to stay productive. While the occasional writer's block or feelings of "I'm done with this" are inevitable, writers have ways to keep going. Today we will learn that when we think we are done, we can always revise, edit, start on a new piece of writing, or study and practice a technique.

INSTRUCT

Explain with Examples

Explain the different strategies that students can use in order to stay productive.

Let me explain. During our precious writing time, it is important to stay focused on one thing—writing! However, since writing is a craft and not an assignment, this can mean a few different things.

For starters, one of the most important things writers do is revise. We think, "How can I make this stronger?" We reread a section and ask, "How can I give the reader a clearer picture?" When we reread a section line by line, we ask ourselves if the information fits or makes sense. If it doesn't, we can move it to another section or remove it all together.

When you've finished revising, it's time to edit. We can edit by pointing under each word and checking its spelling. If we're unsure, we can try to spell it again or use a resource to help. We can check our punctuation, making sure our sentences have the correct end marks. Lastly, we can check for capitals at the beginning of sentences and for proper nouns.

If you have revised and edited, you can start another piece of writing!

Emergent / Transitional You can work on a new booklet for a new topic, or you can think of a side writing project to work on—one of your own choosing in a different genre.

Fluent You can start a second topic, by generating new ideas and writing entries, or play in your notebook by writing in another genre.

We can also use our time to learn from other writers! We can look at books from our classroom library and get new ideas for our writing.

All these strategies can help you stay productive every day!

ALTERNATIVE

Demonstration: **Using your own writing as an example, show students how you might revise and edit a section, start a new entry, or study an author's craft.**

GUIDE

Ask students to think about how they will spend their writing time today.

Now that you know how to stay productive, can you look at your writing and make a plan for your writing time today? Will you continue working on what you had going yesterday? Will you revise? Edit? Study an author's craft?

(Allow 1–4 minutes for students to turn and talk with partners. Share exemplary responses.)

RELEASE

Reiterate the importance of staying productive during writing time.

Remember that when you think you're done, you've really only just begun. Stay productive by revising or editing your work, starting a new writing project, or learning from another writer. This way you don't waste precious writing time but use it to become a stronger writer.

FOR ADDITIONAL SUPPORT, TRY

1.4 Something Old, Something New

1.5 Topics Can Hide in Other Places

1.6 Borrow Ideas from Others

TIPS/RESOURCES

- Create an anchor chart with suggested ways to stay productive.
- Do some whole-class revision or editing.
- Study an author's craft by noticing and naming techniques the author used.

LESSON 1.13

Keep It Together

In this lesson, students learn to manage their writing projects in a folder that separates work in progress from finished pieces. (You will need a folder for each student.)

Writing Stage: Emergent, Transitional • **Genre:** List, Pattern, How-To Book, All-About Book

INTRODUCE

Tell students that writers have ways to keep their projects organized.

Writers keep their projects organized so that they can easily locate what they are working on when it's time to write. However, they also keep their completed and paused writing in a safe place so that they can go back to those projects if needed.

INSTRUCT

Explain with Examples

Show students a two-pocket folder. Explain where finished and unfinished work is placed.

When I am working on a writing project, I know that it might take a few days to finish. There's not always enough time to complete my work in one session. This folder is helpful because sometimes, after a long break, I forget about a piece that I was working on; seeing the folder reminds me it's there.

(Show your two-pocket folder with work in it. Label one pocket for work in progress and the second pocket for work that is complete.)

Since I have finished all of these booklets, I placed them on the left side of my folder. I started this booklet yesterday but didn't finish it. There are still some blank pages to it, so I store it in the side pocket on the right because it is still a work in progress. Today, when I get started during writing time, I will work on finishing this piece first. Once it is done, I will move it to the left side.

I know what you are thinking. "Why are we saving our old pieces?" That is a good question. One reason we save our finished work is because as we learn new things, we may want to go back and add them to an old piece. Another reason is because sometimes looking back at these pieces can give us ideas for new pieces. We also save our older pieces so that we can look back and notice some goals we want to work on or improve. Finally, the most important reason we save our older pieces is so we can choose which one we want to fix up, fancy up, and publish for our big celebration.

ALTERNATIVE

Demonstration: **Model how to decide whether to put pieces in the "finished for now" or "work in progress" sides of a pocket folder.**

 |

GUIDE

Give students their writing and a folder. Prompt them to decide where to place their writing pieces.

(Hand students their previous writing and give each student a labeled, two-pocket folder.)

Here is your writing and your very own writing folder. Notice the side for finished work and the side for unfinished work. Look at your writing and reread all the pages. Once you have read them, ask yourself if this piece is finished or unfinished, and place it on the correct side of your folder.

(Give students 1–2 minutes to reread their writing and place it in their folders.)

Tell your partner your plan for today. Will you be starting a new piece or finishing up the piece you were working on?

RELEASE

Remind students to get started with unfinished pieces and to keep their writing organized.

As you go off to write today, remember that if you have unfinished writing, put it in the right side of your folder. You should finish that first before moving on and starting a new piece. If you do not have unfinished work, get a new booklet to begin a new piece of writing. This process will help you stay organized.

FOR ADDITIONAL SUPPORT, TRY

1.2 All About Me

1.3 Artifacts Can Give You Ideas

1.21 Be Resourceful!

TIPS/RESOURCES

- Use green and red dots to indicate exactly which pieces are work in progress (green) or finished for now (red).
- Keep resources in the folder inside sheet protectors.
- Laminate folders to preserve them longer.

See Where It Takes You

In this lesson, students learn to "brain-dump" their ideas with a fast and furious quick write in their notebooks.

Writing Stage: Transitional, Fluent

Genre: All-About Book, Feature Article, Literary Nonfiction, Expository Nonfiction, Biography, Research Report, Expository Essay

INTRODUCE

Tell students that writers experiment with many topic possibilities before settling on one.

It's important for writers to experiment with different ideas and possibilities before landing on an idea. Some of these ideas may never see the light of day, and others may unexpectedly turn out to be their best work. Today we are going to learn how writers freewrite about a variety of topics to see where that takes them.

INSTRUCT

Demonstration

Model for students how you experiment with a topic by quickly writing whatever comes to mind.

As a writer, I look for topics wherever I go, even when it's not my "writing time." Some of these topics seem insignificant while others seem big and meaningful. However, I never really know until I try them out. The topics I expect to go nowhere sometimes have the greatest energy and excitement behind them. Alternately, some of my best ideas don't take off. I call this kind of writing a rehearsal. I try out a topic, writing a full page fast and furiously, without letting spelling or conventions get in my way. Watch me as I write an entry for a new topic, coffee. *(Quickly write or pretend to write in your notebook as you say your entry out loud.)*

> "Coffee is used around the world and has been around for centuries. Legend has it that it was discovered by a goat herder who noticed that his goats had tremendous amounts of energy after eating the berries off of a coffee tree. People then began experimenting with its energetic powers and shared their knowledge. Coffee spread across the globe. Americans first started using coffee to protest paying high taxes for tea from England. They replaced the need for tea by using coffee instead. Maybe this is why coffee is preferred in the US and tea is still the favorite in England. People drink coffee in many ways. Europeans drink coffee in smaller, strong doses called espresso. Americans drink larger cups and dilute it with water. However, coffee has taken on many forms in recent years. People drink cappuccinos and macchiatos which involve mixing coffee with steamed milk. Some like to blend their coffee with milk and ice and create frappuccinos. Traditional coffee is even served cold as iced coffee or cold brew. Another form of cold brewed coffee is coffee that is mixed with nitrogen and comes out of a keg and tap." (Keep going until a page appears to be filled.)

Do you see how I just started writing quickly to see where the topic would go? I didn't even think it was worth writing about, but I was wrong!

 |

GUIDE

Ask students to help you write another entry through a shared-writing experience.

Will you help me fill the page by brain-dumping everything you know about physical education? What is physical education? What do you do there? What do you enjoy about it? Quickly tell your partner everything!

(Allow students 2–3 minutes to share ideas. Start to synthesize their information and transcribe it on chart paper, in a notebook, or under a document camera.)

RELEASE

Remind students that it is important to experiment with ideas to see where they go.

So, writers, when you are generating ideas for writing, it goes far beyond just making a list. You have to "try on" topics by rehearsing them and seeing where they take you. Remember to do this with many topics before settling on the one you hope to take through the process.

FOR ADDITIONAL SUPPORT, TRY

1.7 Try It On for Size

1.8 Give a Synopsis

1.9 Talk It Out

TIPS/RESOURCES

- Encourage students to write multiple entries per day; an entry doesn't need to feel completed.
- Don't let students spend too much time on an entry.
- Model for students how rereading an entry can give them ideas for sections or subheadings.

A Picture Is Worth a Thousand Words

In this lesson, students learn to write about a picture, photo, or sketch to create detailed explanations.

Writing Stage: Any • **Genre:** Any

INTRODUCE

Tell students that a picture, photo, or sketch can spark ideas for writing.

Pictures, photos, and sketches can help us in our writing in a few different ways. They can help us plan the parts of a topic and how the whole piece might go. Or they can help us write more details about one part of the topic.

INSTRUCT

Demonstration

Model for students how using images helps create detailed explanations for one or more sections.

Watch me get started with my topic, "Visiting New York City." I am going to look at a few photos to get some ideas. *(Print or project photos.)* Here I see some famous landmarks, such as the Empire State and Chrysler Buildings and One World Trade Center. This gives me an idea that I can include a section on famous buildings or landmarks.

As I look closer at this photo, I see Central Park, which has me thinking that I can include a section on parks to visit. This photo of Times Square reminds me to include a section on tourist attractions. I also notice that there are lots of Broadway theaters, which gives me the idea of a section on shows to see. Of course, I see a taxicab. I can include a section on how to get around New York City. Looking at photos really helped spark some ideas!

I can also study just one picture closely to help me write with more detail. Let's say in my section on getting around, I wanted to write about subways. If I look at this subway map closely, it can help me say a lot! I notice that the subway lines aren't only in Manhattan; they also go to Queens, Brooklyn, and the Bronx. I can say that the subways help you get in and around most of the boroughs of New York City. As I look even closer, I can say that New York City has different colored subway lines. Some lines go north and south, some lines go east and west, and some go in all directions. It also seems that each colored line includes letters or numbers. I can add that to my writing. Looking at the full picture, I can say with confidence that the subways can help you get to most places in New York City.

Do you see how pictures can help you develop an entire piece of writing as well as just a section?

 |

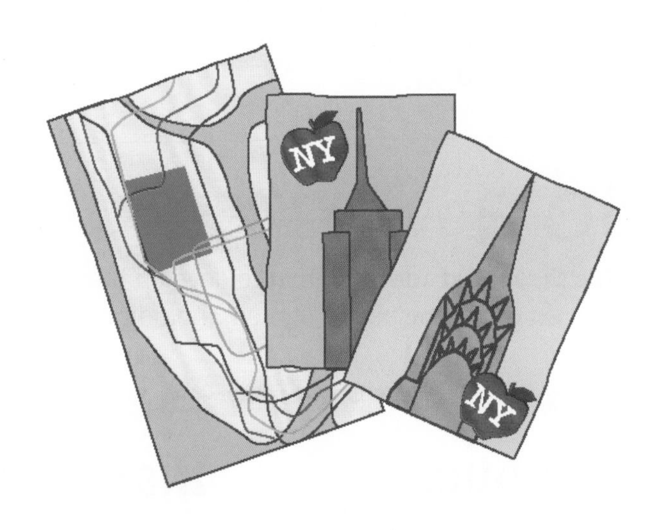

GUIDE

Share an image and ask students to come up with details to write based on it.

Can you help me with this next part while I try out this strategy? In my section on landmarks, there's a part on the Empire State Building. Let me draw it for you. *(Draw or show a predrawn image. Think out loud or name some parts of the drawing to show how you use the image to add detail.)*

What details might I include if I were writing about the Empire State Building?

(Allow 1–4 minutes for students to turn and talk with partners. Share exemplary responses. The more specific the details, the better.)

RELEASE

Remind students that visuals such as photos, pictures, and sketches can help get ideas going.

So, writers, remember that visuals such as photos, pictures, and sketches can help spark ideas for writing. You can use them to help you plan, say more, or get going with ideas when you feel stuck.

FOR ADDITIONAL SUPPORT, TRY

1.2 All About Me

1.3 Artifacts Can Give You Ideas

TIPS/RESOURCES

- For emergent and early transitional writers, have students draw a picture on each page for inspiration.
- For advanced transitional and fluent writers, have students use photos in their notebooks for inspiration.
- Give reluctant writers access to photos and pictures that might help spark ideas.

LESSON 1.16

Be a Writer

In this lesson, students learn to develop their independent writing lives by making choices about what to do when finished or stalled, including starting another piece or an independent project.

Writing Stage: Any • **Genre:** Any

INTRODUCE

Tell students that writing is a practice that needs to be nurtured and developed.

Each and every day, we gather information and I give you a tip to help you in your nonfiction writing projects. Most times, you go off to write and continue to work on those projects. However, sometimes you might feel a little stalled or not in the mood to work on this kind of writing. That's okay because writing can feel hard, especially when you are being told what kind of writing to do. Regardless, you have to write something—ANYTHING! Today we are going to talk about what you can do to keep going and live your writerly life.

INSTRUCT

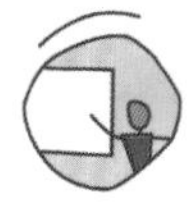

Explain with Examples

Remind students that there are a few ways to keep writing, even if they need a break from a current project.

(Provide students with a variety of options that are developmentally appropriate.)

One thing you can do is write another kind of nonfiction. You can try a How-To Book, an All-About Book, a Biography, a List Book, or an Alphabet, Number, Color, or Shape Book. You can also try writing a magazine or newspaper article.

Another thing you can do is switch the type of writing altogether and try some narrative writing. Perhaps you want to tell a story. You can even create a comic book with familiar characters—or invent your own characters. Maybe you want to try a graphic novel because you love reading that style of writing.

Maybe you are feeling creative. If so, you can write a poem or song. Your song can be a piggy-back song—one that is sung to a familiar tune with new words—or an original song with your own made-up tune.

Maybe you want to share your ideas or opinions with the world, write a speech about something you care about, or write a letter to someone to make a change. You can even share your opinions in reviews or essays.

You can reach out to someone you care about in a friendly letter, email, or with a special greeting card. Just as long as you write something—ANYTHING! Whatever the kind of writing you choose to do, you can always look at another author's writing to help you.

ALTERNATIVE

Demonstration: **Model for students how to push through a stalled piece of writing or how to decide what to do when finished.**

GUIDE

Give students some time to express their interests.

Right now, think about the kind of writing that interests you if you were to start a side project. Share your ideas with a partner.

(Allow 1–4 minutes for students to turn and talk with partners. Share exemplary responses. If possible, provide an additional folder for independent projects.)

RELEASE

Reiterate that students should prioritize their nonfiction writing projects over independent projects.

As you go off to write today, remember that you have a choice to work on your nonfiction writing pieces, or try another kind of writing—one that interests you as a writer. Remember, it is important that we get our nonfiction writing done each day—most of the time. However, on occasion, it is okay to work on something else when you feel finished, or stuck, or during other times of the day.

FOR ADDITIONAL SUPPORT, TRY

1.5 Topics Can Hide in Other Places

1.6 Borrow Ideas from Others

TIPS/RESOURCES

- Offer specialty paper choices for independent writing projects.
- Pull small groups or partnerships to help them plan their writing based on the genre they selected.
- Remind students of other kinds of writing they have learned about and encourage them to use the skills and strategies they learned to create those pieces.
- Offer time weekly or biweekly for independent side projects.

LESSON 1.17

Be a Copycat

In this lesson, students learn to study a mentor text for content, an idea for structure, or a craft move. They notice it, study it, mimic it, and try it on their own.

Writing Stage: Any • **Genre:** Any

INTRODUCE

Tell students that writers get started by studying a mentor text for inspiration.

Have you ever had someone say to you, "Don't be a copycat!" Well, you should know that writers get ideas by looking at what other writers do—that's how we learn and grow! Today I want to teach you that we can look at a mentor for all kinds of inspiration, including ideas for content, structure, and craft. We notice it, study it, mimic it, and then try it on our own. Today we're going to be copycats!

INSTRUCT

Demonstration

Model for students how to look at a mentor text for content, structure, and craft ideas. Remember, ideas do not need to be an exact match; rather, they can be "inspired" by the mentor.

Watch me as I look at a few of our mentor texts to show you how I use them for inspiration.

First, I'm going to look through the lens of topics. What is this author writing about that I can write about, too? We have a book about Amelia Earhart. She is famous for being the first woman pilot to fly solo across the Atlantic. I could write a book about a famous person. Or maybe about a person who is famous for making a difference—like Michelle Obama, the first African American First Lady. She started the Let's Move campaign to fight childhood obesity. I could also just write about famous people I know about, like LeBron James!

Now, I'm going to look through the lens of structure—how the book is organized. This book is comparing lizards and snakes. I could take something I know about and compare it to something else—like soccer versus basketball. I could compare the skills you need for both games. I could compare some of the famous people I know about—for instance, LeBron James and Michael Jordan. Here's another book about climate change. This book is organized to show causes and effects. I wonder how I can use that structure.

Finally, I'm going to look at some of the craft moves the writers have used. I see that they have bold words—some for definitions, some for emphasis. In this book about whales, the author uses comparisons to describe the whale. She writes that the whale's eye is as big as a teacup. And says its skin is smooth and springy like a hardboiled egg. The comparisons help to make things clear. Could I try this when I write about LeBron James?

ALTERNATIVE

***Inquiry:* Ask students to study texts employing the question: How can this inspire me to write?**

GUIDE

Prompt students to talk about what they see as inspiration related to topics, structure, and craft.

Now it's your turn. Use a mentor text to answer these questions:

- What topics does it get you to think about?
- How is it organized?
- What do you notice about the author's craft?

(For each category, allow a few minutes for students to turn and talk with partners. Share exemplary responses.)

RELEASE

Remind writers that they can always look to mentor texts for ideas.

Writers, remember that when you are getting ready to write you can look to other writers—not to copy their ideas exactly, but to be inspired by them. We can think about topics, structures, or craft to gather ideas for our own writing.

FOR ADDITIONAL SUPPORT, TRY

1.3 Artifacts Can Give You Ideas

1.6 Borrow Ideas from Others

1.15 A Picture Is Worth a Thousand Words

TIPS/RESOURCES

- Gather mentor texts with a variety of structures for students to study.
- Break this lesson into three separate lessons: topics, structure, and craft.
- Create a chart of ideas for the class.

LESSON 1.18

Go with the Flow

In this lesson, students learn that to have "flow," it is important to not let spelling slow them down. They should spell words the best they know how and move on so their ideas are not disrupted.

Writing Stage: Any • **Genre:** Any

INTRODUCE

Tell students that writers have strategies to protect their "flow."

Sometimes, when writing really clicks, we can get into something called "flow"—where the ideas are coming easily. When that happens, we don't want to do anything to disrupt it! Instead of stopping to ask someone how to spell a word, or stopping to look something up, there are strategies you can use to apply your best spelling and move on so that you don't disrupt your flow of ideas.

INSTRUCT

Demonstration

Model for students how you can circle a word you're not sure how to spell as a way to remind yourself to come back to it when you finish writing.

Watch me as I show you what I mean. Uh-oh, here's a tricky word. I can't see it on the word wall. I'm having a hard time chunking it, or breaking it into parts. And when I say it out loud and stretch it ... what I'm writing down doesn't look right. But the next sentence I want to write is in my head already. I don't want to forget it! I'm just going to spell this word as best I can. Then I'm going to circle it, so that when I finish writing today, I can come back to it and try a few strategies.

Do you see what I did there? I circled the word I was stuck on. I didn't change it to an easier word I know how to spell, but I also didn't get hung up on it and lose track of my ideas.

 |

GUIDE

Prompt students to brainstorm a list of strategies to try when they come back to a word they circled.

Let's do this next part together. Imagine you've circled some words because you were really in a writing flow, but now writing time is almost over. You still have a few minutes left to go back. What are some strategies you can use to apply your best spelling?

(Give students a minute to talk. Then have them share out. Chart their ideas and create a list of strategies.)*

I'm hearing that you can check the word walls and other charts in the room. Move closer to see them clearly, if you need to. You can check any charts you have in your writing folders for blends or common prefixes and suffixes. I heard you could chunk the words to see if there are words you know within that word. You can ask a friend who is finished writing. And, you can look it up.

That's a great list of strategies!

RELEASE

Remind students to protect their writing flow by circling a word they're stuck on and come back to it later.

Remember, as you're writing today and you feel you're in a flow, you can still do your best spelling. Circle any tough word and come back to it later, applying the strategies from our chart. That way, you can protect your writing flow and do all the best work you can. I can't wait to see what you write today!

FOR ADDITIONAL SUPPORT, TRY

1.1 Dream a Little Dream
1.11 Just Get Started
1.14 See Where It Takes You
1.16 Be a Writer

*See sample chart, "Go with the Flow," on page 70.

TIPS/RESOURCES

- Chart strategies for checking circled words.*
- Notice we didn't say "don't worry about spelling." Writers *do* worry about spelling. This lesson helps writers understand *when* to focus on accurate spelling.

Stronger Than Yesterday

In this lesson, students learn to set goals for writing by reflecting on how much and how long they typically write. They use this information to write a little more and a little longer.

Writing Stage: Any • **Genre:** Any

INTRODUCE

Tell students that writers set goals to push themselves to write more.

Runners are known for training with goals in mind. They think about how far and how long they usually run and plan their training so that they can improve their time and distance. Similarly, we can push ourselves to write a little more, or a little longer, each day.

INSTRUCT

Demonstration

Model for students how you look for patterns across your writing in terms of volume and stamina. Show them how you use that information to set a goal for yourself.

Emergent / Transitional Watch me as I look in my writing folder to see how much writing I do on a typical day. I'm not going to read my writing. I'm just looking at it to see how much writing I usually do. I need to look across my pages and across my booklets. I even look at how many lines are filled on each page.

Let's see. I have a 3-page booklet, another 3-page booklet, a 2-page booklet, and another 3-page booklet. Looks like I write a lot of 3-page booklets! I could say I'm going to set a goal to write a 4-page booklet. But first let me see if I could write more on each page? All of the pages have two lines. I could choose paper with maybe five lines? Hmmm. That might be too big of a jump. How about three lines? That seems like a good goal. I'll write more on each page but still aim to get one booklet done each writing time.

Do you see how I looked first at how many pages and then at how many lines in order to set a goal for myself?

Fluent I'm going to look back through my notebook to see how much I typically write. I know that writing time is typically 30 minutes. It looks like I have one half-page, one three-quarter page, and another half-page. Yikes! I should really be writing more. At least a full page. Do I get started right away? Do I get distracted? Or end early? Let's see. I know I get started right away. But, if I'm honest, sometimes I lose focus. I've never written a full page. Maybe I'll make an "x" three-quarters of the way down the page. I will work hard to get there and then if there is still time, I will work to write a full page. Maybe smaller goals could help me avoid distraction. I could also time myself for five minutes, see how far I get, count the lines, and set that as a goal for every five minutes.

Do you see how I looked at how many lines, or how far down the page I usually get, to determine roadblocks and solutions?

 |

GUIDE

Prompt students to reflect and set goals with their partners.

Now it's your turn. Look across your pages. What do you see? How much do you typically write? What's a good goal?

(Allow 1–4 minutes for students to turn and talk with partners. Check in to see if goals are realistic and offer suggestions to adjust as needed. Share exemplary responses.)

RELEASE

Remind students to check in with their goals to keep themselves on track.

Remember, writers, any time you want to set a goal for yourself, you can reflect on your writing. You can set a goal and then—just like a runner—get ready, get set, go!

FOR ADDITIONAL SUPPORT, TRY

1.1 Dream a Little Dream

1.12 Writers Are Never Done

1.16 Be a Writer

TIPS/RESOURCES

- With transitional writers who are writing in notebooks, use the "Fluent" section during Instruct.
- Remind students to check in with their goals as a midworkshop teaching point.
- Help define realistic goals for students. A goal should not be too easy or too hard.

Word Collectors

In this lesson, students learn to keep a bank of new, beautiful, and interesting words in the back of their notebooks for use in their writing.

Writing Stage: Transitional, Fluent

Genre: All-About Book, Feature Article, Literary Nonfiction, Expository Nonfiction, Biography, Research Report, Expository Essay

INTRODUCE

Tell students that writers gather words they like the sound or the look of.

Writers grow because they pay attention. They notice beauty, pain, nature, and snippets of conversation—and then capture them as best they can. They also pay attention to words. Words that are long, short, funny-sounding, beautiful, or super smart. We're going to make a place for those words in our notebooks so that we can draw on them as we write.

INSTRUCT

Guided Practice

Read aloud to students anything with interesting or beautiful language. Practice choosing words to create a class word bank.

Let's try this together. I'm going to start this read-aloud, and we're all going to pay attention to the language. When you hear a word you like, let me know to stop. Just give me a thumbs up and remember your word.

(Read aloud a text that contains interesting language. Stop to share words you notice and how they impact you. When students put their thumbs up, stop and have them share the word and its impact. If they need a warm-up, have students turn and talk to share words with each other, then share out. Add the words to a word bank—a chart with listed words and definitions. Also, model looking up words quickly.)

ALTERNATIVE

Demonstration: **Model for students how to create a word bank and pay attention to words in daily life.**

 |

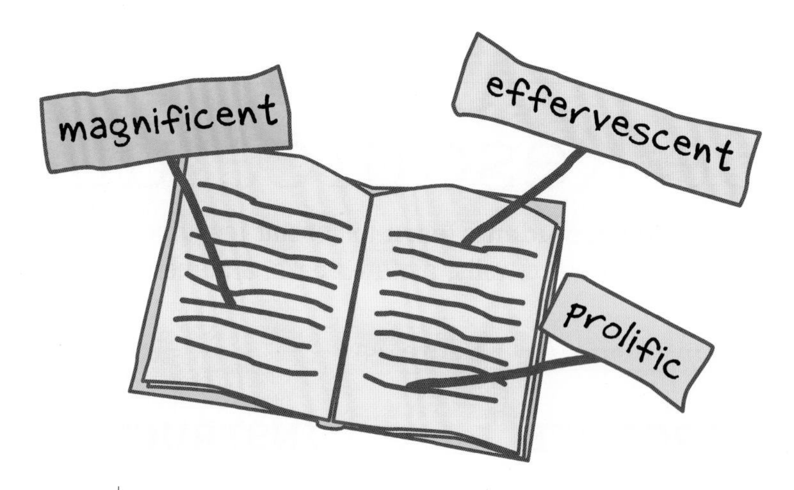

GUIDE

Prompt students to try adding to their own word banks.

Now find a place in the back of your notebook and label it "Word Bank." Take a minute and add one or two words that you particularly love to your word bank. Once you have a few words, share them with your partner. Talk about what you like about the word or words you have chosen and how you think you might try to use each one.

(Allow students 1–2 minutes to share and discuss words. They can add more to their word banks if their partners convince them to like a new word.)

RELEASE

Remind students to add to their word banks at various times during the day.

Remember, as you're reading in this class and in others, pay attention to the words you see and hear. If you like the look, sound, or meaning of a word, add it to your word bank. Then check in with your word bank before you start writing to remind yourself of certain words, to be inspired by certain words, or to be challenged to add new words to your writing.

FOR ADDITIONAL SUPPORT, TRY

6.18 What Does That Mean?

TIPS/RESOURCES

- Create class word banks.
- Launch this lesson by reading Peter H. Reynolds's picture book, *The Word Collector*.

Be Resourceful!

In this lesson, students learn to consult resources for help when they feel stuck—such as charts, word walls, picture books, and more.

Writing Stage: Any • **Genre:** Any

INTRODUCE

Tell students that independence is something you learn by using the resources around you.

Being resourceful is so important in life. It's also important in writing. Luckily, it's something we can learn and work on. Today I want to teach you that as writers we can consult resources to help us when we're stuck. And we can do this independently, without a teacher telling us to.

INSTRUCT

Inquiry

Focus students on this question: What can we use to help us when we're stuck? To support students, describe specific "stuck" scenarios and name resources, around the room or in writing folders, that can help.

Let's answer this question together: What can we use to help us when we're stuck? I'm going to describe some common problems that come up in writing. You're welcome to add any problems that you have had.

You know how sometimes you're making the sound a letter makes, but you're not sure which letter, or maybe you can't remember how to make it? What can we use to help us?

(Give partners a minute to talk. Possible answer: alphabet chart)

Okay, here's another one: What if you're stuck on a blend or digraph? Maybe you're trying to spell *scarf*, and you can't remember what comes after the **s**. What can you look at for help?

(Give partners a minute to talk. Possible answer: blend and digraph chart.)

What if you're trying to write a story about something you and a classmate did, but you don't know how to spell their name?

(Give partners a minute to talk. Possible answers: job or partner chart.)

What should you do if you aren't sure how to revise, but I'm conferring with someone, so you can't ask me?

(Give partners a minute to talk. Possible answers: ask a partner; use an editing checklist.)

(Continue posing questions in this way. Allow students to state their own problems as well to see if classmates can help them find resources to check for solutions.)

 |

GUIDE

Prompt students to get ready for writing time by making a note of where resources are in the room.

Now that we've found resources for so many problems, take a minute and, with your partner, recall some of the resources that you think you're likely to try using today.

(Allow 1–4 minutes for students to talk with partners and make a plan. Share out plans that reinforce habits you'd like students to form.)

RELEASE

Remind students that they can, and should, use resources on their own—not just when directed to by a teacher.

When you're writing today, remember, there are resources all around you. And you're free to use them—that's being resourceful. You don't need me to tell you to do it. You can do it yourselves and be your own bosses!

FOR ADDITIONAL SUPPORT, TRY

1.12 Writers Are Never Done

1.17 Be a Copycat

1.22 Partners Are Resources, Too!

TIPS/RESOURCES

- Notice, and talk up, any and all use of resources—even approximations. Compliments go a long way here!
- Make extra copies of resources for students to have on their own.
- Create an anchor chart with the different strategies writers can use when they are feeling stuck.*

*See sample chart, "Be Resourceful!," on page 70.

Partners Are Resources, Too!

In this lesson, students learn ways partners can be helpful. They can generate ideas, rehearse how their writing will go, share their writing, relieve writer's block, reflect on ideas, and give each other feedback.

Writing Stage: Any • **Genre:** Any

INTRODUCE

Tell students that they can consult their partners as a resource.

Your partners are people whom you're used to talking to—and they can be a huge help while you're writing. They can be a resource in the room, almost like a second teacher! Today let's think together about the ways partners can help each other.

INSTRUCT

Inquiry

Focus students on specific questions to work with a partner. Model with common writing problems.

We're going to work together to think of ways partners can act as resources. I'm going to give you a "What if" statement, and then we're all going to think, "How can a partner help?" I'll start us off. What if ... I can't think of anything to write about! How can a partner help? Well, I could listen to my partner's ideas and see if that gives me an idea. Maybe because my partner knows me, they could give me suggestions. Or maybe we just talk. For instance, my partner could say, "I'm writing about _____. Does that give you any ideas?"

See how I thought of some solutions to that "what if"? I'm going to give you some other "what ifs," and while you're talking about how partners can help, I'll chart the idea I just talked about.

- What if ... you have an idea, but you're not sure how it will go. How can a partner help?
- What if ... you think you might be finished, but you're not quite sure. How can a partner help?
- What if ... you're stuck. You just can't get beyond the problem you're having. How can a partner help?
- What if ... you made some changes, but you don't know if they are very good. How can a partner help?

(*Give partners time to talk after each "What if." Listen in for examples to share and add to the class chart.*)

ALTERNATIVE

Explain with Examples: **Offer examples of the many ways partners can support one another in solving common writing problems.**

 |

GUIDE

Prompt students to plan with their partners to determine what type of support they need.

Do you need a partner as a resource today? Plan for when you might meet a partner and what you might talk about. Check the chart we created for ideas.

(Allow students time to make a plan. Offer guidance when needed. Share exemplary plans.)

Remember, when you're giving feedback think about how it might feel to receive the feedback you're giving. Notice something positive, and then offer assistance—not just criticism.

RELEASE

Remind students that they can use their partners as resources, but they need to prioritize writing time.

Today writers, work with a partner when you need one. Remember to ask your partner first; he or she could be busy. Also, partner time is meant to help you write and should not take over your entire writing time. Now go write and don't be afraid to lean on a partner!

FOR ADDITIONAL SUPPORT, TRY

1.9 Talk It Out

1.21 Be Resourceful!

TIPS/RESOURCES

- Designate spaces for partners to work together without disturbing others.
- Create guidelines to make sure partner time doesn't take up all of students' writing time.

Writers Take a Pause

In this lesson, students learn the habit of pausing periodically to reread their work. They listen for errors and for gaps where more information is needed.

Writing Stage: Any • **Genre:** Any

INTRODUCE

Tell students writers don't wait until they're done to reread and revise their work.

Writers don't wait until a piece is completed to read it over. They pause every so often to reread their writing. As we write, we can go back after a sentence, a few lines, or a paragraph to see what changes we need to make. We can listen for errors, or gaps where information needs to be added, or where we want to go next with our work.

INSTRUCT

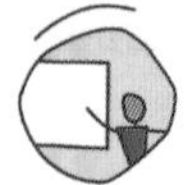

Demonstration

Model how to write a bit, pause, and reread aloud, making sure to fix errors in spelling, punctuation, and missing information.

Watch me as I write for a bit, then pause and reread aloud to myself. I'm going to check for errors in spelling and punctuation, but also I'm going to make sure that all of the words and ideas in my head are actually on the page. Finally, I'm going to see if I'll get some ideas for what I could add.

So I've written a few sentences about Diwali. So now I'm going to pause and reread: "Diwali is the most important holiday in India. It is festival of lights."

Wait—I can see I'm missing "a" in that last sentence, so let me fix that. And while I'm stopping, I also noticed that I should probably say that Diwali is *one* of the most important holidays, since there are other holidays that are celebrated in India, like Ghandi's birthday and other Buddhist, Hindu, and Muslim holidays. So I'll change that, too. Now I have, "Diwali is one of the most important holidays in India. It is a festival of lights."

I should say more about that. What does that mean? "Indian people put lights outside of their houses." I should probably say why, "The lights symbolize the inner light that protects you from darkness."

Do you see how going back and rereading lets me catch mistakes and also helps me think of other things I want to say or clarify?

 |

GUIDE

Support students in making plans to use the strategy during writing time.

I stopped and read to myself after just a couple of sentences because that makes sense for me. Can you take a minute and talk to your partner to make a plan for how you're going to try this? Will it be after a few sentences? A page? A paragraph?

(Allow 1–4 minutes for students to turn and talk with partners. Share exemplary responses.)

RELEASE

Remind students to use the strategy as they write.

When you write today, don't wait until you feel finished to review your writing. Writers check their writing as they work. They pause, reread, check for errors, and make additions.

FOR ADDITIONAL SUPPORT, TRY

1.9 Talk It Out

1.12 Writers Are Never Done

1.22 Partners Are Resources, Too!

TIPS/RESOURCES

- Emergent writers might want to go back and reread after a word or two, whereas fluent writers may want to wait until they have 3–5 lines.

LESSON 1.24

On Your Mark, Get Set, Go!

In this lesson, students learn to draft the body of their piece quickly in one sitting.

Writing Stage: Fluent • **Genre:** Expository Essay

INTRODUCE

Tell students that one way to draft is to use a plan and write all of the piece in one sitting.

One way writers can draft and harness some energy is to do it all at once. Basically, we look at the clock, look at the blank page, get our plan in our minds, and say to ourselves, "Ready, set, go!" We can draft from start to finish in one sitting in order to get all of our information out onto the page.

INSTRUCT

Explain with Examples

Explain how to draft an essay quickly, showing an example of a "speed draft." Point out transitions and sentences that explain.

I have my thesis here with three supports:*

"People make assumptions about pit bulls based on misinformation.
- People assume pit bulls are more aggressive than other breeds.
- People assume pit bulls are always bred for fighting.
- Because people think pit bulls are bad, people assume that bad people own pit bulls."

I know essays start with an introduction. But if I'm drafting quickly, it makes more sense to start with the body, and then come back to the introduction, so I'm going to start with my first point:

"People assume pit bulls are more aggressive than other dog breeds."

So now I have to think, "What do I know about this?" I know that pit bulls aren't just one breed. I also know that the label "aggressive" has led to many pit bulls being euthanized or put in shelters. Now I have to put that into paragraph form:

"People assume pit bulls are more aggressive than other dog breeds. That assumption has led to many problems for these dogs. For example, many states have anti-pit bull legislation that makes owning pit bulls illegal. In states where pit bulls are allowed, landlords often discriminate, making it impossible for renters to keep their dogs. But pit bull isn't really a breed! The term "pit bull" is a catch-all term for a number of breeds, or mixes of breeds, including American Staffordshire Terriers and American Pit Bull Terriers."

Do you see how all of my information supports the idea that people make assumptions based on misinformation? I use transitional phrases such as "For example" and sentences that explain terms and ideas to say more about my facts.

ALTERNATIVE

Demonstration: **Model for students how to write the body of your essay quickly, being sure to emphasize what you know about well-written essays.**

GUIDE

Give students an opportunity to plan their writing.

Look at one of the supporting details on your plan.* Turn and talk to a partner, taking turns discussing how your paragraph will go. You can use the exact words you want to write, thinking about sentences that explain terms and ideas. You can also use transitional phrases such as "For example" or "One way."

(Allow 1–4 minutes for students to turn and talk with partners. Share anything you're noticing that will support students as they write.)

RELEASE

Send students off to do a quick draft.

When you go off to write today, you're going to draft the body of your essay, using what you know about informational essays. Before you leave, share your plan for writing with your partner. That's your exit ticket for today.

FOR ADDITIONAL SUPPORT, TRY

5.22 Rehearse Your Thesis

5.23 Just Give Me a Reason

6.26 Invite Your Reader

6.27 Make It Playful

TIPS/RESOURCES

- Race drafts help prepare students for high-stakes, timed tests.
- Create a "box and bullet" template for students to fill in.
- Color code parts of the paragraph: the support sentence, transitions, and partner sentences.

*See sample chart, "Plan with Boxes and Bullets," on page 70.

Lesson 1.11 Just Get Started

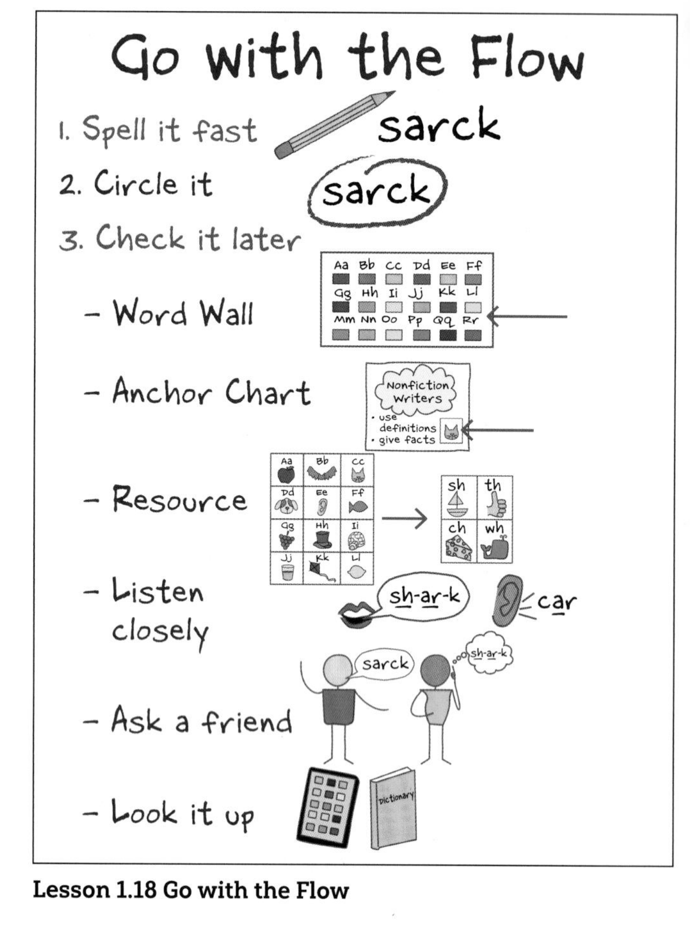

Lesson 1.18 Go with the Flow

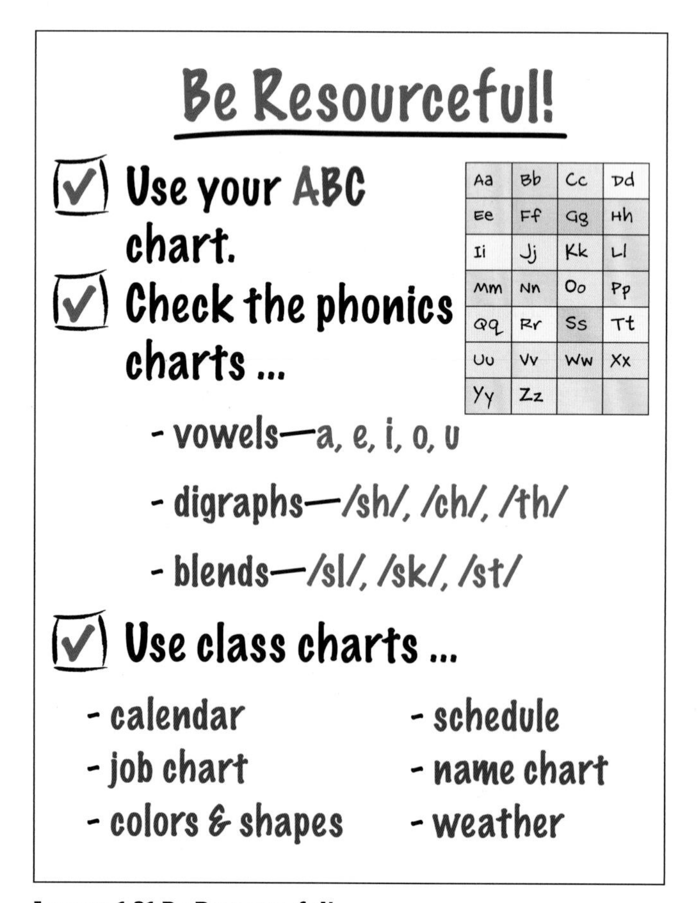

Lesson 1.21 Be Resourceful!

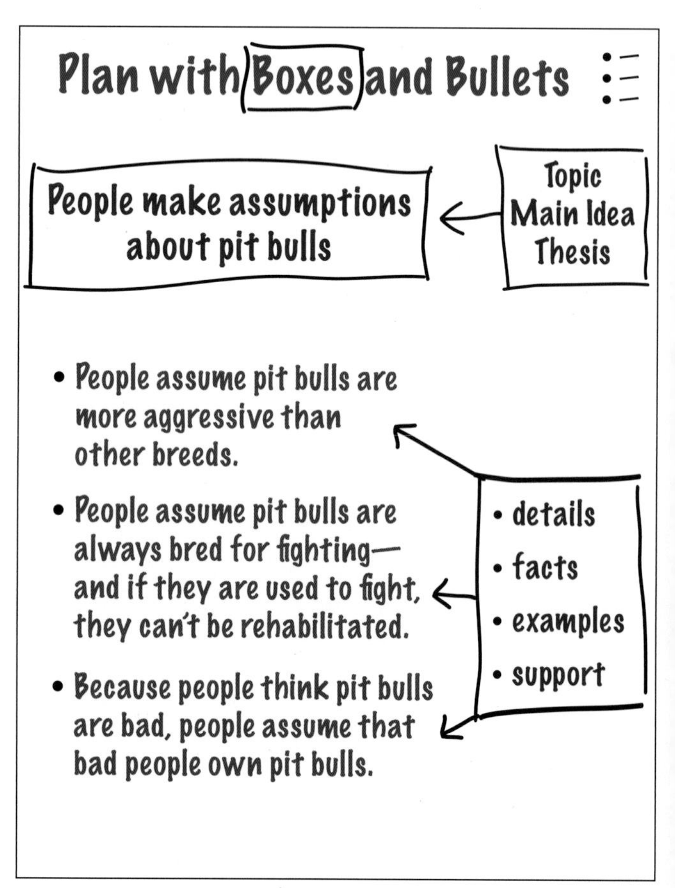

Lesson 1.24 On Your Mark, Get Set, Go!

Foundations & Conventions

The series of lessons in this section relate to the conventions of writing. Sometimes you might decide to create a spotlight on conventions by completing an entire series of lessons in a single unit. Other times you might disperse these lessons across several units as whole-class, small-group, or individualized lessons. The lessons:

- offer strategies to sound out and spell words;
- address punctuation, grammar, and usage; and
- can be used throughout different parts of the writing process.

Descriptors for Independent Use of Foundations and Conventions

Emergent Writers	Fluent Writers
• Spell words beginning with labeling illustrations, moving from hearing only initial sounds; to hearing initial and ending sounds; to hearing initial, medial, and ending sounds. • Develop skills from encoding simple CVC words to using learned spelling patterns (rimes) to experimenting with using parts of known words to write new words. • Use inconsistent spacing between words when writing sentences, moving toward consistent use of spacing. • Write words with a combination of uppercase and lowercase letters, moving toward conventional capitalization rules. • Punctuate sentences inconsistently, moving toward more consistent use of end punctuation. • Use sentence structures that match students' oral language, and move toward more technical structures as students learn transition words and phrases.	• Use simple and complex spelling patterns, prefixes, and suffixes to spell most words correctly. • Spell high-frequency words correctly and with automaticity. • Use appropriate capitalization and a variety of punctuation. • Punctuate dialogue correctly with occasional errors. • Indent to form paragraphs. • Use a variety of sentence structures so that the writing sounds more developed.

At-a-Glance Guide

Foundations & Conventions

Title		Lesson
2.1	**Who's On First?**	Stretch out words by listening for the beginning sound and writing the letter that matches.
2.2	**First and Last**	Stretch out words by listening for the beginning and ending sounds and writing the letters that match.
2.3	**Stretch It Out**	Stretch out a word by saying the word slowly, listening for beginning, medial, and ending sounds, and writing the letters that match.
2.4	**Tap It, Map It!**	Plan a sentence by tapping the words across fingers, mapping it on the page, and writing the words.
2.5	**Say It, Hear It, Write It, Read It, Repeat**	Stretch out a longer word by saying the first part, listening for the sounds, writing the letters, reading it back, and listening for the next sound.
2.6	**Clap It Out, Then Sound It Out**	Sound out longer words by clapping out the syllables, saying them slowly, and writing the sounds heard.
2.7	**That Sounds Like ...**	Spell words by listening for little words or word parts to write new words.
2.8	**Show What You Know**	Spell words by listening for and using spelling patterns.
2.9	**Give Them Some Space**	Write a word, read it back, and place a spacer before writing the next word.
2.10	**Stand Tall, Stand Proud**	Use capitals correctly by focusing on the first word in a sentence, on names, and on the pronoun *I*.
2.11	**Give Them a Break**	Use end marks correctly by first saying and writing a sentence, then placing the appropriate end mark.
2.12	**Who Said That?**	Use quotation marks correctly for information said by a person or copied from a source.
2.13	**Keep 'Em Separated**	Separate descriptors of three or more by placing a comma after each word except for the one that follows *and* or *or*.
2.14	**Give Them Room to Breathe**	Use a comma after a transition word to help readers take a pause.

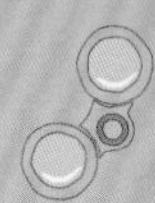

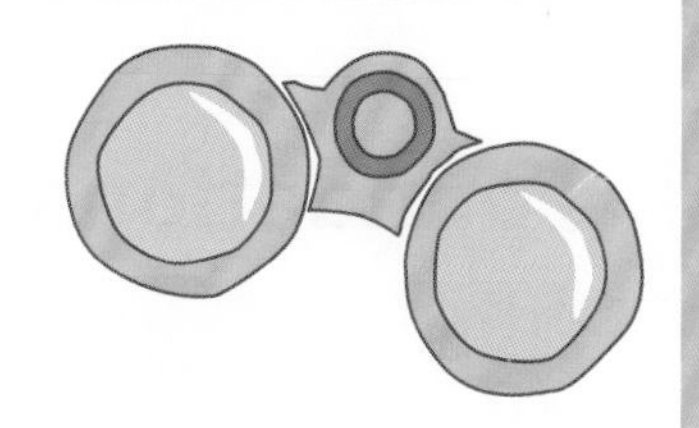

Writing Stage	Genre	
Emergent	List Pattern	How-To
Emergent	List Pattern	How-To
Emergent	List Pattern	How-To All-About
Emergent	List Pattern	How-To All-About
Emergent Transitional	List Pattern	How-To All-About
Emergent Transitional	List Pattern	How-To All-About
Emergent Transitional	List Pattern	How-To All-About
Any	Any	
Emergent	List Pattern	How-To
Emergent Transitional	List Pattern	How-To All-About
Emergent Transitional	List Pattern	How-To All-About
Transitional Fluent	All-About Feature Article Literary Nonfiction Expository Nonfiction	Biography Research Report Expository Essay
Transitional Fluent	Any	
Transitional Fluent	How-To All-About Feature Article Literary Nonfiction	Expository Nonfiction Biography Research Report Expository Essay

Foundations & Conventions continued

Title		Lesson
2.15	**Be Descriptive**	Be more precise by using adjectives to describe nouns.
2.16	**Descriptions Go Beyond Nouns**	Be more descriptive by using adverbs to show where, when, how, how much, and how often.
2.17	**Prepositions Describe, Too**	Be more descriptive by showing the relationship of a noun or pronoun to other words or phrases.
2.18	**Be Consistent**	Keep verbs and other language consistent throughout writing.
2.19	**Nouns and Verbs Must Get Along**	Make sure that the noun and verb agree in number.
2.20	**Put It in a Paragraph**	Write in correct paragraph form with a topic sentence, supporting details, and a concluding sentence.
2.21	**Rhythm Is Gonna Get You**	Create voice and rhythm by varying sentence lengths and beginnings.
2.22	**Conjunction Connection**	Link ideas or create longer sentences by using conjunctions.
2.23	**Come Together**	Write compound sentences that connect two independent clauses.

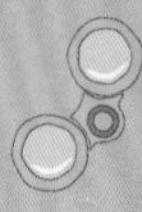

Writing Stage	Genre	
Any	Any	
Any	How-To All-About Feature Article Literary Nonfiction	Expository Nonfiction Biography Research Report Expository Essay
Transitional Fluent	How-To All-About Feature Article Literary Nonfiction	Expository Nonfiction Biography Research Report Expository Essay
Transitional Fluent	How-To All-About Feature Article Literary Nonfiction	Expository Nonfiction Biography Research Report Expository Essay
Transitional Fluent	How-To All-About Feature Article Literary Nonfiction	Expository Nonfiction Biography Research Report Expository Essay
Transitional Fluent	All-About Feature Article Literary Nonfiction Expository Nonfiction	Biography Research Report Expository Essay
Fluent	All-About Feature Article Literary Nonfiction Expository Nonfiction	Biography Research Report Expository Essay
Transitional Fluent	How-To All-About Feature Article Literary Nonfiction	Expository Nonfiction Biography Research Report Expository Essay
Fluent	Feature Article Literary Nonfiction Expository Nonfiction	Biography Research Report Expository Essay

Who's On First?

In this lesson, students learn to stretch out words by listening for the beginning sound and writing the letter that matches.

Writing Stage: Emergent • **Genre:** List, Pattern, How-To Book

INTRODUCE

Tell students that they will stretch out a word by listening for the beginning sound and recording the letter that matches.

As we write, we want to start thinking about the words we are writing. Sometimes thinking about writing big, new words can seem tricky. Instead of giving up, let's just think about the first sound we hear in a word and write only the beginning sound. It's the perfect place to start!

INSTRUCT

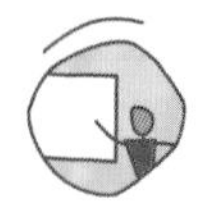

Demonstration

Show students how you stretch out words, listen for the beginning sound, and write the corresponding letter.

Let me show you how I stretch out words and listen for the beginning sound so that I can write the letter that matches.

Here I have my writing about cats. *(Show students your booklet.)* I want to add some writing to match my pictures. To help me, I will listen to the first sound I hear in the word, think about the letter that makes that sound, and then write the letter to match. On this page, I drew a picture of a cat playing with a toy mouse. What are some words I can try to add here? Oh, I know ... *cat*! What's the first sound I hear in the word *cat*? Let me stretch it out, **/k/ /a/ /t/**. The first sound I hear is **/k/**. What letter makes the **/k/** sound? The letter **c**! So let me add that to my writing. *(Jot down the letter **c** to label the cat.)* Let me try this one more time. This part of the picture shows a toy mouse. Let me stretch out the word *toy* and think about the beginning sound I hear in **/t/ /oy/**. Hmmm. I hear the **/t/** sound, which is the letter **t**! So I will write a **t** near the toy mouse to label it. *(Jot down the letter **t** to label the toy.)*

Do you see how I stretched out words to listen for just the beginning sound? And then I thought about what letter makes that sound?

 |

GUIDE

Prompt students to follow your model. Name words from your writing for them to practice with a partner.

Here, on the next page, is a picture of a cat with its food and water dish. Some words that I am thinking of adding on this page are: *cat*, *food*, *water*, and *dish. (Including the word* cat *again gives them a chance to reinforce the strategy before they move on.)* That's four words! With your partner, I want you to think about the beginning sounds you hear. Remember to stretch out each word, listen closely to the beginning sound, and then think about the letter that makes that sound.

(Allow 1–4 minutes for students to turn and talk with partners. Share out correct initial sounds for each word.)

RELEASE

Remind students about the importance of attempting to write words by listening for sounds.

I am so impressed! You started important writing work today by adding letters to your writing to represent words. Don't get discouraged or think "I don't know how to write _____." Instead, slow down and think about just the beginning sound. Then think about the letter that makes the sound and write it. Remember, as informational writers we want to make sure we include as much information as we can, not just in our pictures but also in our words.

FOR ADDITIONAL SUPPORT, TRY

2.2 First and Last

7.1 Do You Hear Me? Do You See Me?

TIPS/RESOURCES

- Use a class ABC chart for letter identification and recall.
- Use dry-erase boards to make the practice visual.
- Practice one word at a time to take it at a slower pace.
- Use a document camera to enlarge your writing.

LESSON 2.2

First and Last

In this lesson, students learn to stretch out words by listening for the beginning and ending sounds and then writing the letters that match.

Writing Stage: Emergent • **Genre:** List, Pattern, How-To Book

INTRODUCE

Tell students that they will stretch out words by listening for the beginning and ending sounds and writing the matching letters.

As we work on our informational writing, we can use what we know about letters and sounds to help us write more words on the page. It's okay if we don't know how to spell the whole word exactly, because that can be tricky sometimes. Instead, we can start taking some more risks as writers and using what we know about letters and sounds. We can do this by stretching out words and thinking about the sounds we hear in the beginning and at the end of the words and then writing down the letters that match.

INSTRUCT

Demonstration

Model how you listen for the beginning and ending sounds, think about what letter makes each sound, and write down the letters that correspond.

Let me show you how I stretch out words—first by listening for the beginning and ending sounds, then by writing down the letters that match.

Here is my writing about transportation. *(Show students your booklet.)* I have so much information already about different types of transportation on each page, but I think it's time for me to try to add some more writing. On this page, I have a picture of a bus, so let me add that word to my writing. I will stretch out the word and listen to the beginning and ending sounds. **/b/ /u/ /s/**. The first sound I hear is **/b/** and I know the letter **b** makes the **/b/** sound so let me write that down. *(Quickly jot down letter **b**.)* Now, let me listen again to the end sound. **/b/ /u/ /s/ ... /s/**—that's an **s**! So let me add that to my writing. *(Quickly jot down letter **s**. Keep in mind you are demonstrating how to approximate spelling so that your students will take risks and apply their letter/sound knowledge to unknown words.)*

Let me give it another try on the next page. On this page, I have a boat—**/b/ /ō/ /t/**. I know. ... It's a **b** again for the first letter. (*Quickly jot down letter **b**.*) Let me stretch it out again to listen for the end sound—**/b/ /ō/ /t/** *(accentuate the end sound)*. I hear the **/t/** sound and I know that the letter **t** makes the **/t/** sound, so I will add that to my writing. *(Quickly jot down letter **t**.)*

Do you see how I stretched out my words? Did you notice how I listened for the beginning and ending sounds, then thought about the letters that make each sound and wrote down the letters?

ALTERNATIVE

Guided Practice: **Have students help you stretch out words for your writing. Ask them to listen for the beginning and ending sounds and think about what letters will match.**

 |

GUIDE

Ask students to work with partners and stretch out words using the process you've shared.

Do you think you can help me with the next page? *(Show students the next page of your writing.)* Here I have a page about cars. Let's stretch out the word *car* with our partners and listen for the beginning and end sounds. What sound do you hear at the beginning? At the end? What letters make those sounds? Turn and talk and give it a go with your partner. *(Allow students 1–2 minutes to turn and talk with partners.)* I heard so many of you say **/k/** and **/r/**, which stand for the letters **c** and **r**. Give me a thumbs up if you and your partner said the same thing. Wow! I am so impressed. Let me add that to my writing. *(Add letters **c** and **r** to your writing to represent the word* car.*)*

RELEASE

Remind students to pay attention to the initial and ending sounds and write the letters that match.

Today we took a big jump in trying to write words that might seem a little tricky at first. We did this by listening to beginning and ending sounds, then writing the letters that match. As you are writing today and every day, remember that it's okay to start taking some more risks in writing new words.

FOR ADDITIONAL SUPPORT, TRY

2.3 Stretch It Out

2.5 Say It, Hear It, Write It, Read It, Repeat

2.6 Clap It Out, Then Sound It Out

7.1 Do You Hear Me? Do You See Me?

TIPS/RESOURCES

- Display a class ABC chart for letter identification and recall.
- Create individual ABC charts for each student.
- Use dry-erase boards in the Guide portion of the lesson.
- Use a document camera to enlarge your writing.

Stretch It Out

In this lesson, students learn to stretch out a word by saying the word slowly, listening for beginning, medial, and ending sounds, and writing the letters that match.

Writing Stage: Emergent • **Genre:** List, Pattern, How-To Book, All-About Book

INTRODUCE

Tell students that they will stretch out words listening for beginning, middle, and ending sounds.

Sometimes it might seem that certain words are too tricky for us to write, but it doesn't have to be perfect. What we need to focus on is what we know about letter/sound relationships and use that knowledge to write our words the best we can. We can do this by listening to each part of the word. We can say the word slowly and listen for the beginning, middle, and ending sounds, and then think about what letters make each sound and write those down.

INSTRUCT

Demonstration

Show students how you stretch out a word, listening for the beginning, middle, and ending sounds.

Watch me as I work on my booklet about soccer. *(Show students your booklet.)* On this page, I have a picture of a soccer net. I would like to add the word *net*, but I am not sure how to spell it. Let me stretch out the word *net* to listen for the beginning, middle, and ending sounds. **/n/ /e/ /t/**. What sound do I hear first? **/n/** ... that's the sound that the letter **n** makes. *(Jot down each letter as you stretch out the word.)* What sound do I hear in the middle of *net*, **/n/ /e/ /t/**? **/e/**, **/e/** ... hmmm, that's a little tricky, but I think the letter **e** makes the **/e/** sound in *net*. Remember, it's okay if I'm not 100 percent sure, but I will try my best to match letters to the sounds I hear. So I will add an **e** to the word *net* to represent the middle sound. Now let me stretch out the word *net* to hear the ending sound. *Net*—**/n/ /e/ /t/**, **/t/**. I hear a "t" at the end, so I will add the letter **t** to my word. *(Finish writing the word* net.*)* "n-e-t" ... *net*! Wow! Look at that. I was able to write the whole word *net* because I stretched it out and listened to each part of the word—the beginning, middle, and ending sounds.

Did you notice how I stretched out my word? Then I listened for the sound in each part of the word. I thought about what letter makes each sound and wrote the letter that matches!

ALTERNATIVE

Guided Practice: **Using dry-erase boards, work with students to stretch out sounds as they write their responses.**

 |

GUIDE

Prompt students to continue practice by sounding out words from your writing.

Do you think you can help me with the next page? *(Show students the next page of your booklet.)* Here I want to write the words *win* and *game*. Let's stretch out the word *win*—**/w/ /i/ /n/**. What sound do we hear at the beginning? The middle? The end? What letters match each sound?

(Allow students 1–4 minutes to turn and talk with partners. Write the word win.*)*

What about the word *game*? This one is a little trickier. For the beginning sound, I heard a lot of you say the letter **g** for **/g/**, so let me write down that letter. Then for the middle sound, we hear **/ā/**, like the name of the letter **a**, so let me jot that down. Then at the end, what do we hear? *Game* ... **/m/** ... what letter makes the **/m/** sound, everyone? The letter **m**! *(Quickly jot down* **g-a-m***. If your students have received instruction on silent* **e***, then it should be expected they apply that knowledge here. This goes for any phonics principle.)*

RELEASE

Remind students to practice sounding out words by stretching them out, listening for sounds, and then writing down the letters that match.

Remember, today and every day when you're writing, stretch out the words. Listen for the beginning, middle, and ending sounds. Think about the letters that make each sound, and then write down the letters that match. The more we do this, the more writing our booklets will have in them—and the more information our reader will have to learn about our topics!

FOR ADDITIONAL SUPPORT, TRY

2.1 Who's On First?

2.2 First and Last

2.5 Say It, Hear It, Write It, Read It, Repeat

2.6 Clap It Out, Then Sound It Out

TIPS/RESOURCES

- Display a class ABC chart. Provide individual ABC charts for each student.
- Have students use dry-erase boards to write the letters to make the practice auditory and visual.
- For Instruct and Guide, you can choose to use words that align practice with your phonics instruction.

LESSON 2.4

Tap It, Map It!

In this lesson, students learn to plan out a sentence by tapping out the words across their fingers, mapping it out on the page, and then writing the words.

Writing Stage: Emergent • **Genre:** List, Pattern, How-To Book, All-About Book

INTRODUCE

Tell students that they will learn how to plan out a sentence by tapping, mapping, and writing.

As we build up our writing muscles, we are ready to start pushing ourselves to write sentences to match our pictures. Sometimes the idea of writing a whole sentence can feel tricky. We are going to learn to plan out a sentence by tapping out each word across our fingers and then mapping it out on the page.*

INSTRUCT

Demonstration

Show students how you tap out the words in your sentence, map it out on paper to see where the words will go, and then write the sentence.

Watch me as I give this a try.

Here I have my writing about transportation. *(Show students your booklet.)* On this page, I have a train and I want to add a sentence to match my picture, "Trains go fast." Let me first tap to see how many words are in my sentence. *(Tap one finger for each word. Show how there is a space between each finger.)* How many words do I have here? Yes, three! Okay, so now I know I have three words in my sentence. Let me look at my page and see where my sentence will go. On this line I will write, "Trains go fast." Let me see where each word will fit. I can put a lightly marked line using my pencil to make a space where the word will go. *(Show students how you lightly make a space for each word.)* Remember, I counted the words for this sentence—I have three words. *Trains* will go here *(motion to the space you're making for each word)*, *go* will be next but we have to remember to leave a little space, and then *fast* will go last. Now I tapped out my sentence and mapped it out, so I am ready to write it! *Trains* goes first. *(Jot down each word as you say it.) Go* is second and I know that word from our word wall. *Fast*, let me stretch this one out, ***/f/ /a/ /s/ /t/***, *fast*. "Trains go fast." I will add a period at the end. That wasn't too tricky after all!

ALTERNATIVE

Guided Practice: **Using dry-erase boards, have students tap, map, and write multiple sentences.**

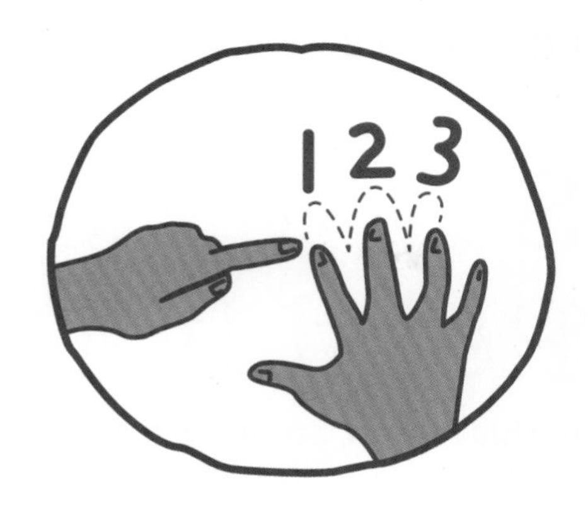

GUIDE

Guide students to use the strategy for your next sentence.

Do you think you can help me with my airplane section? *(Show students your booklet.)*

I want to write words to match my picture: "Airplanes fly in the sky." *(Tap it out as you did earlier.)* We have five words in this sentence. Now we need to map it out. You will use your dry-erase boards for this part. Map out where each word will go. Remember you can put a little line where each word will be written. *(Prompt students to work in partnerships to map out the sentence on their boards and write the sentence.)*

Look at those sentences! I will add the sentence to my writing now. *(Quickly jot down the sentence.)*

RELEASE

Remind students to write sentences by tapping and mapping.

Today we talked about how to tap out sentences using our fingers and map out on the page where each word will be written. We can even make little lines to mark the place where each word will go.

Remember, you can do this anytime to help you add sentences to your writing.

FOR ADDITIONAL SUPPORT, TRY

2.9 Give Them Some Space
2.11 Give Them a Break
6.8 From Labels to Sentences

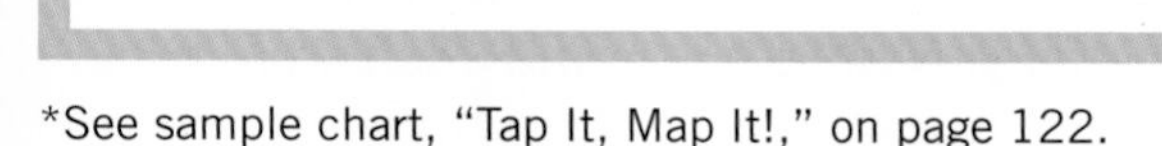

TIPS/RESOURCES

- Instead of dry-erase boards, have students write in the air.
- Use sentences that are appropriate for your group of students.
- Use the same process in interactive writing.

*See sample chart, "Tap It, Map It!," on page 122.

Say It, Hear It, Write It, Read It, Repeat

In this lesson, students learn to stretch out a multisyllabic word by saying the first part, listening for the sounds, recording the letter(s), reading it back, and listening for the next sound.

Writing Stage: Emergent, Transitional • **Genre:** List, Pattern, How-To Book, All-About Book

INTRODUCE

Tell students that it is best to sound out longer words one sound at a time.

Spelling words can seem simple when there are only a few sounds. Long words can sometimes become a jumbled mess, though, when we try to sound them out. Today we are going to learn that we can stretch out longer words one sound at a time.

INSTRUCT

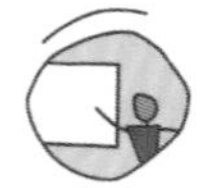

Demonstration

Model for students how you spell multisyllabic words one phoneme at a time as you move across the word.

Watch me as I spell a long word one sound at a time. As I say each sound, I listen closely to hear it, then write the letter that matches. Before I go on to the next sound, I point under what I have written so far. I say it, hear it, write it, and read it back to check it. Then I repeat the process with the next sound! *(Display anchor chart.* Chant the steps with students.)*

Today I am writing my book about insects. This page is going to be about butterflies. My first sentence is, "A butterfly is an insect." *(Begin to write the sentence.)* The first word is easy peasy—*A*. The next word, *butterfly,* is not so easy. Let's look at the chart. Step 1: Say it! I am going to say the first sound, **/b/**. Step 2: Hear it! I hear **/b/**. The letter that makes that sound is **b**. Step 3: Write it! I am going to write the letter **b**. Step 4: Read it! I am going to point under what I wrote so far and read it back, **/b/**. Now, Step 5: Repeat!

As I read it, I will continue to listen for the next sound **/b/ /u/**. I hear **/u/**—the letter **u** makes that sound. Let me write it. Now I read back what I have so far, **/b/ /u/**. I am going to say the next sound **/bu/ /t/**. I hear **/t/**—the letter **t**. Let me write it and read it all back, **/b/ /u/ /t/**. Now I will say the next sound **/b/ /u/ /t/ /r/**. I hear **/r/**. That's the letter **r**. Let me write it and read it back **/b/ /u/ /t/ /r/**. Now I will say the next sound **/but/ /r/ /f/**. I hear **/f/**, the letter **f**. Let me write it and read it all back, **/b/ /u/ /t/ /r/ /f/**. The next sound is **/b/ /u/ /t/ /r/ /f/**, **/l/**. I hear **/l/**; that must be the letter **l**. I will write it, read it back, and say the next sound—**/b/ /u/ /t/ /r/ /f/ /l/** ... **/ī/**. I hear **/ī/**—that must be the letter **y**. Now let's read the whole word back, **/b/ /u/ /t/ /r/ /f/ /l/ /y/**. I think I have all the sounds! *(Approximate spellings are developmentally appropriate at this stage.)*

The next words are easy—*is, an*. The last word is trickier—*insect.*

(Model spelling the word insect *as you did with* butterfly.
Refer to the anchor chart.)

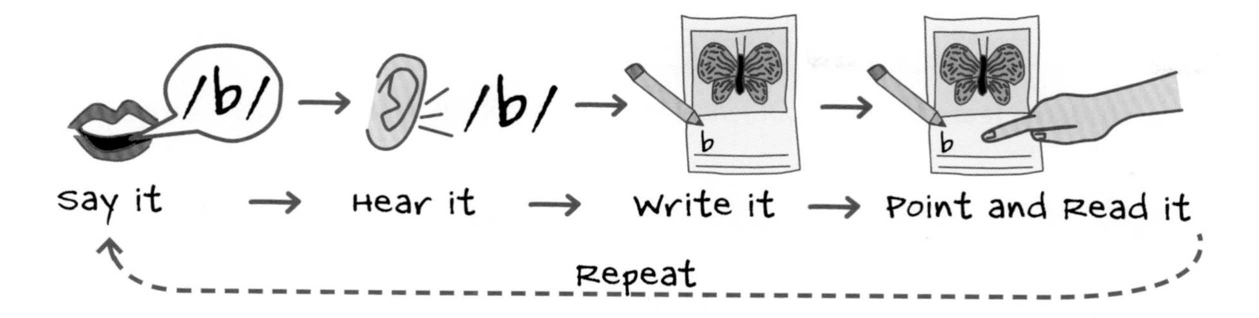

GUIDE

Provide each student with a dry-erase board and guide the class through spelling words together.

Do you think you can help me with the next sentence, "A butterfly begins as a caterpillar." I don't need your help with *A* or *butterfly*, but I do need your help with *begins* and *caterpillar*. Using your dry-erase boards and markers, will you work through these words with me, bit by bit, using the steps on our chart?

(Have students call out the sounds and record the letters on their boards as you write them out.)

RELEASE

Remind students that spelling longer words requires working through them bit by bit, one sound at a time.

So remember, writers, long words often require a little more work. We must work them out, one sound at a time, reading back each bit as we write and moving across the word. Starting with the first sound, we say it, hear it, write it, read it—then repeat with the next sound!

FOR ADDITIONAL SUPPORT, TRY

1.21 Be Resourceful!

2.1 Who's On First?

2.6 Clap It Out, Then Sound It Out

TIPS/RESOURCES

- Use interactive writing activities during other parts of the day and apply the strategy for longer words.
- Encourage students to keep alphabet, digraph, blend, and vowel charts handy.

*See sample chart, "Say It, Hear It, Write It, Read It, Repeat," on page 122.

Clap It Out, Then Sound It Out

In this lesson, students learn to sound out longer words by clapping out the syllables, saying them slowly, and recording the sounds they hear.

Writing Stage: Emergent, Transitional • **Genre:** List, Pattern, How-To Book, All-About Book

INTRODUCE

Tell students that breaking words into parts can make them easier to spell.

Spelling words can seem simple when they are short. But long words can be broken down into smaller parts, making them just as easy to spell. Today we are going to learn that we can sound out longer words by clapping out the syllables, saying each syllable slowly, and writing the sounds we hear.

INSTRUCT

Demonstration

Model for students how you sound out longer words in your own writing by breaking the words into syllables.

I am working on my book about insects. This page is going to be about ladybugs. I am going to write, "A ladybug is an insect."

I know the first word is going to be easy—*A*. However, the second word is a little trickier, *ladybug*. *(Display a chart with picture support for each step.*)* First, I am going to clap out the syllables. Then I am going to say each syllable slowly. Last, I will write the sounds I hear. Let me clap out the syllables for *ladybug—la-dy-bug*. It has three syllables. The first syllable is, **/lā/**. Let me say that one very slowly —**/l/ /ā/**. The letters that match those sounds are **/l/**, the letter **l**, and **/ā/**, the letter **a**. I am going to write **l** and **a**. Let me clap out the word again—*la-dy-bug*. The second syllable is **/dē/**. Let me say that very slowly—**/d/ /ē/**. The letters that match are **/d/**, the letter **d**, and **/ē/**, the letter **e**. *(Note that approximated spelling is acceptable at this developmental stage.)* I am going to write **d** and **e** next to the first part because it is still the same word. Let me clap out the word again to see if there are more parts—*la-dy-bug*. The third syllable is *bug*. Let me say that very slowly—**/b/ /u/ /g/**. The letters that match are **/b/**, the letter **b**; and **/u/**, the letter **u**; and **/g/**, the letter **g**. I am going to write *bug* next to the first parts because it is still the same word. Let me read it back, *ladybug*.

Terrific! Now let me finish my sentence, "A ladybug is an insect." I can write *is* and *an* easily. I know those words. Now I must write *insect*. Since this is a longer word (refer to the chart), let me clap out the syllables, say each syllable slowly, and write the sounds I hear.

(Repeat the process for the word insect.*)*

GUIDE

Provide each student with a dry-erase board and guide the class through spelling long words.

Do you think you can help me with the next sentences? They are, "They are beetles. They like flowers." I don't need your help with *they* or *are* or *like*, but I do need your help with *beetles* and *flowers*. Using your dry-erase boards and markers, will you work through these words with me, one syllable at a time, using the steps on our chart?

(Have students clap out the syllables in unison, say each syllable slowly, and call out the sounds they hear, then record corresponding letters on their boards to write the words.)

RELEASE

Remind students that spelling longer words requires breaking them down into smaller parts.

So remember, writers, long words can be broken down into smaller parts making them just as easy to spell as short words. It's just that longer words require a little extra work. We must first clap out the syllables so that we can stretch each syllable slowly and write the sounds we hear.

FOR ADDITIONAL SUPPORT, TRY

1.21 Be Resourceful!

2.1 Who's On First?

2.5 Say It, Hear It, Write It, Read It, Repeat

TIPS/RESOURCES

- Create small copies of the chart for students to keep handy.
- Use interactive writing throughout the day for longer words.
- Encourage students to keep alphabet digraph, blend, and vowel charts handy.

*See sample chart, "Spell Longer Words," on page 122.

That Sounds Like ...

In this lesson, students learn to spell words by listening for "little words" or word parts to write new words.

Writing Stage: Emergent, Transitional • **Genre:** List, Pattern, How-To Book, All-About Book

INTRODUCE

Tell students that one way to spell new words is to listen for little words or parts of known words inside the unknown word.

Rather than sound out words by listening for each sound, it is sometimes easier to listen for parts of words inside words. When you hear a little word that sounds like another word you already know, you can use that word or part to help you spell the new word.

INSTRUCT

Demonstration

Model how you spell words by listening for parts similar to words you can already spell or find in the classroom.

Watch me as I spell new words in my book about insects. On this page, I plan to write, "Ants are insects. They can hold a lot."

When I say a word out loud, I listen to hear if there is a part that reminds me of another word. When I hear that part, I figure out how some of those letters will help me write the new word. The first word is *ants*. Let me say it out loud—*ants*. I hear **/an/** at the beginning of that word! *An* is a word I know. It is also part of another word I know—*can*. I know that the letters **a** and **n** are how you spell it! (*Record the first part of the word, then sound out and record the rest.*) Now I listen for the other sounds. I hear **/t/ /s/** which must be the letters **t** and **s**.

Let me write the next words. I know how to spell *are* but don't really know how to spell *insects*. I hear **/in/** at the beginning of that word. *In* is a word that I know. It is also part of other words I know—*pin* and *tin*. I know that the letters **i** and **n** are how you spell it, so I can write the first part of *insects*. (*Record the first part of the word, then sound out and record the rest.*)

Do you see how I am listening for parts of words and sounds inside words to help me spell?

GUIDE

Provide each student with a dry-erase board and guide the class through spelling new words.

Will you help me spell some tough words in the next sentence? You will use your dry-erase boards and show me how to spell these words.

I want to say, "They can hold a lot." *They* and *can* are easy, word wall words. However, *hold* is trickier. Do you hear something familiar in that word? *(Ask for responses from students.)* Some of you hear the word *hole*. Some of you hear the word *old*. Some of you said that it reminds you of the word *cold*. Which of those words might be easy for us to find? *(Ask for responses from students.)* Some of you said that we can look on the weather chart for *cold*. Which part of the word will help us spell *hold*? We need to start with the letter **h**. That's right—and the letters **o**, **l**, **d** will help us spell it.

(Repeat with the word lot.*)*

RELEASE

Remind students that one way to spell new words is to listen for little words or word parts they already know.

Remember that another way to help you spell new words is to say the word out loud and listen carefully for little words inside that bigger word. Then you can use those little words to help you spell the bigger word.

FOR ADDITIONAL SUPPORT, TRY

1.21 Be Resourceful!

2.5 Say It, Hear It, Write It, Read It, Repeat

2.6 Clap It Out, Then Sound It Out

TIPS/RESOURCES

- Use interactive writing throughout the day for longer words.
- Have students keep small copies of word wall words handy to use as a resource.
- Encourage students to use their environment to find words that will help them spell.

Show What You Know

In this lesson, students learn to spell words by listening for and using spelling patterns that they have learned previously to help them advance.

Writing Stage: Any • **Genre:** Any

INTRODUCE

Tell students that by listening closely for spelling patterns, we can write new words.

As writers, we want to use our best spelling anytime we write. To do that, we sometimes need to keep in mind not only what we want to say, but what we already know about how words are spelled. We do this by listening for and using spelling patterns we've learned.

INSTRUCT

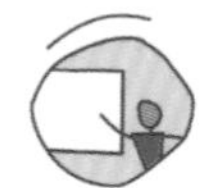

Demonstration

Model how to use words or spelling patterns that you know to spell new words. Use any helpful phonics charts.

When you write, it can help to make sure any tools you need are nearby. I can get out lists of spelling patterns I know I have in my writing folder or be sure to move myself closer to our phonics board.

I can use what we've been learning about word families to help me write. Here I'm teaching about my cat. The first page of my book shows my cat knocking my plant off the table—cats do this kind of thing when they're bored. I want to write: "My cat is so bad." I know *cat* is one of our **-at** family words. So I write: "My c-at is so ..." The words *my, is,* and *so* are already on our word wall. Now what can I use to help me spell *bad*? The first sound is **/b/**. (*Feel free to have students tell you it is the letter* ***b***.) Yes, that is the letter **b**. Is there a word family that can help me? *Bad*. **/b/ /ad/**. Oh! That's the **-ad** family! *b-a-d*. Now I have my sentence: "My cat is so bad."

 |

GUIDE

Prompt students to construct your next sentence using the patterns they know.

Can you help me with the next page of my book? I'm still teaching about my cat. See, she's here on my lap taking a nap. I want to say: "My cat naps on my lap." Let's do it together. Get out your dry-erase boards. *My* is a word wall word. How about *cat*? Is there a word family we know that can help us?

(*Coach students to use the* ***-at*** *and* ***-ap*** *word families to write the words in your sentence. Invite students to write* cat, nap, *and* lap *on their dry-erase boards. You may also ask individual students to come to the front and "pass the pen."*)

Wow! You really used what we know about word families and spelling patterns to help me write my page!

RELEASE

Remind students to use what they know about spelling patterns as they write.

When you go off to write today, be sure to use what you know—not just our word wall words, but what you know about spelling patterns and word families to help. You can take out any word charts that help you or move closer to the phonics board when you need to.

FOR ADDITIONAL SUPPORT, TRY

2.3 Stretch It Out

2.7 That Sounds Like ...

TIPS/RESOURCES

- Make classroom and personal charts of spelling patterns available to students.
- Involve all students during Guide by giving them dry-erase boards to try the sentence.
- Invite students up to the board and "pass the pen" to involve them in the strategy.
- If you don't have dry-erase boards, use paper and clipboards, or have students write in the air.

LESSON 2.9

Give Them Some Space

In this lesson, students learn to record a word, read it back, and place a spacer before writing the next word.

Writing Stage: Emergent • **Genre:** List, Pattern, How-To Book

INTRODUCE

Tell students that writers make spaces between their words by writing one word, reading it back, and using a spacer before writing the next word.

When we're writing, we have to think of our reader. One way we think of our reader is to make our writing easy for them to read. We can do this by making sure there are spaces between the words we write. To do this, we write down one word, then read it back—just to make sure we have put on the paper all the letters of the sounds we hear. Then we use a spacer before we write the next word.

INSTRUCT

Demonstration

Model how you write a word, read it back, and use a spacer (your finger, a craft stick, or other tool) to create a space.

Let me show you. *(Write words and model spacing for students.)* I'm writing about our playground here at school. I have my drawing here of the first thing I see—the swings. I'm going to write: "I see the swings." First, I write "I." Now I'm going to read it back: *I*.

Now I have to write "see." Wait, I need to use my spacer—I'm going to use my finger to make a space. I'll put it right after *I*. Now I can write "see." Hmmm. *See* is a sight word. I can look at our chart. **s**, **e**, and another **e**. There, *see*. I'll put my space finger down again—"I see." Now my next word is *the*. "I see the" Hey, that's another sight word: **t**-**h**-**e**. I only need a little space between the letters, but at the end of the word I need a big space. So now I'll need my spacer again. Who can come up and help me with the spacer?

(Demonstrate the next word, swings, *to complete the sentence.)*

Did you notice how I wrote a word, read it to make sure it was right, and then made a space?

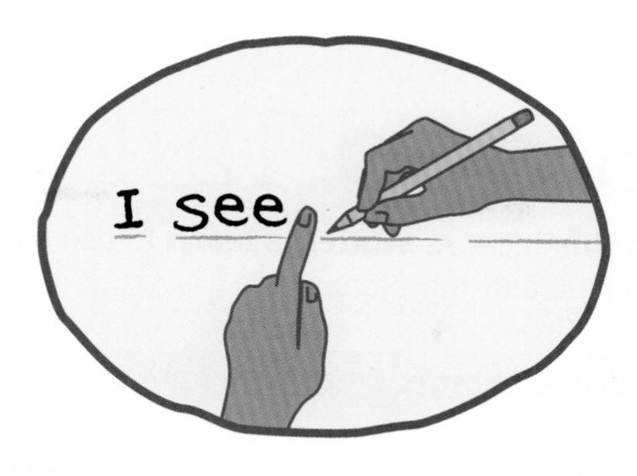

GUIDE

Prompt students to use spaces between words as they each write a sentence on a dry-erase board, paper, or clipboard. Invite students to come and write on the demonstration text.

Let's try this together. My next page is about the slide on our playground. *(Display the page.)* I want to write, "I see the slide." Can you use your dry-erase boards to try it all together? First, we have to write "I." Okay, now everyone, read what's on your dry-erase board. Now what do we need? A spacer! Right. Put your space finger down. And let's say and write our next word: *see*.

(Guide students in this way as you write the sentence "I see the slide." together. Also ask students to come up and write on the Instruct demonstration text.)

RELEASE

Remind students to make their writing easy for readers by making spaces between each word.

As you write today, be sure to think of your reader. Make spaces between your words to make it easy for them to read. Do it by writing a word, going back to read it, and using a spacer after that word before you start writing the next word. That way, your reader can enjoy your writing and read it with ease!

FOR ADDITIONAL SUPPORT, TRY

2.5 Say It, Hear It, Write It, Read It, Repeat

TIPS/RESOURCES:

- Use a physical spacer to help students remember this strategy.
- Involve all students during Guide by giving them dry-erase boards to try the sentence.
- Invite students up to the board and "pass the pen" to get them involved in applying the strategy.

Stand Tall, Stand Proud

In this lesson, students learn to use capitals correctly by focusing on the first word in a sentence, names, and the pronoun *I*.

Writing Stage: Emergent, Transitional • **Genre:** List, Pattern, How-To Book, All-About Book

INTRODUCE

Tell students we need to use capital letters correctly: at the start of a sentence, for a name, and for *I*.

When we're writing, we want to keep our readers in mind so that they will be able to understand our writing with ease. One way to make our writing easy to read is to pay attention to when we use capital letters. We use them to start sentences, for the names of things (or proper nouns), and for the word *I*.

INSTRUCT

Inquiry

Have students look at a sentence and discuss what they notice about capitals.

(*Display sentences.*) Take a moment and look at these sentences:

"My dog is Roscoe. My family and I adopted him from South Carolina."

What do you notice about the capital letters in this sentence? First, where are they? Can you point them out, and I'll highlight them? Good. What do we notice about them? Why do we think some letters are capitalized, or uppercase, and others aren't?

*(Give students a minute to turn and talk. If they're confused about what you mean, you might model by saying: **My** is capitalized in both sentences because the beginnings of sentences always start with a capital letter. What else do we notice?)*

I'm hearing you say that the **R** in *Roscoe* is capitalized. Why is that? Right! That's because names are capitalized—like the name of the state he's from, South Carolina. I also noticed that you said **I** is a capital letter, too. That's because the word *I* is always capitalized.

ALTERNATIVE

Demonstration: **Model for students how to make decisions about capital letters while you are writing.**

 |

GUIDE

Ask students to think about how to use proper capitalization in the next sentence.

Let's try this together. Here's the next page of my book about my dog, Roscoe. *(Display page.)* This page is about how Roscoe loves to play with his friends, Wally and Moose, at his day care, Preferred Pets. See? There's Roscoe, Wally, and Moose, and they're all running and playing in the yard at Preferred Pets. I want to write: "Roscoe loves to play at Preferred Pets with his friends, Wally and Moose." Can you help me remember what I need to capitalize?

(Allow students a minute to talk to a partner. They may write their answers on dry-erase boards, and/or you may ask individual students to come up and write the capitalized letters for you.)

That looks right! *Roscoe* is capitalized because it's both the start of a sentence and a name. *Preferred Pets* is capitalized because it's the name of his day care. *Wally* and *Moose* are also capitalized, because they're the names of Roscoe's friends.

RELEASE

Remind students of the rules for capitalization.

Remember, when you go off to write today, and anytime you're writing, certain words are capitalized: any word that starts a sentence, the word *I*, and specific names of things (proper nouns).

FOR ADDITIONAL SUPPORT, TRY

2.11 Give Them a Break
7.3 Put an End to It
7.4 Stand Up Tall

TIPS/RESOURCES

- Use the language of grammar along with everyday language—so "proper nouns" and "names of things."
- Encourage students to notice capital letters in reading selections by paying attention to when writers capitalize.
- Create a chart with capitalization rules.

Give Them a Break

In this lesson, students learn to use end marks correctly by first saying and writing a sentence, then placing the appropriate end mark.

Writing Stage: Emergent, Transitional • **Genre:** List, Pattern, How-To Book, All-About Book

INTRODUCE

Tell students that they will learn how to use end marks correctly by saying a sentence out loud and considering punctuation options.

As we add more to our booklets, our writing needs to have breaks in between the sentences. This helps the reader know when to pause or change voice. This means that as we write sentences, we need to think about the end punctuation we need to include. This can be a period, a question mark, or an exclamation mark.

INSTRUCT

Demonstration

Show students how you think about the appropriate end marks for your sentences.

Watch me as I use end marks at the end of my sentences before starting another one. *(Use an anchor chart to review ending punctuation. Then display your booklet.)*

Here I have my book about the octopus. Today I was planning on writing about how the octopus can hide and escape. The first sentence I will write is: "The octopus can camouflage." (*Quickly jot down your sentence leaving off the end mark.*) Let me think about what end mark I should use. I will look at our chart. *(Refer to the anchor chart. Pause to consider each type of punctuation.)*

"The octopus can camouflage." Hmmm. Is it a question? I don't think so because I'm not asking anyone anything. Or is it an exclamation? Well, there isn't much excitement involved here, nor is this a part I want the reader to read with a louder voice. "The octopus can camouflage" is just a regular, simple sentence, so it needs a period at the end. *(Place a period at the end of the sentence.)*

Let me give this another try. The next sentence I want to write is: "Can you find the octopus hiding?" *(Jot down the sentence without the end mark. Reference the chart.)* A period? It doesn't sound like a statement or a simple sentence. A question mark? I am asking the reader if they can see the octopus hiding, which is why my voice goes up a little bit. It's a question, so I will put a question mark at the end of my sentence. Let me read it aloud: "The octopus can camouflage. Can you find the octopus hiding?" Now my sentences have a break between them, which will help the reader know when to pause and change voice.

Did you notice how I thought about the different end marks and then put one at the end of each sentence? Do you see how using the appropriate end marks helps my writing flow and have breaks in between sentences?

 |

GUIDE

Prompt students to turn and talk with their partners and to think about the appropriate end mark for the next sentence.

Do you think you can help me with my next sentence? "The octopus can squirt ink out to trick its enemy!" *(Quickly jot down the sentence leaving off the end mark.)* What end mark do you think I should use here? Is it a statement, a question, or an exclamation?

(Prompt students to look at the chart. Allow 1–4 minutes for students to turn and talk with partners. Share that either a period or exclamation point could work, but a question mark would not.)

RELEASE

Remind students about the importance of using end marks in their writing.

Today we focused on making sure our sentences have correct end marks. Just like real authors, we want our readers to know when to pause and when to change their voices as they read our writing. So whenever you are writing, always think about the appropriate end marks for each sentence before writing another one. You can always refer back to this chart to help you remember.

FOR ADDITIONAL SUPPORT, TRY

2.10 Stand Tall, Stand Proud
6.8 From Labels to Sentences
7.3 Put an End to It

TIPS/RESOURCES:

- Add any new punctuation to your existing editing checklist.

Who Said That?

In this lesson, students learn to use quotation marks correctly by placing them before and after words that were said by a person or copied from another source.

Writing Stage: Transitional, Fluent
Genre: All-About Book, Feature Article, Literary Nonfiction, Expository Nonfiction, Biography, Research Report, Expository Essay

INTRODUCE

Tell students that they will learn how to use quotation marks correctly.

Sometimes we want to include specific information about our topic that might come directly from a source—a book, article, website, or even an interview. When we do this, we have to be sure to use the correct punctuation: quotation marks, commas, and end marks. We know that including specific quotes in our writing is important because it gives the reader precise information. But we also need to make sure we are using quotation marks correctly. That way, the reader will know that we are sharing someone else's ideas.

INSTRUCT

Demonstration

Show students how you use quotation marks correctly, placing them before and after words that were said by a person or copied from a source.

Here is my writing on sharks. I have been doing research to gather some facts about how sharks aren't the killers that they are made out to be. Sometimes I want to include exactly what the author said because it is so precise. I don't want to paraphrase or summarize. In the book, *Sharks,* by Seymour Simon, he talks a lot about how sharks are monsters of myth. One of the facts that he includes is, "Sharks have killed fewer people in the United States in the past one hundred years than are killed in automobile accidents over a single holiday weekend." This is a quote I would like to include because it supports my idea that sharks aren't the killers they are perceived to be. I will need to write the exact words and include a quotation mark at the beginning and at the end and then use proper ending punctuation. I will also make note of this source and be sure to include *Sharks,* by Seymour Simon, in my list of references. This is what my quote looks like and sounds like: (*Show students where you put the quotes and punctuation.*)

> In the book, *Sharks*, by Seymour Simon, he says: "Sharks have killed fewer people in the United States in the past one hundred years than are killed in automobile accidents over a single holiday weekend."

Do you see how I placed quotation marks at the beginning and end of the sentence and included the proper end punctuation? Did you notice how I made sure I copied the words exactly as they were written in the book?

 |

According to Nicola Davies,
"There are over 500 different
kinds of sharks."

GUIDE

Prompt students to look through their research and think about when and how they will use quotation marks to give proper credit.

Who and what do you want to quote? Think about your research, the sources you have, or an interview that you conducted. Take a look at your information and think about who you will quote and how you will be sure to use quotation marks correctly.

(Prompt students to look through their writing and research, and then turn and talk to share.)

RELEASE

Remind students of the importance of using quotation marks correctly.

Today we learned how to use quotation marks in our writing. When you include someone else's exact words in your writing, you need to be sure to use quotation marks correctly. Use the example we charted for a reference.

FOR ADDITIONAL SUPPORT, TRY

5.19 Ask an Expert

6.40 What Do the Experts Say?

6.42 Back It Up!

7.5 Watch What You Say

TIPS/RESOURCES

- Show students examples of how quotes are used in books.
- If needed, give students a few opportunities to practice placing the correct punctuation around quotes.

LESSON 2.13

Keep 'Em Separated

In this lesson, students learn to separate descriptors of three or more by placing a comma after each word except for the one that follows *and* or *or.*

Writing Stage: Transitional, Fluent • **Genre:** Any

INTRODUCE

Tell students that they will learn how to separate descriptors by using commas.

As we continue working on our writing, we need to be sure that we are using the correct punctuation when we list things. For instance, if I told you that in this classroom we have twenty chairs, five tables, and four windows, I would need to put a comma in between each descriptor. Today we are going to learn to separate descriptors of three or more by placing a comma after each word except for the one that follows *and* or *or.*

INSTRUCT

Demonstration

Model how you separate descriptors of three or more by placing a comma after each word except for *and* or *or.*

Let me show you how I do this with my writing.

Here I have my writing about the octopus. In this part, I wrote about the different colors that the octopus can change to when it's camouflaging. *(Display your writing so students can see the sentence you are working on.)* I want to write that the octopus can turn many colors, such as red, black, yellow, or brown. The color words in this sentence are the descriptors because they are describing the different colors that the octopus can become. Right before the last word in a list like this, writers usually put the words *and* or *or.* So after each color word, I need to add a comma but not after the word *or.*

(Show students the sentence without commas and read it aloud.)

Do you see how the sentence doesn't look right? Or sound right? All the words run into each other.

(Add in commas, emphasizing the comma placement after each descriptor and not placing one after the word or.*)*

Now let me read my sentence and see how the commas separate my descriptors so the words don't all collide. *(Read the sentence aloud.)* Do you see how I did that? I used commas to separate the descriptors in my sentence. Did you notice how I was careful not to put a comma after the word *or* because it's not a descriptor?

ALTERNATIVE

Explain with Examples: **Using mentor texts, show students examples of how authors separate descriptors using commas.**

 |

Octopuses can turn many colors, such as red, black, yellow, or brown.

GUIDE

Invite students to give it a try with another sentence.

Let's do some of this work together. Here I have the next part where I am writing about what an octopus eats. I have a few descriptors in this sentence that will need commas to separate them. Here's the sentence I want to write: "An octopus eats different crustaceans such as shrimp scallop lobster and clams." Where do we put the commas to make this sentence look and sound right? Read the sentence a few times with your partner to listen to how the sentence sounds with and without the proper punctuation.

(Allow 1–4 minutes for students to turn and talk with partners. Share out a correct response.)

RELEASE

Remind students the importance of using commas to separate descriptors.

Today we focused on an important rule in writing. We learned how to separate descriptors with a comma between each word, except for the last word that follows *and* or *or*. When we use commas, our writing is not only written correctly, it also sounds better to the reader. As you write, keep in mind that when you have a sentence that includes a list of descriptors, you should place a comma in between each word, except for the last one.

FOR ADDITIONAL SUPPORT, TRY

2.14 Give Them Room to Breathe

2.15 Be Descriptive

6.52 Everything Will Flow

TIPS/RESOURCES

- Add this rule to your editing checklist.
- Have a model sentence on an anchor chart for students to refer to during independent writing time.

LESSON 2.14

Give Them Room to Breathe

In this lesson, students learn that when a comma follows a transition word, it helps the reader take a pause.

Writing Stage: Transitional, Fluent

Genre: How-To Book, All-About Book, Feature Article, Literary Nonfiction, Expository Nonfiction, Biography, Research Report, Expository Essay

INTRODUCE

Tell students that a comma after a transition word reminds readers to take a pause.

Writers often use transition words and phrases at the beginning of a sentence to show a relationship between ideas. These transitional words and phrases are often followed by a comma to signal for the reader to take a short pause. This pause can also help emphasize the relationship between the ideas.

INSTRUCT

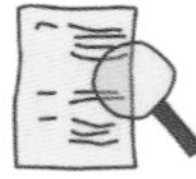

Explain with Examples

Explain the common relationships and provide examples of transition words used in informational writing. Demonstrate using examples that relate to students' background knowledge so that they can focus on the strategy and not the content.

Some common relationships we might use in informational writing are addition, comparison, contrast, summarization, and time. Each relationship can be indicated by different transition words.

Addition To give an idea and then add more to it, use words such as: *In addition, Furthermore, Additionally,* and *Also.*

Comparison To compare things that are similar, use words such as: *Similarly, Comparatively, In comparison, Likewise,* and *Along with.*

Contrast To show how things are different, use words such as: *In contrast, However,* and *On the other hand.*

Summary To draw a conclusion or summarize information, use words such as: *In conclusion, In summary, Altogether,* and *In short.*

Time To show how things are related in time order, use words such as: *First, First and foremost, Second, Next, Then, Finally, Soon after, Last,* and *Last but not least.*

When we use these words, we typically use a comma to bridge the information. Here is an example about bikes:

To show similarity, I might say: "Bikes often have two brakes located on the handlebars. The brake on the left side stops the front tire. *Similarly,* the brake on the right side stops the rear tire." If I were to show a contrasting idea, I might say: "*However,* children's bikes often have brakes on the pedals to make it easier to stop."

 |

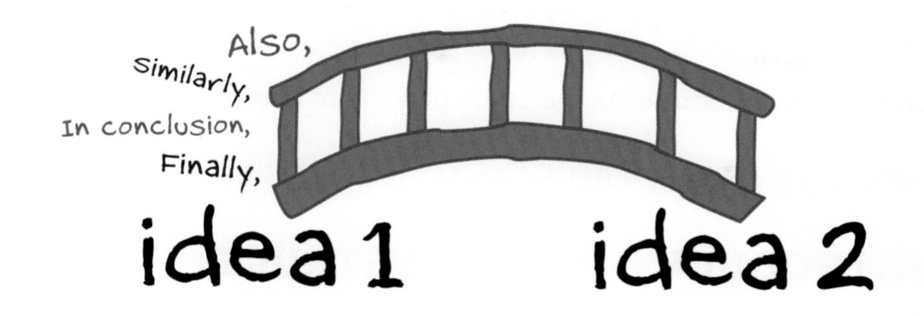

GUIDE

Using interactive writing, write a few sentences together. Invite students up to write the transition word and comma while you fill in the rest of the sentence.

Let's try a few sentences together. Close your eyes and imagine that you are speeding down the street on a bicycle and approaching a stop sign. What would you have to do? Perhaps you can consider the steps in order.

(Allow 1–2 minutes for students to talk. Write out a few examples with time order words and commas.)

RELEASE

Remind students that commas link transition words with information to show relationships and allow readers to pause.

Remember that it is important to use transition words and phrases to show the relationship between information and ideas in your writing. It is grammatically correct to use commas after these words and phrases as a link and a reminder to your reader to take a pause. Now let's transition to writing time!

FOR ADDITIONAL SUPPORT, TRY

2.13 Keep 'Em Separated

TIPS/RESOURCES

- Provide students with a personal chart of transition words to keep as a resource.
- Chart additional transition words such as: *In fact, Indeed, Obviously* or *Hence, Therefore,* and *Thus.*
- Practice examples where the comma does not immediately follow the transition word *Unlike _____; Differing from _____;* etc.

Be Descriptive

In this lesson, students learn the benefits of being precise by using adjectives to describe nouns.

Writing Stage: Any • **Genre:** Any*

INTRODUCE

Tell students that writers use adjectives to be more descriptive about nouns.

Writers use adjectives to be more descriptive. Adjectives give more specific information about a person, place, or thing by adding information related to size, shape, color, number, texture, and quality.

INSTRUCT

Inquiry

Have students compare examples with and without adjectives. Have them identify each adjective and how it makes the writing more descriptive.

When we are writing informational books, we always want to be mindful of our readers and how they will see and understand our information. To help them, you can use one or more adjectives to describe a noun.

Let me show you in my writing about sharks. *(Display the examples below.)* I want you to look at my two examples and think about which one is more descriptive.

"Besides their backbone and teeth, sharks do not have any bones. Instead, their skeletons are made of cartilage."

"Besides their backbone and teeth, sharks do not have any bones. Instead, their skeletons are made of a tough, white, bendable material called cartilage."

Which one is more descriptive? Can you identify the adjectives that make it more descriptive? *(Give students 1–2 minutes to turn and talk. Share the correct responses.)*

Yes, the second one is more descriptive because it uses the words *tough, white,* and *bendable*. How does this help you understand cartilage?

(Give students 1–2 minutes to turn and talk. Share responses.)

**For How-To Books, use steps as examples.*

ALTERNATIVE

Explain with Examples: **Using pages from mentor texts, explain how authors use adjectives to make information more specific and precise for the reader.**

 |

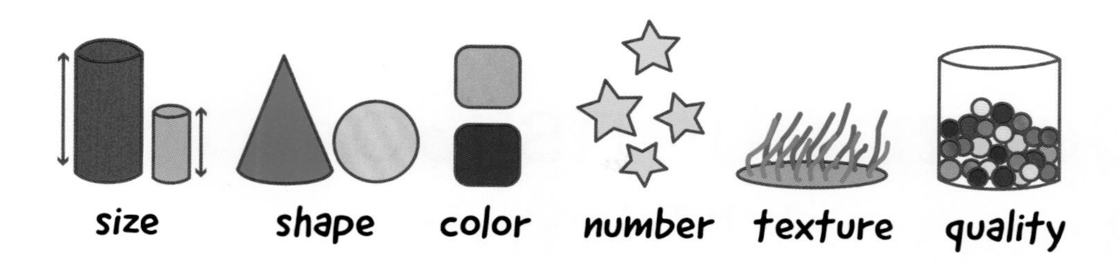

GUIDE

Ask students to help you create a more descriptive sentence.

Let's try one together. Let's make this information more descriptive for readers to understand.

"Fast-swimming sharks have teeth for tearing apart other big fish and marine mammals."

Which word in this sentence can we describe with adjectives? What are some adjectives we can add to this sentences to make it more descriptive?

(Allow 1–4 minutes for students to turn and talk with partners. Share exemplary responses.)

RELEASE

Remind students that writers use adjectives to be more descriptive.

So, writers, remember that when you are explaining information it is important that your reader can understand it and imagine it. One way to do this is by using adjectives to be more descriptive in your writing.

FOR ADDITIONAL SUPPORT, TRY

6.15 Be Specific

6.16 Everything Counts in Exact Amounts

6.22 Use Your Senses

TIPS/RESOURCES

- Encourage students to visualize or use images and videos to help them brainstorm adjectives.
- Photocopy examples from mentor texts and highlight adjectives for students to reference and discuss.
- Have partners look at each other's writing to offer suggestions for additional descriptions.

Descriptions Go Beyond Nouns

In this lesson, students learn to be more descriptive by using adverbs to show where, when, how, how much, and how often.

Writing Stage: Any

Genre: How-To Book*, All-About Book, Feature Article, Literary Nonfiction, Expository Nonfiction, Biography, Research Report, Expository Essay

INTRODUCE

Tell students that writers use adverbs to be more descriptive about verbs, adjectives, and other adverbs.

Being descriptive helps give readers a clear picture in their minds about what they are reading. Adverbs give more specific information about a verb, adjective, or another adverb by providing information related to where, when, how, how much, or how often something occurs.

INSTRUCT

Explain with Examples

Provide students with an anchor chart that lists adverbs in different categories. Provide an example for each.

Adverbs are used to describe verbs, adjectives, and other adverbs. *(Display chart of adverbs by category.)* Adverbs may describe:

How using words like *quietly*, *slowly*, *fast*, *badly*, *well*, and *beautifully*. "How" relates to sound, speed, quality, and feeling. One example is, "Sharks can swim fast." *Fast* describes how they swim.

How Much using words like *enormously*, *completely*, *fully*, *quite*, *very*, *few*, and *too*. "How much" relates to size and quantity. One example is, "A shark can devour its prey completely." *Completely* describes the quantity or size. *Devour* (or eat) is the action.

How Often using words like *always*, *sometimes*, *occasionally*, *hardly*, *often*, and *never*. "How often" relates to frequency. One example is, "Sharks are always on the hunt for their next meal." *Always* describes how often they hunt. *Hunt* is the action.

When using words like *now*, *later*, *yesterday*, *tomorrow*, *last week*, and *soon*. "When" relates to time. One example is, "I watched a documentary about sharks yesterday." *Yesterday* describes when the action happens. *Watched* is the action.

Where using words like *above*, *outside*, *upstairs*, *behind*, *anywhere*, and *everywhere*. "Where" relates to place. One example is, "Hammerhead sharks can see above and below them at all times. *Above* and *below* describe where the sharks can see. The action is *seeing*.

**For How-To Books, use steps as examples.*

GUIDE

Prompt students to compare examples with and without adverbs. Have them identify how the adverbs impact the writing.

I want you to look at two examples from my writing. Which is more descriptive? Can you locate the adverbs and describe their impact? *(Display the examples below for students to see.)*

"Great white sharks swim, which makes them some of the best hunters in the sea. They can reach speeds of 43 miles per hour, which allows them to surprise their prey."

OR

"Great white sharks swim underwater very fast, which makes them some of the best hunters in the sea. They can reach high speeds of 43 miles per hour, which allows them to surprise their prey from above, below, behind, and straight ahead."

(Allow 1–4 minutes for students to turn and talk with partners. Share exemplary responses.)

RELEASE

Remind students that writers use adverbs to be more descriptive.

So, writers, remember that when you are explaining information it is important to help your reader understand it and see it. One way to do this is by using adverbs to be more descriptive in your writing.

FOR ADDITIONAL SUPPORT, TRY

6.15 Be Specific

6.16 Everything Counts in Exact Amounts

6.19 We Can Do It

TIPS/RESOURCES

- Have partners look at each other's writing to offer suggestions for using adverbs.
- Encourage students to use images and videos to help them brainstorm adverbs.
- Photocopy examples from mentor texts and highlight adverbs for students to reference.

Prepositions Describe, Too

In this lesson, students learn to be more descriptive by using prepositions to show the relationship of a noun or pronoun to other words or phrases that highlight time, place, or direction.

Writing Stage: Transitional, Fluent

Genre: How-To Book, All-About Book, Feature Article, Literary Nonfiction, Expository Nonfiction, Biography, Research Report, Expository Essay

INTRODUCE

Tell students we can use prepositions to create phrases that describe time, place, and direction.

When we write, we often use adjectives to describe. For example, we include color, shape, size, or sensory details. But prepositions can help us describe, too! We can use prepositions to help us describe time, place, or direction to teach our readers more about our topics.

INSTRUCT

Demonstration

Model for students how to describe and say more using prepositions.

Let me show you what I mean. First of all, prepositions are words that express the relationship of nouns and pronouns to other words in a sentence. It sounds confusing, but once you hear what the prepositions are, it will make more sense. Some prepositions are: *in*, *on*, *at*, *under*, *through*, *into*, *above*, *before*, *after*, *around*, or *below*. We can use these words to describe by thinking of the prepositions associated with time, place, and direction.

In this piece, I've been writing about our school. I'm talking about the playground outside. So far I have, "We have swings. We also have a climber." I can use prepositions to help me add more. I can think about place and use *at*, *in*, or *on*. I could say, "We have swings *at* our school." Or, "We have swings *on* the playground *at* our school." Now my reader knows where they are. With my next sentence, I could think of the same thing. "We also have a climber." I could write, "We have a climber *next to* the swings." Or I could switch it around and start with the prepositional phrase, "*Next to* the swings, we have a climber." Because I started with that phrase, I need to add a comma after *swings*. I could even look at the list of prepositions to get me thinking of more I could add—how you can climb *up* the climbing structure, or how we like to climb *on* it, or sit *on top of* it.

ALTERNATIVE

Inquiry: **Look at a number of sentences that use prepositions to describe time, place, and direction. Point out the prepositions. Discuss how they are used.**

 |

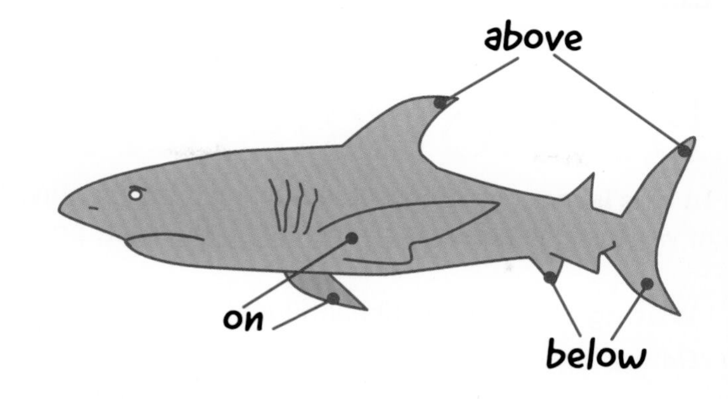

GUIDE

Prompt students to use prepositions to describe place, time, and direction.

Now it's your turn. Look at these next sentences about the playground.

We have two slides. One is straight. One is curvy.

How can I use prepositions to describe and say more?

(Allow 1–4 minutes for students to turn and talk with partners. They could work to write the sentence on a shared dry-erase board, do it individually, or just have a conversation.)

RELEASE

Remind students to think about using prepositions and prepositional phrases—not just adjectives — to say more.

Remember, adjectives aren't the only way writers have to describe. We can use prepositions to give more information about place, time, and direction to teach our readers more about our topics.

FOR ADDITIONAL SUPPORT, TRY

2.15 Be Descriptive

2.16 Descriptions Go Beyond Nouns

TIPS/RESOURCES

- Chart prepositions in categories of time, place, and direction:
  - Time: *in, on, at*
  - Place: *in, on, at, above, among, over*, etc.
  - Direction: *across, along, around*, etc.

Be Consistent

In this lesson, students learn to keep their writing consistent by staying aware of whether the action is happening in the past, present, or future.

Writing Stage: Transitional, Fluent

Genre: How-To Book, All-About Book, Feature Article, Literary Nonfiction, Expository Nonfiction, Biography, Research Report, Expository Essay

INTRODUCE

Tell students that we check our writing to make sure our verb tenses agree and are consistent throughout.

When we write, we need to be consistent. This means we need to make sure that our verb tense is consistent throughout our writing. When we write, we make a choice to write in the past, the present, or the future, and then we stick with it. One strategy is to reread and make sure we're consistent in our language so that our reader can follow our thinking.

INSTRUCT

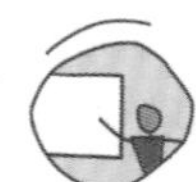

Demonstration

Model for students how to consider verb tense and check for consistency.

Verbs either take place in the present, past, or future. We can talk about what sharks eat, what they ate yesterday, or what they will eat tomorrow. So I might have a page that says: "Sharks eat almost anything, including mollusks and crustaceans." That's the present tense.

I could say the same facts this way in the future tense: "Sharks will eat almost anything, including mollusks and crustaceans." Take a minute and think about how writing this way changes, not the meaning really, but the tone or the feeling of the sentence. You might notice that the future "they will eat" here implies a willingness, a want. To me, this connects to the way sharks behave—always hunting, always moving, on the lookout for their next meal.

Let's see what it might look like in the past tense: "Sharks ate almost everything" Hmmm. I'm not sure that makes sense. If we put it in the past, it might make sense for telling a story or recounting an anecdote such as, "Sharks in the aquarium ate almost anything." The point is, we want to think about what tense we're using, what it conveys, and how to be consistent with it throughout our writing.

For my writing on sharks, I think I want to stick with the present tense. I'm giving my reader current, accurate information.

ALTERNATIVE

Explain with Examples: **Show examples of the different verb tenses and how they impact meaning.**

 |

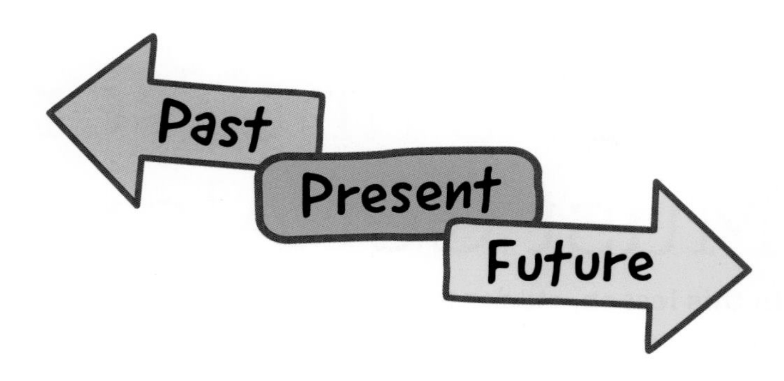

GUIDE

Prompt students to read for consistency of verb tense and then make a plan for their own writing.

So let's read this paragraph I've already written to make sure it's consistent. Here's what I have so far:

> "Sharks eat almost anything, including mollusks and crustaceans. Because they are always hunting, they have sometimes confused surfers for something they usually eat—seals—resulting in shark attacks. Shark attacks don't happen often, but when they do they will always be in the news."

Take a minute and talk to your partner. What tense makes the most sense here? What changes should be made to maintain it?

(Allow students a few minutes to discuss with partners. Share and listen to suggestions, talking through choices that make sense.)

Before we go off, think about the writing you're about to do today. What tense do you imagine will best suit your purpose for writing? Take a minute and tell your partner.

(*Allow students 1 minute to share a plan.*)

RELEASE

Remind students to maintain tense as they're writing.

When you're writing today, and any time you're writing, be sure to think about the tense you're writing in. Make sure your choice makes sense for the content. Then stop periodically to make sure you're keeping that tense consistent throughout.

FOR ADDITIONAL SUPPORT, TRY

1.1 Dream a Little Dream

2.19 Nouns and Verbs Must Get Along

TIPS/RESOURCES

- When reading, spend time noticing and talking about the verbs and verb tense.
- Chart verb tenses.
- Point out how "non-action" verbs that refer to states of being also indicate tense.

LESSON 2.19

Nouns and Verbs Must Get Along

In this lesson, students learn that when writing a sentence, they need to make sure the noun and verb agree in number.

Writing Stage: Transitional, Fluent

Genre: How-To Book, All-About Book, Feature Article, Literary Nonfiction, Expository Nonfiction, Biography, Research Report, Expository Essay

INTRODUCE

Tell students that as we write we notice whether the subject is singular or plural, and we make sure the verb matches.

As we write, we have to keep in mind so many things—what we're saying and how we're saying it. That's part of what makes writing tricky sometimes. One of the things we need to pay attention to is that the nouns, specifically the subject of each sentence, must agree in number with the verb or the predicate of the sentence. We do this by first identifying the subject of the sentence, then deciding if the subject is singular or plural, and, lastly, deciding which verb form will match with the subject.

INSTRUCT

Demonstration

Model for students how to think about subject and verb agreement as you write.

Let me show you what I mean. If I'm starting my sentence with the subject, or noun, *sharks*—that's plural. Now I know that whatever verb I attach to that subject needs to be plural. I want to write about how they find food: "Sharks find their prey by using their senses." I wrote, "Sharks find" See how I made sure they agree? If I were writing about one shark, a shark, or the shark, what would need to change? (*Give students a minute to think.*)

If you're thinking I would write, "A shark *finds*," you're right!

I can do this as I'm writing, but I can also go back and check my writing to make sure my nouns and verbs agree.

ALTERNATIVE

Explain with Examples: **Show models of subject-verb agreement, talking through verb forms and changes.**

GUIDE

Prompt students to try the strategy with a partner, coaching them as they talk it through.

Let's look at this next part. Check the first sentence with your partner, and then complete the sentence to make sure the subject and verb agree.

> "Sharks uses their sense of smell to locate prey, but they also use their sense of hearing. A shark _____ prey from far away, helping it zone in for the kill."

(Allow 1–4 minutes for partners to talk about what makes sense. You might coach them to ask if what they're saying sounds or looks right.)

I heard you say that *uses* in the first part of the first sentence should be changed to *use*, which is correct for multiple sharks. In the second sentence, *smells* is correct for one shark.

RELEASE

Remind students to check for subject and verb agreement.

When you write today, and any time you're writing, pay attention to the nouns and verbs in your sentences. Make sure they agree in number so that your reader will understand what you're teaching them.

FOR ADDITIONAL SUPPORT, TRY

1.12 Writers Are Never Done

1.23 Writers Take a Pause

2.18 Be Consistent

TIPS/RESOURCES

- During read-alouds, take notice of subject and verb agreement, paying particular attention to irregular verbs.
- Use interactive writing where students decide what noun or verb to use.

Put It in a Paragraph

In this lesson, students learn to write in correct paragraph form with topic, supporting, and concluding sentences.

Writing Stage: Transitional, Fluent
Genre: All-About Book, Feature Article, Literary Nonfiction, Expository Nonfiction, Biography, Research Report, Expository Essay

INTRODUCE

Tell students that today they will learn to write in correct paragraph form.

As we write, one thing we need to keep in mind is making sure our writing is in correct paragraph form. When we use proper paragraphing, it is easier for the reader to navigate our writing because it's clear and organized. We want to make sure that we are grouping our information with facts and ideas that go together.

INSTRUCT

Demonstration

Model for students how you think of a topic sentence, come up with supporting details, and then write a concluding sentence.

Here, I am writing about how the octopus is able to hide and escape from predators. I will group the information together in paragraph form with topic, supporting, and concluding sentences.*

Let me first think about my main idea for this paragraph. Maybe my topic sentence can be: "The octopus can hide and escape from its predators in many ways." *(Jot down the topic sentence.)*

Now for supporting details. I want to make sure that every sentence connects back to my topic sentence. I could include that the octopus turns different colors to camouflage itself among sea life. Or that the octopus can squirt ink to trick its predators or uses poison to paralyze its prey. I also want to include how it can swim really fast to escape. Do all of these connect back to my main idea? *(Restate the topic sentence.)* Camouflaging definitely connects to hiding and escaping. So does using ink. What about how it poisons its prey? I don't think that connects back because it's not about hiding or escaping. My last detail, about it swimming away fast, does connect. So I have three supporting details.

A concluding sentence should complete the idea and transition to the next paragraph. Maybe I can write: "The octopus is skillful at hiding and escaping from its predators, but what about when the octopus is the predator?" I like that because it connects back the main idea and it also sets up the reader for the next part of my writing.

This is what my paragraph looks like. Note how the first line is indented. *(Display the completed paragraph.)*

ALTERNATIVE

Guided Practice: **Using a shared topic, guide students to think of a topic sentence, supporting details, and a concluding statement to write in proper paragraph form.**

 |

GUIDE

Prompt students to write down possible topic sentences and supporting details.

Okay, it's your turn to talk to a partner about your topic sentence and supporting details. This will give you some time to talk through your ideas before putting pencil to paper.

(Allow 1–4 minutes for students to turn and talk with partners. Share exemplary responses.)

RELEASE

Remind students of the importance of writing in correct paragraph form.

As we write paragraphs, remember to think first about your main idea and write a topic sentence. Then, write a few supporting sentences, including facts and details that connect back to your main idea. Last, write a concluding statement that sums up and transitions to the next paragraph.

FOR ADDITIONAL SUPPORT, TRY

5.12 Build Me Up
6.29 Tell Me More, Tell Me More
6.30 Connect Your Ideas
6.45 Give Me a Sign

TIPS/RESOURCES

- Use markers to highlight the different parts of a paragraph.
- Create an anchor chart with paragraphing steps.
- Construct paragraphs in shared writing.
- Use mentor texts to show students how authors use paragraphs effectively.

*See sample chart, "Build a Paragraph," on page 122.

Rhythm Is Gonna Get You

In this lesson, students learn to create voice and rhythm in their writing by varying sentence lengths and beginnings.

Writing Stage: Fluent
Genre: All-About Book, Feature Article, Literary Nonfiction, Expository Nonfiction, Biography, Research Report, Expository Essay

INTRODUCE

Tell students that writers try to write in ways that flow and sound like natural conversation.

Nonfiction writers want to engage and interest their audiences. One way they do this is with rhythm and voice—writing in ways that sound as if they are discussing, teaching, or talking directly to the reader about the topic. They do this by varying their sentence beginnings and sentence lengths, and by finding their own ways of creating voice in their writing.

INSTRUCT

Explain with Examples

Explain to students how their unique personalities should come through in their writing. Provide examples to let them compare "dry," fact-driven writing versus writing with rhythm and voice.

Even though we are writing nonfiction, we don't want our writing to sound too technical. We aren't walking encyclopedias just giving facts. Instead, we are experts who are excited about our topics. When we write, our voices and personalities must come through. Let's take a look at this writing about sharks. *(Display the excerpt below.)*

> "Sharks come in many different sizes. Sharks come in many different shapes. Sharks also come in many different colors. They can be as small as your hand. They can be as big as a school bus. Some sharks have long, lean bodies. Some sharks have short, stout bodies. Some sharks have flat bodies. Sharks can be brown. Sharks can be blue. Sharks can even have spots."

As you read this, does this information sound interesting to you?

(Give students 1–2 minutes to turn and talk. Share exemplary responses. Possible responses: Sentences are too short and choppy. The writer overuses the word *shark*. The writing lacks engagement.*)*

Now I would like you to compare it to a similar piece of writing. *(Display the excerpt below.)*

> "Sharks come in many different sizes, shapes, and colors. They can be as small as your hand or as gigantic as a big, yellow, school bus! Can you imagine a shark as big as a bus? Sharks have different body types, too. Some have long, lean bodies like a torpedo. Others have short, stout bodies like a blob. Some are even flat like a scrap of carpet. Not only are sharks' sizes and body shapes different, they also come in many different colors. I bet you thought that all sharks were gray or black. Wrong! They can be brown, blue, or spotted with polka dots."

Do you hear how this second excerpt sounds different?

 |

GUIDE

Ask students to compare two examples for rhythm and voice.

Now, with a partner, I want you to compare and contrast both excerpts. Look closely, line by line, keeping rhythm and voice in mind.

(Allow 1–4 minutes for students to turn and talk with partners. Share exemplary responses. Possible response: They provide the same information but the second excerpt sounds more like a conversation.*)*

RELEASE

Remind students to sound conversational in their writing and let their personalities shine through.

Remember, writers, as you are writing, we (the readers) need to know that it is coming from you. Your uniqueness needs to shine through in your conversation with your readers. The writing should sound like you are talking. Varying your sentence beginnings and lengths, and incorporating your own language style, will help bring rhythm and voice to your writing.

FOR ADDITIONAL SUPPORT, TRY

2.22 Conjunction Connection
2.23 Come Together
6.30 Connect Your Ideas
6.52 Everything Will Flow

TIPS/RESOURCES

- Encourage students to orally rehearse with a partner.
- Tell students to write a sentence or two, then reread and listen for rhythm.

Conjunction Connection

In this lesson, students learn to link ideas and create longer sentences by using conjunctions.

Writing Stage: Transitional, Fluent

Genre: How-To Book, All-About Book, Feature Article, Literary Nonfiction, Expository Nonfiction, Biography, Research Report, Expository Essay

INTRODUCE

Tell students that one way to create longer sentences is to use conjunctions to combine ideas.

As we write, we often think about how we can express our ideas in more sophisticated ways. One way to do that is to create longer sentences by using conjunctions. One conjunction we probably all know is the word *and*. However, if we use *and* over and over again, we will likely make boring or run-on sentences. To avoid run-on sentences when creating longer, sophisticated sentences, we can use different conjunctions to combine ideas.

INSTRUCT

Demonstration

Model how to combine sentences using conjunctions and create longer, more sophisticated sentences.

There are many conjunctions in the English language. Some of the most common are: *and, or, but, because, so, if, then, until, while.* There are many ways we can use these words to combine ideas:

Conjunctions can connect two nouns: "Bats eat fruits *and* insects."

They can connect two verbs: "Flying rays swim fast *then* jump out of the water."

They can connect adjectives: "Hippos are large *yet* graceful swimmers."

They can also connect phrases:

"Dogs wag their tails *and* pant with their tongues to show excitement."

Or they can connect dependent and independent clauses:

"*Because* of movies like *Jaws,* people are often fearful of sharks."
Or "People are often fearful of sharks *because* of movies like *Jaws.*"

Let's look at some sentences in my writing to see if I can use conjunctions to create longer, more sophisticated sentences by connecting ideas. *(Display the sentences below.)*

"There are many different names for cows. Cattle refers to a group of adults. Babies are called calves."

I could use the conjunction *and*, but that's not how I want my writing to sound. Instead, I could say: "There are many different names for cows. Babies are called calves *while* adults are called cattle."

Or I could say: "There are many different names for cows. Babies are called calves *until* they grow into adults, then they are called cattle."

ALTERNATIVE

Explain with Examples: **Show students examples of sentences where phrases are combined with conjunctions.**

 |

GUIDE

Prompt students to try the strategy on a shared text.

Now it's your turn. Look at this next group of sentences. *(Display sentences.)* How can I use conjunctions to make my writing sound more sophisticated?

"Male cattle are called bulls. They have horns on their heads. Females are called cows. Some females have horns. Others don't. All females have udders."

(Allow 1–4 minutes for students to turn and talk with partners. Share exemplary responses.)

RELEASE

Remind students that they can use conjunctions to connect simple sentences and make longer, more sophisticated sentences.

Remember, look back on your writing periodically to see if you're using simple sentences. Try using conjunctions to connect ideas. You can also keep conjunctions in mind as you're writing to create sophisticated sentences right from the start!

FOR ADDITIONAL SUPPORT, TRY

2.13 Keep 'Em Separated
2.14 Give Them Room to Breathe
2.21 Rhythm Is Gonna Get You
2.23 Come Together

TIPS/RESOURCES

- Gather mentor sentences to discuss and display around your classroom.
- Avoid talking here about coordinating, subordinating, and correlative conjunctions.
- Give students dry-erase boards during the Guide portion.
- "Pass the pen" to individual students to model the strategy.

LESSON 2.23

Come Together

In this lesson, students learn to write compound sentences that connect two independent clauses or sentences together.

Writing Stage: Fluent

Genre: Feature Article, Literary Nonfiction, Expository Nonfiction, Biography, Research Report, Expository Essay

INTRODUCE

Tell students they will write compound sentences by using coordinating conjunctions.

As we have more sophisticated ideas, we learn ways to make our sentences more sophisticated to match those ideas. One way to do this is to use compound sentences rather than simple sentences. We can accomplish this by connecting two independent clauses (or sentences) together using coordinating conjunctions.

INSTRUCT

Demonstration

Model how to combine sentences using conjunctions to create longer, more sophisticated sentences.

A compound sentence is a sentence that has a least two independent clauses connected by a conjunction. Conjunctions are words that connect. An independent clause is a group of words in a sentence that can function as its own complete sentence—so, something that has a subject and a predicate. Some coordinating conjunctions are: *for*, *and*, *nor*, *but*, *or*, *yet*, *so*. We remember them by the acronym FANBOYS:

For And Nor But Or Yet So

We can use them to combine sentences. Let me show you:

"Hamsters make great pets. They are relatively quiet and clean."

I could say: "Hamsters make great pets *and* they are relatively quiet *and* clean." But that's too many *ands*! Maybe I could use *for*? It has a similar meaning to *because*.

"Hamsters make great pets for they are relatively clean and quiet."

Here's another:

"Hamsters are great diggers. In the wild, they burrow in the soil. In captivity, they burrow in their bedding."

I could say: "Hamsters are great diggers, *so* in the wild they burrow in the soil *and* in captivity they burrow in their bedding."

I used two conjunctions!

ALTERNATIVE

Explain with Examples: **Show students examples of sentences where phrases are combined with conjunctions.**

GUIDE

Prompt students to try the strategy on a shared text.

Can you help me with this one?

"Hamsters love to eat leafy greens and fruit. They don't like apple seeds and skin."

(Allow 1–4 minutes for students to turn and talk with partners. Share exemplary responses.)

RELEASE

Remind students they can use conjunctions to combine simple sentences.

As you write today, go back and look at some of your sentences. If you're writing in simple sentences, use FANBOYS to see if you can connect some of the ideas to create longer, more sophisticated sentences.

FOR ADDITIONAL SUPPORT, TRY

2.13 Keep 'Em Separated

2.21 Rhythm Is Gonna Get You

TIPS/RESOURCES

- Create an anchor chart of conjunctions: *for, and, nor, but, or, yet, so.*
- Pass the pen to individual students to model the strategy.
- Gather mentor sentences from reading to study as examples.

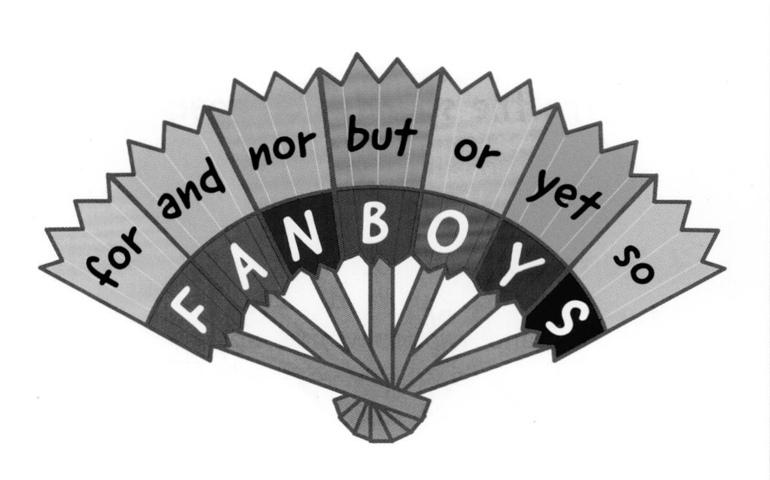

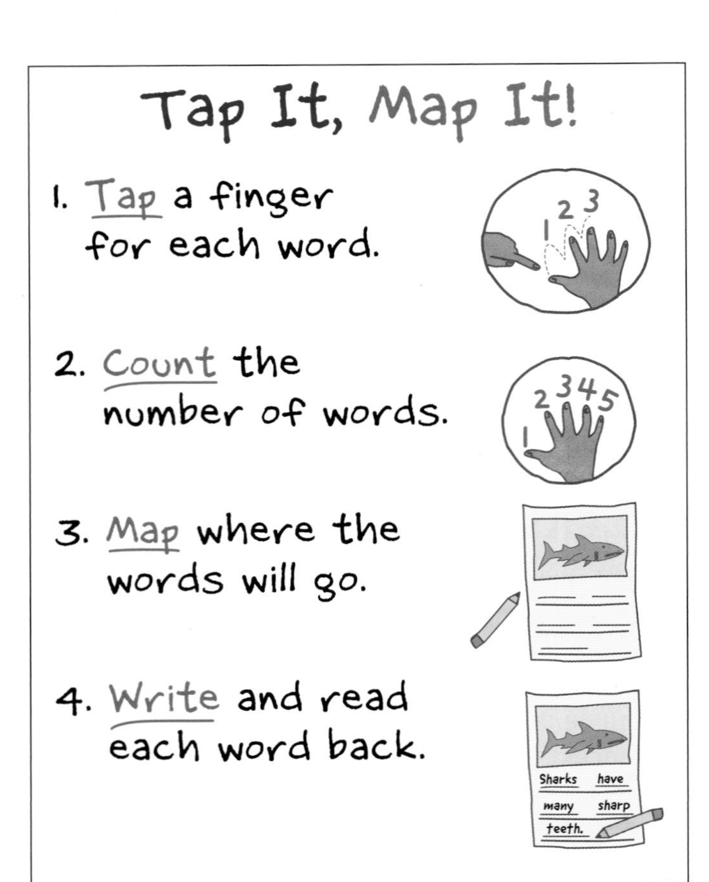

Lesson 2.4 Tap It, Map It

Say it /b/

Hear it /b/

Write it

b

Point and read it

b

Repeat

Lesson 2.5 Say It, Hear It, Write It, Read It, Repeat

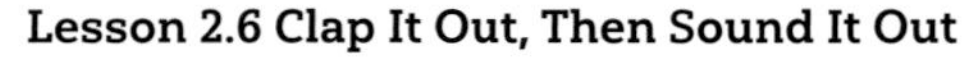

Lesson 2.6 Clap It Out, Then Sound It Out

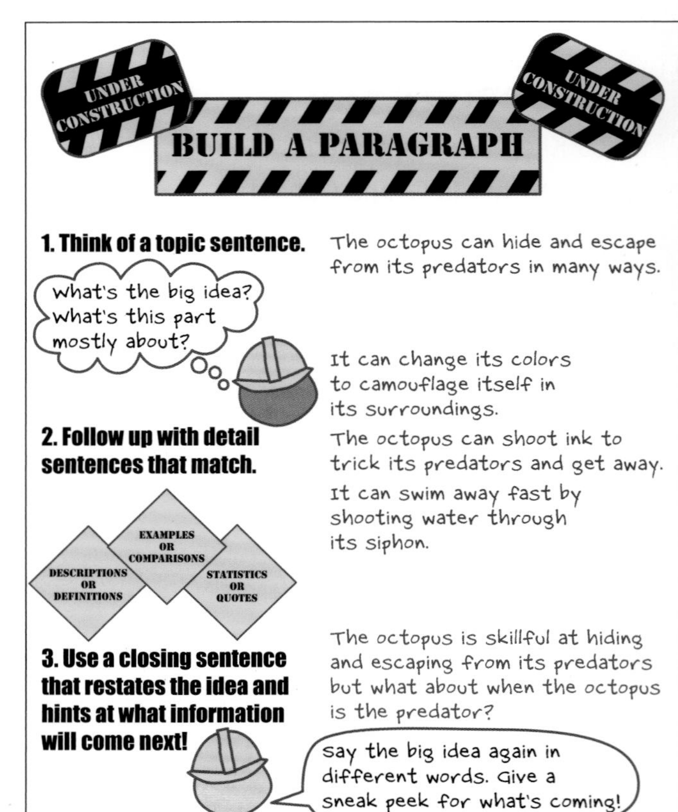

Lesson 2.20 Put It in a Paragraph

 |

Generate & Experiment

The series of lessons in this section contain strategies to help writers generate ideas. Students will often try out and experiment with several topics before landing on one topic to bring to publication. The lessons:

- provide students with strategies to brainstorm multiple ideas for writing topics.

Descriptors for Idea Generation and Experimenting with Entries

Emergent Writers	Fluent Writers
• Generate an idea and quickly plan that idea across pages in stapled booklets of 3+ pages. In Kindergarten and first grade, students can often write an entire booklet in 1–2 days.	• Brainstorm multiple topics, then choose a few to experiment with in short form as entries.
• Orally rehearse to experiment with an idea to see if they have enough to say about that topic.	• Create entries that consist of sketches, webs, notes, or longer forms of writing in a structure.
• Experiment by beginning to write about a topic, and then abandoning that topic and moving to a new one if they do not have enough to say.	• Generate and experiment with many ideas for the first few days of a unit before landing on the topic they will take through the writing process.
• Generate new ideas throughout the unit until the final week when one topic is selected and prepared for publication.	• Experiment with a topic by writing snippets about the topic with summaries or incomplete sections.

At-a-Glance Guide

Generate & Experiment

Title		Lesson
3.1	**I Spy with My Little Eye**	Use the classroom or other useful environments to get ideas.
3.2	**Think with Your Heart**	Think of things that you love to help you find a topic.
3.3	**This Is FUN!**	Think about enjoyable activities to help you find a topic.
3.4	**I Can Do It!**	Think about things you can make, build, cook, or prepare to help you find a topic.
3.5	**What's Your Hobby?**	Think of hobbies and pastimes to help you find a topic.
3.6	**Oh, The Places You Go!**	Think about different places to help you find a topic.
3.7	**Power of the People**	Think about people of notoriety to help you find a topic.
3.8	**You Better Work**	Think about routines to help you find a topic.

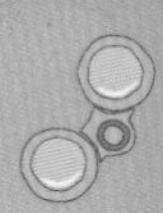

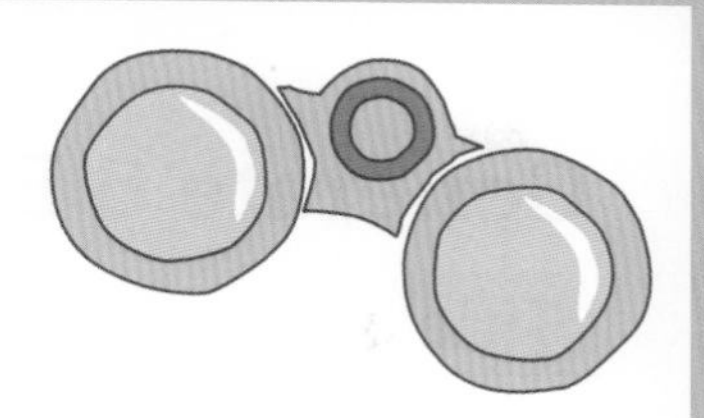

Writing Stage	Genre	
Any	Any	
Emergent Transitional	Any	
Any	Any	
Any	List Pattern All-About Feature Article	Research Report Expository Nonfiction Expository Essay
Any	Any	
Any	Any	
Transitional Fluent	All-About Feature Article Research Report	Biography Expository Nonfiction Expository Essay
Any	List How-To All-About Feature Article	Research Report Expository Nonfiction Expository Essay

Generate & Experiment continued

Title		Lesson
3.9	**Natural Wonders**	Think of topics related to the natural world.
3.10	**Flaunt Your Expertise**	Think about topics relating to personal expertise.
3.11	**This I Believe**	Think of passions to find a topic.
3.12	**Get Schooled**	Look at other parts of the school day to find a topic.
3.13	**A Bit of Advice**	Generate topics by thinking about a problem and possible solutions.
3.14	**Inquiring Minds Want to Know**	Think of things that spark curiosity to find a topic.

 |

Writing Stage	Genre	
Any	List All-About Feature Article Research Report	Literary Nonfiction Expository Nonfiction Expository Essay
Any	Any	
Transitional Fluent	All-About Feature Article Research Report Biography	Literary Nonfiction Expository Nonfiction Expository Essay
Any	Any	
Any	How-To All-About Feature Article	Expository Nonfiction Expository Essay
Transitional Fluent	How-To All-About Feature Article Literary Nonfiction	Expository Nonfiction Biography Research Report Expository Essay

I Spy with My Little Eye

In this lesson, students learn to generate ideas by using the classroom environment, or any space around them, to make observations and get ideas.

Writing Stage: Any • **Genre:** Any

INTRODUCE

Tell students that they can use their environments and observations as a way to think of ideas for their writing.

Sometimes we think that we don't have any ideas to write about. However, if we just look up, we might find inspiration all around us! Our environment can give us many ideas to fuel our writing. Today we are going to learn that when we look closely at the spaces around us and make observations, we can get lots of ideas for informational writing.

INSTRUCT

Demonstration

Model for students how you use your home environment to come up with ideas.

Watch me as I try this. I do a lot of writing at home—sometimes in my office, at my kitchen table, or on the couch. I will picture and scan those places in my mind to see what I come up with.

Emergent / Transitional In my kitchen, I look around and see cookbooks, kitchen tools, and the oven. That makes me think of some things I make—such as cookies, smoothies, and grilled cheese sandwiches. My husband is the real cook in my house. That makes me think I could write a book about dads in the kitchen. If I'm in my office, I see books about animals, music, and art. I could teach about sharks, dogs, or some other topic. If I'm sitting on my couch, I see a piano, guitars, a trombone, and a clarinet. I could teach about those instruments. I also see plants; I could teach about plants, flowers, or gardening.

Fluent If I'm writing in my kitchen, I look around and see my cookbooks, kitchen tools, and the oven. This makes me realize that I'm not the cook in my family—my husband cooks. I could teach about our ideas related to jobs and gender roles or the history of the division of labor in our lives. If I'm in my office, I look around and see books about animals, music, art, and teaching. I could teach about the importance of a varied reading life or how having varied interests make me well rounded. If I'm sitting on my couch, I see a piano, guitars, a trombone, and a clarinet. I could teach about the importance of music in my family, or how music affects the brain.

I originally thought I didn't have anything to write about, but now look at all of the topics I could teach you!

ALTERNATIVE

Guided Practice: **Together with students, observe a shared environment to find new topics. Chart ideas.**

 |

GUIDE

Ask students to look around the classroom to brainstorm some ideas.

Let's look around our classroom. What is something in our classroom environment that you can teach someone about? Go ahead, look at the charts on the walls, our library, the materials around us, the people, and the relationships. What are some topics that you can write about? Once you have one idea, look to see if you can find another one.

(Allow 1–4 minutes for students to turn and talk with partners. Share exemplary responses.)

RELEASE

Encourage students to consider different environments in their lives to find topics.

So remember, you can look around the classroom for inspiration, or even consider another familiar place such as your home or a place you visit often. Picture those places in your mind, and as you scan around those places in your mind's eye, think, "What are some topics I can teach about that live in these spaces?"

FOR ADDITIONAL SUPPORT, TRY

3.2 Think with Your Heart
3.3 This Is FUN!
3.4 I Can Do It!
3.5 What's Your Hobby?

TIPS/RESOURCES

- Have students make a sketch or draw a map of a familiar environment. Encourage them to label the map and think of topics that "hide" in those places.
- Remind students to not only look at objects, but to also look at people, interactions, situations, and relationships.

Think with Your Heart

In this lesson, students learn to generate ideas for writing by thinking of things they love—people, activities, and other things such as, pets, special toys/games, and memorabilia.

Writing Stage: Emergent, Transitional • **Genre:** Any

INTRODUCE

Tell students that today they will come up with writing ideas by thinking of things they love.

One of the important things we know about authors is that their best writing happens when they write about topics they love. When authors write about topics they love, they feel connected to the topic and enjoy teaching others about it. We love so many things in our world—people, activities, and things like pets, special toys, games, and memorabilia. Once we tap into our heart, we will find that we have more ideas than we ever imagined!

INSTRUCT

Demonstration

Model for students how you think about things you love to come up with ideas.

Watch me as I think about things I love and how I can come up with many different ideas for my writing. I am going to look inside my heart and think about the different people, activities, and things I love and want to teach people about.

In my heart, I have some very important people that I love. My family and friends are the first people that come to mind. I could write a whole book about all the different people in my family. Or I could zoom in on just one family member and write my entire book about him or her, such as my sister. I could also think about activities I love, like gardening or bike riding. I could teach someone about gardening because it's something I love to do and know a lot about. Lastly, I could think about things that I love like cats or my bike. I could think about cats and everything I know about them and then turn it into a whole book that teaches all about cats. I would have so much to write because I love cats and know so much about them.

I can't believe I have so many ideas for my writing! I thought about my family, gardening, my blanket, cats, and riding my bike! Once I started to think about the people, activities, and things that I love, I was able to come up with so many writing ideas.

ALTERNATIVE

Explain with Examples: **Using a variety of mentor texts, show students examples of how authors write about topics they love and feel connected to.**

GUIDE

Prompt students to brainstorm a list of topics that they love.

Let's try this together. We are going to take a minute and think inside our hearts—what are some things that we love? Let's think about the people, activities, and things that we love and know so much about that we could teach others about them. As you think of some ideas, push yourself to think about one or two people, one or two activities, and one or two things that are topics you feel strongly about. Once you have some ideas, share them with your partner.

(Allow 1–4 minutes for students to turn and talk with partners. Share exemplary responses.)

RELEASE

Send students off to write independently. Encourage students to think through a few different topics before deciding on which one they will write about.

Today, when you go off to get started on your writing, remember to think from your heart—what do you love? Let that drive your thinking today and tap into all the things that you love in your world before choosing one to write about. Writing about things you love gives you an opportunity to teach others and also helps you stay connected to your topic.

FOR ADDITIONAL SUPPORT, TRY

3.3 This Is FUN!
3.4 I Can Do It!
3.5 What's Your Hobby?

TIPS/RESOURCES

- Have students sketch, draw, label, or write the topic ideas that they love for later use.
- Have them use a heart template as a place to house all the topics that they love.

This Is FUN!

In this lesson, students learn that one way writers get ideas is to think about things they do for fun, including games, sports, or other activities they play or watch.

Writing Stage: Any • **Genre:** Any

INTRODUCE

Tell students that they are going to come up with topics by thinking of activities they watch or play.

One of the things that makes writing fun is when we write about things we like to do. We can think of ideas for our writing by focusing on the activities we like to participate in, the games we play, and the sports we play or watch. Writing about topics that we think are enjoyable is important because we are able to share our excitement for the topic.

INSTRUCT

Guided Practice

Create a chart with the class, listing activities, games, and sports as possible writing topics.

Let's brainstorm some ideas. *(Create an anchor chart titled: "This is FUN!" with three columns for activities, games, and sports.*)*

Emergent / Transitional We are going to think about one thing at a time, starting with activities. Let's think—what are some activities you like to participate in? What activities do you like to do at home? With your friends? At school? *(Give students 1 minute to think before prompting them to turn and talk with a partner. Add their ideas to the chart under the "activities" column. Repeat the process for games and then for sports.)*

Fluent Think about the activities, games, and sports that could be potential writing topics. You can think about ones you know a lot about, have participated in for a long time, or ones that are new to you. This would give you an opportunity to pursue a topic that you might want to learn more about later in the writing process. Take a few minutes and think of a few games, sports, or other activities that could be possible topics. *(Give students 1 minute to think before prompting them to turn and talk with a partner. Add their ideas to the chart under the appropriate columns.)*

ALTERNATIVE

Demonstration: **Model how you brainstorm a list of the activities, games, and sports you enjoy and know enough to possibly write about.**

 |

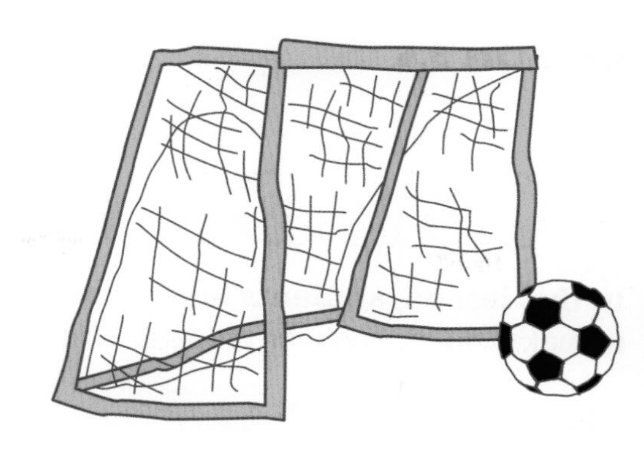

GUIDE

Ask students to choose an idea and prompt them to think about what they already know about that topic.

Let's see how some of the topics feel when we think about them a bit more.

Emergent / Transitional Which idea from our chart do you want to try on? List what you know across your fingers and try to make each fact sound different. For example, if I choose dance, I might say: (1) Dancing is exercise; (2) There are different types of dances; (3) Dance can be just for fun or more serious; (4) You can do it by yourself or with others; and (5) There are interesting dance costumes and shoes.

Fluent Which idea from our chart do you want to try on? Consider the topic you find interesting, are knowledgeable about, or are interested to find out more through research. What would be some possible sections, chapters, or headings? Jot them down in your writer's notebook. For example, if I chose surfing as my topic, I might say: Section 1: History of Surfing; Section 2: Different Types of Surfboards; Section 3: Best Places to Surf; and Section 4: How to Surf.

(Allow 1–4 minutes for students to turn and talk with partners. Share exemplary responses.)

RELEASE

Send students off to write independently, thinking about how well a topic fits them.

Remember, you can think of all the activities, games, and sports you enjoy to come up with ideas for your writing. Try one out, and if it doesn't feel like a good fit, you can always try another and another, until you find the one that fits.

FOR ADDITIONAL SUPPORT, TRY

3.1 I Spy with My Little Eye
3.2 Think with Your Heart
3.4 I Can Do It!
3.5 What's Your Hobby?

TIPS/RESOURCES

- Remind students that activities don't have to be popular or well known. A unique, family game can be an appropriate topic.

*See sample chart, "This is FUN!," on page 156.

I Can Do It!

In this lesson, students learn that one way writers think of ideas is to consider what they like to make, build, cook, or prepare. Writers can describe information or share how to do a task.

Writing Stage: Any
Genre: List, Pattern, All-About Book, Feature Article, Research Report, Expository Nonfiction, Expository Essay

INTRODUCE

Tell students that they can think of writing ideas by thinking about what they make, build, cook, or prepare.

Oftentimes when we think of writing ideas, we lean on topics we know a lot about or love. Sometimes it helps to think about things we do, too. We can think about the things we make, build, cook, or prepare. These can be things we do automatically or tasks that take a lot of focus. Today we are going to use this as our source to find writing ideas.

INSTRUCT

Demonstration

Model for students how you come up with writing ideas by thinking about the things you do well or are learning how to do.

Watch me as I think about some things that I like to make, do, build, or prepare.

Emergent / Transitional What are some things I make? Build? Or cook? I like to make homemade birthday cards because I think it's more fun and meaningful. So that could be a writing idea. What else could I write about? Let me think of things I cook or prepare. I cook eggs all the time—I could teach someone how to make a fried egg. That would be easy for me. Now let's see if I can come up with one more idea ... maybe something I can build. I love to build race car tracks with my son. I could teach someone how to build a race car track—that could be another writing idea!

Fluent Sometimes we can think of things we already know how to make, build, cook, or prepare—other times we might want to write about something we are still learning to do. Writing gives us the opportunity to share our expertise or to further our own. Let me show you what I mean. I love gardening so I decided to make my own greenhouse last spring. It didn't fully work—it blew over, the cover kept coming off, and my seeds looked like they were fried from the sun. But I am not giving up! I need to do some research to gather more information on how to make it work. So I can use the idea of building a greenhouse, research more about it, and write a how-to piece on making one. I could also add a section to my piece on the importance of greenhouses in the environment, the effects of greenhouses on plants, and the materials and steps to make one.

 |

GUIDE

Prompt students to think of ideas that can be topics to teach others. Push them to broaden their ideas.

Now it's your turn. Think of some things that you make, build, cook, or prepare. Remember, it can be something you do every day or that you are learning to do. Try to think of a few tasks that fall into different categories.

(Allow 1–4 minutes for students to turn and talk with partners. Share exemplary responses.)

RELEASE

Send students off to write independently about the things they do. Encourage them to continue brainstorming ideas.

So today, when you go off to write, remember to use the things you make, build, cook, or prepare as a source of ideas for what you can teach others. Try to think of simple things that you do all the time as well as the things that you want to learn more about. You can teach someone how to do it or just write all about it.

FOR ADDITIONAL SUPPORT, TRY

3.2 Think with Your Heart

3.3 This Is FUN!

3.5 What's Your Hobby?

3.8 You Better Work

TIPS/RESOURCES

- For students who are stuck, have a list of some things you've observed they do well to share.

What's Your Hobby?

In this lesson, students learn that one way writers think of ideas is by considering their hobbies and pastimes. They can write about them to spark interest in the reader or teach readers a new skill.

Writing Stage: Any • **Genre:** Any

INTRODUCE

Tell students that they can think of hobbies and pastimes for writing topics.

Sometimes when we are thinking about topics we can teach others, we can focus on our hobbies or pastimes. These can be things we do to fill our downtime or things we are so interested in that we actively and frequently pursue them. This is important because when you choose writing ideas that you think are fun and interesting, then you will be engaged in your writing and excited to share what you know. You also might spark someone else's interest in that hobby or pastime.

INSTRUCT

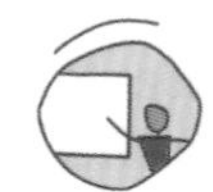

Demonstration

Show students how you come up with ideas by thinking about your hobbies and pastimes.

Watch me as I think about my hobbies and pastimes to help me come up with ideas for my informational writing. One thing that comes to mind is playing the piano. I love to play the piano even though I don't consider myself very good at it. I don't take lessons, but I do find it fun and relaxing. So playing the piano could be an idea that I can write about and teach others. Let me see if I can come up with another idea. What are some things I do to pass the time, like when I am bored? Or when there is a snowstorm? Puzzles! Sometimes I start a puzzle with a lot of pieces so that it takes a while to complete. Whether I have just a few minutes or an hour, it's there waiting for me. It's a great pastime and something I enjoy doing. I love it when my family joins in and I see pieces and parts coming together. It's always fun seeing the finished product.

Did you see how I was able to come up with writing ideas by thinking about my hobbies and pastimes? I thought about a hobby that I enjoy doing and one of my favorite pastimes. As I thought about these things, I realized I had a lot to say about them and now feel excited to get started on my writing!

ALTERNATIVE

Guided Practice: **Together with the class, brainstorm a list of hobbies and pastimes. Chart their ideas.**

 |

GUIDE

Prompt students to share their ideas, hobbies, and pastimes. Remind students that they don't need to be an expert at something to write about it and share their enthusiasm.

Now it's your turn. Think about your hobbies and the things you do to pass time. What are some ideas you have that you can write about and teach others? Share with your partner your ideas—remember, your ideas can be a hobby like mine, playing the piano, or something that is more of a pastime like doing puzzles.

(Allow 1–4 minutes for students to turn and talk with partners. Share exemplary responses.)

FOR ADDITIONAL SUPPORT, TRY

3.3 This Is FUN!

3.4 I Can Do It!

3.8 You Better Work

RELEASE

Send students off to write, reminding them to think about their hobbies and pastimes as writing ideas.

So today, when you sit down to begin writing for the day, think about your hobbies and pastimes as possible writing ideas. Remember, it doesn't have to be something you do all the time or something you're an expert at, but just something you have an interest in and enjoy doing. Once you have an idea, start to write about it and see how much you have to say. You can always go back and brainstorm more ideas.

TIPS/RESOURCES

- Chart students' ideas for later reference. Add more ideas as needed.
- Students will benefit from hearing each other's ideas and may use them as possible topics for their own writing.

Oh, The Places You Go!

In this lesson, students learn that one way writers gather ideas is to think about both the ordinary and extraordinary places they go.

Writing Stage: Any • **Genre:** Any

INTRODUCE

Tell students that they can use the places they go as a way to think of ideas for their writing.

Writers are often most inspired by their own personal experiences. These experiences can be both small, ordinary, everyday kinds of experiences, or they can be once in a lifetime experiences. Today you are going to learn that the places you go, ordinary or extraordinary, can give you ideas for informational writing.

INSTRUCT

Demonstration

Model for students how you consider the places you go to come up with ideas.

Watch me as I use this concept for informational writing. To help me narrow down some places, I might first consider indoor versus outdoor places. *(Begin to create a two-column chart.)* I might also consider the seasons in the year. *(Divide the T chart into quadrants for each season.)* Now I can think of both ordinary and extraordinary places that I have experienced both indoors and out across the year.

In summer, I went to some ordinary outdoor places, such as Jones Beach, Taghkanic State Park, and the Bronx Zoo. However, I also traveled to some extraordinary places, like Paris in France, Venice in Italy, and even Pompeii. During colder months, I prefer indoor activities like The Metropolitan Museum of Art or Broadway Theaters. During the fall, some ordinary places I go include school and stores. On weekends, I like to visit Fix Brothers Farms in Hudson for apple and pumpkin picking and Kaaterskill Falls for hiking and enjoying the foliage. With any of these topics, I can think of something to teach.

Emergent / Transitional I could teach about zoos and the different animals you see there. I could teach about school or places new students might need to know about, like the cafeteria.

Fluent I could teach or share research about Pompeii. If I consider the Bronx Zoo, I might want to write my opinions about animals in captivity.

Did you notice how I first narrowed it down by considering both indoor and outdoor places and then the seasons to help me brainstorm? I considered geographic locations, landmarks, and places of recreation.

ALTERNATIVE

Explain with Examples: **Using a variety of mentor texts, show students examples of titles that include geographic locations, landmarks, and places of recreation.**

 |

GUIDE

Ask students to brainstorm some places that they have been.

Let's see how many more ideas we can brainstorm. Using the seasons as a guide, consider the ordinary and extraordinary indoor and outdoor places that you have been. What are some topics that you could write about? What are some things you might teach or say about those places?

(Allow 1–4 minutes for students to turn and talk with partners. Share exemplary responses.)

RELEASE

Encourage students to think of a broad range of places for writing ideas.

So today, when you go off to write, remember that your own personal experiences and the places that you have been can help you come up with ideas. You can consider geographic locations, landmarks, and places of recreation or fun.

FOR ADDITIONAL SUPPORT, TRY

3.3 This is FUN!

3.5 What's Your Hobby?

3.9 Natural Wonders

3.12 Get Schooled

TIPS/RESOURCES

- Scaffold this lesson by focusing on ordinary or extraordinary places first.
- Create a class anchor chart that lists the four seasons in one column and columns for ordinary and extraordinary places.

Power of the People

In this lesson, students learn that one way writers discover ideas is to think about people of notoriety throughout history—either individuals or groups/categories.

Writing Stage: Transitional, Fluent
Genre: All-About Book, Feature Article, Research Report, Biography, Expository Nonfiction, Expository Essay

INTRODUCE

Tell students that they can use people of notoriety to think of ideas for their writing.

Writers often get inspired by people—either individuals or groups that fascinate them in different ways. The types of people that they write about usually seem extraordinary in some way—either because they have accomplished great things, or because they have lived a life that is very different from their own. These notable subjects can be historical or present day. Today we are going to learn that extraordinary people can give us ideas for informational writing.

INSTRUCT

Demonstration

Model for students how you brainstorm possible subjects because you know a lot about them, admire them, or feel awestruck by their accomplishments.

I am going to think about people who I admire or with whom I am awestruck. I might consider people who have overcome adversity, people who are great leaders, or people who have made great contributions to the world. I can also think of my own passions and interests and the people who have made contributions in those fields.

Let me first consider people in history. One person might be Harriet Tubman. I am awestruck by her ability to help more than 70 people find their way to freedom. She overcame tremendous obstacles. Another subject might be the ancient Egyptians. I am fascinated by their ability to build the pyramids and how advanced their ancient civilization seemed. I desperately want to visit the pyramids one day!

If I were to consider people from the present day, I might choose Barack Obama as a great leader who become the first black president of the USA. I also might consider inventors and innovators in technology because I love computers, phones, and other gadgets. Therefore, Steve Jobs might be a subject I choose to write about because Apple has made tremendous contributions to the world of technology. I also love music, so I might consider performers who have achieved greatness like Taylor Swift. She lives an extraordinary life worth writing about.

Did you see how I thought about both historical and present-day people who fascinate me through their leadership, bravery, and contributions? Did you notice that the subjects were all from different walks of life, yet connected to my own interests in some way?

ALTERNATIVE

***Guided Practice:* Brainstorm a list with the class considering subjects from different walks of life throughout history to present day.**

 |

GUIDE

Prompt students to make connections between their passions and noteworthy people.

Now let's try it together. First, think about the kinds of things that really interest you. Then, consider people in those areas or fields who you might find inspiring or awesome. These can be people in history or present day. Consider people who have overcome adversity, leaders of movements or groups, or people who have achieved greatness. You can name subjects across your fingers with a partner or jot some names down on a list.

(Chart student responses.)*

RELEASE

Send students off to write and remind them that people of notoriety are a way to think of ideas for their writing.

So today, remember that people or groups that fascinate us are one way that writers come up with ideas. These can be people throughout history or people from the present day. As you think of some ideas, go ahead and write a little something about why these subjects are so great—much like a summary blurb on the back of a book or the book jacket's inside flap.

FOR ADDITIONAL SUPPORT, TRY

3.3 This Is FUN!

3.5 What's Your Hobby?

3.9 Natural Wonders

3.12 Get Schooled

TIPS/RESOURCES

- Display mentor texts such as biographies, magazine covers, and nonfiction books that profile individuals or groups. Be sure to include diverse subjects and topics.

**If students have difficulty identifying people, but have identified an area of interest, help them research people or groups who are connected to those fields.*

You Better Work

In this lesson, students learn that one way writers think of ideas is to consider the routines, jobs, tasks, or chores across their day.

Writing Stage: Any
Genre: List, How-To Book, All-About Book, Feature Article, Research Report, Expository Nonfiction, Expository Essay

INTRODUCE

Tell students that they can use the routines, jobs, tasks, or chores across their day to think of ideas for their writing.

Sometimes we don't realize that the ordinary things we do across our day are things that we can write about. Today we are going to learn that the routines, jobs, tasks, or chores we do can give us ideas for informational writing. This is important because others may need or want to learn how to do them, or they might be curious to understand someone else's perspective on them.

INSTRUCT

Demonstration

Model for students how you consider the routines, jobs, tasks, or chores you do to come up with ideas. Chart your ideas.

I am going to break up my day into parts: the morning, the school day, the afternoon, dinner time, and bedtime.

If I were to zoom into when I first wake up, I can think about the things I do across the morning every day. First, I get out of bed. What are some things I do when I get out of bed? Oh, I know! First, I make my bed. Then I pick out my clothes. Let me close my eyes again and picture what comes next. I make my way into the bathroom and wash my face, brush my teeth, and put in my contact lenses. Then I get dressed. Finally, I walk into the kitchen to make a smoothie and prepare my lunch. Let's see—which of these ideas could I use for my writing?

List Books and How-To Books I could make a book about *Getting Ready for School*, or *How to Make a Bed*, or *Getting Dressed*, or *How to Brush Your Teeth,* or *How to Wash Your Face*, or *How to Make a Smoothie.*

All-About Books I could make an all-about book on *Good Hygiene*, or *All About Smoothies* or *All About Fashion.*

Feature Article, Expository Nonfiction, Expository Essay, or Research Report I could write about *Oral Hygiene, Healthy Breakfast Alternatives, Dressing Professionally and Comfortably,* or *Smoothies: A Recipe for Every Palate.* I could even do some research on *The Benefits of Protein Powders.*

ALTERNATIVE

Guided Practice: **With the class, brainstorm a list of routines, jobs, tasks, or chores you do. Chart the ideas.**

 |

GUIDE

Prompt students to brainstorm some routines, jobs, tasks, or chores across the school day.

Let's try this together and see how many more ideas we can brainstorm to add to this chart. This time, we will zoom into the school day. Let's take a look at our daily schedule. What are some routines, jobs, tasks, or chores across our school day that we can write about? Look at each of our periods in the day and think about what we do during that period.

(Allow 1–4 minutes for students to turn and talk with partners. Share exemplary responses.)

RELEASE

Remind students that seemingly ordinary routines are a way to think of ideas for their writing.

So today, when you go off to write, remember that the ordinary routines, tasks, jobs, and chores are topics that you can write about. Others might need or want to learn to do these things, or they may be curious to learn how you do them through your writing. As you brainstorm ideas, remember to think about different parts of your day, such as mornings, afternoons, and evenings. You can even think about different parts of the week or year, like weekends or seasons.

FOR ADDITIONAL SUPPORT, TRY

3.3 This Is FUN!

3.4 I Can Do It!

3.5 What's Your Hobby?

TIPS/RESOURCES

- Have students consider both indoor and outdoor routines.
- Have students consider jobs that they do independently.

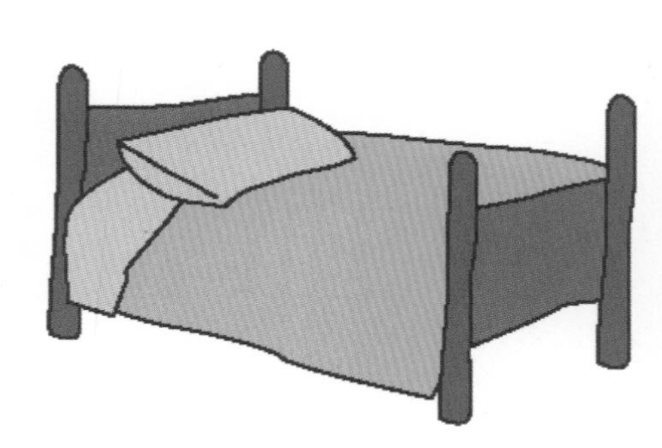

Natural Wonders

In this lesson, students learn that one way writers think of ideas is to consider the natural world around them, including the environment.

Writing Stage: Any
Genre: List, All-About Book, Feature Article, Research Report, Literary Nonfiction, Expository Nonfiction, Expository Essay

INTRODUCE

Tell students that they can use topics related to nature or the environment as ideas for writing.

Even though there are a wide range of informational topics that authors write about, many texts are about the natural world or the environment. Today we are going to look here to find some ideas for our pieces. This is important because readers are forever curious about nature.

INSTRUCT

Guided Practice

Prompt students to come up with numerous ideas of potential topics. Chart the responses for reference.

Let's brainstorm a list of potential topics related to the natural world or the environment. Before we begin calling out topics, let's consider a few important details. First, we must be interested in the topic and learning more about the topic. Next, we should also have a considerable amount of background knowledge about the topic. Starting from scratch would require too much research. Lastly, we should make sure that our topics aren't too broad. For example, the topic "animals" is better for a reference book rather than an informational text. Instead, we might consider a single category, such as "sharks" or "pets" so that our writing is more focused, organized, and manageable to write.

Consider different parts of the natural world such as land, sky, and sea. Consider different climate zones or parts of the world. Consider the different disciplines in science. Lastly, consider effects on our environment.

(Give students time to brainstorm and/or discuss in partnerships or small groups. Chart their responses for reference.)

ALTERNATIVE

Explain with Examples: **Display a variety of nonfiction texts related to the natural world. Include topics of high interest to your class.**

 |

GUIDE

Give students a moment to consider some of the topics that might interest them.

We have quite a list here. Let's choose one of these topics. You can choose an idea of your own a bit later.

Emergent / Transitional Once you have picked a topic that interests you, tell some facts across your fingers. Be sure the facts are different. For example, if I chose dogs, I might say: (1) There are many kinds of dogs; (2) Dogs eat special dog food to stay healthy; (3) Dogs can be trained to do tricks and follow directions; (4) Dogs make great pets; and (5) Dogs have puppies.

Transitional / Fluent After you pick a topic that interests you, think of some possible chapters or subheadings. Jot them on a page in your notebook. Be sure each subheading is different. For example, if I chose the moon, I might say: Chapter 1: Geography of the Moon; Chapter 2: Phases of the Moon; Chapter 3: Traveling to the Moon; and Chapter 4: Life on the Moon.

Remember to ask yourself if you have enough knowledge on this topic. If not, choose a new idea.

(Allow 1–4 minutes for students to turn and talk with partners. Share exemplary responses.)

RELEASE

Send students off to write and remind them that topics in nature can fuel new ideas.

So today, when you go off to write, remember that topics related to the natural world are a good place to look for topics. Think of topics that excite you and for which you have background knowledge. Once you have some ideas, try them on for size by rehearsing how they might go.

FOR ADDITIONAL SUPPORT, TRY

3.10 Flaunt Your Expertise

3.12 Get Schooled

TIPS/RESOURCES:

- Have students look at books, photos, or videos of the natural world to get ideas.
- Review the table of contents in mentor texts to discuss ideas about text structures.

LESSON 3.10

Flaunt Your Expertise

In this lesson, students learn that writers get ideas for topics by thinking about topics of personal expertise. Writers ask: What am I an expert at that I could teach to someone else?

Writing Stage: Any • **Genre:** Any

INTRODUCE

Tell students that they can get ideas for writing by thinking about topics in which they are experts.

When we hear the word *expert*, we might feel a little intimidated. "Who me? I'm no expert!" Of course you are! You know about many things. Today we are going to learn that one way to get ideas for informational writing is to ask ourselves what topics we know a lot about and could teach someone else.

INSTRUCT

Demonstration

Show writers how you think of the things you know a lot about as a way to get ideas for writing.

Watch me think about things I know a lot about—things I'm an expert on—and could teach someone else.

Emergent / Transitional I know a lot about basketball. I watch it all the time. I could teach someone all about it—from the uniforms, to the rules of the game, to facts about famous players. I also know a lot about pets. I have a dog and two cats; I've also had fish, tadpoles and frogs, guinea pigs, and rabbits. I could teach people about animals. I know about sharks, lemurs, and cows. I walk to school. I know a lot about some of the things I see on those walks, such as the stores and places I pass.

Fluent I know a lot about basketball—I watch it and read about it. I could teach about the leagues, teams, and specific players like Steph Curry and LeBron James. I can also write about the rules of the game. I could also teach about pets. I have a dog and two cats; I've had fish, tadpoles and frogs, guinea pigs and rabbits. I could teach about the life cycle of a frog or how to train a dog. I could teach people about sharks, lemurs, and cows. I could write about shark types, where they live, their teeth and what they eat, or how people are destroying their environment. As another topic, I walk to school each day so I could teach about some of the things I see. I pass a library—I could tell you about how to find the right book there, or what they have besides books, or the spaces in the library for studying and gathering.

Did you notice how I thought about specific things I know a lot about and could possibly teach others?

ALTERNATIVE

Guided Practice: **Together with students, brainstorm a list of topics of personal expertise that you could teach to others.**

 |

GUIDE

Ask students to share topics of personal expertise with one another. Chart their ideas.

Let's try this together. Take a moment to think about the topics in which you are an expert—the topics you could teach others. You might think about the things you do, some experiences you've had, or just things you know a lot about. Share your ideas with your partner.

(Allow 1–4 minutes for students to turn and talk with partners. Share exemplary responses. Remind students it is okay to be inspired by their partner's or others' ideas.)

RELEASE

Remind students that topics of personal expertise are worth writing about because often they will have the most to say about these topics.

So today, when you go off to write, remember that you really are an expert on so many topics. You can think of the things you know about and can teach to others to get ideas for writing. You can make a list or begin with a sketch to help you, and then try writing about one of those topics.

FOR ADDITIONAL SUPPORT, TRY

1.2 All About Me

3.3 This Is FUN!

3.4 I Can Do It!

3.12 Get Schooled

TIPS/RESOURCES

- Encourage students to be inspired by a partner's ideas. This communication can help jog a student's memory of their own interests.
- Tell fluent writers they have reached "expert status" if they can name 3–5 facts about a topic.

This I Believe

In this lesson, students learn one way writers think of ideas for informational writing is to consider their passions—topics they feel strongly about. They can then teach others to show their passion.

Writing Stage: Transitional, Fluent
Genre: All-About Book, Feature Article, Research Report, Biography, Literary Nonfiction, Expository Nonfiction, Expository Essay

INTRODUCE

Tell students they can think of topics they're passionate about as a way to generate ideas for writing.

We often think of informational writing as very factual, devoid of emotion. In reality, historians, scientists, doctors, researchers—people who write informational texts—are very passionate about their topics. This enthusiasm carries them through the hard work of research and writing; they want you to "catch" their curiosity for and excitement about their topic. Today I want to teach you how we can use our emotions by thinking of topics we are passionate, or very enthusiastic, about to generate ideas for our informational writing.

INSTRUCT

Demonstration

Model for students how you think of your passions—things you're enthusiastic about—as ideas for writing.

Watch me as I think of my passions—things I'm enthusiastic about—as a way to get ideas for writing.

Transitional I'm passionate about animals. I love them, and I know about different kinds of animals. I know about pets: cats, dogs, fish, hermit crabs, and frogs. But I also know about unusual animals like sharks, octopuses, lemurs, and manatees. I could teach about all of those topics. One way I know I'm enthusiastic about something is if it comes up in conversation and I can't stop talking about it. I love talking about basketball, reading, and authors I love, like Jacqueline Woodson. I feel strongly about equality and people being treated the same. I could write about any of those things.

Fluent I'm passionate about animals. I love them, and I know about different kinds of animals. I know about pets: cats, dogs, fish, hermit crabs, and frogs. I could write about these animals, but I could also write about animal rescue and the important role it plays in our community. I also know about unusual animals like sharks, octopuses, lemurs, and manatees. I could write about how the changes in our environment are endangering their existence. One way I know I'm enthusiastic about something is if it comes up in conversation and I can't stop talking about it. I love talking about basketball, the game, but also the teams and coaches I like. I love reading and there are authors I love, like Jacqueline Woodson and Jason Reynolds. I feel strongly about equality and people being treated the same. I could write about movements in our country for equality, too.

ALTERNATIVE

Guided Practice: **Together with students, think of things you know they are passionate about. Be careful to steer them to topics, rather than opinions on topics.**

 |

GUIDE

Prompt students to turn and talk about their passions with a partner.

Let's try this together. Take a minute and think about something you're passionate about—something you're enthusiastic or have strong feelings about. It might be something you love to talk about or enjoy sharing with others.

(Allow 1–4 minutes for students to turn and talk with partners. Share exemplary responses.)

RELEASE

Send students off to write independently on topics they're passionate about.

So today, when you go off to write, remember that your passions are sources for writing—topics you feel strongly about or that fill you with strong emotions like excitement and enthusiasm. You can think of those topics, make a list or a sketch, then pick one and start writing about it. If you finish before writing time is over, you can return to your list or make another sketch and write on a different topic you're passionate about.

FOR ADDITIONAL SUPPORT, TRY

3.3 This Is FUN!

3.4 I Can Do It!

3.5 What's Your Hobby?

TIPS/RESOURCES:

- If students are stuck, it might be helpful to think about passions in terms of a category (their life, friends, school, history, etc.).

LESSON 3.12

Get Schooled

In this lesson, students learn that one way to gather ideas for writing is to think about topics they've learned related to social studies, science, or other parts of their school day.

Writing Stage: Any • **Genre:** Any

INTRODUCE

Tell students that they can use ideas they've learned in content-area classes, or other parts of their day, as ideas for writing.

We learn so much in our content-area classes like social studies and science, and during other times of our day, like our special events. Why keep all of those ideas just in one part of our day? We can bring them to writing to share what we know. Today we are going to think about what we've learned about outside of reading and writing, as topics for writing. We can make a list or sketch those ideas to teach to our reader.

INSTRUCT

Guided Practice

Guide students to think together about topics you've covered in social studies or science, or that you know they've learned about in art, music, etc.

Grade-Level Teachers Let's think about some things we've learned about in other times of our day. How about social studies or science? It could be something we're studying right now or from a previous unit. Let's think of things you've learned in other classes. You might think about art, P.E., or music. Take a moment to share your ideas with your partner. (*Give students a minute to turn and talk, then share out ideas. Chart student responses.*)

Departmentalized Teachers Let's think about some of the topics we have learned during our unit of study that we can write about. These can be smaller topics that live inside of a big topic.* Share ideas with your partner. (*Give students a minute to turn and talk, then share out ideas. Chart student responses.*)

*For example, in a larger topic such as the American Revolution, guide students toward topics like the Boston Tea Party, Paul Revere's ride, etc.

ALTERNATIVE

Demonstration: **For departmentalized teachers, demonstration might be a better fit (or have conversations with colleagues about topics they've covered with students before trying guided practice).**

 |

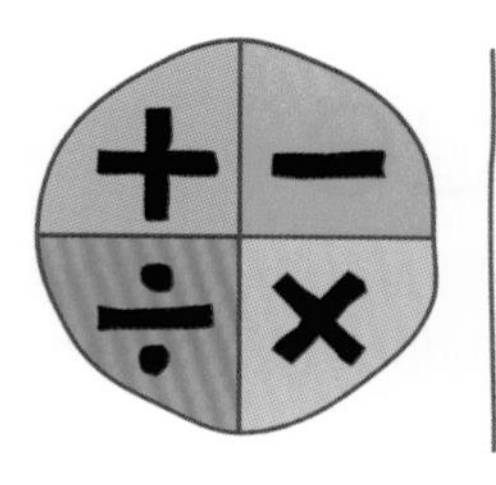

GUIDE

Ask students to take one of the topics from the class chart and talk it through with a partner. Have them tell their partners what they could teach within that topic.

Let's take a minute to try this. Choose something off of our list or something you thought of that isn't written on our list. When you have a topic you're interested in, give me a thumbs up. Think about what you could teach someone about that topic. Start to list those ideas in your mind or across your fingers. Turn and talk to your partner; tell them what you could teach about your topic.

(Listen in and voice over topics you hear students discussing. Add any new ideas to the class chart. You might also coach students to teach their partners more to encourage students to elaborate.)

RELEASE

Send students off to write independently. Encourage them to think of topics from social studies, science, or other classes.

So today, when you go off to write, one way to think about topics is to think of the things you've learned about in other times of the school day. You can use our class chart to help you or just think about what you've learned in other classes. You might even think about things you learned or loved learning in previous years.

FOR ADDITIONAL SUPPORT, TRY

1.4 Something Old, Something New
1.6 Borrow Ideas from Others
3.1 I Spy with My Little Eye
3.9 Natural Wonders

TIPS/RESOURCES

- Talk with content-area specialists to see which topics have been taught and are most engaging for students.
- If you teach other content-area classes, make past resources available to jog students' memories.

A Bit of Advice

In this lesson, students learn one way to get ideas for writing is to think about a problem that they, or others, face. They can write to teach about the problem and how it might be solved.

Writing Stage: Any
Genre: How-To Book, All-About Book, Feature Article, Expository Nonfiction, Expository Essay

INTRODUCE

Tell students that they can think of problems in different parts of their lives and then teach about how to solve them as ideas for writing.

I often turn to my close friends for advice—the friends who can help me solve a problem. As writers, we can be those kinds of friends for our readers. Today we are going to learn how we can think about a problem and write to teach someone how they can solve it.

INSTRUCT

Guided Practice

Guide students to think about problems in the classroom or school, and discuss some ways the problems could be solved.

Emergent What are some problems that we have right here in our classroom or school?* (*Have students turn and talk. Share out exemplary responses.*) I am hearing great ideas such as children running in the hall, students being mean to one another, and classmates not sharing supplies. If we were to write to solve these problems, perhaps we can make a book about school safety or kindness, or being a good friend, or sharing.

Fluent What are some problems that we see in our world that we can write about to raise awareness and propose solutions? (*Have students turn and talk. Share out exemplary responses.*)

I am hearing some great ideas such as pollution, recycling, climate change, cyber-bullying, and racism. These are all topics that we can write about to inform our readers and raise their awareness. In our writing, we can even propose solutions to these problems!

(If time permits, have students turn and talk to brainstorm additional problems and solutions.)

ALTERNATIVE

Demonstration: **Model for students how you think about problems and solutions related to problems. Use problems students likely connect with.**

GUIDE

Give students an opportunity to take one problem and talk it through with a partner.

Now it's your turn. Take one of the problems on our list—one that you think you can explain and give some advice on. Now turn and talk to your partner and say the words you think you would write.

(Listen in and voice over topics you hear students talking about. Add any new ideas to the class chart. You might also coach students to think through solutions to their problems.)

RELEASE

Encourage students to write about a specific problem and some advice they might give a reader to solve it.

So today, when you go off to write, one thing you can do is think about some advice you might give to a reader for a problem that you see. It could be a problem in our classroom, school, or your neighborhood, or community, or in the world. You can sketch these problems or list them, then pick one to write about. Explain the problem to your reader and give them some advice for how to solve it—like a good friend would!

FOR ADDITIONAL SUPPORT, TRY

1.9 Talk It Out

1.22 Partners Are Resources, Too!

3.11 This I Believe

TIPS/RESOURCES

If students need support, encourage them to think about categories.

- For emergent writers, think of places (cafeteria, gym) or times of day (arrival, pack-up).
- For fluent writers, think of problems affecting their social groups (gender, race, age). You might need to coach students on multifaceted solutions.

*See sample chart, "Where Can We Find Problems to Solve?," on page 156.

Inquiring Minds Want to Know

In this lesson, students learn to generate ideas by thinking about things they are curious about.

Writing Stage: Transitional, Fluent

Genre: How-To Book, All-About Book, Feature Article, Literary Nonfiction, Expository Nonfiction, Biography, Research Report, Expository Essay

INTRODUCE

Tell students that they can use what they know, and what they are curious about, to brainstorm topics.

Sometimes with informational writing, it's our curiosity that drives us to write. We think about the things we know or wonder about. Today I want to teach you how we can think about what we want to know and do some freewriting about those ideas. By asking questions and wondering, we can let our inquisitive minds be our guide.

INSTRUCT

Demonstration

Show students how you use what you know as a springboard for what you want to know.

Watch me as I use what I know to help me wonder.

Transitional I know about sharks—where they live, different types, and the fact that some of them are very unusual. But I wonder if there have been any recent discoveries of new shark species? I have also heard that climate change is causing sea levels to rise and oceans to warm. I wonder how those changes are affecting sharks? Is it affecting the food they eat? The places they live? I also know that sharks are hunted by humans, but I never see people eating sharks, at least I don't think I do. What could sharks be used for?

Fluent I know about Brown vs. the Board of Education, the landmark 1954 Supreme Court case that ruled segregated public schools were unconstitutional. But I also know that public schools in many areas across our country are segregated—even though they aren't supposed to be. I wonder why that is, and I also wonder why it is allowed to continue. I'm sure that there must be people fighting this, but where are they and what are they doing?

Do you see how I thought about a topic I know about and that I'm interested in learning more? I pushed myself to reflect, wonder, and ask questions. I'm going to write those questions down, just like I talked through them.

ALTERNATIVE

***Guided Practice:* Guide students to think about topics they've studied together and the questions, wonderings, and hypotheses they have about those topics.**

GUIDE

Prompt students to try the strategy by orally rehearsing their ideas with a partner.

Now it's your turn. Think of a topic you know about. It might be something you've even written about before. Once you get that idea in your head, give me a thumbs up. Now try to think of what you're still curious about with regards to that topic. Turn and talk to your partner. Share your questions.

(Allow 1–4 minutes for students to turn and talk with partners. Share exemplary responses.)

RELEASE

Send students off and invite them to try the strategy independently.

So today, when you go off to write, one thing you might try is to think of topics you know but still have burning questions about. You may also be curious about topics that you have yet to study, and you can write about those topics, too, by generating lots of questions.

FOR ADDITIONAL SUPPORT, TRY

1.4 Something Old, Something New

1.6 Borrow Ideas from Others

1.9 Talk It Out

3.12 Get Schooled

TIPS/RESOURCES

To support students' curiosity, provide an anchor chart* with sentence starters like:

- I wonder _____.
- Why do/does/are _____?
- How can/do/does _____?

You may combine this idea with *1.9 Talk It Out* by having partners ask each other questions about the topic.

*See sample chart, "Inquiring Minds Want to Know," on page 156.

Lesson 3.3 This Is FUN!

Where Can We Find Problems to Solve?

places

school: auditorium, library, classroom, lunch room, hallways, gym

home: pets, bedroom, kitchen

times of day

arrival: desks/tables, buses, coat area, class library

dismissal: announcements, hallways, packing up, line up, bus, bathroom

Lesson 3.13 A Bit of Advice

Lesson 3.14 Inquiring Minds Want to Know

Choose & Refine

The series of lessons in this section contain strategies to help students select a topic to write about or take through publishing. They also include strategies to narrow a focus and consider one's audience. The lessons:

- include selecting a topic from brainstorming lists and reviewing notebook entries to decide which topic to take through the writing process;
- show students how to refine a topic when topics are too broad; and
- encourage students, especially fluent writers, to "write small" with greater elaboration.

Descriptors for Choosing and Refining Ideas

Emergent Writers	Fluent Writers
• List ideas "in the air" and then choose one to write about. • Choose topics from displayed anchor charts containing lists of ideas generated by students that the teacher has scribed. • Refine topics by orally rehearsing a few different ways the book could go before settling on how they will write it. • Rehearse a topic by talking with a partner and sharing what they will say about it before writing.	• Choose a topic from their entries that they will commit to moving forward in the writing process. • Reread and reflect in order to get to the "heart" or focus of their work. • Refine their writing by focusing on structures in smaller sections or an overall structure for the entire piece.

At-a-Glance Guide

Choose & Refine

Title		Lesson
4.1	**Chatterbox**	Choose the topic with the most information.
4.2	**Find Out More**	Choose an idea based on curiosity.
4.3	**Stay Connected**	Choose an idea that you care about the most.
4.4	**Narrow It Down**	Ask strategic questions connected to knowledge, audience, interests, and perspective.
4.5	**What's Your Angle?**	Develop an angle.
4.6	**Discover What You Want to Say**	Freewrite about a topic in long form to see which aspect of the topic generates the most ideas.
4.7	**Go Back!**	Reread notebook entries to notice recurring ideas and emerging patterns.
4.8	**Switch It Up**	Try the topic as a poem or a story.
4.9	**Who's Your Audience?**	Consider the audience to develop ideas.
4.10	**Make a Commitment**	Choose a long-term writing project.

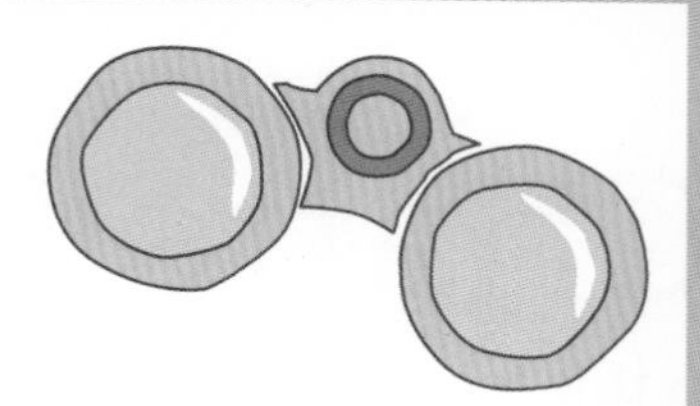

Writing Stage	Genre	
Any	Any	
Any	Any	
Any	Any	
Any	Any	
Transitional Fluent	All-About Feature Article Literary Nonfiction Expository Nonfiction	Biography Research Report Expository Essay
Fluent	Feature Article Literary Nonfiction Expository Nonfiction	Biography Research Report Expository Essay
Fluent	Feature Article Literary Nonfiction Expository Nonfiction	Biography Research Report Expository Essay
Fluent	Feature Article Literary Nonfiction Expository Nonfiction	Biography Research Report Expository Essay
Any	Any	
Fluent	Feature Article Literary Nonfiction Expository Nonfiction	Biography Research Report Expository Essay

LESSON 4.1

Chatterbox

In this lesson, students learn that one way writers choose an idea is to think about which topic they have the most to say about.

Writing Stage: Any • **Genre:** Any

INTRODUCE

Tell students that they can choose a topic by considering which topic they have the most to say about.

Writers often choose a topic to develop or publish that they care a great deal for and that they have a lot to say about. These two elements are important because in order to fully develop a topic, an author has to feel a great deal of passion about it.

INSTRUCT

Demonstration

Look through your writing and choose a topic based on how much was already written and how easily you can think of ways to add more information.

Watch me as I choose my topic by thinking about my ideas and noticing which ones I have the most to say about.

Emergent / Transitional Let me start by opening up my writing folder to look at my writing. I want to make sure I choose a topic that I have a lot to say about, not just my favorite one. I am going to ask myself: "Did I have a lot to say about this topic?" and "Can I say more about this topic?" These questions will help me figure out which ideas to publish. I will make two piles: one for those I have a lot to say about and one for those that I do not. The first piece of writing I have is about gardening. I love to garden, but not only do I not have a lot of writing on the page, I also can't think of anything else to add. I will put this writing in the pile of ideas that I don't have enough to say about. This next piece of writing is about cats. Look at how much I wrote about cats! Not only do I have a lot of writing, but I also can think of more information to add. This tells me this might be a good idea for me to choose.

Fluent Let me start by opening up my writer's notebook. I might have an idea of what I want to choose, but I want to make sure I pick a topic that I have a lot more to say about beyond my notebook entries. I'm going to go back and review my entries. My first entry is about gardening. Reading through it, I can see that I wrote mostly about planting and the different vegetables someone could plant. I actually can say more about gardening, such as planning a garden, diversifying plants, and the availability of fruits and vegetables to everyone in our community. I could write about community gardens and their impact on food deserts. I'm going to mark this entry as one I might choose and jot down possible subtopics in the margin. I can really see there is some potential here. Then I will move on to consider my next entry.

 |

GUIDE

Prompt students to look at the first entry of their own writing and question themselves.

Now it's your turn. Open to your very first topic. Ask yourself: "Do I have a lot to say about this topic? Are there parts of my topic I can say more about?"

Fluent Ask yourself, "Can I create more subheadings or parts for this topic?"

(Allow 1–4 minutes for students to turn and talk with partners. Share exemplary responses.)

RELEASE

Send students to independently look through their topics and see which ones are worth developing.

So today, when you go to write independently, remember that writers don't only choose the topics that they love, but they consider which ones they have the most to say about. Once we identify those topics, we can continue to add to them.

FOR ADDITIONAL SUPPORT, TRY

4.3 Stay Connected
4.7 Go Back!
4.9 Who's Your Audience?

TIPS/RESOURCES

- Create an anchor chart with the guiding questions from the lesson.

LESSON 4.2

Find Out More

In this lesson, students learn that one way writers choose an idea is to think about a topic they are curious about and excited to study more.

Writing Stage: Any • **Genre:** Any

INTRODUCE

Tell students that they can choose an idea by thinking about the ones they are curious about and want to learn more.

Sometimes writers ask themselves questions to help them choose which idea they want to write about. They ask, "Which topics am I most curious about?" and "Which ones do I want to learn more about?" These questions can help us narrow down our ideas to the ones we most want to pursue. This is important because when we are curious about an idea, we can use that excitement to motivate us to learn more about it.

INSTRUCT

Demonstration

Model how you look through your writing folder or notebook to choose an idea based on curiosity and desire to learn more.

Watch me as I think about my ideas and consider which ones I'm most curious about and want to learn more.

Emergent / Transitional I have so many writing ideas to choose from in my folder! I want to focus on the ideas that I am most curious about and want to learn more. Two ideas that I am curious about are gardening and cats. I am not sure if gardening is a good fit for me. I only know a little bit about it, and it's almost wintertime so I won't be able to try some gardening at home. Let me think about my other idea—cats. I love, know a lot about, and am very curious about cats. I wonder, "How long do they nap? And what are their favorite toys and treats?" Wow, I am actually more curious about cats than I even thought. If I choose cats as my idea, I could easily observe my cats at home to gather more information.

Fluent I have so many different writing ideas in my notebook, but today I want to look through my entries and ask myself, "Which ideas do I want to learn more about, have questions about, and am excited to do some research on to find answers?" As I go through my entries, I am noticing that some of these ideas are things I like, but I am not that curious about them. I have a few entries on bike riding, but I am not really interested in learning more. I notice I have an entry or two about martial arts. That's something that I have recently become curious about and would like to learn about. Actually, now that I think about it, I am excited to learn more about martial arts, research it, and write about it as my topic.

Did you see how I chose an idea by thinking about what I'm curious about and want to learn more?

 |

GUIDE

Prompt students to look at their writing and ask guiding questions to choose a topic.

Emergent / Transitional Open up your writing folders. Take a look at your writing ideas. Ask yourself, "Which ideas am I curious about and want to learn more?" Remember that your topic also needs to be something that you know enough about to share your information with an audience.

Fluent Open up your notebooks. Take a look at your entries and ask yourself, "Which ideas am I curious about and want to learn more?" Remember, your idea can be something that you want to gather information on to add to what you already know.

(Allow 1–4 minutes for students to turn and talk with partners. Share exemplary responses.)

RELEASE

Send students off to continue looking through their ideas for the ones with the most potential.

So today, look through your ideas to see which ones spark curiosity and the desire to learn more. When we choose our topics this way, we will be more motivated to write and share.

FOR ADDITIONAL SUPPORT, TRY

4.1 Chatterbox

4.3 Stay Connected

4.4 Narrow It Down

TIPS/RESOURCES

- Brainstorm a list as a class of some possible ideas so students have a shared resource.

Stay Connected

In this lesson, students learn that writers can choose an idea by thinking about the one they feel the most connected to or care the most about.

Writing Stage: Any • **Genre:** Any

INTRODUCE

Tell students that they can choose ideas by thinking about what they feel most connected to.

The connections we have in life are what make it meaningful and fun. Perhaps it's the way you connect with a teacher and the safe feeling he or she gives you. Or maybe it's a connection you have to a fun game and how it calms you down. When we are connected to our ideas, writing will be more meaningful and enjoyable.

INSTRUCT

Demonstration

Model for students how you look through your writing and think about which ideas you are connected to, distinguishing between liking and loving an idea.

Watch me as I choose my topic by thinking about the ideas I am connected to.

Emergent / Transitional Let me start by taking a look at the writing in my folder. Here is one piece where I started to write about the beach. Let me think deeply about the beach for a moment. Well, I do love the beach and I go all the time. I also always pick up garbage to keep it clean and to protect the animals. I have many memories of going there with my friends and family. The beach is definitely an idea I am connected to. Here is another piece of writing about bicycles. When I think about bikes, I don't think I feel very connected. I care about bikes but not nearly as much as I do about the beach. That settles it for me, the beach is my topic! I am going to take a self-stick note and put it on my piece of writing about the beach and quickly draw a heart on it. This is exciting because now I get to see what else I have to say about the beach.

Fluent Let me start by taking a look at some of my notebook entries. Here I have one about gardening. Gardening is interesting, but I don't feel connected to the idea. Let me keep looking. Here is one about the beach. I love the beach and I have endless memories of my family and friends all going to the beach together. I would go to the beach every day if I was able to! I also care a lot about the beach and protecting the environment and wildlife from erosion and pollution. In fact, I have volunteered at a few beach cleanups and also helped plant new dune grass to prevent erosion. This is definitely a topic that I am connected to so I am going to put a heart on this entry. This will help me remember how I feel about this idea and possibly use it as the topic I move forward with in writing.

 |

GUIDE

Prompt students to look at their own writing and to place a heart to signify if it's an idea they love.

Emergent / Transitional Open up your writing folders. Take a look at your writing ideas. Think about which idea you feel connected to, not just one you like a little bit. Place a self-stick note with a quick sketch of a heart on it so you know it's the one you chose.

Fluent Open up your notebooks. Take a look at your entries and think about which ideas have great meaning to you and don't just simply represent something you like. Once you find a strong idea, sketch a little heart on the page or margin so it's easy to find in case it becomes the idea you decide to move forward with.

Once you have your idea, share with your partner why you're connected to it.

(Allow 1–4 minutes for students to turn and talk with partners. Share exemplary responses.)

RELEASE

Remind students to look through all their ideas and clearly identify the one that moves them most.

So today, when you go off to write, remember that writers write best when they are connected to their ideas and feel strongly about them. You might have some ideas that you already know you are connected to and care about, but still take some time to consider other ideas, too.

FOR ADDITIONAL SUPPORT, TRY

3.2 Think with Your Heart

4.1 Chatterbox

4.2 Find Out More

TIPS/RESOURCES

- Show students mentor texts that easily demonstrate the author's connection to the topic.

Narrow It Down

In this lesson, students learn that writers narrow a broader topic by asking themselves strategic questions connected to their knowledge, audience, interests, and perspective.

Writing Stage: Any • **Genre:** Any

INTRODUCE

Tell students that they can narrow down the focus of their writing when it feels "too big."

Sometimes, as writers, we choose ideas and then later realize that the topic is too big! This can make our writing feel unorganized, messy, and overwhelming. That's why it's important to narrow ideas down. Writers narrow a broader topic by thinking about their knowledge, audience, interests, and perspective.

INSTRUCT

Demonstration

Model for students how you narrow down a topic by thinking about what you want to focus on.

To help me do this work, I am going to use these questions: "What part of my topic do I know more about?" "What might my audience want to know more about?" "What aspect am I most interested to learn about?" and "What do I want to say about this topic?"*

Emergent / Transitional As I look at the writing in my folder, I see one of my favorite ideas is cats. "Cats" feels like such a big idea! I can write about house cats, wild cats, cats that do tricks, how to care for a cat, and more. Let me see if I can use these questions to help focus my idea. I think I know the most about house cats and how to take care of them. I don't really know too much about wild cats and different breeds, so I would leave that information out and narrow my topic. I also think that my audience is people who love cats, like me, or perhaps want to get a cat as a pet. My writing will give them information about house cats. That went from a big idea of cats to a more focused one—house cats.

Fluent I am going to go through my entries and think about how I can narrow some of my ideas down. Here I have an idea about the beach. That's a pretty big idea! I can write about everything from ocean animals, beach activities, surfing, erosion, tides, ocean pollution, the most popular beaches, and more! That feels overwhelming! Let me think about which aspect of the beach I am the most interested in learning more about. I feel very strongly about protecting the beach from erosion. I also think the audience for my writing might be people who want to learn how they can help, too. I took the big idea of the beach and narrowed it down to beach erosion—now it feels focused!

Did you see how I narrowed down my idea? I thought about aspects of my topic to narrow it to something more specific and focused.

ALTERNATIVE

Explain with Examples: **Gather mentor texts and talk through how authors narrowed down a topic from a big idea to a more focused one.**

GUIDE

Prompt students to look at their ideas and think about how they can narrow them down.

Now you are going to give it a try. Think about your idea and how you can narrow it down. Use the same questions I used to guide your thinking. (*Display an anchor chart with questions.**) Go though your writing and choose an idea that feels big and talk to your partner about how you will narrow it down.

(Allow 1–4 minutes for students to turn and talk with partners. Share exemplary responses.)

RELEASE

Have students use strategic questions to refine their focus.

So today, when you go off to write, remember that it's important to narrow down your ideas to think about what you want to focus on in your writing. You can try this with a few different ideas that feel too big to help you decide which idea feels like a good fit.

FOR ADDITIONAL SUPPORT, TRY

4.3 Stay Connected
4.5 What's Your Angle?
4.6 Discover What You Want to Say
4.8 Switch It Up

TIPS/RESOURCES

- Make an anchor chart with key questions from instruction.*

*See sample chart, "Zoom In on What's Important," on page 180.

What's Your Angle?

In this lesson, students learn that one way writers focus a topic is to develop an angle. They do this by reflecting on what they would like to share and what their audience might want to know.

Writing Stage: Transitional, Fluent
Genre: All-About Book, Feature Article, Literary Nonfiction, Expository Nonfiction, Biography, Research Report, Expository Essay

INTRODUCE

Tell students that they should consider an angle for their topic with a specific audience in mind.

Writers often develop an angle for their topics so that their writing is more focused on something that they want to say or teach to others. This is important because having an angle can interest a reader, provide them with particular insight, or answer certain questions about a topic.

INSTRUCT

Demonstration

Model for students how you consider a topic from your notebook to find an angle.

Sometimes when we begin to plan or write about a topic, the possibilities for subtopics seem endless. We may get excited about having so much to say. However, this can be a problem if our writing loses focus. Readers might think, "What's the point?" This is why it is important to develop an angle for our topic. This way we can plan our subtopics so that they support one specific angle.

To develop an angle, we might consider guiding questions, such as:

- What aspect or part of the topic might interest readers most?
- What's my particular stance or belief, and why is it important?
- What misconceptions might I want to clear up?
- What might be the less popular or lesser known aspect of the topic?

(Display the questions on an anchor chart or give students copies of the questions to glue into their notebooks.)

Watch me come up with an angle for my topic. In my notebook, I have an entry about cars. I could write about types of cars, speed of cars, history of cars, maintaining cars, and on and on. I have to think about what might interest a reader. Perhaps I could just focus on sports cars! Developing the angle further, I could just write about European Sports Cars. I could even develop an angle, such as The Evolution of the Sports Car, and write about how these cars have changed over the last 125 years. I might experiment with all three to see what kinds of subtopics I could come up with now that I have a better focus.

ALTERNATIVE

Explain with Examples: **Collect a variety of nonfiction books and articles that have clearly angled titles or subtitles. Explain how the author angled the topic and show how the subtopics fit the focus.**

 |

GUIDE

Prompt students to look at one of their topics, or their chosen topic, to experiment with an angle.

Now take a look at your topic. Ask yourself, "What do I really want to say about this topic?" and "What aspect might interest my readers?" It's okay if you don't have a definite answer right now, as you will have more time during independent writing.

(Allow 1–4 minutes for students to turn and talk with partners. Share exemplary responses.)

RELEASE

Have students continue to work on their angle and refine their topics.

So today, when you go off to write, remember how important it is to find a focus for your topic. Rather than say everything, find an angle that might interest your audience. Consider the guiding questions we discussed and experiment with a few different angles to see which one works best.

FOR ADDITIONAL SUPPORT, TRY

4.2 Find Out More
4.4 Narrow It Down
4.6 Discover What You Want to Say
4.9 Who's Your Audience?

TIPS/RESOURCES

- Give students informational books and articles to identify the ways in which authors angle or focus a topic. Advise them to look at the titles, introductions, and conclusions.

Discover What You Want to Say

In this lesson, students learn that writers freewrite in long form to see which aspect of a topic generates the most ideas.

Writing Stage: Fluent
Genre: Feature Article, Literary Nonfiction, Expository Nonfiction, Biography, Research Report, Expository Essay

INTRODUCE

Tell students that they can find a focus for a topic by freewriting and looking for patterns.

Writers know the importance of having a focus that defines the main idea. Sometimes they freewrite in long form to see what aspect of a topic they have the most information to include. Once they discover a focus for a main idea, they reflect on whether or not that particular focus can be expanded into a full informational piece.

INSTRUCT

Demonstration

Model for students how you write a long, full-page entry in your notebook so that you can reread it to discover a focus.

Watch me reread a long freewrite that I wrote about my topic to see if I can discover a focus. *(Display a full-page entry about your selected topic.)* Here is what I wrote:

"Dogs make really great pets. They are much like another member of the family. They are always around, and they participate in all of the family events. They even make the family picture for holiday cards and celebrations. Some people celebrate dogs' birthdays as if they were a member of the family! These parties often involve cakes, and even gifts. People share their spaces with dogs. The dog often sleeps in the bed with his owners or has his own spot on the couch. At dinner time, dogs often eat alongside the family to share in that sacred time. Like children, people treat dogs in similar ways. Some people never leave them home alone and some hire a dog sitter or bring their dogs to day care! Some people bring their dogs out to run errands like going to the hardware store and other pet-friendly localities. People even take their dogs on vacations!"

(After rereading your entry, name for students a focus that you were able to discover in your freewriting; for this example, the focus could be that dogs are like family.)

Did you see how I just began writing fast about my topic without overthinking it? Did you notice how, when I reread what I wrote, I started to discover an idea about my topic—dogs are like family? This idea can be the focus of my piece.

GUIDE

Ask students to help you develop subheadings considering the angle of your topic.

Let's try this next part together. Will you help me brainstorm some subheadings that would fit with my focus?

(Allow 1–4 minutes for students to turn and talk with partners. Listen for exemplary responses and chart ideas.)

I heard some great ideas for subheadings such as: Family Activities with Dogs, Making Space for Dogs, Celebrating with Dogs, Vacationing with Dogs, Alone Time with Dogs, and Dogs for Every Family.

Each of these subheadings could surely include information and examples that support the angle or main idea. Each subheading describes how dogs are much like another member of the family—how they are more than just pets!

RELEASE

Have students work independently to freewrite and discover a main idea and possible subheadings.

Remember that as you go back to your notebooks to write, it is important to have a focus or main idea for your informational writing. One way to help you discover that focus is to not overthink it, but just freewrite for as long as possible and see if something emerges. Once you read it back, see if you can discover a focus and brainstorm some subheadings that would fit.

FOR ADDITIONAL SUPPORT, TRY

4.4 Narrow It Down
4.5 What's Your Angle?
4.8 Switch It Up
4.9 Who's Your Audience?

TIPS/RESOURCES

- Have students orally rehearse with partners and transcribe their conversations into their notebooks.
- Have students consider an audience for their topic to focus their information.

LESSON 4.7

Go Back!

In this lesson, students learn to reread notebook entries to notice recurring ideas and emerging patterns worth developing.

Writing Stage: Fluent

Genre: Feature Article, Literary Nonfiction, Expository Nonfiction, Biography*, Research Report, Expository Essay

INTRODUCE

Tell students that they can choose a topic and focus by looking across a variety of entries in their notebooks for patterns.

Writers know the importance of choosing a good topic to turn into a full writing piece. It must be a topic that they are connected to and have enough to say about in order to work on it for a long stretch of time. Sometimes no single entry in our notebooks seems to fit, so we must look across multiple entries to see if we can come up with a combined topic that will work.

INSTRUCT

Demonstration

Model for students how you skim through your entries for ideas that can be combined.

Watch me skim through my notebook to see if I notice a pattern or ideas that fit together in some way.

(Out loud, read through your notebook entry titles and ask yourself questions about ideas that seem alike and that could be combined to create one solid topic; see example below.)

As I read through my entries, I notice some ideas that seem to follow a pattern—Food! I have an entry about smoothies, another one about energy balls, and another about yogurt parfaits. None of these seem strong enough to be an idea on their own. However, if I were to combine these topics, I could have a topic titled Healthy Sweets: Alternatives for Your Favorite Indulgences. As I read on, I see I have an entry about meditation, sleep, healthy eating, and another about yoga. I could combine those ideas for a topic on Self Care or Alleviating Stress. I also have one on dogs and one on cats. Perhaps I can do a comparison piece on The Pros and Cons of Pet Dogs versus Cats!

Did you see how some of my topics on their own seemed vague or general, but when I put them together with others that were similar I was able to develop a bigger idea for a topic?

**For Biography, rather than choose a single subject, a student might write about a few individuals who are connected such as: Teen Idols, Tech Inventors, Important Women in History, etc.*

GUIDE

Prompt students to skim through some of their entries to identify a pattern and group a few ideas together.

So now it's your turn. Quickly skim through several of your entries to see if you notice a pattern or if you can group a few ideas together.

(Allow 1–4 minutes for students to turn and talk with partners. Share exemplary responses.)

Once you have grouped a few ideas, consider, "How can I link these topics with an idea?" For example, you might notice that all of your ideas are about sports. What idea might link them? You may notice they are linked together with the theme of working together, working hard, or being a good sport.*

RELEASE

Remind students to look for patterns as they review their entries.

So when you write today, remember that sometimes patterns in entries help you choose and refine a topic. Remember that an idea or theme that connects the topics or entries is more important than just a category. It is a way to link the ideas together with a theme, message, or thesis.

FOR ADDITIONAL SUPPORT, TRY

4.4 Narrow It Down
4.5 What's Your Angle?
4.6 Discover What You Want to Say

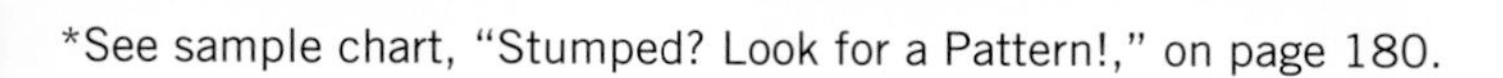

TIPS/RESOURCES

- Collect a variety of nonfiction books and articles grouped together around a topic for students to browse through to spark ideas.

*See sample chart, "Stumped? Look for a Pattern!," on page 180.

Switch It Up

In this lesson, students learn to try their topics as poems or stories—to narrow their focus and get to the heart of what they want to say.

Writing Stage: Fluent

Genre: Feature Article, Literary Nonfiction, Expository Nonfiction, Biography, Research Report, Expository Essay

INTRODUCE

Tell students that trying out an idea in a poem or story form can help them focus their writing.

Trying a different form of writing can help us see our ideas more clearly. Turning our information into a poem or a story can help us get to the heart of what we want to say. This exercise helps us narrow our focus.

INSTRUCT

Demonstration

Model for students how you narrow your focus by trying your topic as a poem or story, pointing out the "heart" of your topic.

Watch me as I try my topic as a poem to get to the heart of what I want to say. My topic is sharks—it's a broad topic. Let me try a Haiku. It's short. Three lines, 5 syllables, 7 syllables, 5 syllables. After a lot of crossing out, and trying different words, and counting syllables, I came up with:

"Sharks glide through warming
Water, parting schools of fish.
Snaggled teeth. Tall tales."*

Wow! When I look at these images and word choices, I now know that I want to write about how warming oceans and the "tall tales" people circulate about sharks are impacting shark populations on our planet. I want my audience to care about sharks and combating climate change as much as I do. Did you notice how writing a poem, and thinking carefully about my word choices, helped me get to the heart of what I want to say in my informational piece?

ALTERNATIVE

Guided Practice: **Using a class topic, begin a poem or story and have partners work to finish it.**

 |

GUIDE

Prompt students to discover an angle in an informational poem that you read together.

Let's read this poem I wrote about bats and see if we can discover an angle, or focus, for writing.

Bats at Night

She wakes at dusk and finds herself upside down.
Hungry for a snack
She swoops, she flies, she flutters her wings
High across the night sky.

She sings a high-pitched song, one only she can hear.
When it echoes back, insects are near.
She goes in for a bite and a hundred more
Until morning light, when she returns to her roost.

With your partner, discuss what kind of angle you could develop for a piece about bats from this poem. What would be some subtopics?

(Allow 1–4 minutes for students to turn and talk with partners. Share exemplary responses.)

RELEASE

Send students off to try this strategy using different narrative and poetic forms.

So today, when you go off to write, remember that one way you can narrow the focus of your topic and get to the heart of what you're trying to say, is to try your topic as a poem or a story. After trying a poem or story, you can look back and see how your topic has changed, and then do some writing based on that new focus.

FOR ADDITIONAL SUPPORT, TRY

4.4 Narrow It Down
4.5 What's Your Angle?
4.6 Discover What You Want to Say

TIPS/RESOURCES

- Notice student work and interrupt the class to briefly share successful tries. Name the specific steps you observed.

*See sample chart, "Switch It Up," on page 180.

LESSON 4.9

Who's Your Audience?

In this lesson, students learn to consider the audience for their writing and to develop ideas by thinking about what a specific audience might need or want to learn.

Writing Stage: Any • **Genre:** Any

INTRODUCE

Tell students that thinking of a specific audience—who they are writing to—can help them develop an idea.

When we're writing nonfiction, imagining our audience can help us to focus and refine our topic. We imagine the aspect of the topic they may be interested in learning.

INSTRUCT

Guided Practice

Think through a shared topic together, discussing the ways different audiences might require different information.

Have you ever noticed that the way you talk about something with someone changes based on the person's level of experience? The way my son and his friends talk about video games is very different from the way he talks to me about them. I don't play video games. When he talks to me, he keeps his information basic, and he explains a lot of terms and names to me. When he talks to his friends, they share examples, tips, and tricks, using more advanced words and terms.

As we plan our piece, we can ask, "Is our audience a beginner or an expert? Someone our own age or someone older or younger who might have a different perspective?" By thinking about our audience, we can select an angle for our piece and details that are just right.

Let's try this together. Imagine we're writing about our school. Our audience is young children who are new to our school. What information do we want to give them? What are some things they need to know?

(Give students 1–2 minutes to turn and talk. Share responses.)

Now let's think for a minute about the kind of information we might give to a graduating class from our school. They've been here for years. What information can we give them that would be meaningful to them?

(Give students 1–2 minutes to turn and talk. Share out ideas focusing on the shift in details.)

Last one. Imagine you're writing for parents. What kind of information would they need to know or is important to them?

(Give students 1–2 minutes to turn and talk. Share responses.)

ALTERNATIVE

Explain with Examples: **Show models of writing—or even video—with the same topics, but different audiences. Name, specifically, how the authors made changes based on the intended audience.**

GUIDE

Prompt students to think through possible audiences for their topics with a partner.

Take a minute with a partner and think through some possible audiences for your writing. What information would you include?

(Allow 1–4 minutes for students to talk and plan with partners. Share exemplary responses.)

RELEASE

Send students off to try out different audiences for a topic, noting the kinds of information each audience would want and need.

So today, when you go off to write, think about your audience. You might write a few lines, then think about your audience. Or, you might choose your audience first, and then start your entry based on their interests and needs.

FOR ADDITIONAL SUPPORT, TRY

4.5 What's Your Angle?
4.6 Discover What You Want to Say

TIPS/RESOURCES:

- List audience categories (classmates, beginner, expert, parent, young child, etc.).
- Let students write a letter to a particular person to get comfortable with the process.

Make a Commitment

In this lesson, students learn that writers choose a long-term project after they have rehearsed a few possibilities.

Writing Stage: Fluent

Genre: Feature Article, Literary Nonfiction, Expository Nonfiction, Biography, Research Report, Expository Essay

INTRODUCE

Tell students that they must commit to a long-term project at some point.

When writers have been considering a few possible topics or angles by rehearsing how each one might go, they eventually commit to one for a longer term project. This is important so they can take one idea through the entire writing process and see it through to publication.

INSTRUCT

Explain with Examples

Present students with guiding questions to support their decision-making.

Sometimes writers are lucky enough to have several strong possibilities for writing projects. Today I am going to provide you with some guiding questions to help you select the one project that you will commit to take through the rest of the writing process.

Here are some questions to consider:

- Is this topic one that both myself and my audience will be enthusiastic about?
- Is this topic one that I have enough to say about across several sections?
- If this topic requires research, will I be able to find enough information about it and will I be able to understand it?

(Display the questions on an anchor chart or give students copies of the questions to glue into their notebooks.)*

Let me explain: First and foremost, if you or your audience aren't enthusiastic or excited about the topic, it will be difficult to sustain the energy for it long-term. Secondly, regardless of your enthusiasm, you must be realistic as to whether you have enough to say about this topic beyond an introduction. The idea needs to have several strong subtopics. Third, you must consider your access to research. Has this topic been widely written about so that you can lean on resources to learn more? If resources are available, you need to be sure they aren't too difficult for you to understand. Lastly, be realistic: does your gut tell you that the topic is strong enough to support your best work?

ALTERNATIVE

***Demonstration:* Using your own notebook, read through some of the topics that you rehearsed with possible angles or foci.**

 |

GUIDE

Assign student partners and have each partner name their topics to one another.

I am going to assign each of you to a consulting editor. He or she will be your partner for the remainder of this project. You will be each other's sounding board and advisor. You will have time to read your work to one another and give each other feedback daily. Right now, you will quickly tell one another the different topics you have to choose from. You will have time to read through your entries and reflect on the guiding questions together when you go off to work independently.

(Allow 1–4 minutes for students to turn and talk with partners. Share exemplary responses.)

RELEASE

Ask partners to work together to choose their topics for publication using the guiding questions.

Remember that there's a lot to consider when choosing the topic that you want to take through the writing process. Each guiding question does not stand alone. You must take all of them into consideration when deciding if an idea is worthy of a long-term project.

FOR ADDITIONAL SUPPORT, TRY

4.4 Narrow It Down

4.5 What's Your Angle?

4.6 Discover What You Want to Say

*See sample chart, "Make a Commitment," on page 180.

TIPS/RESOURCES

- Similar ability partnerships support conversations.
- Create research clubs if several students are working on the same topic.

Lesson 4.4 Narrow It Down

Stumped?
Look for a Pattern!

This entry is about smoothies!

This entry is about tropical fruit salad!

How do some of my ideas connect?

This entry is about yogurt parfaits!

This entry is about energy balls!

Healthy snacks!

Lesson 4.7 Go Back!

Lesson 4.8 Switch It Up

Make a Commitment

Is this topic one that ...

- both myself and my audience will be enthusiastic about?
- I have enough to say about, across several sections?
- requires research and for which I will be able to find enough information?

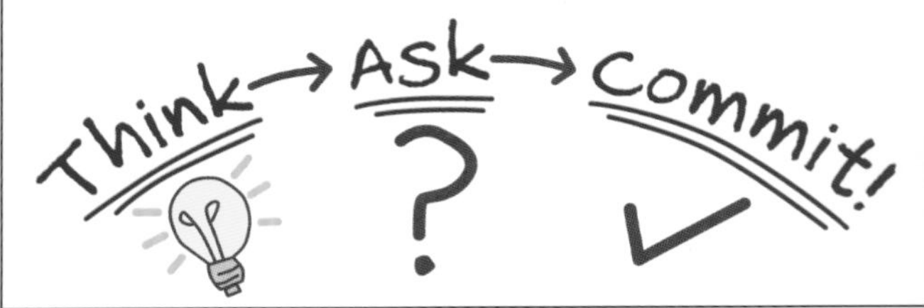

Lesson 4.10 Make a Commitment

 |

Plan & Develop

The series of lessons in this section contain strategies to help students structure their writing. The lessons:

- have students consider a structure and plan for the entire piece or part of their writing;
- have students consider the details and information that will go into each part of the piece; and
- include strategies for research, note-taking, and organizing ideas.

Descriptors for Planning and Developing Ideas

Emergent Writers	Fluent Writers
• Plan through oral rehearsal (e.g., list facts across fingers or touch each page of a book and say what they will writ. • Develop their writing by considering different paper choices or chapter types that might be added to their books. • Consider the sketches and drawings that convey the meaning of each part of their writing.	• Plan within a structure to list or sketch the parts of their pieces. • Create graphic organizers to arrange their ideas. • Develop chapters by brainstorming the details they might include. • Make plans for research. • Collect illustrations and graphics they plan to include. • Experiment with elaboration techniques such as description and adding examples before they move on in the writing process.

At-a-Glance Guide

Plan & Develop

Title		Lesson
5.1	**How Will It Go?**	Plan for the text structure of their books.
5.2	**Make a List, Check It Twice**	List information about a topic across fingers; make a page for each.
5.3	**Pattern Power!**	Pick one pattern type and use it to plan writing across pages.
5.4	**Try, Try Again**	Try different pattern structures; rehearse a few different ways books might go.
5.5	**The Notorious TOC (Table of Contents)**	Create a table of contents to sort topics into categories that may be revised later.
5.6	**Easy as 1, 2, 3 ...**	Tell the steps across fingers.
5.7	**Step by Step**	Sketch each step across pages.
5.8	**You Missed a Step!**	Make sure each step is included by acting it out with a partner.
5.9	**Flip It and Reverse It**	Decide on the order of the pages based on ideas and information taught.
5.10	**Step in Time!**	Create a time line for a topic by organizing ideas sequentially.
5.11	**Talk It Out**	Try out different points of view for a topic.
5.12	**Build Me Up**	Try out different structures for a topic.

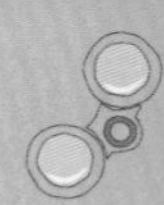

Writing Stage	Genre	
Emergent Transitional	List Pattern	All-About
Emergent Transitional	List Pattern	All-About
Emergent	Pattern	
Emergent	Pattern	
Any	All-About Feature Article Biography	Expository Nonfiction Literary Nonfiction Research Report
Emergent	How-To	
Emergent	How-To	
Emergent	How-To	
Emergent Transitional	List Pattern	All-About
Any	List Pattern All-About Feature Article	Biography Expository Nonfiction Literary Nonfiction Research Report
Transitional Fluent	All-About Feature Article Biography	Expository Nonfiction Literary Nonfiction
Transitional Fluent	All-About Feature Article Research Report	Expository Nonfiction Literary Nonfiction

Plan & Develop continued

Title		Lesson
5.13	**Learn from a Mentor**	Consider additional sections by studying mentor texts.
5.14	**Multimedia Mentors**	Gather more information by observing a topic in person, looking at pictures, or watching videos.
5.15	**Get in Character**	Try a topic in narrative form by imagining it as a character.
5.16	**Fact Weaver**	Use a hybrid text structure to bring topics to life.
5.17	**The Best Laid Plans**	Make a plan for research—not just what facts are needed but where they can be found.
5.18	**5Ws (and 1H)**	Ask questions to research more: Who? What? When? Where? Why? How?
5.19	**Ask an Expert**	Develop interview questions for an expert to acquire firsthand information.
5.20	**Writers Take Note**	Take notes in different formats.
5.21	**Say That Again, Please**	Paraphrase when taking notes during research.
5.22	**Rehearse Your Thesis**	Craft a clear thesis.
5.23	**Just Give Me a Reason**	Try out various reasons to support a thesis.
5.24	**Grow Your Word Banks**	Create a word bank of domain-specific vocabulary.

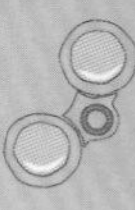

Writing Stage	Genre	
Transitional Fluent	All-About Feature Article	Expository Nonfiction Research Report
Any	Any	
Fluent	Research Report Literary Nonfiction	Expository Nonfiction Expository Essay
Fluent	Literary Nonfiction Biography	
Fluent	Feature Article Research Report Biography	Literary Nonfiction Expository Nonfiction Expository Essay
Transitional Fluent	All-About Feature Article Research Report Biography	Literary Nonfiction Expository Nonfiction Expository Essay
Transitional Fluent	All-About Feature Article Research Report Biography	Literary Nonfiction Expository Nonfiction Expository Essay
Fluent	Feature Article Research Report Biography	Literary Nonfiction Expository Nonfiction Expository Essay
Fluent	Feature Article Research Report Biography	Literary Nonfiction Expository Nonfiction Expository Essay
Fluent	Expository Essay	
Fluent	Expository Essay	
Fluent	Any	

How Will It Go?

In this lesson, students learn to plan how their books can be organized or structured.

Writing Stage: Emergent, Transitional • **Genre:** List, Pattern, All-About Book*

INTRODUCE

Tell students that once writers have an idea for a book, they think about its structure.

Once writers select an idea for a book, they have some important thinking to do. They need to think about which structure they will use before they begin to write. They can start with a big idea and then share details, or they can arrange the book by headings that name different parts of the topic. Knowing how your book will go is important because it will make your teaching clear to the reader.

INSTRUCT

Demonstration

Model for students how you consider different structures for your writing.

Watch me show you how I try out different ways my book could go.

(Share mentor texts or examples as you talk about each possibility.)

List Books / Pattern Books Today I plan to write a book about sharks. (*Hold up a stapled booklet, 3–5 pages. Turn each page as you orally rehearse.*) If I want to teach about:

- "big idea and details," I might consider "Shark Food." That means each page of my book will be about a detail of what sharks eat: plankton, fish, sea lions, seals, etc.
- "different kinds" of sharks, then each page will teach about a different shark: hammerheads, wobbegongs, great whites, etc.
- "parts of" a shark, each page will teach about a different part of its body: gills, fins, tail, head, etc.
- a "list that describes" the topic, then I might teach different things sharks do: swim, eat, feel, hide, etc.
- "compare and contrast," I might compare sharks to whales: a shark breathes through its gills while a whale breathes through its blowhole; sharks can be big or small while all whales are big.
- the "order of things" in a sequence, I can show the life cycle of a shark: egg, pup, newborn, juvenile, and adult.

To decide, I have to ask myself, "What do I really want to teach my reader?" I want to teach my reader about different kinds of sharks, because most people don't realize that there are so many.

ALTERNATIVE

Explain with Examples: **Show students examples of informational books and highlight the structure of each. Explain how to use each one as a mentor text for planning.**

***For All-About Books:** Today I plan on working on my book, *All About Beaches*. I can think about using different structures for different chapters. If I want to include "big ideas and details," I can imagine having some chapters like: "Beach Activities," "Wildlife at the Beach," and "What Beaches Look Like." I might also consider including a part of my book that explains the different kinds of beaches, like "Rocky Beaches" or "Black Sand Beaches." Maybe I could compare and contrast the kinds of beaches, such as: "Ocean Beaches versus Lake Beaches." I could even have a part of my book that has a sequence or procedure, like: "How to Make a Dribble Castle" or "How to Dig for Sand Crabs."

GUIDE

Prompt students to turn and talk as they try one possible structure for their topics.

Think about your topic. Then ask yourself, "What is one way that my book could go?" Share your idea with your partner.

(Allow 1–4 minutes for students to turn and talk with partners. Share exemplary responses.)

RELEASE

Remind students to try out a few possibilities before settling on a structure.

Remember, writers, it is important to not only think about what you will write, but how your book will go. Writers always plan by considering all of the possibilities and then settling on a structure that seems to make the most sense.

FOR ADDITIONAL SUPPORT, TRY

5.2 Make a List, Check It Twice

5.3 Pattern Power!

5.5 The Notorious TOC

TIPS/RESOURCES

- Consider modeling one structure per day.
- Make an anchor chart with visuals.
- Have students orally rehearse a structure by telling it across their fingers.

Make a List, Check It Twice

In this lesson, students learn to make a plan for their writing by listing all they know about a topic across their fingers.

Writing Stage: Emergent, Transitional • **Genre:** List, Pattern, All-About Book

INTRODUCE

Tell students that once writers have an idea, they plan by listing all they know about it across their fingers.

Now that we have ideas for our writing, we need to think about what we are going to say and how we are going to arrange the facts. Today we will make a plan for our writing by listing all that we know about our topic across our fingers. This is an important step for writers because when you have a plan, your writing is likely to be focused.

INSTRUCT

Demonstration

Model for students how making a plan helps you determine the number of pages in your book.

Watch me as I list across my fingers what I know about my topic.

Today I am going to begin writing a book about sharks. Before I start, I need to list all the things I know about sharks across my fingers and plan how I will include them in my book. (*Hold up your hand and show each finger as you list each idea.*)

List Books / Pattern Books I know the different parts of their bodies, so I can plan my book to sound like this: "Sharks have fins," "Sharks have teeth," "Sharks have gills," and "Sharks have eyes." That's four simple facts that I know about sharks. So I would need four pages. Or I could describe sharks in more detail. I could write: "Sharks are big and small," "Sharks swim fast," "Sharks eat fish and seals," and "Sharks are blue, black, grey, and brown." (*Hold up five fingers to show that you would need five pages.*) Now I have two different ways my book can go. I know how many parts there are to my book based on how many fingers I used to list what I know across my fingers!

All-About Books I have a lot of ideas about sharks so perhaps my book could go as follows. First, I could write about what sharks look like and include a diagram of a shark. Second, I could write about different kinds of sharks. Then, where sharks live. Next, what sharks eat. And last, surprising facts about sharks. That really helps me plan out how many parts I will have in my book, which is five! I also know the different types of pages I want to include in my book, such as a diagram and pictures showing the different types of sharks.

Did you see how I didn't start with the pencil and paper? I started by talking out loud as I listed all that I know across my fingers.

ALTERNATIVE

***Guided Practice:* Using a shared topic, together list all the things you know about the topic across your fingers. Guide students to see different ways the writing can go.**

 |

GUIDE

Prompt students to turn and talk to list all that they know about their ideas across their fingers.

Now it's your turn to try. Think about your topic. What will you write about today? Once you have an idea, list all the things you know about your topic across your fingers. Turn to your partner and plan out your writing.

(Allow 1–4 minutes for students to turn and talk with partners. Share exemplary responses.)

RELEASE

Remind students to use their fingers to list ideas so that their writing is clear, focused, and organized.

Remember, it is important to plan out your writing so you know what you want to include in your book. Writers can make a plan by listing across their fingers all the things they know about a topic. They also consider the different parts of their books so that their writing is clear, focused, and organized.

FOR ADDITIONAL SUPPORT, TRY

5.1 How Will It Go?

5.5 The Notorious TOC

5.9 Flip It and Reverse It

TIPS/RESOURCES

- Have students point to each finger as they plan out their writing. It should be a clear, crisp, 1:1 correspondence.
- Provide premade booklets.

Pattern Power!

In this lesson, students learn to use their knowledge of pattern books to plan how they want to structure their writing.

Writing Stage: Emergent • **Genre:** Pattern

INTRODUCE

Tell students that once writers have an idea, they plan their writing by thinking about the patterns they know as readers.

Let's think about what we know about pattern books as readers to help us in our writing. We know that in pattern books the pattern repeats on every page and only one or two words change. For example, "The dog plays. The dog eats. The dog sleeps." As writers, we can use our knowledge of pattern books to plan how we want our writing to go. We can use a simple repeating pattern to get started in planning our pattern book across pages.

INSTRUCT

Demonstration

Model for students how you consider different patterns for your book. Show how you plan your writing across pages.

Watch me as I think about what I know about pattern books to plan my writing. I will use my idea about the beach to write a pattern book today.

(Hold up a stapled booklet, 3–5 pages. As you orally rehearse, turn the blank pages to show what you might write.)

Let's see, if I want to think about using a simple repeating pattern to teach about what you can see at the beach, my book might go like this—"I see the sand. I see the ocean. I see the sun." That's one way my pattern book can go. Let me think of another possible pattern for my book. If instead I wanted to describe beaches, my pattern book could sound like this—"Beaches are warm. Beaches are fun. Beaches are big."

Did you notice how I thought about what I wanted to say about beaches and then thought of a pattern to match that idea? I tried a few different patterns and rehearsed my ideas across pages of my booklet so I can have a plan of how the book could go. This helps me think about the words I will need to build my sentences as I write.

ALTERNATIVE

Explain with Examples: **Show students examples of pattern books and highlight each pattern. Explain how to use each mentor text for planning.**

GUIDE

Prompt students to turn and talk as they try different pattern structures for their books.

Now it's your turn to give it a try. Think of an idea that you are going to write about today. Then think about a pattern sentence that will go with that idea. What pattern do you think will go with what you want to say, show, or teach? Remember, there are many different ways your pattern book can go, so it might be fun to try a few like I did with my book about beaches. Turn and share with your partner.

(Allow 1–4 minutes for students to turn and talk with partners. Share exemplary responses.)

RELEASE

Remind students to think about the patterns they can use to help them plan out their pattern books.

Today we focused on how we can use some of what we know about pattern books to help us with our writing. As we continue to write our books, we should always first think about what we want to say, show, or teach, and then think of a pattern that will match. Once we choose a pattern, we can plan across pages so that we know how our books will go and what we are going to write.

FOR ADDITIONAL SUPPORT, TRY

5.1 How Will It Go?

5.4 Try, Try Again

TIPS/RESOURCES

- Have students tap out their ideas on each page.
- Encourage students to use the word wall to help construct a pattern.
- Gather pattern books for read-alouds and book baskets.

Try, Try Again

In this lesson, students learn to plan out their writing by trying out different pattern structures. They rehearse a few different ways their books might go before settling on a structure for their books.

Writing Stage: Emergent • **Genre:** Pattern

INTRODUCE

Tell students that they will try different pattern structures in their writing to rehearse how their books might go.

As writers, we know the importance of trying out different things before deciding what our next step will be in writing. Today we are going to try different pattern structures. We can change the pattern on the first/last page, use a seesaw pattern, or have a "one or two" sentence pattern and think about which parts of each sentence will change and which will repeat. Making this decision will help us organize our writing based on what we want to teach others.

INSTRUCT

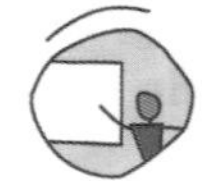

Demonstration

Model for students how you consider different pattern structures for your book.

Watch me as I try different pattern structures for my book on the beach.

(Hold up a stapled booklet, 3–5 pages. As you orally rehearse a pattern, turn the blank pages to show what you might write.)

I want people to know that there are many things you can do at the beach, so perhaps a question/answer structure could go like this: "What do you do at the beach? I play in the sand. What do you do at the beach? I swim in the water. What do you do at the beach? I build sandcastles."

If I want to describe the beach, I could change the question: "What do you see at the beach? I see waves. What do you hear at the beach? I hear seagulls. What do you eat at the beach? I eat ice cream."

Maybe I will write two sentences as my pattern and repeat those two sentences: "The beach has sand. The sand is soft. The beach has waves. The waves are blue. The beach has shells. The shells are colorful." Here I am repeating some words: "The beach has _____" and then "The _____ are _____."

I could also keep my pattern book simple using just one pattern sentence, but maybe the first and last page do not follow the pattern. It might sound like, "There are so many things to do at the beach. You can play at the beach. You can swim at the beach. You can eat at the beach. You can surf at the beach. What will you do at the beach?"

Did you notice how first I thought about what I want to say about my topic? Then I tried out a few different pattern structures.

ALTERNATIVE

Inquiry:* Gather different types of pattern books that have clear, strong examples. Pass them out to partners to determine the pattern structure in each book. Create an anchor chart with their ideas.

 |

GUIDE

Prompt students to turn and talk as they try different pattern structures for their topics.

Now it's your turn to try. Think of your idea and what you want to say about it. What is one way it can go? Which words will repeat and which words will change? How many sentences will you use?

(Allow 1–4 minutes for students to turn and talk with partners. Share exemplary responses.)

FOR ADDITIONAL SUPPORT, TRY

5.1 How Will It Go?

5.2 Make a List, Check It Twice

5.3 Pattern Power!

6.9 Producing Patterns

*See sample chart, "Pattern Possibilities," on page 234.

RELEASE

Remind students to try out a few possibilities before settling on a pattern structure.

Today, when you go off to write, remember to think about the different pattern structures for your book and try a few different ones for your topic. You want to think about what you want to say about your topic and then plan out how you are going to say it so your book is clear and focused.

TIPS/RESOURCES

- Use books that are familiar to students and that have a clear, strong sense of pattern using a variety of pattern structures.
- Create a chart that lists pattern book titles and the different pattern structures used in each for students to reference while planning their own books.

LESSON 5.5

The Notorious TOC (Table of Contents)

In this lesson, students learn to plan their writing by creating a table of contents to sort a topic into categories. This can be a preliminary table of contents that gets revisited and revised.

Writing Stage: Any
Genre: All-About, Feature Article, Biography, Expository Nonfiction, Literary Nonfiction, Research Report

INTRODUCE

Tell students that today they will create a table of contents that will help them plan out the different parts of their writing.

Imagine your idea is a big umbrella and underneath it are different categories, chapters, or subtopics that connect to your big idea. Some nonfiction books have a table of contents that shows you these different categories. Today we will take our idea and create a table of contents. This table of contents can be revisited and revised as you write to make sure it accurately reflects your book.

INSTRUCT

Demonstration

Model for students how you think about different categories to plan out a table of contents.

Watch me as I plan for my writing by creating a table of contents.

Emergent / Transitional First, let me think through some ideas that I have about sharks. Then, I will sort them out into categories for my table of contents. Sharks have cool features—rows of teeth, no eyelids, and a strong sense of smell. There are different types of sharks and they eat different types of food, including plankton, seals, and fish. So one chapter might describe sharks, perhaps titled "What Are Sharks?" The next chapter could be "What Do Sharks Eat?" and then a third chapter could be "Different Kinds of Sharks." That's three chapters! And maybe I'll include a "Did You Know?" to add some fun facts about sharks. Now I have four chapters for my All-About Book.

Fluent I am going to write about Jane Goodall. Let me sort through my ideas to see what categories they fall into for my table of contents. I want to give my readers background information about Jane—where she was born, where she grew up, and what her childhood was like. I also want to include a part about how she always had an intense love for chimpanzees and a fierce desire to protect them. I also think it's important to include a section about Jane's current work as a conservationist in support of animal welfare issues. Now I have an idea about the sections, parts, categories, or subtopics I want to include about Jane Goodall. This helps me envision how my writing can go, so I will jot this down to keep track of my writing and stay organized. If needed, I can change my table of contents as I go and revise my ideas.

ALTERNATIVE

Explain with Examples: **Use a text to highlight how an author might have planned out writing by using a table of contents.**

GUIDE

Prompt students to think about the different categories within their topics.

Now it's your turn to give this a try. What categories will you write about?*

(Allow 1–4 minutes for students to turn and talk with partners. Share exemplary responses.)

*Have fluent writers write in their notebooks before sharing.

RELEASE

Remind students that planning out a table of contents will help organize their writing.

Today, as you go off to write, create a table of contents to help you organize and plan your writing. Remember, you can always go back to revisit and revise your table of contents to reflect sections you no longer want to include or new ideas you want to add.

FOR ADDITIONAL SUPPORT, TRY

5.2 Make a List, Check It Twice

5.13 Learn from a Mentor

TIPS/RESOURCES

- Leave space in the table of contents as you model so that you can show students how you revise your plan.

LESSON 5.6

Easy as 1, 2, 3 ...

In this lesson, students plan their how-to books by listing the steps across their fingers.

Writing Stage: Emergent • **Genre:** How-To Book

INTRODUCE

Tell students that today they will plan by listing their steps across their fingers.

When we are teaching someone how to do something, it's good to name all the steps. If we miss even just one step, the outcome can be ruined! Today we are going to plan the steps for our how-to writing by listing the steps across our fingers. This is important because it will help us make sure we don't miss a step.

INSTRUCT

Demonstration

Model for students how you plan for your how-to book by listing the steps across your fingers.

Watch me as I plan my how-to book by listing the steps across my fingers.

I am writing a how-to book about how to feed a cat. Let me think of the steps for a minute and gather my ideas, picture myself doing it, and think about the order. I see myself getting the food and bowl, and the spoon, too. Then I have to put the food into the bowl and give it to the cat. The last thing I do is clean up. Okay, I think I got it. Now, watch me plan out my how-to book by telling each step across my fingers. (*Motion to your fingers as you list the steps.*) First, take out the cat food, the cat bowl, and a spoon. Second, open the cat food. Third, spoon some cat food into the bowl. Fourth, give the food to the cat. Last, clean up. Did you see how I did that? First, I thought about it in my head, pictured myself feeding a cat, and then I told the steps across my fingers. Now I know that I have five steps to my how-to writing, which means I can plan for the paper I need; and I already know the steps for my book!

(If needed, you can model this with a few different how-to topics to show students how it sounds with different ideas.)

ALTERNATIVE

Guided Practice: **As a class, brainstorm the steps of a how-to idea and have students join you in listing the steps across their fingers.**

GUIDE

Prompt students to think about their how-to ideas and list the steps across their fingers.

Now it's your turn. Think of the how-to book idea that you want to teach someone to do. In your head, just like I did, picture yourself doing it and think about the steps and order. Then turn to your partner and tell the steps for your how-to across your fingers. If you finish doing it with one how-to idea, you can try it with another one.

(Allow 1–4 minutes for students to turn and talk with partners. Share exemplary responses.)

RELEASE

Remind students that they can plan their how-to writing by listing their steps across their fingers.

Today we focused on planning out our how-to books by listing the steps across our fingers. This helps us plan our books to ensure that we have all our steps and that the steps are in the correct order. Once you have all the steps planned out, then you are ready to start writing your how-to!

FOR ADDITIONAL SUPPORT, TRY

5.7 Step by Step

5.8 You Missed a Step!

TIPS/RESOURCES

- Add color-coded ordinal words to your word wall.
- Have a hand drawn with an arrow pointing to the words *first*, *second*, *then*, and *last* written on each finger.

Step by Step

In this lesson, students learn that writers can plan out their how-to books by sketching their steps across the pages in their booklets.

Writing Stage: Emergent • **Genre:** How-To Book

INTRODUCE

Tell students that they will plan their how-to books by sketching steps across the pages in their booklets.

As writers, we know that sometimes we might forget our ideas or lose track of our thinking. We want to make sure this doesn't happen! To solve this, we are going to sketch each step to help us hold onto our ideas. When we sketch, we don't have to worry about the picture looking perfect. So today we are going to plan our how-to books by sketching the steps across the pages in our booklets so that we remember each step.

INSTRUCT

Demonstration

Model for students how you plan your how-to book by sketching the steps across pages.

Watch me as I sketch the steps for my how-to book across my pages to help me plan out my writing. I am writing a how-to book on how to feed a cat. *(Hold up a stapled booklet, 3–5 pages. Use a pencil and sketch a quick drawing as you think aloud each step.)* My first step is to take out the cat food, the cat bowl, and a spoon, so I want to be sure to include these things in my sketch. Step two is to open the cat food, so my sketch will show the cat food being opened. Step three is to spoon the food into the bowl, so I will make sure my sketch includes a picture of the spoon and the food in the bowl. Step four, give the food to the cat—my sketch will show how to place the food on the floor for the cat. And the last step is to clean up, so I will sketch a picture of a sink.

Did you see how I used a quick sketch to represent each step for my how-to book? Did I include detailed drawings? No! I sketched enough to help me hold onto my thinking, plan out my how-to book, and include all the steps in the correct order. Now, I can add words and details when I am ready.

GUIDE

Ask students to talk with a partner about the sketches they will use for each step.

Now it's your turn to try. You are going to talk through your ideas and tell your partner each step and what you plan on sketching for that step. Remember, sketches are quick drawings that are clear enough to help us hold onto our ideas, but they do not include details. We save the details for later. Turn and talk to your partner and plan out the steps to your how-to book by thinking about what you will sketch on each page.

(Allow 1–4 minutes for students to turn and talk with partners. Share exemplary responses.)

RELEASE

Remind students that sketches help them plan and remember their ideas.

Today, when you go off to write, remember to start with sketches. Think about the steps for your how-to book and sketch each one across the pages. Then your how-to book will be well planned for you to go back and add details to your pictures and your words.

FOR ADDITIONAL SUPPORT, TRY

5.6 Easy as 1, 2, 3 ...

5.8 You Missed a Step!

6.2 How Do I Draw That?

TIPS/RESOURCES

- For how-to books, have 1–2 steps on each page rather than a list of the steps all on one page.

You Missed a Step!

In this lesson, students learn to make sure they include every step by acting out each one with a partner.

Writing Stage: Emergent • **Genre:** How-To Book

INTRODUCE

Tell students that they will act out the steps for their how-to book ideas with a partner.

Have you ever played the game, Charades? Charades is when you act something out and the other person has to guess what it is. Today we are going to use this game to help us plan out our how-to writing. This will help us make sure we don't skip any steps in our how-to books. We will do this with a partner. Your partner will say each step for you to act out. It will be your job to tell your partner when you are confused. This will help us make sure we have all the necessary steps in our books.

INSTRUCT

Guided Practice

Together as a class, have students act as your partner and act out the steps of your book.

We are going to do this work together. All of you will be my partner and act out the steps for my idea, "how to feed a cat." As I say each step, it will be your job to act it out quietly to notice if I miss a step. Ready? Everyone stand up and listen to the steps.

(Give students time to act out each step and join in to help them with the gestures and motions. Pause in between steps and reiterate as needed. Exaggerate the movements so they get the point.)

Ready? First, take out the cat food, the cat bowl, and a spoon. Second, open the cat food. Does this make sense so far? I think it's clear and nothing is missing yet. Let's go on. Third, give the food to the cat. Wait a minute! Open the cat food was step two and then step three was give the food to the cat. Am I missing something here?

(Act out how after you open the food you don't know what to do because you are missing a step.) What am I missing? Let me go back to step two—open the cat food. Oh, I know. I need to spoon the food into the bowl before giving it to the cat! Did you see how it didn't make sense to keep going? It's like being on pause or a glitch in the how-to! Now we have step three, so let's act it out—spoon the food into the bowl. Step four, give the food to the cat. Last, clean up!

 |

GUIDE

Prompt students to work with their partners and act out each step of their how-to topics.

Now it's your turn to try. You are going to do this work with a partner, and you might need some space to do the charades. You will take turns acting out each other's how-to idea to make sure that you aren't missing any steps.

(Prompt students to act out each other's how-to idea. Guide them to notice when steps are missing and how to add them in.)

RELEASE

Remind students that this is a strategy that will help them make sure they have all their steps.

Today was a different kind of lesson for writing because we took time to act out our ideas to figure out if we are missing any steps. This is something you can always do with a partner or even by yourself—act out each step and make sure you have all the steps in the right order so that someone else can learn what it is that you are teaching them. Some of you might want to spend a little more time making sure you have all your steps, and others might be ready to get started on writing your how-to books.

FOR ADDITIONAL SUPPORT, TRY

5.6 Easy as 1, 2, 3 ...

5.7 Step by Step

TIPS/RESOURCES

- Act out some warm-up activities such as brushing your teeth, riding a bike, etc.
- Encourage creativity for the last step to keep it fun.

Flip It and Reverse It

In this lesson, students learn to decide on the order of the pages in their books based on what they want to teach and say. They will try it out a few ways to see which feels the best.

Writing Stage: Emergent, Transitional • **Genre:** List, Pattern, All-About Book

INTRODUCE

Tell students that once writers consider an order of the pages or chapters, they check to make sure it makes the most sense.

Writers know how important it is to make a plan for their writing before they write. Once writers have their ideas, they often think about an order that makes the most sense for their topics. Today we are going to learn how writers organize their writing so that the reader has an easy time understanding the information.

INSTRUCT

Demonstration

Model for students how you consider different ways to organize your writing.

(Hold up a stapled booklet, 3–5 pages. As you orally rehearse your book, turn the blank pages to show what you might write on each page.)

Today I will work on a book about soccer. In this book, I plan to teach the reader about soccer practice as my main idea. I will include details such as how to: play a game, practice drills, rehydrate, warm up, and stretch. I know what I want to say on each page, but I also have to think about the order of this information. Right now, this information seems pretty random. Perhaps it would make the most sense to tell the order in which we do these things, such as: warm up, practice drills, play a game, stretch, rehydrate. This way the reader will understand what happens at soccer practice from beginning to end.

If I decide to work on my book about different kinds of sharks, I will need to organize my writing for that as well. I plan to teach the reader about dwarf lanterns, tigers, wobbegongs, great whites, and hammerheads. In this type of book, I can't show things in time order like I did with my soccer idea. So perhaps I could go in size order! Should I go from biggest to smallest or smallest to biggest? Perhaps I can go from least deadly to most deadly?! If I go from biggest to smallest, I could surprise my reader in the end because they probably don't know that dwarf lantern sharks are only 6 inches long. So my book could start with tiger sharks, since they are 16 feet long; then great whites, since they are 14 feet long; followed by hammerheads, since they are 13 feet long; then the 4-foot wobbegongs; and finally on the last page, dwarf lanterns, since they are only 6 inches long.

ALTERNATIVE

Explain with Examples: **Show students examples of information books and highlight the organization of each.**

 |

GUIDE

Ask students to help you organize the content of another book.

Do you think you can help me organize another book? I was thinking of making a color book about fruits because including different colored fruits in your diet helps you get all of the vitamins your body needs. It will include: yellow bananas, green grapes, red apples, orange clementines, purple plums, and blue blueberries. What order might make sense?

(Allow 1–4 minutes for students to turn and talk with partners. Share exemplary responses.)

RELEASE

Encourage students to consider organization when planning a piece of writing.

Writers, remember that whenever you are making a plan for writing, it is important to think about the order of the information. If you are starting a new book today, put a little extra thought into how you will organize your writing. If you decide you need to reorder your writing, simply pull your booklet apart and put the pages in a different order.

FOR ADDITIONAL SUPPORT, TRY

5.1 How Will It Go?
5.5 The Notorious TOC
5.10 Step in Time!

TIPS/RESOURCES:

- Create an anchor chart with some common organizational structures, such as time order, life cycle, size order, etc.
- Have students work in partnerships to determine an order.

LESSON 5.10

Step in Time!

In this lesson, students learn to create a time line for their topics. They can organize their ideas across a lifetime, a time period, or a day.

Writing Stage: Any

Genre: List, Pattern, All-About Book, Feature Article, Biography, Expository Nonfiction, Literary Nonfiction, Research Report

INTRODUCE

Tell students that sometimes writers consider structuring their writing using a time line.

Writers know that when planning out their books, they can structure them in a variety of ways. One way is by using time. There are a few ways we can use time to shape our texts.

INSTRUCT

Explain with Examples

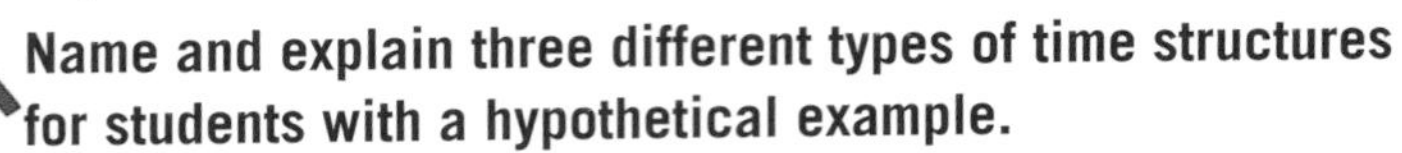

Name and explain three different types of time structures for students with a hypothetical example.

Let me explain. When writers use time to structure a piece, they might create a time line to help them plan.

(Note: Adjust examples to match the needs of your class.)

For example, if I wanted to write about a topic across a lifetime, my time line can show a subject's life from the time they were born until they grow up or reach the end of life. If my topic was frogs, I might write my book so that it shows its life cycle: from egg, to tadpole, to tadpole with legs, to froglet, to adult. If I were to write about a person such as Abraham Lincoln, I might tell about when he was born in 1809, to his childhood growing up in Indiana, to when he studied and got his law degree, into his adult life when he got married, became president, and was later assassinated.

If I wanted to write about just a period of time, I would pick the years that span an important era. For example, if my topic were about tigers, I might only write about cubs from when they are babies to when they leave their mothers. Or if I wanted to write about a person, I might only focus on one part of their life. For example, if I were to write about Ariana Grande's music career, I could start with her first record and write about her musical journey up until today.

Lastly, I could just focus on a single day in a life. For example, if my topic were bats, my whole book could just focus on when they wake up in the evening, then go hunt for food, escape predators, and how they return to their roosts to sleep. If it were a famous pop star, like Taylor Swift, maybe I would focus on a day in her life on tour—from waking in a hotel, to working out, to doing a TV interview, to going to a sound check at the arena, to getting ready for a show, to performing, to jumping on a private jet to go to the next city.

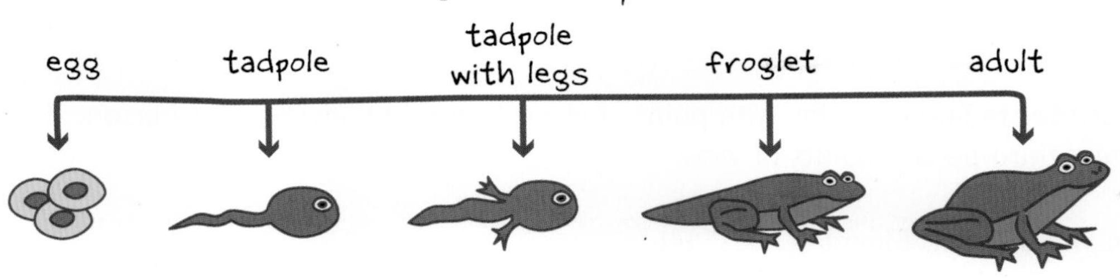

GUIDE

Ask students to help you plan one particular structure.

Let's say we are going to write an information book about students. Should we tell about Kindergarten to twelfth grade, focus on one grade, or a "day in the life" of a student? Since we haven't made it through high school yet, it might be hard to do an entire school career. And since we all have had different teachers and experiences, that might be difficult, too. Perhaps, we can try a "day in the life" structure. What are the important parts of our day?

(Allow 1–4 minutes for students to turn and talk with partners. Share exemplary responses.)

RELEASE

Remind students that planning using a time line structure can go a variety of ways.

So, writers, remember that if you would like to structure across time, consider what you really want to show your reader. Is there a moment in time that has dramatic action you want to capture? Will it be about a life span, a period of time, or just a "day in the life" of a subject?

FOR ADDITIONAL SUPPORT, TRY

5.1 How Will It Go?

5.9 Flip It and Reverse It

TIPS/RESOURCES

- Use a recent history or science topic as an example.
- Provide mentor texts and have students identify the time structures.

LESSON 5.11

Talk It Out

In this lesson, students learn to play with point of view. They will consider first-person, second-person, and third-person points of view.

Writing Stage: Transitional, Fluent
Genre: All-About Book, Feature Article, Biography, Expository Nonfiction, Literary Nonfiction

INTRODUCE

Tell students that one way authors give voice to their writing is through playing with point of view.

In many nonfiction books, you might notice that writers often use a technical voice—one that gives straight facts and information. However, writers also enjoy engaging their readers using a different point of view—one where they pretend to be the topic (first person), talk about the topic as an observer (third person), or talk to the reader as if they were the topic (second person).

INSTRUCT

Demonstration

Model for students how you consider different points of view for how you want your writing to sound.

Watch me plan for how my writing can go if I experiment with different points of view. Let's say I'm writing about tigers, specifically tigers hunting. If I use a regular technical voice, it might sound like this: (*Display the writing samples for students to see.*)

> "Tigers rely on their senses of sight and hearing rather than on smell when hunting their prey. They cautiously stalk their unsuspecting prey from behind in order to get as close as possible. Then they take down their prey with a powerful bite to the neck or throat."

If I want to engage my reader differently, I can write from the tiger's perspective:

> "I use my senses of sight and hearing rather than my nose when hunting my prey. I cautiously watch and stalk my prey from behind, in order to get as close as possible to my unsuspecting victims. Then I take them down with a powerful bite to the neck!"

Lastly, I could talk to the subject as if the reader is the tiger:

> "You use your senses of sight and hearing rather than smell when hunting your prey. You cautiously watch and stalk your prey from behind in order to get as close as possible to your unsuspecting victims. Then you take them down with a powerful bite to the neck!"

Did you see how I tried out my writing in a few different voices? I could use any one of these techniques across my writing, depending on how I want my readers to experience my topic.

ALTERNATIVE

Explain with Examples: **Show students examples of informational books that use different points of view.**

 |

GUIDE

Ask students to discuss the differences that they notice and experiment with each technique.

Take a moment to review these different points of view with your partner to decide which one I should use with my writing. Discuss which one might engage my reader the most?

(Allow 1–4 minutes for students to turn and talk with partners. Share exemplary responses.)

RELEASE

Restate the various points of view and encourage students to experiment.

Remember that whenever you are writing informational texts, you may use different techniques depending on how you want to engage your reader. You can choose to be serious or you can be more playful. Try on a few different points of view to see which feels best.

FOR ADDITIONAL SUPPORT, TRY

5.15 Get in Character

5.16 Fact Weaver

TIPS/RESOURCES

- Have mentor texts so that students can see examples of different points of view across an entire text.
- Have students sketch or draw a scene of the topic to put a point of view in context.

Build Me Up

In this lesson, students learn to try out different structures, such as: description; cause and effect; question and answer; and compare and contrast to help develop and organize their ideas.

Writing Stage: Transitional, Fluent
Genre: All-About Book, Feature Article, Research Report, Literary Nonfiction, Expository Nonfiction

INTRODUCE

Tell students that one way to develop subtopics is to consider different structures.

In order to develop and organize their ideas about a topic, writers often brainstorm the different sections, subheadings, or chapters that will support it before they begin to write. Often, many of those sections, subheadings, or chapters are easy to come up with because the writer is an expert and knows what they want to say. However, writers can come up with more possibilities by considering different text structures that they could use in their writing, such as description, cause and effect, question and answer, compare and contrast, or sequence.

INSTRUCT

Demonstration

Model for students how you consider different structures for developing your topic.

Watch me brainstorm possibilities for my topic, Soccer in Motion, by considering a variety of text structures. *(List and define each structure on an anchor chart.*)*

If I consider using description for a section, I will think of information related to a category or bigger idea, and the details that can define it, describe it, or give examples. Perhaps I can start with talking about teams. I could include information about the number of teams in a game, the number of players on a team, why teams wear the same uniforms, and different positions on a team.

If I want to use cause and effect, I can think about something that happens in soccer and why it happens. I know—fouls! There are nine major fouls and I can describe each one. So kicking or tripping an opponent is a cause, and the effect would be a foul. I can say what happens when there is a foul—the opposing team gets a free kick!

If I want to try a question and answer structure, I might consider my readers' questions or my own questions if I interview someone like David Beckham. Perhaps, how do players work together in order to score a goal? Then I can write an elaborate answer to that question.

If I want to try a compare and contrast structure, I might consider something that I could describe similarities and differences about. Perhaps I can compare and contrast the different moves used in soccer.

If I use sequence as a structure, I can consider things that I can teach in steps, order, or time. Perhaps I can write a section on the sequence or order of a soccer game so my reader can understand the flow of it.

ALTERNATIVE

Guided Practice: **Using a topic of shared knowledge, brainstorm sections for a class book using different text structures.**

 |

Description

IDEA

Cause and Effect

CAUSE EFFECT

Compare and Contrast

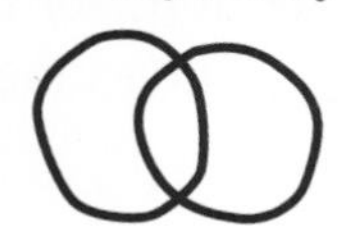

Problem and Solution

Sequence

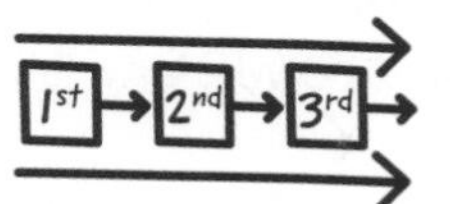

GUIDE

Ask students to consider one text structure that could work with their own topics.

Now it's your turn to give this a try. Take a moment to talk with your partner about one text structure that you could use with your topic.

(Allow 1–4 minutes for students to turn and talk with partners. Share exemplary responses.)

RELEASE

Remind students that text structures can help them brainstorm subtopics.

So, writers, today as you develop your own topics, you may already have some sections in mind. However, you can consider new possibilities by brainstorming how you could use different text structures with your topic.

FOR ADDITIONAL SUPPORT, TRY

5.5 Notorious TOC

5.13 Learn from a Mentor

TIPS/RESOURCES

- Photocopy parts of mentor texts that show different text structures for students to study.

*See sample chart, "Nonfiction Text Structures," on page 234.

Learn from a Mentor

In this lesson, students learn to consider additional sections for a topic by studying mentor texts that include "How-To's," "Diagrams," "Different Kinds," "Time Lines," and more.

Writing Stage: Transitional, Fluent
Genre: All-About Book, Feature Article, Expository Nonfiction, Research Report

INTRODUCE

Tell students they can develop their topics by studying mentor texts.

Sometimes when we look at informational texts, especially ones that are in a series, we notice that the books are organized in similar ways. They may have predictable chapters or sections in them. Today we are going to learn that writers can study mentor texts for ideas on how to structure and organize their own books.

INSTRUCT

Explain with Examples

Collect a variety of mentor texts to explain the different sections that students can replicate with their own topics.

Let's look together at these mentor texts to see what kinds of chapters or sections they include and which ones could work with our topic. *(Create an anchor chart. Consider including photocopies of examples.)*

How-To Writers include an embedded how-to or procedure section. For example, in a book about the history of ice cream, you might find a step-by-step procedure for how to make ice cream at home.

Diagrams Writers include diagram sections with labels, arrows to show movement, and descriptions of how parts function. For example, in a book about sharks you might find a diagram that labels body parts.

Different Kinds Writers include a section or page that lists and describes varieties. For example, a book about apples might contain a section on all the different varieties with descriptions or historical facts.

Time Lines Writers include time lines or information about elapsed time. For example, a book about the moon might include a time line of events leading up to the first moon landing or the phases of the moon.

Famous Examples Writers include information related to popular culture or notoriety. For example, in a book about dogs, an author might include a section on famous dogs from television, film, or history.

Fun Facts Writers include information that may not fit in another section but might be of interest, like fun facts in sidebars or callout boxes.

Profiles Writers include information related to people who made significant contributions related to the field of the topic. In a book about airplanes, you might find a profile about the Wright brothers.

ALTERNATIVE

Inquiry: **Go through a variety of (familiar and new) mentor texts with students. Ask them to notice what kinds of sections each author included and create an anchor chart of possibilities.**

 |

GUIDE

Ask students to consider one or more additional sections that could work with their topics.

Quickly share with your partner which one or more of these different sections might work with your topic. Consider why it would be especially helpful to your reader based on the topic you are teaching.

(Allow 1–4 minutes for students to turn and talk with partners. Share exemplary responses.)

RELEASE

Reiterate that studying a mentor text for ideas can help students develop their topics.

Today, when you work on your writing and you are thinking of ways to develop your topics, remember that leaning on a mentor author can help. It might even be particularly useful to look at mentor texts that are about topics similar to your own.

FOR ADDITIONAL SUPPORT, TRY

5.5 The Notorious TOC

5.12 Build Me Up

TIPS/RESOURCES

- Photocopy some examples for students.
- Remind students that added sections must enhance the overall meaning of the topic.

Multimedia Mentors

In this lesson, students learn to gather more information by observing in person, looking at pictures, or watching videos on a topic.

Writing Stage: Any • **Genre:** Any

INTRODUCE

Tell students that they can research a topic through observation.

Writers of informational texts are observers and researchers. They take note of the world around them and pay attention to the subtlest details in order to teach specific information about their topics. Today we are going to learn that being a keen observer is a great way to develop and elaborate on our topics.

INSTRUCT

Explain with Examples

With your own topic, explain what details you observe in live action, in a photo, or by watching a video.

There are different ways to research. Sometimes a project calls for in-depth research where it's necessary to consult many resources like primary documents, books, and interviews. However, sometimes we just need a little more information, such as getting the answer to some specific questions. In this case, simply observing is enough. We can observe a few different ways. We can watch live action, study a photograph, or watch a video about our topic.

Let me explain. If I were writing about basketball, it might be helpful for me to attend a live game and closely watch what is happening. I might notice how well the players block one another and this might remind me that I need to include a section on blocking. Maybe I notice that there are players on the bench. Then I remember that I should include information about how some players are benched and called to the court for different reasons.

Let's say I was studying a team photograph. I might notice how many players are on the team, which was a question that I had. I might notice the uniform design that supports quick arm and leg movements. I might notice a coach or referee in the picture and remember to include sections or chapters about their roles.

If I had the opportunity to watch a video about basketball, I could pause, rewind, or slow it down to notice subtle details that I might miss during a live game. While watching the video, I might notice how the players use jolts or movements to confuse or get around a defensive player. I might notice the smooth and delicate movements a player uses when shooting a basket.

ALTERNATIVE

Demonstration: **Have a photograph and video segment of your selected topic to demonstrate how you notice details to include in your writing.**

 |

GUIDE

Prompt students to make a plan for potential research that will support their own writing.

Now it is your turn to consider if your topic needs a little bit of observing and research in order to find more details to include. If so, would you use live action, a photo, or video to help? What information would you hope to get?

(Allow 1–4 minutes for students to turn and talk with partners. Share exemplary responses.)

RELEASE

Remind students that being an observer is one way to gather more information about a topic.

So, writers, remember that research doesn't have to be very involved. When you need to find answers to specific questions that you have, or if you need help to recall information that you may have forgotten to include, observing is a great way to gather that information. You can watch it live, study a photo, or find a video that you can look at closely to notice more.

FOR ADDITIONAL SUPPORT, TRY

5.18 5Ws (and 1H)
5.19 Ask an Expert

TIPS/RESOURCES

- Visit a place in the school that allows an opportunity for observations.
- Partner with the school media specialist to help students search video platforms to find usable clips.
- Give students time to collect photos online.

Get in Character

In this lesson, students learn to try a topic in narrative form by imagining it as a character and thinking about what that character could teach.

Writing Stage: Fluent
Genre: Research Report, Literary Nonfiction, Expository Nonfiction, Expository Essay

INTRODUCE

Tell students that informational writing can be written as a narrative.

Sometimes informational writing can take on a narrative form. This is especially true in literary nonfiction. When writers use narrative writing, it tends to bring an emotional component to their work which helps the reader empathize with the topic. Today we are going to learn how your topic can play the part of the main character in a story.

INSTRUCT

Demonstration

Using your own writing, personify your topic as if it were a character in a story. Consider the parts of your story from beginning to end.

Watch me as I experiment with this. First, I will consider the story I want to tell and how it unfolds from beginning, to middle, to end. Then, I will consider the point of view of the story.

I am going to try it with my topic, the Freedom Tower—One World Trade Center in New York City. Even though my topic is an object, I am going to personify it by making it seem as if she is a living thing. I will call her Freedom. I could begin with the history of how she came to be, then how she was built, followed by how she serves as a symbol of strength. Second, I have to decide if I should tell it from the narrator's point of view and use "she" or from the character's point of view, using "I." For this piece, I think the narrator's point of view is more powerful because it can show how impressive she is without it seeming like bragging or boasting.

I will begin with the setting to introduce my story. *(Display a photo of the Freedom Tower.)*

> "As the dawn breaks, and the sun emerges, Freedom glows like a golden torch, illuminating lower Manhattan. She reflects the sun's amber waves, making the city appear as if it were made of gold. Freedom is tall, nearly 100 stories high, and she towers over her neighbors. Her spire, a sword she holds straight up to the heavens, only makes her seem more impressive. She is the tallest in the country and in the western hemisphere. In total, she stands 1,776 feet tall, a symbol of freedom and reference to when the country declared its independence. She watches over and guards the city she calls home, along with Lady Liberty, who defends the nearby shores."

ALTERNATIVE

Explain with Examples: **Using several literary nonfiction texts, select parts to read aloud so students get a sense of the techniques used.**

GUIDE

Ask students to consider how they might try a narrative technique for their topics.

Now it's your turn. Think about your topic. How might you turn it into a story with a character?

Consider who the character is? What will that character's name be? Will it be general, like "Baby Bear," or will it have a human name? Will its name be a symbol or trait?

Once you have an idea of your character, consider the plot of your story. How might it begin, where will it go next, how will it end? Take a moment to talk it out with your partner.

(Allow 1–4 minutes for students to turn and talk with partners. Share exemplary responses.)

RELEASE

Encourage students to work on their topic in narrative form, imagining it as a character, and considering point of view.

So, writers, today we learned that informational writing can sometimes take a narrative form. Today you might take some time to develop your topic as a character. Bring it to life by thinking about its traits and characteristics. Lastly, decide on the point of view you want to use.

FOR ADDITIONAL SUPPORT, TRY

5.10 Step in Time!
5.11 Talk It Out

TIPS/RESOURCES

- Encourage students to include elements of tension to elicit emotions.
- Give students the option of applying these elements to just one part of the text.

Fact Weaver

In this lesson, students learn to use a hybrid text structure to bring their topics to life. Students may weave in factual information within the story, in a sidebar, or as an appendix.

Writing Stage: Fluent • **Genre:** Literary Nonfiction, Biography

INTRODUCE

Tell students that once they have an idea for a story, they can weave in facts.

You know how there are some nonfiction pieces that just pull you in? Hybrid structures such as narratives and biographies are great at this. But we want to make sure we focus on the facts! So today I'm going to teach you how to weave in factual information into your stories, including in the story itself, in a sidebar, in a text box, or as an appendix. We can try it a few ways to determine which way makes the most sense.

INSTRUCT

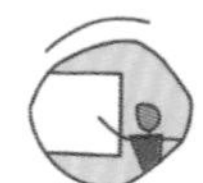

Demonstration

Model for students how you can add information to your piece in a variety of ways: by weaving it into the story or by adding a sidebar, text box, or appendix.

Watch me as I try adding facts to my story.

As you know, I'm telling a story about the life cycle of a shark. In this scene, my shark is looking for a place to lay eggs. See, she's swimming and saying that she needs to find a safe spot to lay her eggs, like in a mangrove or in a coral reef. And then here she finds a secure place to lay her eggs. I could teach my reader more information about her eggs—that some shark eggs are actually leathery pouches that kind of look like leaves underwater. They are called mermaid's purses and have tendrils that wrap securely around plants or coral to keep the shark's eggs safe and secure. Other sharks lay eggs that corkscrew into rocks. I could add this information in an appendix; I could make a whole heading on shark eggs and write about it; or I could put the information in a sidebar right on the same page. I could also weave it into my story. I could add, "She looks for a place that the leathery pouch of her eggs, also known as a mermaid's purse, could hang on to, allowing it to blend into the surrounding plants, and therefore, keep her babies safe."

ALTERNATIVE

Guided Practice: **Have students work together on a shared topic to add information in a variety of ways.**

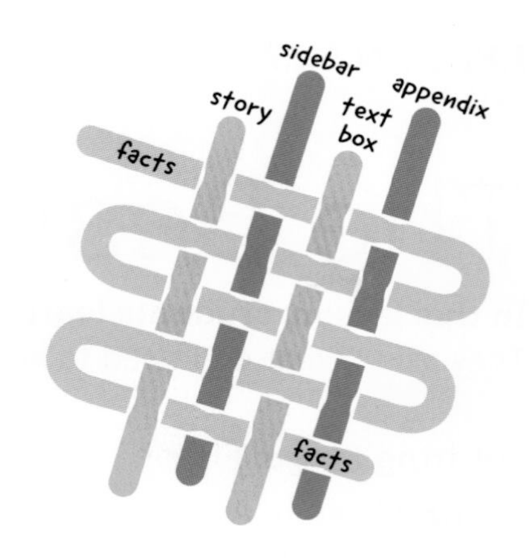

GUIDE

Prompt students to discuss the merits of one fact over another and where the facts should go—sidebar, appendix, or weaved throughout. Give them a moment to plan with a partner.

Can you take a minute and talk about what you noticed that I was doing? Specifically, I'd like you to talk about which way—appendix, sidebar, or incorporating the facts right into the story through definitions and details—works the best in this part of my draft.

(Allow 1–4 minutes for students to turn and talk with partners. Share exemplary responses.)

Now, before you head off to write, make a quick plan with your partner how you might incorporate more facts into your writing.

(Allow students 2–3 minutes to plan. Quickly share some students' plans if writers need more support.)

RELEASE

Remind students that they have multiple ways to weave in facts.*

As you go off to write today, remember you have a number of ways to teach your reader more. You don't always have to choose the same way for each part. Choose the way that best conveys your information to your reader.

FOR ADDITIONAL SUPPORT, TRY

5.11 Talk It Out

5.14 Multimedia Mentors

5.15 Get in Character

TIPS/RESOURCES

- Create an anchor chart listing techniques from mentor texts.

*See sample chart, "Fact Weaver," on page 234.

The Best Laid Plans

In this lesson, students learn that writers make a plan for research. They ask: "What do I need to know?" and "Where can I find it?"

Writing Stage: Fluent
Genre: Feature Article, Research Report, Biography, Literary Nonfiction, Expository Nonfiction, Expository Essay

INTRODUCE

Tell students that writers make plans for their research by asking questions.

When writers know they want to add some research to their writing, they make plans. They think not only about what they need to research, asking "What do I need to know," but they also ask themselves where they might find that research.

INSTRUCT

Demonstration

Model for students how you ask yourself questions to plan your research.

Watch me as I look back at my entries (or draft or draft plan) on my topic and ask myself: "What do I need to know?" and "Where can I find it?"

In this first part, I have information about sharks' bodies—what they look like, externally and internally. As I reread my notes, it feels a bit thin, like I am just listing surface facts. I've read a couple of books about this, and I'm wondering if it might help to see some sharks with commentary to add more details. Maybe I could look for some video sources? I can do an online search for videos, check them out, and make sure the sources are trustworthy. I'm also thinking that I could use some more information about the inside of sharks' bodies. I know that I've read a couple of picture books, including *Surprising Sharks* and *Neighborhood Sharks*, that give details about the inside of their bodies. I should go back and reread those pages to add that research to my writing. And now I'm wondering if a diagram might help me—I could learn the different parts, both inside and outside. If I searched "shark bodies" and then clicked "images," I might find some diagrams that would give me information.

Did you notice how I didn't just run to the computer and search "sharks"? Instead, I thought about the specific information I was looking for, and then I thought about places I could find that information.

ALTERNATIVE

Guided Practice: **Using a shared topic, ask questions to plan research together.**

GUIDE

Prompt students to turn and talk to plan out their research.

Now it's your turn. Look back at your topic (entries, draft plan) or your subtopics. Ask yourself: "What do I need to know?" and "Where can I find it?" Make a T-chart in your notebook. Once you have some ideas written down for "What do I need to know?" take a minute and talk to your partner. Help each other think about the "Where can I find it?" part of your plan.

(Allow students 1–2 minutes to jot down what they need to know and 2–3 minutes to talk about where they can find it.)

RELEASE

Send students off to plan their research, going through each part of the topic.

Remember, researchers don't just type a topic into the computer to see what's out there. They go through the parts of the topic, thinking about what they need or want to know, then they think about where they might find that information. Above all, we have to make sure we have a plan.

FOR ADDITIONAL SUPPORT, TRY

5.5 The Notorious TOC

5.13 Learn from a Mentor

5.18 5Ws (and 1H)

5.23 Just Give Me a Reason

TIPS/RESOURCES

- Make a T-chart (topic/research plan); invite students to create their own charts, too.

LESSON 5.18

5Ws (and 1H)

In this lesson, students learn to ask questions to conduct additional research, including the words: Who? What? When? Where? Why? How?

Writing Stage: Transitional, Fluent
Genre: All-About Book, Feature Article, Research Report, Biography, Literary Nonfiction, Expository Nonfiction, Expository Essay

INTRODUCE

Tell students that writers ask questions in order to research more.

Informational writers often do additional research to add to their topics. To do that work, they reread any writing they have and think of questions that might guide their research. Today I want to teach you that when writers ask questions, they often think about the 5Ws (and 1H). They ask: Who? What? When? Where? Why? and How?

INSTRUCT

Demonstration

Model for students how you take a part of your topic and ask the 5Ws (and 1H) to uncover opportunities for research.

Watch me as I try this. I've chosen octopuses for my topic. I have information about where they live, their bodies, what they eat, and their behaviors. I can use the questions to find out even more.

I'll start with *who*. Wait a minute. That seems tricky. I'm going to come back to that one. I'll start with *what*. When I ask *what*, I'm really asking myself, *what else*? Let me give you an example. When I look at this part about an octopus body, I know that it has 8 tentacles with suctions on them, and I know the suctions almost work like fingers. But what else do the suctions on their tentacles do? I can ask *how*: How do they control their suctions? And *why*: Why do they need to touch things or feel things like fingers—do they grab things for hunting? What do the suctions help them to do?

I don't think *who* works for the tentacles and suction cups part. So I can move on to some other information I already know. I know that an octopus changes color to camouflage itself. But I'm curious: *Why* else do they change color? Do the colors ever change to express emotions or other feelings—like feeling sick, or injured? *What* are some of the colors and patterns that change? *How* do they change colors? *Who* are the researchers who have made discoveries about octopus behavior?

Do you see how I took a section of my topic, and a fact that I already know, and then I used the 5Ws and an H to push myself to find out more information?

ALTERNATIVE

Guided Practice: **With a shared topic, ask the 5Ws and 1H together.**

GUIDE

Prompt partners to ask each other who, what, when, where, why and how to develop their research questions.

Now it's your turn. Pick a part of your topic. When you have that in your mind, give me a thumbs up. Partner A, you're going to go first with your topic or fact, and Partner B, you're going to name the 5Ws and an H. So, Partner B, you might start off by saying "How?" to your partner. Partner A, you're going to try to think of a *how* question for your topic. If you can't right away, you can say "Pass." Partner B, make sure to come back to the questions your partner has passed on if you have time. Then you'll switch.

(Allow 1–2 minutes for each partner to try.)

RELEASE

Send students off to develop more research questions.

One way to push our research is to ask questions. Push yourself to ask many questions about your topic so that when you start researching, you can find answers and teach your readers even more.

FOR ADDITIONAL SUPPORT, TRY

5.2 Make a List, Check It Twice
5.14 Multimedia Mentors
5.17 The Best Laid Plans
5.19 Ask an Expert

TIPS/RESOURCES

- Create a T-chart with the fact or subtopic on one side and questions on the other.
- Have students make space under their questions to jot notes.
- Suggest to students that they color-code questions.

LESSON 5.19

Ask an Expert

In this lesson, students learn to develop interview questions and ask an expert for firsthand information on a topic.

Writing Stage: Transitional, Fluent
Genre: All-About Book, Feature Article, Research Report, Biography, Literary Nonfiction, Expository Nonfiction, Expository Essay

INTRODUCE

Tell students one way to gather information is to develop interview questions for experts.

Research doesn't always mean reading books and articles or searching websites. Sometimes it means going straight to the source—an expert source! Today I want to teach you how we can develop interview questions to ask an expert for firsthand information on our topic.

INSTRUCT

Demonstration

Model for students how to think about a part of your topic, who an expert might be, and questions to ask.

Watch me as I think of my topic and then think of what questions to ask and who to direct them to.

My topic is dogs and my categories are: "Physical Appearance," "Caring for Dogs," and "Dog Behavior." I'll start with physical appearance. It might make more sense to do research online through images or video to research this part. Okay, next, "Caring for Dogs." I can interview a veterinarian! I could also interview a breeder, but I don't know any of them. I know people who have fostered and rescued dogs; they know a lot about caring for dogs. I might even talk to a groomer. Next category: "Dog Behavior." That seems like something I could also ask the experts. I wonder if I could interview someone at the dog rescue where I got my dog? I could ask a dog trainer some questions, too.

On to the questions. I can make a three-column chart in my notebook to keep these organized. I'll focus on a specific category and my audience to ask key questions. If I think about "Dog Behavior," and the person I'm going to interview is a dog trainer, I'll start with *what* questions: What do dogs do to communicate their emotions? What behaviors are the most misunderstood by humans? I can do the same with *how*, *why*, *where* and *when* questions. When someone is rescuing a dog, what behaviors should we be aware of? How can humans best communicate with dogs?

Do you notice how I'm thinking about questions and follow-up questions? And my questions are aimed at my specific audience?

ALTERNATIVE

Guided Practice: **With a shared topic, consider the audience and questions together.**

Inquiry: **Study an article set up in an interview format to notice the kinds of questions the author asks.**

GUIDE

Ask students to share ideas with a partner for experts and questions on particular subtopics.

Now it's your turn. With a partner, get started thinking about the categories of research and possible experts. Talk with your partner about the expert you might talk to and your access to that expert, or who else might help you gain access.

(Allow 1–4 minutes for partners to talk. After talking, suggest that "Fluent" writers make a 3-column list in their notebooks: Subtopic; Possible Expert(s); Questions.)

RELEASE

Send students off to write interview questions.

As you go off to write today, remember, we're thinking about experts in the field and what we could ask them. Think of questions and even follow-up questions for your specific audience.

FOR ADDITIONAL SUPPORT, TRY

5.18 5Ws (and 1H)

TIPS/RESOURCES

- Ask for community support by bringing local experts to your classroom

Writers Take Note

In this lesson, students learn that research writers can take notes in different formats. They can label pages in notebooks, cut and paste using computers, write on index cards, and more.

Writing Stage: Fluent
Genre: Feature Article, Research Report, Biography, Literary Nonfiction, Expository Nonfiction, Expository Essay

INTRODUCE

Tell students that researchers and writers have different ways of organizing their notes.

I'm sure you've noticed different teachers organize their rooms and their spaces differently—the same is true for students. Researchers and writers also have many different systems for organizing the notes they take from their research. Today I want to show you some options to organize your research notes so that you can choose a system that works best for you.

INSTRUCT

Explain with Examples

Show students examples of different ways to organize research, explaining the merits and drawbacks of each system.*

(Be prepared to show a personal model for each system.)

First, here's a research section in my notebook. For this, I can label the top of a page with my source and then jot my notes underneath. It's helpful because everything from that source is in one place. The only drawback is that I have to anticipate how many pages I need to reserve for each source. Later I can transfer any self-stick notes I have from my reading right into my notebook. If you always have your notebook, this will work. If you tend to leave things at home, this could be a problem.

Another idea is a digital system. I've created a "Research" folder in my drive, and I have a document started for each source. I can add notes, copy and paste direct quotes from articles, or add images. I can organize by source or by subtopic. I like that I can copy and paste things, but I prefer to write on paper.

Taking notes on index cards is a third method I want to show you. Note cards are compact and I can move the information around. Typically on an index card you include the source. If you have more than one index card on a subtopic, you number them to keep them organized.

You can also use regular paper and envelopes or folders. If you use both, the folder can hold everything, and the envelopes can be labeled with the subtopics. If you print an article, you can tuck it in there, jot notes from a video, etc. You're basically putting the things you gather into little containers. I end up just shoving things anywhere thinking I can put it in the right envelope or folder later, and then I don't and things are a mess. But for others, this system works really well.

ALTERNATIVE

Demonstration: **Choose one (or maybe 2 ways) to model in-depth how a particular note-taking format works.**

 |

GUIDE

Prompt students to talk through their note-taking systems and choose one that matches their style.

Reflect a little bit with a partner—which system do you think will work best for you and why?

(Allow students a few minutes to talk over their choices—coach them to consider their work habits and organizational style.)

RELEASE

Send students off to research, trying out their note-taking systems.

Writers often pause to reflect and see what's working or not working for them, and then they make changes. So when you go off to research today, try out your system. Then be sure to pause, reflect, and be honest about how well it works for you.

FOR ADDITIONAL SUPPORT, TRY

5.17 The Best Laid Plans

5.18 5Ws (and 1H)

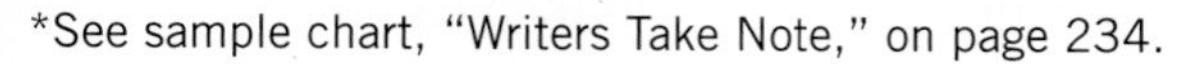

TIPS/RESOURCES

- Make envelopes, folders, index cards, etc. available.
- Remind students to cite sources in their notes and in their writing.
- Set aside time for students to reflect and see how a note-taking system is working.

*See sample chart, "Writers Take Note," on page 234.

Say That Again, Please

In this lesson, students learn how to paraphrase when taking notes during research.

Writing Stage: Fluent
Genre: Feature Article, Research Report, Biography, Literary Nonfiction, Expository Nonfiction, Expository Essay

INTRODUCE

Tell students one way to paraphrase is to read, cover, stop and retell, then write.

You've heard a teacher say: "Put it in your own words! Don't plagiarize!" But that can be hard when the information you're reading has so many useful facts. So today I'm going to teach you how one way we can paraphrase is to read a chunk of text, close the book (or cover the part you've just read), stop and retell in your mind, then write what you've learned.

INSTRUCT

Demonstration

Model for students how to read a chunk of text, cover it, and retell the important parts to yourself.

Watch me as I try this strategy using an article about sharks' senses. Notice how I read, cover, retell, and then write. (*Display paragraph.*)

> "Sharks are literally wired for hunting. The finned predators of the high seas are equipped with a special sense called electroreception that allows them to home in on prey with deadly accuracy. Other members of the elasmobranch fish family—rays and skates—also share this trait, but sharks' electroreception abilities are the most finely tuned."[1]

Now I cover it and retell. Basically this part is about how sharks, rays, and skates all have this special sense called electroreception. But sharks are better at it than rays and skates. Next I will jot down what I just said. *(Write down for students to see.)*

That seemed easy. Let me try a chunk packed with facts. I'll read it first:

> "Electroreception simply means the ability to detect electrical currents. What does electricity have to do with sharks' underwater habitat? Any muscular movement or twitches in living animals and fish create small electrical currents. At hospitals, electrocardiogram machines track the electricity resulting from our heart beating."

Now cover and retell. This is saying that sharks detect the electrical currents that sea creatures send out through the water as they move.

Note that there will be parts you want to copy directly, or quote, because they are particularly powerful the way they are worded, but for the most part we find our own language.

ALTERNATIVE

Guided Practice: **Using a shared text, practice the strategy: read, cover the text, and retell to a partner. Then have some partners share what they would jot, inviting other partnerships to add on.**

GUIDE

With a shared text, prompt students to practice the strategy: read, cover the text, and retell to a partner.

Now I'm going to show you the next chunk of text. Then I'm going to cover it and you will retell:

> "Open air does not conduct this electricity away from our bodies, but thankfully for sharks, salt water does. Salt in salt water contains sodium and chlorine ions. Ions are particles that have an electrical charge because they have lost or gained an electron. In water, these sodium and chlorine ions in salt separate and move freely, transporting electricity."

(Allow partners 2–3 minutes to retell.)

RELEASE

Send students off to practice the strategy on their own research.

So today, when you go off to research, think about what parts you need to paraphrase. That way our readers get the opportunity to hear our unique voice and enjoy how we chose to put together information.

FOR ADDITIONAL SUPPORT, TRY

5.20 Writers Take Note

TIPS/RESOURCES

- Partners can be used for oral rehearsal.
- Focus on purpose—students don't need complete sentences here.

[1] Conger, C. (2019, December 15). *What is electroreception and how do sharks use it?* Newsela. https://newsela.com/read/lib-electroreception-and-sharks/id/56749/?collection_id=339&search_id=2aa59f1b-df05-4183-9ff6-d1a0074bff5d

Rehearse Your Thesis

In this lesson, students learn to try out different thesis statements and push themselves to use the exact words that express their ideas.

Writing Stage: Fluent • **Genre:** Expository Essay

INTRODUCE

Tell students that writers try different theses for their essays before settling on one.

Today we're going to work on our thesis statements. Remember, a thesis statement is the big, controlling idea of your essay, so it's important to get it just right. And when you're working to get something just right, you don't settle for your first try. So today, I want to teach you that writers rehearse a thesis statement multiple times.

INSTRUCT

Demonstration

Model for students how to try a thesis statement a few ways to get the right words.

The topic for my expository essay is sharks. I could start with "Sharks are extraordinary." Now I have to hint at some of my supports without sharing details that are too small. For example, "Sharks are extraordinary because they have thousands of teeth, and when they lose one, there's another right behind it." That won't work.

My subtopics are bodies, varieties, and behavior. So I could say, "Sharks are extraordinary because of their bodies." Or, "Sharks are extraordinary because of their bodies, the way they act, and how many different kinds there are." Those are all categories of information, but it sounds kind of clunky. There has to be a better way to say that. Maybe I should say what they are, "Sharks are extraordinary creatures? Animals?" Maybe I should be more specific? "Sharks are extraordinary fish." I'll list that. Do you see how I'm listing a new thesis each time?

I'm going to keep pushing myself to think: Is this the right word? Is it specific? Precise? Is it clear to my reader? Does it sound right?

(*Model this a few more times for students, ending with reading the entire list which may go something like:*

- Sharks are extraordinary.
- Sharks are extraordinary animals.
- Sharks are extraordinary fish because of their bodies, the way they act, and because there are so many different kinds.
- Sharks are extraordinary fish because of their internal and external features and the way they act.
- Sharks are extraordinary fish because of their bodies, their behavior, and because there are so many different kinds.)

ALTERNATIVE

Guided Practice: **Coach students to try multiple theses on a shared topic by considering both specific words and the overall sentence.**

 |

GUIDE

Prompt students to talk through a couple of thesis statements with a partner.

Now it's your turn. Start doing what I just did using your own topic. Think about your word choices—are they specific? Do they make your idea clear to your reader?

(Allow 1–4 minutes for partners to talk and share ideas for their thesis statements.)

RELEASE

Send students off to write multiple thesis statements.

Before you go off to work, take a moment to capture some of your thesis ideas. Be sure you push yourself to change your words and change the order of the words. This is a time for rehearsal.

FOR ADDITIONAL SUPPORT, TRY

5.2 Make a List, Check It Twice

5.5 The Notorious TOC

5.14 Multimedia Mentors

5.15 Get in Character

TIPS/RESOURCES

- Look at some essay samples so students understand the purpose and intention behind a thesis statement.

LESSON 5.23

Just Give Me a Reason

In this lesson, students learn to try out various reasons to support a thesis and push themselves to think of as many reasons as they can.

Writing Stage: Fluent • **Genre:** Expository Essay

INTRODUCE

Tell students one way to develop their ideas is to have many reasons to support their thesis.

Writers, selecting strong, clear, reasons turns your piece into a persuasive argument. So today, I'm going to show you how essay writers come up with as many reasons as they can, knowing they will go back later to select the best ones. Essay writers do this by saying their thesis aloud, and adding a "because" to it.

INSTRUCT

Demonstration

Model how to come up with as many reasons as possible using *because*.

Let me show you what I mean. I have a thesis about basketball: basketball builds confidence. Now I have to think of supporting reasons. Basketball builds confidence *because* ... I know I feel confident when I play because it's not just me out there; I'm part of a team. Basketball builds confidence because you're part of a team. That's one reason.

Basketball builds confidence because I'm working on something, with drills and practice, as a way to get better. Reason two.

Why else? Oh! I know—I've made a lot of friends playing basketball. Basketball builds confidence because of the friendships you make.

What's another way? Maybe I can break it into parts? The parts of basketball. Basketball builds confidence because there are so many things you can improve on. I can get better at footwork, my ball handling skills, passing, and my knowledge of the game.

That seems like a lot of reasons, but I can do more! I can think about times. What are the times in basketball when I feel most confident? I know if we've practiced a play a lot and then we run it in a game and it works, I feel great! How can I say that? Basketball builds confidence because you can see the results of your hard work.

I can also think of kinds, as in the kinds of confidence. Confidence in myself, my knowledge of the game, but also my fitness and stamina. So basketball builds confidence in your physical fitness.

Finally, I can think of famous examples. LeBron James is famous for his confidence, which stems from his hard work. Basketball builds confidence even for the best of players.

ALTERNATIVE

Guided Practice: **Together, develop reasons for a shared topic using reasons, ways, parts, kinds, times, and famous examples.**

 |

GUIDE

Prompt students to begin thinking of reasons for their topics by sharing them with a partner.

Now name your thesis and use *because* to list several supporting reasons across your fingers. See if you can think of ways, kinds, parts, times, or even famous examples.

(Allow 1–4 minutes for students to turn and talk with partners. Share exemplary responses.)

RELEASE

Send students off to write. Remind them to push themselves to write as many reasons as they can.

Writers, you're going to go off today to develop supports for your thesis. And you know you can do that by asking: What are the ways my topic does this? You can restate your thesis, add a *because*, and list your reasons. List as many reasons as you can think of.

FOR ADDITIONAL SUPPORT, TRY

5.14 Multimedia Mentors

5.15 Get in Character

TIPS/RESOURCES

- Make sure students are clear on the definition of a thesis.
- Coach students to add more by asking: What qualities do the strong reasons share?
- Push students on ways, parts, kinds, times and famous examples to develop supports.

Grow Your Word Banks

In this lesson, students learn to create a word bank of domain-specific vocabulary that they will use in their writing.

Writing Stage: Fluent • **Genre:** Any

INTRODUCE

Tell students that writers grow their vocabulary on informational topics by gathering words connected to their topics.

Writers don't just sit down to write about a topic and know every word and definition connected to it. They are always on the lookout for new words connected to their topics in order to teach the reader more, or to just expand their own vocabulary. And so today we're going to create word banks of domain-specific vocabulary words that pertain to our topics and help us say more about an idea.

INSTRUCT

Demonstration

Model for students how to both create a word bank for specific topics and how to refer back to that word bank as they write or revise.

Watch me as I try this strategy.

First, I have to decide how I'm going to organize my word bank. I can find a space in my writer's notebook, create my own little personal dictionary, or make a document online. I'm going to use my writer's notebook and place a self-stick note on the page so I can turn to it easily.

I'm writing about Ancient Egypt, so I'll use that as the heading. I already know some words that I'm thinking of writing about: *mummy*, *hieroglyphics*, *the Great Sphinx*. I'm going to jot some definitions here. Now I can look and use my word bank to plan. But it's also there so that if I learn something in Social Studies, or if I read a book about my topic, I can add new words I learn or find.

I can do this for any topic. I can think about terms associated with soccer (*corner kick*, *header*), or figure skating (*axel*, *crossover*, *death spiral*), or even some science writing I'm thinking of doing about plants (*photosynthesis*, *roots*, *shoots*, *seeds*). See how I can get started thinking about the words I know, but then add to them as I learn new words?

 |

GUIDE

Prompt students to think about words connected to a shared topic.

Let's try this together. Here's a topic I know you all know about because we've been learning about our country's symbols and landmarks. If we were to write a book about that—symbols and landmarks of the United States—what words might go into our word bank?

(Allow 1–4 minutes for students to turn and talk with partners. Share exemplary responses.)

RELEASE

Remind students to be on the lookout across the school day for new words.

As you go off to write today, take a minute to create a word bank for your topic. Just listing the domain-specific words you know can spark ideas. But then, throughout your day, be sure to pay attention to words you're learning that you can add to your word bank, and later, to your writing.

FOR ADDITIONAL SUPPORT, TRY

1.2 Dream a Little Dream

1.24 On Your Mark, Get Set, Go!

TIPS/RESOURCES

- For emergent/transitional writers, help by jotting down key words.
- Remind students to have their word banks handy in reading and other content areas.
- Consider the best format for students for their word banks (in or outside of their notebooks or digital tools).

Lesson 5.4 Try, Try Again

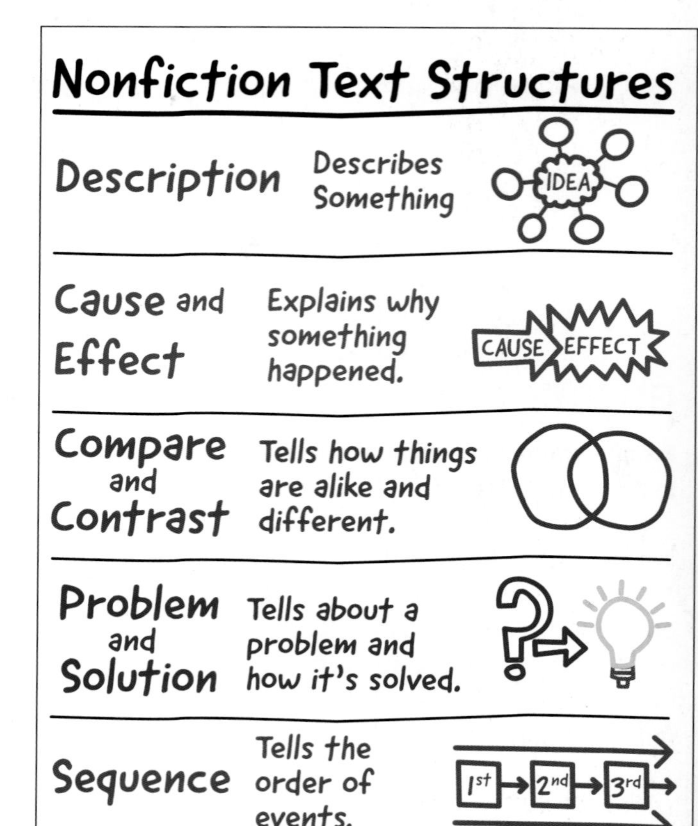

Lesson 5.12 Build Me Up

Lesson 5.16 Fact Weaver

Lesson 5.20 Writers Take Note

 |

Draft & Revise

The series of lessons in this section contain strategies for drafting and revising. While they are separate stages of the writing process, the lessons overlap considerably because they often happen simultaneously. The lessons:

- teach strategies for drawing illustrations that communicate meaning;
- guide students to add details and labels to drawings;
- contain tips for elaboration techniques; and
- help students add more, remove, or reorder information in a draft.

Descriptors for Drafting and Revising

Emergent Writers	Fluent Writers
• Use detailed drawings to convey meaning. • Add labels to illustrations and words (phrases and sentences) to represent ideas. • Incorporate different text features (e.g., headings, labels, diagrams, sidebars, etc.). • Elaborate with details (in pictures and/or in words) that define, describe, and compare. • Use cross outs and carets to substitute and change words and sentences. • Revise and reorganize the order of the pages in their books.	• Draft outside of the notebook on loose-leaf paper or an electronic device. • Use the plan in their notebooks as a guide to draft in one or two sittings. • Leave room for revision when drafting by writing on one side of the page and skipping lines. • Revise directly on the draft, making cross outs and changes visible. • Attend to quality and intentions with large-scale revisions, rather than word for word changes.

At-a-Glance Guide

Draft & Revise

Title		Lesson
6.1	**Pictures Can Teach**	Draft each page of the book by drawing the "big idea."
6.2	**How Do I Draw That?**	Draw ideas by using basic shapes and lines.
6.3	**Put It Under a Microscope**	Show details by zooming in and drawing an object large.
6.4	**Label It**	Use labels in drawings to identify objects, name the parts, or provide a title for a page.
6.5	**Make It Move**	Use arrows and action lines to show direction and movement.
6.6	**Text Features Enhance Understanding**	Use visual text features to clarify and amplify information.
6.7	**Make It Match**	Write words to match the picture in each part of the book.
6.8	**From Labels to Sentences**	Use words *the*, *my*, *a*, *an*, *our*, *this*, and describing words to create simple sentences.
6.9	**Producing Patterns**	Use high-frequency words to create repeated sentence frames.
6.10	**Patterns Come in Pairs**	Add a second sentence on each page of a pattern book.

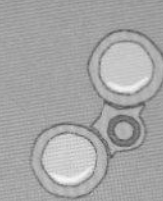

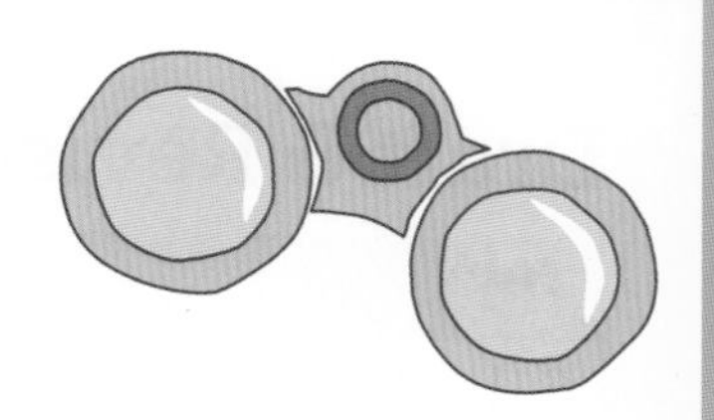

Writing Stage	Genre	
Emergent Transitional	List Pattern	How-To All-About
Emergent	List Pattern	How-To All-About
Any	List Pattern How-To All-About Feature Article	Literary Nonfiction Expository Nonfiction Biography Research Report
Any	List Pattern How-To All-About Feature Article	Literary Nonfiction Expository Nonfiction Biography Research Report
Any	List Pattern How-To All-About Feature Article	Literary Nonfiction Expository Nonfiction Biography Research Report
Any	List Pattern How-To All-About Feature Article	Literary Nonfiction Expository Nonfiction Biography Research Report
Emergent Transitional	List Pattern	How-To All-About
Emergent	List Pattern	How-To
Emergent	Pattern How-To	
Emergent	Pattern How-To	

Draft & Revise continued

Title		Lesson
6.11	**Say Hello and Goodbye**	Add an introduction page and a conclusion to a book.
6.12	**Get Your Things**	Create a page for all the materials a reader might need in order to complete a task.
6.13	**What's Your Order?**	Use pages, numbers, pictures, and words to show order.
6.14	**What's Your POV?**	Consider a consistent point of view to connect with an audience.
6.15	**Be Specific**	Use precise language for nouns and action words.
6.16	**Everything Counts in Exact Amounts**	Give information related to time, temperature, quantity, and quality.
6.17	**Watch Out!**	Add tips, cautions, and warnings, so the reader can be safe.
6.18	**What Does That Mean?**	Use domain-specific words and terms.
6.19	**We Can Do It**	Act out the steps in how-to's to make sure nothing is left out.
6.20	**Extend Your Facts**	Start with a fact and then write a second sentence to add more information.
6.21	**Say More**	Use the sentence starters *most*, *all*, *some*, *many*, and *few* to elaborate.
6.22	**Use Your Senses**	Add information by giving details related to size, shape, color, number, and more.
6.23	**Do They Fit?**	Look across the writing to make sure the sentences on each page fit with the topic.
6.24	**Out of Order**	Consider changing the order of the pages to see what makes the most sense.
6.25	**Check It Together**	Read with a partner to see if pages or sections make sense.
6.26	**Invite Your Reader**	Create an introduction that explains why the topic matters.

 |

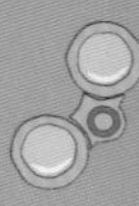

Writing Stage	Genre	
Emergent	List Pattern	How-To
Any	How-To	
Any	How-To	
Any	List Pattern How-To All-About	Feature Article Literary Nonfiction Expository Nonfiction
Any	Any	
Any	Any	
Any	Any	
Any	Any	
Any	How-To	
Any	Any	
Any	List How-To All-About Feature Article	Literary Nonfiction Expository Nonfiction Research Report
Any	Any	
Emergent Transitional	List Pattern	All-About
Emergent Transitional	List Pattern	How-To All-About
Any	Any	
Any	How-To All-About Feature Article Literary Nonfiction	Expository Nonfiction Research Report Biography Expository Essay

Draft & Revise continued

Title		Lesson
6.27	**Make It Playful**	Create an introduction that uses creative elements to engage the reader.
6.28	**New Beginnings**	Write an introduction that speaks to the reader.
6.29	**Tell Me More, Tell Me More**	Start with a topic sentence and then elaborate by explaining with definitions, descriptions, or examples.
6.30	**Connect Your Ideas**	Use transition words and phrases so that the writing flows.
6.31	**Bring It to Life**	Use imagery rather than a dictionary definition to describe.
6.32	**What's It Like?**	Use comparing and contrasting to make information clearer.
6.33	**What Are Your Stats?**	Use exact numbers to sound more knowledgeable.
6.34	**Lean or Extreme**	Use exaggeration to drive home a point.
6.35	**Your Opinion Counts**	Include personal opinions to show how the thinking has evolved.

Writing Stage	Genre	
Any	How-To All-About Feature Article Literary Nonfiction	Expository Nonfiction Research Report Biography Expository Essay
Transitional Fluent	How-To All-About Feature Article Literary Nonfiction	Expository Nonfiction Research Report Biography Expository Essay
Any	Any	
Transitional Fluent	All-About Feature Article Literary Nonfiction Expository Nonfiction	Research Report Biography Expository Essay
Fluent	All-About Feature Article Literary Nonfiction Expository Nonfiction	Research Report Biography Expository Essay
Transitional Fluent	All-About Feature Article Literary Nonfiction Expository Nonfiction	Research Report Biography Expository Essay
Transitional Fluent	All-About Feature Article Literary Nonfiction Expository Nonfiction	Research Report Biography Expository Essay
Transitional Fluent	All-About Feature Article Literary Nonfiction Expository Nonfiction	Research Report Biography Expository Essay
Transitional Fluent	All-About Feature Article Literary Nonfiction Expository Nonfiction	Research Report Biography Expository Essay

Draft & Revise continued

Title		Lesson
6.36	**Something to Think About**	Ask readers a question so that they take a moment to consider the information.
6.37	**Tell It Like It Is**	Include information that pertains to the good, the bad, and the ugly of the topic.
6.38	**So What?**	Support facts and ideas with reasons, vivid examples, and anecdotes.
6.39	**I Don't Know What Else to Say!**	Ask questions to help fill in gaps.
6.40	**What Do the Experts Say?**	Include quotes from experts (including critics) to give writing journalistic heft.
6.41	**Not Everyone Agrees**	Include opposing viewpoints to provide a more complete picture.
6.42	**Back It Up!**	Decide when to quote in full and when to paraphrase.
6.43	**How Can I Help You?**	Consider if the reader needs visuals to help them understand the information.
6.44	**On a Side Note ...**	Include sidebars for fun facts, definitions, quizzes, or other important information.
6.45	**Give Me a Sign**	Include headings and subheadings that organize the writing and orient the reader.

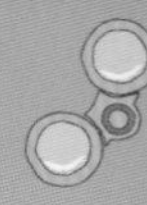

Writing Stage	Genre	
Any	Any	
Transitional Fluent	All-About Feature Article Literary Nonfiction Expository Nonfiction	Research Report Biography Expository Essay
Transitional Fluent	How-To All-About Feature Article Literary Nonfiction Expository Nonfiction	Research Report Biography Expository Essay
Transitional Fluent	All-About Feature Article Literary Nonfiction Expository Nonfiction	Research Report Biography Expository Essay
Fluent	Feature Article Literary Nonfiction Expository Nonfiction	Research Report Biography Expository Essay
Fluent	Feature Article Literary Nonfiction Expository Nonfiction	Research Report Biography Expository Essay
Fluent	Feature Article Expository Nonfiction Research Report	Biography Expository Essay
Transitional Fluent	All-About Feature Article Literary Nonfiction Expository Nonfiction	Research Report Biography Expository Essay
Transitional Fluent	All-About Feature Article Literary Nonfiction Expository Nonfiction	Research Report Biography Expository Essay
Transitional Fluent	All-About Feature Article Literary Nonfiction Expository Nonfiction	Research Report Biography Expository Essay

Draft & Revise continued

	Title	Lesson
6.46	**I Didn't Even Think of That**	Consider including additional chapters or sections for the topic.
6.47	**Try On a New Structure**	Consider text structure when revising.
6.48	**Look Through a New Lens**	Revise with a more sophisticated lens including geography, breakthroughs, and history.
6.49	**Get in Line**	Reread and evaluate the order of sections or chapters.
6.50	**Revise Reasons and Order**	Draft or revise the order of reasons in an essay so they start and end with the strongest ideas.
6.51	**Wrap It Up**	Write a conclusion that summarizes the key points and leaves the reader with a feeling or call to action.
6.52	**Everything Will Flow**	Read the writing out loud to see if it mimics the sound of conversation.
6.53	**Make It Pop**	Look to make words "pop" by bolding, using capitals, or applying playful fonts.
6.54	**Weigh It Out**	Weigh parts of the writing for volume and depth.
6.55	**Revising the TOC (Table of Contents)**	Revise the table of contents to reflect new, removed, or reordered sections.

Writing Stage	Genre	
Any	All-About Feature Article Literary Nonfiction Expository Nonfiction	Research Report Biography Expository Essay
Transitional Fluent	All-About Feature Article Literary Nonfiction Expository Nonfiction	Research Report Biography Expository Essay
Fluent	Feature Article Literary Nonfiction Expository Nonfiction Research Report	Biography Expository Essay
Fluent	Feature Article Literary Nonfiction Expository Nonfiction Research Report	Biography Expository Essay
Fluent	Expository Essay	
Fluent	Feature Article Literary Nonfiction Expository Nonfiction Research Report	Biography Expository Essay
Fluent	Feature Article Literary Nonfiction Expository Nonfiction Research Report	Biography Expository Essay
Any	Any	
Transitional Fluent	All-About Feature Article Literary Nonfiction Expository Nonfiction	Research Report Biography Expository Essay
Transitional Fluent	All-About Literary Nonfiction Expository Nonfiction	Research Report Biography

Pictures Can Teach

In this lesson, students learn to draft each page of the book by thinking, "What is the big idea on this page?" and then drawing a picture to show it.

Writing Stage: Emergent, Transitional • **Genre:** List, Pattern, How-To Book, All-About Book

INTRODUCE

Tell students one way to draft each page of a book is to name the big idea, visualize it, and then draw it in detail.

Nonfiction writers teach information in their books using both pictures and words. The pictures they choose to include not only match the words in that section, but teach more information as well. When writers draft a picture they want to include, they think about the big idea in that part, then draw with details to match.

INSTRUCT

Demonstration

Model for students how to think of the big idea for each page and draw a detailed picture to show it.

Watch me as I think about what the big idea is for each page of my book and then draw a detailed picture that matches.

My book today is about different kinds of transportation. As I draw each page, I must think, "What does this part teach?" This part is about buses. Let me picture it in my mind. I'm going to draw a bus, but is there anything else I want to teach here? I think I want to teach that buses can fit a lot of people in them. But how can I put that information into my drawing? Oh, I know! Maybe I can make windows, and put a person in each window, looking out of the bus. I can also draw the bus at a bus stop with a line of people waiting to get on it. That would show my reader a bus is a form of transportation that can fit many people. I am going to make sure that the bus is front and center, and that it fills the page. *(Draw an illustration on one page of your booklet as an example.)*

The next part of my book is about bicycles. Now I must picture it in my mind and think, "Is there anything else I want to teach here?" I want to teach that there are different kinds of bikes that people ride for transportation like: bicycles, e-bikes, tandem bikes, unicycles, and tricycles. How will I fit all that into my drawing? I know. I can draw a bike lane with each kind of bike in it! *(Draw an illustration on another page of your booklet as an example.)*

Even though my book is about transportation, did you notice how I only drew one big idea on each page? I didn't draw every kind of transportation on every page. Rather, I only drew what that part was about and the details that matched what I wanted to teach!

ALTERNATIVE

Explain with Examples: **Using simple list books, show students how writers teach with their pictures and the words on the page that match the pictures.**

 |

GUIDE

Prompt students to assist you with the next page of your book, being sure to talk through the details that teach the reader.

Will you help me with the next part? The next part of my book is about trains. Close your eyes and picture a train. What else should we teach about trains? Tell your partner what I should draw.

(Allow 1–4 minutes for students to turn and talk with partners. Share exemplary responses.)

RELEASE

Remind students that detailed drawings can teach the reader more information.

When you draft today, I want to remind you to think about what you really want to teach your reader, picture it in your mind, and draw a detailed picture that teaches about each part in your book. You can then go back to add your words.

FOR ADDITIONAL SUPPORT, TRY

6.2 How Do I Draw That?

6.3 Put It Under a Microscope

6.4 Label It

6.5 Make It Move

TIPS/RESOURCES

- Point out to students that color details can also teach information.
- For struggling artists, provide clip art or photos for students to trace or cut and paste.
- Keep nonfiction mentor texts handy to show students how the central idea is enhanced through pictures in each section.

How Do I Draw That?

In this lesson, students learn to draw ideas by using basic shapes and lines.

Writing Stage: Emergent • **Genre:** List, Pattern, How-To Book, All-About Book

INTRODUCE

Tell students that they are going to learn how to use basic shapes and lines to represent their ideas.

As we write, we might feel like we aren't a good enough artist to draw our ideas. However, almost everything around us is made out of basic shapes and lines, such as: circles, triangles, squares, rectangles, ovals, and more! These are the tools that illustrators use to represent their ideas. As we write about our topic today, we are going to think like an illustrator.

INSTRUCT

Demonstration

Model for students how you use basic shapes and lines to draw your idea.

Watch me as I use basic shapes and lines to represent my ideas. *(Show students a blank booklet and have an anchor chart displaying basic shapes and different types of lines.*)*

Today I am writing a book about cats. Let me think about the basic shapes and lines that I can use. Let me picture a cat in my mind and see what lines and shapes I can use. I think I can use a circle for the cat's head and body, and perhaps rectangles for the legs. Maybe triangles will work for the ears and circles for the eyes and nose? Let me get started on my drawing and see how it looks.

(Model for students as you draw.) I used a circle for the head, but now I think it might look funny if I use another circle for the cat's body—maybe a long oval will work better? I'll give that a try. Now, I am going to add rectangles for the four legs, circles for eyes and nose, and triangles for the ears.

Now that I am looking at my cat, I think I can add some lines—a squiggly line for the tail and some straight lines as whiskers. I think that works! Now my cat is starting to really look like a cat! It felt like it was going to be tricky for me, but using basic shapes and lines helped!

ALTERNATIVE

Guided Practice: **Complete the Guide portion of this lesson with students to show all the different things you can make using basic shapes and lines.**

 |

GUIDE

Prompt students to turn and talk about the basic shapes and lines that can be used to draw a car.

Let's get started on a new book, one about transportation. The first idea that we are going to draw is a car. Picture a car in your mind—what shapes do you see? Let's share with our partners and see if their ideas are similar. Name the shapes and the lines you would use to draw a car. Which part of the car would you use each shape for?

(Allow 1–4 minutes for students to turn and talk with partners. Share exemplary responses.)

You all had such great ideas. I heard some of you say a long rectangle for the main part of the car and then smaller ones for the doors, and lines for the windows. *(Using the students' ideas, begin to draw a car. Name the shapes and lines that you use.)*

RELEASE

Remind students to use basic shapes and lines to represent their ideas.

Remember, we have our chart to help us, but there are even more lines and shapes that we might use. The important thing to remember is not to get discouraged and think, "I don't know how to draw that." The more we draw, the better we will get!

FOR ADDITIONAL SUPPORT, TRY

6.1 Pictures Can Teach

6.3 Put It Under a Microscope

6.5 Make It Move

TIPS/RESOURCES

- Frequently reference the anchor chart during the lesson to add new ideas.*
- Use guided drawing sessions where students copycat a variety of demonstration drawings on dry-erase boards in a step-by-step fashion.

*See sample chart, "How Do I Draw That?," on page 356.

Put It Under a Microscope

In this lesson, students learn to show details by zooming in and drawing an object large so that the reader can see it closely.

Writing Stage: Any

Genre: List, Pattern, How-To Book, All-About Book, Feature Article, Literary Nonfiction, Expository Nonfiction, Biography, Research Report

INTRODUCE

Tell students that they are going to learn how to show details in their writing using two techniques.

Have you ever looked at something and wished you could zoom in to notice the tiniest of details? For example, consider the tiny pores under a shark's nostrils that help them sense when prey is near. Today we are going to take our own ideas and show details by zooming in and drawing an enlarged object.

INSTRUCT

Explain with Examples

Collect a variety of mentor texts to show how authors use zoom-in or picture-in-picture images to show details.

To help us do this work today, we are going to lean on some of our mentor texts that show us strong examples of zooming in to see small details.

As we look at our mentor texts, let's think about how and why authors and illustrators use zoom-in or picture-in-picture images to show the details of their topics.

(Display examples of zoomed-in pictures and illustrations where illustrators use a picture-in-picture technique, where they pop out a section of an illustration using a callout box to show up-close details. Have students study each picture to notice the details. Demonstrate how you ask and answer questions, such as: "What do I see? What are the tiniest details that I notice? What does this help me understand? What is it teaching me? If the author didn't zoom in, would I have noticed these things? What helped me notice these details?")

ALTERNATIVE

Demonstration: **Using your own topic, show students how you zoom in to show details. Then model how you draw an object large.**

 |

GUIDE

Prompt students to think about what they will zoom in on for their writing.

Emergent As you think about your topic, what parts do you think you will zoom in on to show your readers more detail? Where might you try a picture-in-picture? When do you think it would be helpful to your reader to show something up close?

(Allow 1–4 minutes for students to turn and talk with partners. Share exemplary responses.)

Transitional / Fluent Look in your notebook for any sketches you might have done already on your topic. Look for places where you might create new illustrations or revise any of your current sketches by zooming in or using the picture-in-picture technique to show more details. Where might you try it? What will it teach your reader?

(Allow 1–4 minutes for students to turn and talk with partners. Share exemplary responses.)

RELEASE

Remind students to try to incorporate zoom-in or picture-in-picture images to show details about their topics.

As we write about our topics, we want to think about the types of pictures we can use that will show readers important details. We can use zoom-in pictures and draw the picture large so our reader can see it clearly and notice all the tiny details. Today, when you go off to write, remember the mentor texts we looked at and how you can use the same techniques in your writing.

FOR ADDITIONAL SUPPORT, TRY

6.2 How Do I Draw That?

6.6 Text Features Enhance Understanding

6.43 How Can I Help You?

TIPS/RESOURCES

- Prior to this lesson, expose students to the different kinds of pictures authors use.
- Make an anchor chart and include zoom-in pictures and picture-in-picture examples.

LESSON 6.4

Label It

In this lesson, students learn to use labels in drawings to identify objects, name the parts, or provide a title for a page.

Writing Stage: Any

Genre: List, Pattern, How-To Book, All-About Book, Feature Article, Literary Nonfiction, Expository Nonfiction, Biography, Research Report

INTRODUCE

Tell students that they can use labels in drawings to identify objects, name their parts, or to provide a title for a page.

Think about when you put something new together, say a toy that has different parts. When you open the directions and just see words, it can be very overwhelming! But when the directions have labels to identify different parts, then you are set up for success. We are going to use labels in our writing to identify objects, name their parts, or to provide a title for a page so that our readers can learn more about the topic.

INSTRUCT

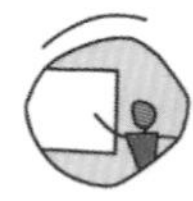

Demonstration

Model for students how you use labels to teach the reader and make the information clearer.

Watch me as I use labels in my drawings.

Emergent Let's look at my book on transportation. Here on this page, I have some ideas about jet skis, cruise ships, sail boats, and submarines. Maybe I can label this page "Water Vessels" since all of these belong in the water. That would help my reader keep track of the information better. Then I can label each different water vessel. *(Show students how you label each one by its name.)* To take it one step further, perhaps I can add labels to one of the water vessels to show more detail. Let me try it with the cruise ship. I can label the cabin rooms, the pool, the deck, the engine, the bow, and the stern. Now I have labels in my writing, which makes it clear for my reader to learn more about my topic.

Transitional / Fluent I am going to think about the labels I could add to my writing on sharks that will teach my reader more and make my information crystal clear. In this part, I am talking about the different fins that sharks have. Perhaps I can label this part of my writing "Shark Fins" and use additional labels that show the different types of fins. Then, in my writing, I can explain the different features and purpose for each type of fin. *(Model how you add the labels described above in your writing.)*

ALTERNATIVE

Explain with Examples: **Collect a variety of mentor texts that show how authors use labels.**

GUIDE

Prompt students to think about their ideas and how they can use labels.

Now it's your turn to give this a try. Take out your writing and think about a part where you could add labels. The different objects? The parts of an object? The page?

(Allow 1–4 minutes for students to turn and talk with partners. Share exemplary responses.)

RELEASE

Remind students to think about adding labels to their writing.

Today we learned a lot about labels and how they can help make our information clear to the reader. As you write, think about the places in your writing that you can add labels. Remember that you can add labels to more than one place in your writing.

FOR ADDITIONAL SUPPORT, TRY

6.6 Text Features Enhance Understanding
6.43 How Can I Help You?
6.45 Give Me A Sign

TIPS/RESOURCES

- Share that several parts of a book can be labeled.
- In content areas, showcase how labels are used to teach more about a topic.

Make It Move

In this lesson, students learn to use arrows and action lines to show direction and movement.

Writing Stage: Any

Genre: List, Pattern, How-To Book, All-About Book, Feature Article, Literary Nonfiction, Expository Nonfiction, Biography, Research Report

INTRODUCE

Tell students that today they will learn how to use arrows and action lines to show direction and movement.

When we are writing, we might want to include specific details that show direction and movement. For example, if you are reading a book about hockey, action lines might show the hockey stick, puck, and/or players in motion. Arrows might show the direction of the puck down the ice or toward another player in a pass. If you are reading a how-to book, arrows might show the direction to turn a knob or the placement of an object when putting things together.

INSTRUCT

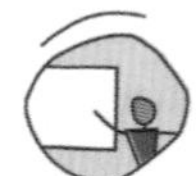

Demonstration

Model for students how you add arrows and action lines to your writing to show direction and movement.

Watch me as I add arrows and action lines to my writing to show direction and movement.

Emergent Here I am writing about cats. One part of my book is "How to Feed a Cat." This might be a good place for me to think about where I can add some arrows to help my reader. Maybe in the part where I am spooning the food into the bowl, I can add an arrow that shows where the food goes, starting the line from the can of food and putting an arrow into the bowl. *(Add the arrow to the picture.)* I also have another part of my book where I teach the reader about what cats like to play with. In my picture, I have a cat playing with a mouse toy, but it looks like the cat is just sitting there. Let me add some action lines to show how the cat is chasing the mouse toy. *(Add some lines to show movement.)* Now it looks like the cat is moving!

Transitional / Fluent Let me look through my writing on octopuses to see if there are any parts where I can add some arrows or lines. In this part, I sketched a little picture to show an octopus encountering one of its enemies. Perhaps, if I add some action, it will show the reader that the octopus is jetting away really fast because of the water that is being pushed out of its funnel. I can even add more lines to show how the water is shooting out, causing the octopus to swim away fast—kind of like a turbo button. *(Add arrows and lines to your picture.)* I also write about the life cycle of an octopus. I have each stage of the life cycle sketched out and labeled, but maybe I can add some arrows to show how the cycle goes around. *(Add arrows to your picture.)*

ALTERNATIVE

Guided Practice: **Prompt students to help you think of how you can add arrows and lines in your own writing.**

 |

GUIDE

Ask students to find places in their writing where they can add arrows and lines.

Now take a look at your writing and find places where you can add arrows and lines to show direction and movement. Think about the parts of your writing where the reader would benefit from seeing the direction of things or how something moves.

(Allow 1–4 minutes for students to turn and talk with partners. Share exemplary responses.)

RELEASE

Remind students that adding arrows and lines in their pictures helps give the reader more information.

Today we focused on how we can add arrows and lines to our writing to show direction and movement. As you write, consider places in your writing that you might add an arrow or a line to your pictures to help the reader better understand movement, directions, or how things work together.

FOR ADDITIONAL SUPPORT, TRY

6.1 Pictures Can Teach

6.2 How Do I Draw That?

TIPS/RESOURCES

- Make an anchor chart that shows how you can use arrows and action lines for different purposes.*
- Gather a few mentor texts to show how arrows and lines are used to enhance the information.

*See sample chart, "Make It Move," on page 356.

Text Features Enhance Understanding

In this lesson, students learn to use visual text features. They learn how to draw illustrations, maps, diagrams, cross sections, cutaways, and time lines to clarify and amplify information.

Writing Stage: Any

Genre: List, Pattern, How-To Book, All-About Book, Feature Article, Literary Nonfiction, Expository Nonfiction, Biography, Research Report

INTRODUCE

Tell students that they can use visual text features to make their writing clear and engaging.

When we think about nonfiction texts, one of the things that usually stands out to us are the text features that the author uses. There are many types of text features that authors can use to present their ideas in a clear and engaging way. Today we are going to think about how we can use visual text features in our own writing to enhance our topics.

INSTRUCT

Explain with Examples

Gather a variety of mentor texts that clearly show how authors purposefully use text features to showcase parts of their topics.

I have collected a variety of mentor texts for us to look at text features. Together we will think about which ones might work with our topics. *(Create an anchor chart. Consider including photocopies of examples.)* Here are some examples you might find:

Illustrations Writers use illustrations to show the reader a drawing of the topic. Sometimes it can be a zoom-in picture. Illustrations help readers visualize the information and connect it to the text.

Maps Writers use maps to show the location of people, places, and things. Maps can show location, size, shape, features of, and relative distance to other places. Maps help readers orient the information.

Diagrams Writers use diagrams with labels, arrows to show movement, and descriptions of how certain parts function to show the reader the different parts of the topic.

Cross Sections and Cutaways Writers use cross sections to illustrate and label the different parts of the topic. A cross section allows readers to see how things are arranged. A cutaway is a type of cross section that shows what's inside a 3D object, the layers and inner workings.

Time Lines Writers use time lines to show important events across many years or a shorter time period. The time line includes dates indicated by points or slashes in the line; each point is labeled with an event.

ALTERNATIVE

Inquiry: **Go through a variety of mentor texts with students and have them take notice of the different text features the author used.**

 |

GUIDE

Ask students to think about the text features that they might try using for their topics and the purpose for each feature they may include.

Think about your topic and which text features are best suited for your writing. Which text features would you like to include? What will it look like? Why do you want to include that feature?

(Allow 1–4 minutes for students to turn and talk with partners. Share exemplary responses.)

RELEASE

Remind students to think about the text features they can include in their writing.

Today we took some time to study the visual text features that authors use in their writing. We know authors not only do this to give the reader more information but also to make it more engaging. Whenever you are writing about a topic, think about the text features that you could include.

FOR ADDITIONAL SUPPORT, TRY

6.3 Put It Under a Microscope

6.5 Make It Move

6.43 How Can I Help You?

TIPS/RESOURCES

- Decide which text features you will expose to your students and have clear examples of each.
- Prior to this lesson, it's helpful if students know about text features.

Make It Match

In this lesson, students learn to write words to match the picture in each part of a book.

Writing Stage: Emergent, Transitional • **Genre:** List, Pattern, How-To Book, All-About Book

INTRODUCE

Tell students that they are going to match words to their pictures, focusing on adding details.

As we prepare to write or add more details to our books, we want to make sure that our pictures and words match. One way we can do this is to look at photographs we've collected or the pictures that we've drawn on each page and ask ourselves, "What am I trying to teach here? What is the picture showing that I want my words to say?"

INSTRUCT

Demonstration

Model for students how you make sure your pictures and words match and how you elaborate content.*

Watch me as I say more and write words in my booklet to match each picture.

Here I have my book about octopuses. Let me see if my pictures and words match on each page and how I can say more to add details to my writing. On this page, I have a picture of an octopus and the suction cups on each leg. So far I wrote, "An octopus has eight legs." That matches the picture, but it's not saying much about the details. Maybe I could add a few more details about octopus legs, such as, "On each leg there are rows of suction cups." That would match my picture and also give the reader more details about my topic. I could also add, "The octopus uses its legs to swim, crawl, and catch prey."

**For How-To Books, model with one of the pages of a step.*

ALTERNATIVE

Explain with Examples: **Gather mentor texts that show clear word-to-picture matching. Emphasize that this helps readers get the key details the author wants them to know.**

GUIDE

Using your own writing, prompt students to think about what you could add on the next page.

Now you are going to give it a try and can help me with my next page.

List, Pattern, All-About Books Here I drew the different things the octopus eats, such as crabs, shrimp, and lobster. I didn't add words yet, so we need to think about what we want to say and the details we want to include.

How-To Books In this "How to Feed a Cat" book, the next page is about Step 3. I didn't add words yet. The picture is showing how to spoon the cat food into the bowl. What words can I add that will match the picture? What details can I include to say more?

(Allow 1–4 minutes for students to turn and talk with partners. Share exemplary responses and add their ideas to your writing.)

RELEASE

Remind students as they write to make sure their pictures and words match.

Today, when you are writing, remember to make sure your pictures and words match on every page. As you make sure that they match, you also want to think about the details you can add to say more on each page so that the information is clear to the reader.

FOR ADDITIONAL SUPPORT, TRY

6.1 Pictures Can Teach

6.2 How Do I Draw That?

TIPS/RESOURCES

- Prior to this lesson, it would be helpful if students were taught Lessons 6.1 and 6.2.
- Use mentor texts where there is simple text that clearly matches the picture on each page.

LESSON 6.8

From Labels to Sentences

In this lesson, students learn to use the words: *The*, *My*, *A*, *An*, *Our*, *This*, and describing words to create simple sentences.

Writing Stage: Emergent • **Genre:** List, Pattern, How-To Book

INTRODUCE

Tell students that they can add words to a label to say more on each page.

You have been working hard to add labels to your books because you know that pictures and words are important for teaching about your topics. Writers try to use more than one word on a page so that it sounds more like how they speak when they are teaching. Today we are going to learn that we can add just one or two simple words to turn our labels into sentences.

INSTRUCT

Demonstration

Model for students how you can either write or revise a simple label book by adding an additional word or two.

Watch me show you how I can revise a book that I've started by turning my labels into sentences. *(Hold up and read aloud a prewritten book with labels.)*

Here I have a book that I wrote about vegetables. Across the pages it reads: "tomato, pumpkin, squash, broccoli, potato, eggplant." As you can see, the word in each picture labels my drawing. I could say more at the bottom of the page to add a sentence. Perhaps I can write: "My tomato," or "A tomato," or "The tomato," or even, "Our tomato." I could also add another word that describes the vegetable. So I could write: "The red tomato" or "The round tomato."

Maybe I'll turn this into a color book and write: "The red tomato," "The orange pumpkin," "The yellow squash," etc. Since I can find these words on the word wall and on the color chart, this should be easy to do. Now it reads more like a book!

ALTERNATIVE

Explain with Examples: **Using a variety of simple label books, show students how authors use a group of two or more words to make a meaningful sentence.**

GUIDE

Ask students to help you brainstorm a phrase for a new book that you create together.

Today I wanted to write a book about school supplies. *(Display the pages with predrawn pictures.)*

I have already drawn the pages of my book and have added the labels: "pencil, marker, eraser, scissors, crayons." Let's start with "pencil." Rather than just write "pencil," what more can I say to teach and turn this into a sentence? What words can I put before the word "pencil"? Should we use *The*, *A*, *Our*, or *My*? What is another word that describes the pencil?

(Allow 1–4 minutes for students to turn and talk with partners. Share exemplary responses. Repeat on more pages as time permits.)

RELEASE

Remind students to use what they know about spelling patterns as they write.

As you work on your own books today, you already know how to add labels to your drawings. Now you are ready to turn those labels into sentences on each page to teach information. You can use the sentence starters *A*, *An*, *The*, *My*, *Our*, or *This* to help. Then, if you are ready, you can try to add a describing word, too.

FOR ADDITIONAL SUPPORT, TRY

2.9 Give Them Some Space

6.4 Label It

TIPS/RESOURCES

- Point out words in the classroom environment that can help students create simple sentences.
- Keep examples of AA-level guided reading books handy for additional ideas.

Producing Patterns

In this lesson, students learn to use high-frequency words to create a sentence frame and repeat the frame on each page.

Writing Stage: Emergent • **Genre:** Pattern, How-To Book*

INTRODUCE

Tell students that pattern books are easy to write once a sentence frame is created.

Nonfiction writers make pattern books by thinking of a sentence frame for what they want to say, and then repeating it on every page while only changing a word or two. Today we are going to learn how to use the word wall to help us make a sentence frame.

INSTRUCT

Demonstration

Model for students how you create your own pattern book by developing a sentence frame using high-frequency words.

A sentence frame is a group of words that are the same on every page with the exception of one or two words that change.

Today I am writing a pattern book about toys—dolls, games, trains, and blocks. I have an idea for how my book will go, but I need to think of a sentence frame. I will use the word wall to help me. *(If possible, manipulate words off your word wall into a pocket chart or magnetic board.)*

Hmmm. I could create a sentence frame using the words *this*, *is*, and *a* to make the pattern: "This is a doll. This is a game. This is a train. This is a block." That would be a good frame if I want to teach the reader about different kinds of toys.

Perhaps I could try a different one. I could create a frame using the words *here*, *is*, and *the* to make the pattern: "Here is the doll. Here is the game. Here is the train." That would be good if I wanted to teach the reader where to find the toys.

Maybe I could create a frame using the words *look*, *at*, and *the*: "Look at the doll. Look at the game. Look at the train." That would be a good frame if I wanted to show the reader my different toys.

I could try a different kind of frame where the second word changes. For instance, "A doll is a toy. A game is a toy. A train is a toy. A block is a toy." Do you notice how only the second word changes?

**For How-To Books, use a different example, such as "How to Make a Pizza: Put the crust on. Put the sauce on. Put the cheese on." etc.*

ALTERNATIVE

Explain with Examples: **Read a variety of guided reading Level A and B pattern books to students. Point out and discuss which high-frequency words make up each sentence frame.**

 |

GUIDE

Prompt students to help you develop a sentence frame and pattern using high-frequency words.

Can you help me come up with a sentence frame for a new book? Let's make a book about desserts—cookies, cake, brownies, and ice cream! Using the word wall, can you and your partner come up with an idea for a sentence frame? Remember to think about what you would want to say or teach about desserts.

(Allow 1–4 minutes for students to turn and talk with partners. Share exemplary responses.)

RELEASE

Remind students to create a sentence frame using high-frequency words.

Writers, remember that when you go back to work on your books, you can use the word wall to help you create your own sentence frames. But don't just pick any words, try to think of a sentence that will help you show or teach what's important for your reader to learn or know.

FOR ADDITIONAL SUPPORT, TRY

2.3 Stretch It Out
2.6 Clap It Out, Then Sound It Out
2.7 That Sounds Like ...

TIPS/RESOURCES:

- Provide students with a small replica of the word wall to use on their own.
- Provide students with an envelope or storage bag of high-frequency word tiles.
- As a class, make an anchor chart of possible patterns.

Patterns Come in Pairs

In this lesson, students learn to add a second sentence on each page of their pattern books —either one that repeats or one that changes on each page.

Writing Stage: Emergent • **Genre:** Pattern, How-To Book*

INTRODUCE

Tell students that pattern books can have two sentences on a page.

Writers of pattern books sometimes have more to teach or say on each page. When that is the case, they add a second sentence to add more detail. The second sentence can use the same pattern, or it can change by one or two words.

INSTRUCT

Demonstration

Model how you revise your own pattern book by developing a second sentence frame using high-frequency words.

Watch me revise to add a second sentence frame to my pattern book about toys. *(Read a prewritten pattern book to your students that has one sentence per page.)*

First, I am going to reread my book, "Here is the doll. Here is the game. Here is the train. Here is the block. Here is the puppet." Next I think, "What more do I want to say about these toys?" Well, if I think about what I do with my toys, I could say, "I can play." Since these are word wall words, I can easily write them! On each page, I can add the sentence, "I can play." So now it will read: "Here is the doll. I can play. Here is the game. I can play. Here is the train. I can play. Here is the block. I can play. Here is the puppet. I can play."

I could also make that sentence change on each page. Maybe I want to show that all types of children play with toys. Then my book could go, "Here is the doll. I can play. Here is the game. We can play. Here is the train. She can play. Here is the block. They can play."

If I wanted to teach what we can do with different toys, then I could add something like, "Here is the doll. I can feed it. Here is the game. I can play it. Here is the train. I can push it. Here is the block. I can build it. Here is the puppet. I can show it."

**For How-To Books, use a different example, such as, "How to Make Pancakes: Add the flour. Mix it. Add the eggs. Mix it. Add the sugar. Mix it. Add the oil. Mix it."*

ALTERNATIVE

Explain with Examples: **Read a variety of guided-reading Level C and D pattern books to students. Point out and discuss how the author uses a second sentence to add additional details.**

GUIDE

Prompt students to help you develop a second sentence frame for several pages in a book.

Do you think you can help me revise this book about desserts? It reads: "We love cookies. We love cake. We love brownies. We love ice cream. We love pie." Can you think about something else that we would want to say or teach about desserts?

(Allow 1–4 minutes for students to turn and talk with partners. Share exemplary responses, such as: "They are yummy!" or "It is yummy!"*)*

RELEASE

Remind students that a second sentence in a pattern book can give more information.

Remember that whenever you are writing or revising a pattern book, you can teach more information by adding a second sentence frame to each page of your book. That sentence can be the same, or it can change by a word or two.

FOR ADDITIONAL SUPPORT, TRY

2.3 Stretch It Out

2.6 Clap It Out, Then Sound It Out

2.7 That Sounds Like ...

2.9 Give Them Some Space

TIPS/RESOURCES

- Use popular class texts and allow students to play with sentence patterns.
- Keep a collection of early level pattern books to read aloud or for students to use as mentor texts to get ideas.

Say Hello and Goodbye

In this lesson, students learn to add an introduction page and a conclusion to their books. They will start or end with a question, big idea, feeling, or call to action.

Writing Stage: Emergent • **Genre:** List, Pattern, How-To Book

INTRODUCE

Tell students that introductions and conclusions are important for conveying a topic's message.

Writers write informational books in order to teach their readers a message about the topics they teach. They usually use an introduction or a conclusion page to hint at what they want their readers to know, feel, or do. Today we are going to learn how writers say hello and goodbye to their readers through questions, big ideas, feelings, or by giving advice.

INSTRUCT

Demonstration

Model for students how you begin your book by starting with an introduction page and ending with a conclusion page.

Watch me write my book using an introduction and conclusion to say hello and goodbye to my reader with a message about my topic. Today I am writing a book about dinosaurs. In it, I plan to write, "Dinosaurs have big teeth. Dinosaurs have big feet. Dinosaurs have big tails. Dinosaurs have big claws. Dinosaurs have big roars."

To say hello or goodbye, I think, "What do I want to say about dinosaurs?" Well, I want my reader to know that dinosaurs were huge! I need an introduction page and an ending page. I could use:

- A question: "Are dinosaurs big?"
- A big idea: "Dinosaurs are big!"
- A feeling: "Dinosaurs are scary!"
- Advice that tells the reader to do something like, "Beware of dinosaurs!"

I think I will start with my big idea, "Dinosaurs are big!" On the pages that follow, I show the ways that dinosaurs are big. I give the details about their teeth, feet, tails, claws, and roars. When I end my book, I have to think about how I can make my idea clearer for the reader. I am not just saying they're big, but that they are huge and terrifying! I think my ending should say, "Dinosaurs are scary!" (*Write the pages quickly.*)

So then, the pages of my book will go: "Dinosaurs are big. Dinosaurs have big teeth. Dinosaurs have big feet. Dinosaurs have big tails. Dinosaurs have big claws. Dinosaurs have big roars. Dinosaurs are scary!"

ALTERNATIVE

Explain with Examples: **Read a variety of early level informational books that use clear introductions or conclusions. Discuss the idea each author is conveying.**

GUIDE

Prompt students to help you develop an introduction and a conclusion for a new book.

Will you help me come up with an introduction and a conclusion for a new book about fruit? My plan is for the pages to read: "Apples are crisp. Oranges are juicy. Bananas are sweet. Grapes are tart." We have to think about what we want to say about fruit. Can you come up with ideas or a message about fruit for our readers?

(Allow 1–4 minutes for students to turn and talk with partners. Share exemplary responses.)

I heard: "Fruit is healthy. Fruit is a good snack. Fruit is delicious. And I love fruit!" So we could write:

- A question - "Is fruit delicious?"
- A big idea - "Fruit is healthy."
- A feeling - "We love fruit!"
- Advice - "Eat more fruit."

RELEASE

Remind students of the importance of introductions and conclusions.

As you write today, remember that introductions and conclusions are great places to share your message with a reader. If you want to revise a book, just attach a blank page onto your booklet at the beginning and at the end. If you are starting a new book, think of how you might say hello or goodbye as you write about your topic.

FOR ADDITIONAL SUPPORT, TRY

4.4 Narrow It Down
4.9 Who's Your Audience?

TIPS/RESOURCES:

- Create an anchor chart with examples of introductions and conclusions from the lesson.

Get Your Things

In this lesson, students learn to consider all the materials a reader might need in order to complete a task by creating a "Things You Need," "Materials," or "Ingredients" page.

Writing Stage: Any • **Genre:** How-To Book

INTRODUCE

Tell students that how-to books sometimes list the materials needed at the beginning so that the reader can perform the steps efficiently.

Writers list the materials needed at the beginning of a how-to book so that the reader can gather them before they start a task. This is important so the reader does not need to stop the task to find things. Today we will learn that writers use either pictures with labels or a list in a "Things You Need," "Materials," or "Ingredients" section at the front of their how-to books.

INSTRUCT

Explain with Examples

Explain to students that some how-to books require materials to be gathered beforehand.

Sometimes, a how-to process requires many things to complete the task successfully. For example, if you decided you wanted to bake a chocolate cake, you would need flour, sugar, eggs, baking powder, vanilla extract, chocolate, salt, and butter. Imagine halfway through mixing you realized you didn't even have the vanilla extract. You would have to run to the store and by the time you returned home, the batter might be ruined! This is why most recipes list the ingredients at the beginning, so you can gather them on the counter before you start.

This isn't only true for recipes, but also holds true for crafts, toys, games, projects, and all sorts of procedures.

Materials are also important for safety as well. For instance, it would be very dangerous for someone to begin a science experiment without goggles and a lab coat to protect their eyes and clothing. Would you want your baby sister or brother attempting to ride a bike for the first time without a helmet or knee pads?

However, some how-to books don't necessarily require these materials. For example, "making a bed" or "doing a cartwheel" are examples where the materials are already there!

ALTERNATIVE

Demonstration: **Model for students how you create a "Things You Need" page for your how-to book.**

 |

GUIDE

Brainstorm a "Things You Need" page with students.

Let's try one together. I thought you could help me write "How to Make a Peanut Butter and Jelly Sandwich." First, what are the materials we need?

(Allow 1–4 minutes for students to turn and talk with partners. Write out exemplary responses. Listen carefully for missing items such as a plate or napkin.)

RELEASE

Remind students that they should consider using a "Things You Need" page for their how-to books.

So, writers, remember that when you work on your own how-to books, you may want to include a "Things You Need," "Materials," or "Ingredients" section at the beginning to help your readers either stay safe or gather the materials needed to complete the task easily.

FOR ADDITIONAL SUPPORT, TRY

6.1 Pictures Can Teach
6.13 What's Your Order?

TIPS/RESOURCES

- Have a collection of How-To mentor texts available that include "Materials" sections.
- Have students draw and label the objects in each step to cross-check their "Things You Need" section.

What's Your Order?

In this lesson, students learn to show order in several ways including: using pages in order, placing numbers in the picture box, using steps, using number words, or using sequence words.

Writing Stage: Any • **Genre:** How-To Book

INTRODUCE

Tell students that in most how-to books, sequence order is important.

For many how-to's, it is important that the steps be done in a very specific order. Today we are going to learn how writers either put their pages in order, use numbers in the picture box, or use steps, numerals, number words, or sequence words to help the reader follow along.

INSTRUCT

Explain with Examples

Show students the different ways that authors typically show sequence and order in how-to books.

Let me show you what I mean. When readers follow a how-to, many times steps cannot be skipped or done out of sequence. For example, you cannot put icing on a cupcake before you have baked it unless you want a messy treat with dripping icing all over it. However, the writer decides how they are going to show order based on their own style and how they want their how-to book to look when it's published. Here are some ways to show order:

(Create an anchor chart with the examples below.)

Pages in Order When an author is using only one step per page, they make sure that the pages in the book are in the right order.

Numbers in the Picture Box When an author uses pictures to show steps and/or when they put a few steps on a page, they sometimes put the number of the step in the top left corner of the picture box.

Steps When an author has either one or a few steps on a single page, they sometimes use the word *step* along with the number word or numeral to show the step number. Some authors use the number symbol (#) with the numeral.

Sequencing Words Some authors prefer to use words like *first*, *next*, *then*, *after that*, and *last* or *finally* to show order.

Some authors use a combination. For example, they can have their pages in order with one step per page, use the word *step* along with the number symbol and numeral, and use sequencing words, too! This way the order is very clear to the reader. Whichever way the author chooses to show order, they do it the same with each step of the book so that all the steps match.

 |

GUIDE

Prompt students to consider and plan how they will show sequence and order in their how-to books.

Now it's your turn to think about how you might show the order of steps in your how-to book. Will you just put the pages in order, use numbers in the picture box, use the word *step* along with numerals or number words, and/or use sequencing words? Will you use just one way or a few ways? Tell your partner which way you think fits your style.

(Allow 1–4 minutes for students to turn and talk with partners. Share exemplary responses.)

RELEASE

Remind students of the importance of order in most how-to books.

So remember that when you are writing your how-to books, it is very important that your readers follow the steps in order. There are many ways to show order and it all depends on your own style and how you want your how-to book to look when it's published.

FOR ADDITIONAL SUPPORT, TRY

5.6 Easy as 1, 2, 3 ...

5.7 Step by Step

5.8 You Missed a Step!

5.10 Step in Time!

TIPS/RESOURCES

- Have word banks displayed with sequencing words, number words, and the word *step* as a resource.
- Have a collection of how-to mentor texts available for students to see examples of how authors show order.

LESSON 6.14

What's Your POV?

In this lesson, students learn to consider the point of view they want to use to connect with an audience and to use it consistently.

Writing Stage: Any
Genre: List, Pattern, How-To Book, All-About Book, Feature Article, Literary Nonfiction, Expository Nonfiction

INTRODUCE

Tell students to consider the point of view they want to use throughout their writing.

Informational writers try to engage their readers in different ways, including topic choice, illustrations, and text features. Another way writers engage is through point of view. Authors decide, "Am I going to use *I*, *you* or *they*?" Once you choose a point of view, it is important to keep it consistent throughout the piece so you don't confuse your reader.

INSTRUCT

Demonstration

Model for students how you think about your topic, connecting it to the point of view that might best reach your audience.

Let me show you what I mean.

Emergent *(Display your book and flip through pages.)* Here's my book about dogs. What point of view do I want to use? On my first page I have, "Dogs can be big. Dogs can be little. They are many colors." That's using a third-person narrator. I sound like a teacher—like I really know what I'm talking about. I like that. However, I could change it to talk to the reader and say, "Your dog can be big. Your dog can be little." I'm not sure yet. I'm going to keep reading. The next page says, "Dogs like to play. You have to walk your dog every day." Hmm, that's different. On this page, I'm talking like a teacher: "Dogs like to play." But I'm also telling you what to do, so that doesn't match! I prefer talking like a teacher. So I'll say, "Dogs like to play. Dogs need to go on walks every day." *(Read more examples to stress consistency.)*

Transitional / Fluent *(Read aloud from your own writing.)* I'm going to look at this one part about dogs' senses: "Dogs and humans have the same senses, but some of a dog's senses are better than humans. I know that dogs have a keen sense of smell. They sniff out drugs, track missing persons, and find explosives. You can hide a treat for a dog and they will find it! There are differences between dogs, though. For example, I know a German shepherd or a bloodhound has a much better sense of smell than a pug or Boston terrier."

In this book, I want to sound like an expert. So maybe using the third person might be the better choice than having a first-person narrator (using *I*) because it gives an air of credibility.

ALTERNATIVE

Explain with Examples: **Use mentor texts to note and name a variety of points of view. Consider the benefits and drawbacks of each perspective.**

GUIDE

Prompt students to talk to their partners about how they will try the strategy in their own writing.

With your partner, talk about which point of view you want to use. Check your draft. Are you using that point of view? Are you using it consistently?

(Allow 1–4 minutes for students to turn and talk with partners. Share exemplary responses.)

RELEASE

Remind students to choose a consistent point of view that will appeal to their readers.

Remember, as you write today, choose the point of view that you think will connect with your reader, and make sure you use it consistently throughout your draft.

FOR ADDITIONAL SUPPORT, TRY

2.18 Be Consistent

2.19 Nouns and Verbs Must Get Along

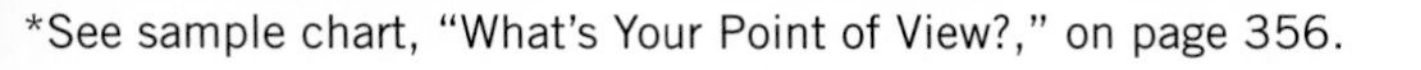

TIPS/RESOURCES

- Create an anchor chart with examples of points of view.*
- Notice how the writer addresses the reader during read-alouds.
- Play with point of view in shared writing.

*See sample chart, "What's Your Point of View?," on page 356.

LESSON 6.15

Be Specific

In this lesson, students learn to use precise language for nouns and action words so that readers can better visualize a piece of writing.

Writing Stage: Any • **Genre:** Any

INTRODUCE

Tell students that they can revise their work by using precise language for nouns and verbs.

When you're teaching, it's important that you're precise. When you're teaching about a topic, your reader needs to know exactly what you mean. Today I want to teach you to use precise language for nouns and verbs so that readers can better visualize the information you're teaching them.

INSTRUCT

Demonstration

Model for students how to use precise language for nouns and verbs.

Watch me as I read my writing. Notice when I need a precise word to help my readers visualize what I'm teaching them. I'm going to look particularly at the nouns and verbs I'm using. Remember, a noun is a person, place, or thing, and a verb is an action word.

Here is my book about my cats. This page says, "Cats eat food. They like to play with yarn." First, I will look at the nouns. "Cats eat food." *Food* is the noun. Can my reader see "food"? Food can look like a cheeseburger or a bowl of cat food. We know cats don't eat cheeseburgers! So I can change it to, "Cats eat _____." What do they eat? Cat food? Fish? Tuna? Those nouns are more precise. *Eat* is the action word. However, I could add another sentence using a more precise verb. I can write, "A cat who loves its food will gobble it up!"

The next part says, "They like to play with toys. Here the noun is *toys*. Can my reader see "toys"? What kind of toys? I could write, "Cats like to play with stuffed mice, crinkly balls, and ribbon." Now let's go back and look at the action words. One is *play*. That's what they're doing. But can my reader see how the cats play with these toys? They might bat with their paws or jump and pounce. I will write, "Cats like to pounce on stuffed mice, crinkly balls, and ribbon." Now, my reader can really see it!

ALTERNATIVE

Guided Practice: **With a shared draft, revise nouns and verbs together.**

GUIDE

Prompt students to try the strategy on another part of your demonstration piece.

Can you help me in this next part? The next part says, "Cats climb things. Cats look for food." With your partner, look at the nouns and the verbs and try to make them precise so that your reader can picture it in their minds.

(Allow 1–4 minutes for students to turn and talk with partners. Then have them share out exemplary responses such as changing things *to* trees. *If needed, scaffold identifying the nouns and verbs.)*

RELEASE

Remind students that precise nouns and verbs make their information clearer for the reader.

When you go off to write today, remember to draft or revise in ways that allow your reader to really see what you're teaching them. Use precise nouns and verbs—just like you helped me to do in my writing.

FOR ADDITIONAL SUPPORT, TRY

6.16 Everything Counts in Exact Amounts

6.18 What Does That Mean?

TIPS/RESOURCES

- Take the opportunity to teach grammatical terms (nouns and verbs).
- Add in conversations about adjectives and adverbs.
- Display charts for precise words; group words in categories; add images to clarify.

Everything Counts in Exact Amounts

In this lesson, students learn to give information related to time/duration, temperature, quantity, and quality.

Writing Stage: Any • **Genre:** Any

INTRODUCE

Tell students that they can revise by giving information related to time/duration, temperature, quantity, and quality.

When writers are teaching about a topic, they write with precision. Sometimes that means considering just the right word, adding definitions, or adding more information to make ideas clear. Today I want to teach you how we can add information to our pieces related to time or duration, temperature, amount, and/or quality.

INSTRUCT

Demonstration

Model for students how to add information by using categories.

Emergent Here's my picture of planting seeds—there's a shovel digging a hole, and I'm dropping the seed into the hole and covering it up with dirt. I wrote, "I dig a hole and put the seed in." To be exact, I can ask myself, "How long?" No, that doesn't work here. Maybe, "How many?" I didn't say how many seeds go in the hole. I can change it to, "I dig one hole and put one seed in it." That's more exact. Can I add anything else? Maybe something about the time of year. Oh! I know, "I plant seeds in the spring. I plant bulbs in the fall." *(Reread your updated sentences all together.)* I added exact information by asking myself questions like, "When? How long? How many? What kind? How hot or cold?"

Transitional / Fluent I wrote, "Start by choosing a place for your vegetable plot. Mark out the space and clear the soil. This means, get rid of grass and weeds, but also any rocks that might make it hard for vegetables to grow. If the soil needs improving, you can add topsoil soil to it, or even compost." Let me think about those categories—time or duration, temperature, amount or quality—to see what I can add to this part. Time. I didn't really say anything about when you should start preparing a garden. You can choose the plot at any time, but you should start digging in the spring. I can add that after the first sentence. Amount. Maybe that's thinking about how much space and how many plants you are going to grow? So I can add, "When making space for the plot, think about the crops you are going to grow. Tomatoes and lettuce don't require that much space, but corn does!"

ALTERNATIVE

Explain with Examples: **Using mentor texts, find examples that illustrate these categories.**

 |

GUIDE

Prompt students to try the strategy in their own writing with a partner.

Now it's your turn. Find a place in your draft and think about our categories of time, temperature, quantity, and quality. Ask yourself: "When? How long? How hot or cold? How many or how much? What kind?" When you find a place you want to try this work, give me a thumbs up.

(Allow 1–4 minutes for students to turn and talk with partners. Share exemplary responses.)

RELEASE

Remind students to try to add exact details to their writing.

When you revise today, look over all parts of your draft and think, "Where can I add exact details?" Ask yourself questions: "When? How long? How hot or cold? How many or how much? What kind?" Make those additions to help your reader learn even more about your topic.

FOR ADDITIONAL SUPPORT, TRY

6.15 Be Specific
6.18 What Does That Mean?
6.21 Say More
6.22 Use Your Senses

TIPS/RESOURCES

- Create an anchor chart showing the different categories: time/duration, temperature, quantity, and quality.
- If students need more support, in the Guide have them try it on a shared piece of writing.

Watch Out!

In this lesson, students learn to add tips, cautions, and warnings so the reader can be safe.

Writing Stage: Any • **Genre:** Any (but most often How-To Books)

INTRODUCE

Tell students one way to revise work is to add tips for what to look out for or be aware of.

Do you have that one person in your life who is very cautious? They're always thinking ahead to make sure you're safe. Sometimes when we're revising our informational writing, we can think about that cautious person in our lives and how they teach us. Today I want to teach you how we can add tips, cautions, and warnings to help our readers stay safe.

INSTRUCT

Demonstration

Model for students how to add more to your writing using tips, cautions, warnings, and advice.

Let me show you what I mean with my gardening draft. You might think, what's there to warn people about with gardening? But I'm going to challenge myself because that's how we grow. So I'm going to look at each part and try this strategy out.

Emergent Look at this page on why it's important to water plants. I wrote, "Plants need water and sun to live." What can I add? You can't hurt yourself watering a plant. Oh, wait! I know! Maybe it's not being careful about yourself, but being careful about the plant. Too much water can kill the plant. So I could add, "Don't pour in too much water! Too much water can kill a plant." Anything else? I can give a tip about the sun. I can say, "Watch out for too much sun. Too much sun can dry plants out."

Fluent Look at this first part about caring for vegetables in a garden. I wrote, "Companion planting is where you grow different kinds of plants together and those groupings benefit each other. The most famous example of companion planting originates with indigenous Americans. Known as the "three sisters," beans, corn, and squash work well together. Bean vines grow on the corn stalks and they provide nitrogen to the soil (which is good for plants). So what warnings can I give? I mean, you're not going to hurt yourself planting things together. Maybe I can think of what not to do? Wait! I read about some plants you shouldn't plant together. I could add, "Be careful not to plant onions or garlic near your peas and beans. Onions and garlic stunt the growth of those vegetables."

Do you see how I thought of warnings and cautions to add to my writing? Furthermore, I was able to add to parts of my writing that, at first glance, seemed fine to me.

ALTERNATIVE

Guided Practice: **Using a shared topic, add cautionary tips together.**

 |

GUIDE

Prompt students to talk through the strategy with a partner, giving them some sentence frames if they need support.

Now it's your turn to try this out. Take out your draft and quickly reread one part. Now push yourself to think, "What caution can I add? I could say, Watch out for _____, or Make sure _____, or Don't _____."

(Allow 1–4 minutes for students to talk through their "Watch out!" additions with partners. Share exemplary responses.)

RELEASE

Remind students they can add tips to watch out for in all parts of their drafts.

When you revise today, challenge yourself to look at all parts of your draft. Think about what tips, cautions, warnings, or advice you can give your reader. Remember, even if you think there's nothing dangerous, maybe you can suggest something to your reader that will make them more successful at whatever it is you're teaching them.

FOR ADDITIONAL SUPPORT, TRY

6.15 Be Specific

6.16 Everything Counts in Exact Amounts

6.21 Say More

TIPS/RESOURCES

- Chart some sentence frames such as:
  - It's important to _____.
  - Don't forget _____.
  - Be careful _____.
  - Watch out for _____.

What Does That Mean?

In this lesson, students learn to use domain-specific words and terms. They will embed definitions in the sentence, with a call out, or by adding a glossary.

Writing Stage: Any • **Genre:** Any

INTRODUCE

Tell students that one way they can revise their writing is to use domain-specific words.

I love our nonfiction reading units because I'm always learning! I now know an octopus is a cephalopod and that there's a "barking" frog—the Barking Tree Frog! As you learn more about a topic, you all become teachers, helping me learn cool facts and new words. Today I want to teach you that we can revise our writing by embedding definitions within a sentence, in a sidebar, or in a glossary.

INSTRUCT

Demonstration

Model for students how to add domain-specific language.

Emergent Here's my draft about fish. On the first page I write, "Fish swim in water." My next page reads, "Fish breathe in water." I don't know that I can add a topic word to this sentence because everyone knows those words. Let me look at my labels. Here is my drawing of a fish. I could use domain-specific words to label the parts of the fish. I'll add *fin* and *tail*. What else on their bodies helps them swim? They don't have skin, but they have scales. I can add that to my drawing. (*Quickly label drawing.*) Now I need to think, "Will my readers know what those are? Should I add a glossary or a text box?" I could add that scales protect the fish so readers know what they are. I can put that in a text box here on the side.

Transitional / Fluent Here's my draft about fish. "All fish live in water and have a backbone. Beyond that, they are all very different and diverse. They breathe through gills and have fins and scales. They are all cold-blooded. Fish have been on the earth for more than 500 million years!" I am using some specific terms, like *gills*, *fins*, and *scales*. But I also think there is a domain-specific word for things with backbones—*vertebrates*. I could say, "All fish live in water and have a backbone or are part of a group called *vertebrates*." Another way I could add it is to say: "All fish live in water and are *vertebrates* (have a backbone)." Or I could say, "All fish live in water and are *vertebrates*." I could then make a glossary at the back, or a text box on this page, that defines *vertebrates*.

ALTERNATIVE

Guided Practice: **Using a shared topic, stop and work with students to add domain-specific language to a draft.**

 |

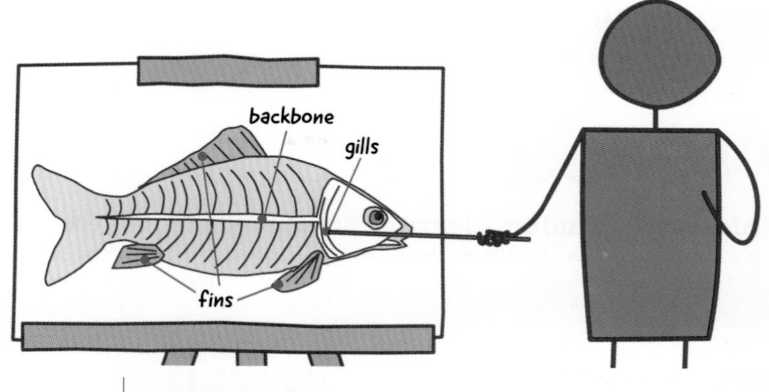

GUIDE

Prompt students to try the strategy with a partner.

Now let's look at this next part of my piece. Can you help me use the strategy here?

Emergent Here's the next page: "Fish breathe in water." What topic words can I add here—either in the sentence, the label, or a callout box or glossary?

(Allow 1–4 minutes for students to turn and talk with partners. Share exemplary responses.)

Transitional / Fluent Let's look at this part: "They breathe through gills and have fins and scales. They are all cold-blooded. Fish have been on the earth for more than 500 million years!"

(Allow 1–4 minutes for students to turn and talk with partners. Share exemplary responses.)

RELEASE

Remind students how and why to add domain-specific language.

When you're revising today, look for places where you can teach your reader more by adding domain-specific language. Try it in a sentence, a glossary, or a callout box.

FOR ADDITIONAL SUPPORT, TRY

6.16 Everything Counts in Exact Amounts

6.20 Extend Your Facts

TIPS/RESOURCES

- Use a topic everyone knows about but that students are unlikely to write about on their own.
- Allow transitional and fluent writers to use quick research to add to their writing.
- Stress key punctuation: commas, parenthesis, etc.

LESSON 6.19

We Can Do It

In this lesson, students learn to act out the steps in their writing to make sure nothing is left out.

Writing Stage: Any • **Genre:** How-To Book

INTRODUCE

Tell students one way to revise a how-to book is to act it out themselves or with a partner.

If there's one thing that's important in a how-to book, it's that your reader can actually do what you're teaching them. But sometimes, when we're teaching someone something we know how to do really well, it can be easy to miss a step. Today I want to teach you that one way to make sure this doesn't happen is to act out the process. We can do this on our own or have a partner act it out while we watch and guide.

INSTRUCT

Demonstration

Model for students how you perform the steps of your own how-to book to check for missed steps or inaccuracies. Make additions and changes as needed.

Watch me as I act out my steps. My how-to book is for new students, helping them learn how to come into our classroom and get ready for the day. Step one says, "Walk into the classroom." Now it says, "Put your backpack on the peg with your name on the back wall." Wait a minute. Acting this out, I'm noticing that there are a lot more steps to this. I have to look at the back wall, walk there, take my backpack off, look for the peg with my name, *then* put the backpack on the peg. Wait, now all of my stuff is in the backpack! And my next step says, "Bring anything you need for class to your desk." I have to move that. I should take my stuff out before I hang it up. So let me make some changes. Now my how-to steps read "1. Walk into the classroom. There is a row of pegs on the back wall. 2. Look for the peg with your name. 3. Take your backpack off and take out any books or materials you need for class. 4. Hang your backpack up on the peg. 5. Take your books to your desk."

(Act out the steps again and make any other additions you see necessary.)

Did you see how, when I acted it out, I saw the steps that were missing?

ALTERNATIVE

Guided Practice: **Using a shared topic, have students serve as your writing partners, acting out the steps of your how-to book.**

GUIDE

Prompt students to try it out on another part of a shared how-to topic.

Now it's your turn. Consider the steps for getting ready to go to P.E. Partner A, you're going to act it out. Partner B, you're going to think about the changes you need to make.

(Allow students a few minutes to act out and make the additions they suggest. Have them try again with Partner B acting it out and Partner A noticing changes. Have students share any additions and make those to the shared how-to text.)

RELEASE

Remind students they can act out individually or with a partner.

Today when you go off to revise, act out your how-to's—either on your own or with a partner. Notice if there are steps missing, or if steps need to be more detailed. Remember, the whole point of a how-to book is for your reader to be able to accomplish the task or topic you are teaching, without question or difficulty.

FOR ADDITIONAL SUPPORT, TRY

6.5 Make It Move
6.7 Make It Match
6.12 Get Your Things
6.13 What's Your Order?

TIPS/RESOURCES

- Assign partners so that students can switch roles.
- Act out every small detail in a step.
- If students have all of the steps, help them use more precise language.

Extend Your Facts

In this lesson, students learn to start with a fact, then write a second sentence to add more information.

Writing Stage: Any • **Genre:** Any

INTRODUCE

Tell students that they can build on facts by adding a second sentence.

As we write about our topics, we need to think about how we can expand on our facts. We want to be careful to make sure we stay on topic and connect our ideas. One way we can do this is by starting with a fact and then adding a second sentence to say more about that fact.

INSTRUCT

Demonstration

Model for students how to write a fact about the topic and then add a second sentence. Think aloud how you use the first fact to stay on topic.

First, I start with a fact about my topic. Then I add a second sentence to say more about that fact.

Emergent / Transitional Here I have my book about transportation. *(Hold up your booklet.)* I am starting this page about trains. Let me think of a fact about trains and then I will add a second sentence to match that fact. I know trains have big engines, so that will be the fact I include in the first sentence. *(Quickly jot down the sentence "Trains have engines.")* Now let me think of a second sentence that matches this fact. Let me reread the first sentence: "Trains have engines." I am going to start with the word *engines.* I'll write,"Engines are big and loud." *(Quickly jot down the sentence.)* Did you see how I wrote down a fact and then added a second sentence to match that fact?

Fluent *(This can be demonstrated in your notebook or on drafting paper.)* Here I have been writing about the benefits of martial arts. I wrote, "Martial arts is an activity that promotes a healthy lifestyle because it improves cardiovascular activity." Now let me think about how I can say more by adding another sentence. In my first sentence, what am I mainly talking about? Am I talking about how martial arts is fun? Or the different types of martial arts? No, I am talking about how martial arts help you have a healthy lifestyle. How about "Martial arts' moves and techniques help improve your reflexes and flexibility"? That connects back to the first fact about martial arts helping you improve cardiovascular activity. Did you see how I wrote a fact and added another sentence by connecting it to the first fact? I can even add a third or fourth sentence for more information!

ALTERNATIVE

Guided Practice: **Using a shared topic or your own writing, guide students to help you write a fact and then add a sentence that builds on or elaborates that fact.**

 |

GUIDE

Prompt students to try the strategy using their own ideas.

Now it's your turn to give it a try. Look at your writing and think about what you want to say. What is the first fact you will write? Then what is a second sentence you can add to connect to that fact? *(For fluent writers, have them jot it down in their notebooks. For emergent writers, have them list the sentences on their fingers and encourage them to come up with a third or fourth sentence.)*

(Allow 1–4 minutes for students to turn and talk with partners. Share exemplary responses.)

RELEASE

Remind students to have their sentences build on one another.

Today, when you're writing, keep in mind that you want to try to extend your facts and not jump around from one idea to the next. You can come up with one fact for your first sentence and then add a second sentence to say more about that fact. If you come up with a second sentence, try for a third or even a fourth!

FOR ADDITIONAL SUPPORT, TRY

6.21 Say More
6.29 Tell Me More, Tell Me More
6.38 So What?

TIPS/RESOURCES

- Jot down some guiding questions on an anchor chart:
  - Does my second sentence connect to the first?
  - Does it say something similar or different?
  - Can I come up with a third or fourth sentence?
- Use mentor texts that match the level of your students' writing.

Say More

In this lesson, students learn to use sentence starters *All, Most, Some, Many,* and *Few* to elaborate ideas.

Writing Stage: Any
Genre: List, How-To Book, All-About Book, Feature Article, Literary Nonfiction, Expository Nonfiction, Research Report

INTRODUCE

Tell students that they will learn how to use sentence starters to elaborate ideas and make comparisons.

As writers, we are always thinking about how we can say more about our topic to give the reader more information. We also want to think about the different ways we can start our sentences to make our writing engaging for readers. To help us do this, we can start our sentences with the words *all, most, some, many,* and *few* to elaborate our ideas.

INSTRUCT

Demonstration

Model for students how you say more about your topic by using sentence starters.

Watch me as I use sentence starters like *all, most, some, many,* and *few* to elaborate and compare my topic and ideas. *(Have the list of sentence starters written out and visible so students can see them during the lesson.*)*

Emergent / Transitional I am working on my book about transportation. *(Hold up your booklet.)* On this page, I am writing about trains. I would like to say more by using one of the sentence starters here on our list. I already wrote, "Trains have engines." I know that different trains have different types of engines—some are big, small, loud, quiet. So maybe I can add, "Most trains have big engines. Some engines are loud." *(Quickly add the two new sentences to your book.)* Now let me read what I have so far: "Trains have engines. Most trains have big engines. Some engines are loud." Wow, my writing sounds much better now that I added more information.

Fluent I am working on my writing about martial arts. Here I wrote, "Martial arts is an activity that promotes a healthy lifestyle because it improves cardiovascular strength." Maybe I can say more by adding details on how it improves your body and on specific martial arts moves. I will write, "Most martial arts moves improve aim, reflexes, and flexibility. *Some* punches, *like* jabs and cross punches, improve aim and reflexes. A *few* of the moves, such as spin kicks and punches, are difficult yet powerful moves to improve speed and flexibility." *(Quickly add the sentences to your writing.)*

ALTERNATIVE

Explain with Examples: **Gather a few different examples of how authors use similar sentence starters to say more about their topics.**

 |

GUIDE

Prompt students to try the strategy with a partner.

Now it's your turn to give it a try. What is something about your topic that you can say using the words *all*, *most*, *some*, *many*, or *few*? Or, what is something you can compare to show the difference between ideas?

(Allow 1–4 minutes for students to turn and talk with partners. Share exemplary responses.)

RELEASE

Remind students that as they write they can use the sentence starters to say more about their topic.

Today, as you write, I want you to think about the different ways you can say more about your topic. You can refer to this list of sentence starters to expand your ideas and give your reader more information about your topic.

FOR ADDITIONAL SUPPORT, TRY

6.29 Tell Me More, Tell Me More
6.32 What's It Like?
6.39 I Don't Know What Else to Say!

TIPS/RESOURCES

- Write starter words in different colors so they stand out.
- Add words to the class word wall. Use different colored paper so they can be found easily.

*See sample chart, "Words That Help Us Say More," on page 357.

Use Your Senses

In this lesson, students learn to add information to their writing by giving details related to size, shape, color, number, texture, sound, flavor, and scent.

Writing Stage: Any • **Genre:** Any

INTRODUCE

Tell students that today they will learn how to add more details to their writing by using their senses.

Imagine you are ordering ice cream. Do you just say, "I would like an ice cream sundae." Or, do you describe the kind of sundae you would like? By giving these extra details, you will get the exact sundae you imagined ... hopefully! As writers, we need to think about how we can add more information to our writing. We can do this by using our senses.

INSTRUCT

Demonstration

Show students how you use your senses to add more details to your writing.

Emergent / Transitional Here I have my writing about the octopus. I wrote, "This is an octopus. It lives in the ocean." Now let me use my senses to add details. Let me think about what the octopus looks like; its body is round and it has eight legs. It has two eyes and it changes color. So I can add that to my writing. Now let me think about the other senses. This might be a little tricky. I don't know how an octopus feels because I have never touched one nor do I know how it smells. Let me go back to what it looks like and try to push my thinking to say more. Perhaps I can add more about its size. I know that the octopus can be as small as your hand and as big as a school bus—so let me add that to my writing. Wow, look at how much information I added using only one of my senses!

Fluent Here I have my writing about the beach. Let me use my senses and think about the beach. The only sense that might not work is taste, but I am going to give the rest a try. First, what do I see? I see waves crashing on the shore, seagulls hovering over the water, and boats on the horizon. I also see the dunes, which look like they're slowly disappearing. I see crushed shells mixed with driftwood, seaweed, and garbage. What do I hear? I hear the waves crashing and the seagulls calling out to each other. What do I feel? I feel the warm, fine sand under my feet. I feel the cool ocean breeze and the sun on my face. What do I smell? I can smell low tide ... which means it smells a little fishy and stinky! Wow, by using my senses, I was able to think of so many details that I can add to my writing!

ALTERNATIVE

Explain with Examples: **Gather a few different examples of how authors use different senses to add details to their writing.**

 |

GUIDE

Prompt students to work with a partner and describe a familiar topic using their five senses.

Now let's practice using a shared topic: pizza. Using your five senses, what details can we include in our writing? What does pizza look like? Taste like? Smell like? Feel like?

(Allow 1–4 minutes for students to turn and talk with partners. Share exemplary responses.)

RELEASE

Remind students to use their five senses as they add detail to their writing.

As you write today, keep in mind that you don't have to use all five senses since some senses can't be used for certain topics. Most of the time you can add a lot of details by just thinking about one or two senses.

FOR ADDITIONAL SUPPORT, TRY

6.15 Be Specific

6.16 Everything Counts in Exact Amounts

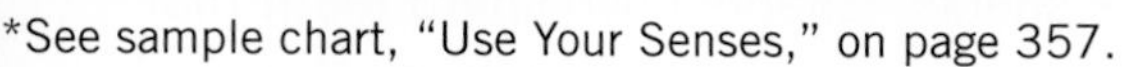
6.29 Tell Me More, Tell Me More

TIPS/RESOURCES

- Quickly review the five senses if necessary.
- Create an anchor chart that illustrates the five senses with guiding questions.*
- Make a game where you use your senses to describe something, and have students guess what it is.

*See sample chart, "Use Your Senses," on page 357.

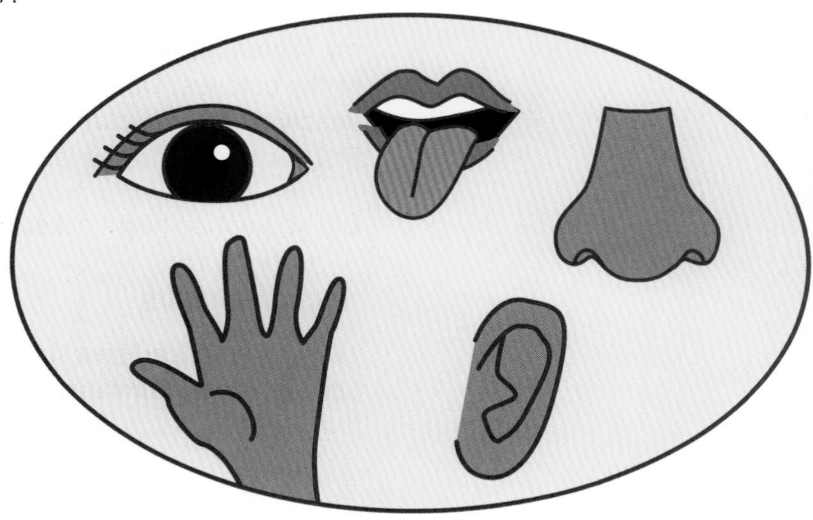

Do They Fit?

In this lesson, students learn to look across their writing to make sure that the pages, or the sentences on each page, fit with the topic.

Writing Stage: Emergent, Transitional • **Genre:** List, Pattern, All-About Book

INTRODUCE

Tell students that they will look at their writing and determine if every page or sentence fits well with the topic.

Now that our books are full of information, it's time to ask ourselves if everything fits. Think about when you go to the grocery store and how it is organized. For example, I know that all the bread will be in one aisle and the fruits and veggies will be in another. If the bread and fruits were together, that would be strange! Today we are going to look across our writing to make sure that the pages, or the sentences on each page, fit with our topic.

INSTRUCT

Demonstration

Show students how you read your writing and ask yourself if the information fits.

Watch me ask myself if everything fits. *(Read aloud from your own book.)*

List and Pattern Books I am going to name my topic and as I read each page, I will ask myself, "Does that fit?" Here I have my book about transportation. Let me read one page at a time to make sure everything connects back to transportation. "Here is a bus." Does that fit with my topic? Yes! A bus is a form of transportation. Let me go to the next page and do the same thing. "Here is a bike." Does that fit? Yes! It does—a bike is another form of transportation. Let me keep going. "Here is a remote-control car." My topic is transportation. Is a remote-control car a type of transportation? Nope, it doesn't fit. I am going to take that page out of my book!

All-About Books Let me look at my book, *All About Octopuses.* As I read each page, I will make sure my sentences all connect to the main idea on that page. I will look at this section called "Octopus Enemies." I have written, "Octopuses have many enemies. Some enemies are deadly, such as sharks. Sharks have sharp teeth that can cut right through the octopus. Sharks are deadly enemies." Do my sentences fit together? Well, each sentence is about the enemies of the octopus. Do I repeat anything? I think I wrote that sharks are deadly twice. *(Quickly reread the sentences again.)* Yes, I did. In the first sentence and the last, so I will remove the last sentence.

Did you notice how I asked myself if all my information fit?

ALTERNATIVE

Guided Practice: **Have students help you go through your writing and decide if the information fits well together.**

GUIDE

Read aloud a demonstration text and have students turn and talk about how well the information aligns with the topic.

(Prior to this lesson, create an additional demonstration text in the same genre as your students.)

We are going to do some of this work together. This time you and your partner will think about how well the information fits together.

(Read aloud the demo text. Allow students 1–4 minutes to turn and talk with partners. While they are talking, repeat aloud the questions: "Does it fit with _____?" "Was anything repeated?" After a few minutes, share out some of their ideas.)

RELEASE

Remind students of the importance of making sure all the information fits.

As we write, we should always think about the clarity and organization of our writing. To do this, we need to reread our writing. Today take a closer look at your writing and ask yourself, "Does that fit?" Move or remove any parts that don't fit with the topic.

FOR ADDITIONAL SUPPORT, TRY

6.24 Out of Order

6.25 Check It Together

TIPS/RESOURCES

- Share more examples during Introduce or Instruct if students need support.
- Slow down the process for transitional writers with multiple sections in their writing.

Out of Order

In this lesson, students learn to consider changing the order of their pages so that they go in time order, size order, or natural order.

Writing Stage: Emergent, Transitional • **Genre:** List, Pattern, How-To Book, All-About Book

INTRODUCE

Tell students that they will consider changing the order of their pages to improve organization.

What happens when things are out of order? Imagine you're baking a cake. Can I just jump right in and start frosting it? No! I have to follow a certain order. I have to mix the ingredients together, then bake it, and after that I can frost it! As writers, we need to make sure we consider the order our pages are in so that our writing makes sense and isn't confusing to our reader. We can think about time order, size order, natural order, or another way that makes the most sense to present the information about our topic.

INSTRUCT

Demonstration

Show students how you look at your writing and consider the order of the pages—thinking about time order, size order, or the way that makes the most sense.

Watch me as I think about the order of my pages.

List and Pattern Books Here is my book about transportation. Let me read my book. "This is a bus. It has wheels. This is a train. It has an engine. This is a car. It has four tires. This is an airplane. It can fly. This is a bike. It has two wheels." I am going to take my pages and lay them out in front of me so I can shuffle them around in different orders. I don't think time order would work because time isn't connected to my topic of transportation. What about size order? That could work—I could reorder my pages to go from the smallest to biggest. Or slowest to fastest, which would be bike, bus, car, train, airplane. (*Read aloud your book in the new order.*) Now my book follows an order that makes sense.

All-About Books Here is my book about the octopus. The first page is my introduction, so that makes sense to go first. Then the rest of my book is laid out like this: "Octopus Enemies," "Different Types of Octopuses," "What Octopuses Eat," "Fun Facts," and "Hiding and Escaping." This order seems a little confusing. Let me lay out the pages and see what order makes more sense. After my introduction, it would probably make more sense to move to "Different Types of Octopuses" and "What Octopuses Eat" so that my reader can learn some general information about octopuses. Now I have a few pages left to figure out. I think moving "Octopus Enemies" next would make sense and then "Hiding and Escaping." That way my reader learns about the enemies and then how octopuses hide and escape. Then my last page is "Fun Facts."

Did you see how I looked at my writing and asked myself if the order makes sense? Laying out the pages helped me think about the different ways I can order my pages so that my writing is clear and organized.

ALTERNATIVE

Explain with Examples: **Use examples from mentor texts to show how authors organize their pages to go in a certain order.**

 |

GUIDE

Prompt students to try out a few ways to organize the book to find the best fit.

Now it's your turn to try. Look at your books and decide if the order makes sense. If not, try on a different organization. What order might make your writing clearer and more organized?

(Allow 1–4 minutes for students to turn and talk with partners. Share exemplary responses.)

RELEASE

Remind students the importance of considering the order of the pages in their books.

As you continue to work on your writing, think about the order of your pages. We want to make sure our writing is organized in a way that is clear and makes the most sense. We can order our pages by time, size, natural order, or the way that makes the most sense.

FOR ADDITIONAL SUPPORT, TRY

6.23 Do They Fit?

6.25 Check It Together

TIPS/RESOURCES

- Create an anchor chart that lists and shows the different orders: time, number order, size order, or natural order.

Check It Together

In this lesson, students learn to read with their partner and ask, "What can I add or change on each page/section?" and "Does the order of my pages/sections make sense?"

Writing Stage: Any • **Genre:** Any

INTRODUCE

Tell students that they will work with a partner to give suggestions on what to revise or remove.

Sometimes when we are looking at our own writing, it can be a little tricky to find the places that need some revision. As writers, we know the importance of revising our writing because it's how we make sure the writing is clear. It can be helpful to have a fresh eye so that you can be nudged to add, change, or remove parts of your writing to make it even better than it already is! We are going to work with our partners and read each other's writing.

INSTRUCT

Explain with Examples

Explain a process for students to use to revise each other's work.

Today we are going to help each other revise our writing by using some questions to guide us. For example, if I am reading my partner's writing about the octopus and on one page they are writing about how the octopus hides and escapes, but then they also have details about what they eat, I might suggest that they move that to a different section. Or if I come to a part where they forgot to add details, I might suggest adding more information. If I find a part that seems repetitive, I can suggest removing that part.

(Have a premade anchor chart with a process and guiding questions similar to those below.)

This is the process we will follow for today's lesson. You will complete it twice, once for your writing and then for your partner's writing.

- First, you will take out your writing. You can either read it to your partner or let them read it themselves. Read one page or section at a time.
- Then, using the anchor chart, ask your partner some of the questions and listen to their suggestions.
- Last, make some revisions to your writing!

As you read your partner's writing, think about if it makes sense. Is the writing clear? Is any information missing? Is any of it confusing? What can be added to make it clearer? Does anything need to be moved? Or removed? Does anything repeat? You can use these questions to help guide your partner work.

ALTERNATIVE

Demonstration: **Using your own writing and a partner, show students how you give each other feedback using a specific process.**

GUIDE

Ask students to work with a partner to read each other's writing and offer suggestions.

Let's start this work together. Take out your writing and get ready to work with your partner. Using the process I just described and the questions we have on our chart, take a look at each other's writing and start checking it together.

(Allow students a few minutes to start this work. Voice over as they work to remind them of the possible suggestions they can offer their partners.)

RELEASE

Remind students that working with a partner is one way they can revise their writing.

Today we focused on how we can check our writing together with a partner to help make our writing clearer and more organized. As you continue to write, think about some of the suggestions your partner gave you and how you can incorporate them into your writing. If you need more time to read each other's writing, you can take that time now. Remember, we have our chart with the questions to consider as you read your partner's writing. We are here to help each other and make our writing even better than before!

FOR ADDITIONAL SUPPORT, TRY

1.22 Partners Are Resources, Too!
6.23 Do They Fit?
6.24 Out of Order
6.39 I Don't Know What Else to Say!

TIPS/RESOURCES

- It would be helpful if students are familiar with lessons 6.23 and 6.24.
- For fluent writers, encourage them to use self-stick notes to flag the places in their partner's writing where they notice something to prepare for a partner conference.
- Prior to this lesson, students should have an understanding of what it means to revise their writing.

Invite Your Reader

In this lesson, students learn to create an introduction that explains why they chose the topic and why it matters.

Writing Stage: Any

Genre: How-To Book, All-About Book, Feature Article, Literary Nonfiction, Expository Nonfiction, Research Report, Biography, Expository Essay

INTRODUCE

Tell students that an introduction can help orient the reader to what they will learn about and why.

Nonfiction writers don't just jump to the facts about a topic, they warm up their readers with an introduction. Introductions help readers understand why an author might have written about a particular topic and what they want their readers to learn.

INSTRUCT

Demonstration

Using your own topic, model how you create an introduction.

Watch me create an introduction for my topic.

Emergent / Transitional If I were writing an introduction to my book about ice cream, I would consider why I chose to write about this topic. Well, I chose this topic because I love ice cream! Then I think, "What is my reader going to learn in this book?" I will write about different flavors, toppings, and ways to eat ice cream. So my introduction might go:

> "Do you love ice cream as much as I do? I bet you do. Most people LOVE ice cream! Read on to find out all the different kinds of ice cream that exist. Learn about toppings. Learn about all the different ways to eat ice cream. By the end, you will scream for ice cream!"

Fluent If I am writing an introduction to my book about sharks, I need to consider, "What do I want my reader to understand?" For starters, I want people to know that sharks aren't the killers movies make them out to be. My sections share that not all sharks are predators, that most sharks only feed on plankton, and that shark attacks are rare. Perhaps my introduction should sound like this:

> "Sharks are one of the most misunderstood creatures of the sea. They are often portrayed as man-eating monsters , yet most only eat plankton. More importantly, very few humans have ever been attacked by sharks. Read on to learn how these myths give sharks an unwarranted reputation."

Do you see how my introduction gives the main ideas that I want the reader to think about?

ALTERNATIVE

Explain with Examples: **Briefly read aloud the introductions to a few mentor texts and ask students to think about what the author wants readers to gain from the text.**

GUIDE

Ask students to think about introductions for their own topics.

Now it's your turn. Take a moment to think about these questions:

- Why did you choose to write about this topic?
- What main idea(s) do you plan to teach your readers about this topic?

(Allow students 1–4 minutes to turn and talk with partners. Share exemplary responses.)

RELEASE

Remind students that introductions help prime a reader for what they will learn and why.

So remember, when you are writing about a topic, avoid jumping right into the facts. Instead, you want to give your readers a heads up to what they are going to learn and why you think it's important. This way, you set your reader up for the big things you want them to know and learn.

FOR ADDITIONAL SUPPORT, TRY

6.27 Make It Playful

6.28 New Beginnings

TIPS/RESOURCES

- Use a shared-writing experience to write an introduction with students who need more support.
- Provide sentence frames for students who need additional support.

Make It Playful

In this lesson, students learn to create an introduction that uses a poem, song, chant, or riddle to engage and interest the reader.

Writing Stage: Any

Genre: How-To Book, All-About Book, Feature Article, Literary Nonfiction, Expository Nonfiction, Research Report, Biography, Expository Essay

INTRODUCE

Tell students that writers sometimes introduce a topic playfully to engage their readers.

Some nonfiction writers get their readers excited to learn about their topics by writing catchy introductions. Today we are going to learn how to use a poem, song, chant, or riddle to grab your readers' attention.

INSTRUCT

Explain with Examples

Use multiple texts with different types of introductions to show students a variety of ways writers engage their readers.

If writers want to introduce their topics seriously, they will often write an introduction that gives background information. However, if writers want to spark a reader's curiosity through mystery or playfulness, they might begin the piece in a way that mixes in fun facts. Let me show you. In the National Geographic Kids book, *Frogs!*, by Elizabeth Carney[1], she begins with a poem. In it, she writes:

Splish, splash.

What is that sound?

What is hopping and jumping around?

What loves to swim?

What loves to eat bugs?

It's a frog!

Can you hop like a frog?

In the Read, Listen, and Wonder book, *Tigress*, by Nick Dawson[2], he begins with riddle-like questions. He writes:

Twigs with whiskers?

A tree with a tail?

Or is it a tigress hiding?

Do you see how the first writer opened with a playful poem and the other with mysterious questions like a riddle? Writers make these decisions about tone based on their audience.

ALTERNATIVE

Demonstration: **Using your own topic, create different introductions and explain how you would decide which one to use.**

GUIDE

Use a shared-writing experience to create an introduction together.

Let's write a playful introduction for the topic of ice cream—a chant and a song to see which we like best. Can you think of a popular chant for ice cream?

(Give students time to turn and talk to think of the "I scream. You scream. We all scream for ice cream!" chant.)

Let's try a song. Although a little trickier, we can make it easier by writing a piggy-back song to an old tune, such as "Frère Jacques" (Brother John).

(Allow students 1–4 minutes to turn and talk with partners. Share responses that work well to create an original song.)

RELEASE

Remind students to consider a tone for their introductions.

As you write introductions for your own topics, consider the tone you want to use. It often depends upon the topic. For example, if you are writing about a serious topic like pets being abandoned, you probably would take on a serious tone. You might even consider trying a few different techniques to see which fits best.

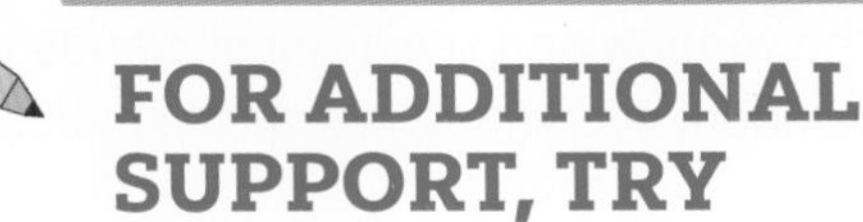

FOR ADDITIONAL SUPPORT, TRY

6.11 Say Hello and Goodbye
6.26 Invite Your Reader
6.28 New Beginnings

TIPS/RESOURCES

- Create an anchor chart with examples of riddles, songs, poems, chants, or rhymes.
- Encourage students to share with the class creative openings they come across in their reading.

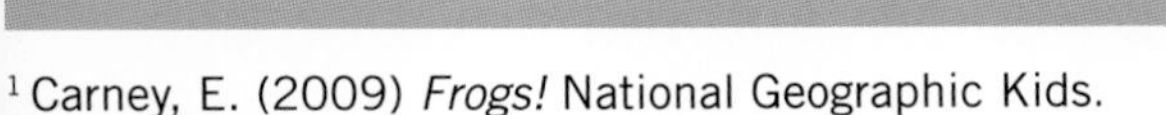

[1] Carney, E. (2009) *Frogs!* National Geographic Kids.
[2] Dawson, N. (2008) *Tigress.* Candlewick Press.

LESSON 6.28

New Beginnings

In this lesson, students learn to write an introduction that speaks to the reader: defining the topic, providing background information, posing a question, using imagery, or sharing surprising facts.

Writing Stage: Transitional, Fluent

Genre: How-To Book, All-About Book, Feature Article, Literary Nonfiction, Expository Nonfiction, Research Report, Biography, Expository Essay

INTRODUCE

Tell students that nonfiction writers introduce their topics in a variety of ways.

Today we are going to learn that introductions can define the topic, provide background information, pose a question, paint a picture of a scene, or use interesting, surprising, or startling facts that grab the reader's attention.

INSTRUCT

Demonstration

Using your own topic, model for students how different introductions have different intentions.

Watch as I share a few ways I could write an introduction for a book on airplanes. *(Display the examples below.)*

If my book focused on what airplanes were, I would just define the topic:

> "Airplanes are fix-winged aircrafts that are pushed forward by the force of jet engines or propellers. Planes come in many shapes, sizes, and wing types. Read on to learn more about these fascinating flying machines."

If I wanted to teach about their history, I would use background information: "People have dreamed of flying throughout time. However, flying only became a possibility in the last 200 years."

Let's say I want to focus on the science behind planes. Then I would pose a question: "Have you ever looked up into the sky and wondered how does that gigantic, 735,000 pound machine stay up in the sky?"

If I wanted to teach about safety, I might paint a picture for the reader:

> "You're sitting comfortably enjoying your peanuts and watching your favorite movie. You look out the window and see a sea of clouds. You lean back and smile. All of a sudden, everything begins to shake. The airplane rumbles ..."

Lastly, if I wanted to argue that flying is safe, I might use interesting or surprising facts: "Did you know that 80 percent of the population is scared to fly? It makes sense when you think about how unnatural it seems for a 735,000-pound flying machine to cross the Atlantic. But do you realize that you have a greater chance of dying from lightning?"

ALTERNATIVE

Explain with Examples: **Select a variety of mentor texts with different introductions. Discuss each author's intentions.**

GUIDE

Prompt students to consider introduction styles for their pieces.

Now it's your turn to consider what kind of introduction would work for you. With your partner, decide which introduction(s) you might try.

(Allow students 1–4 minutes to turn and talk with partners. Share exemplary responses.)

RELEASE

Remind students to consider their intentions when selecting an introduction.

Remember, consider what you are trying to show your reader about your topic. Try a few different ones to see which fits best.

FOR ADDITIONAL SUPPORT, TRY

6.11 Say Hello and Goodbye

6.26 Invite Your Reader

6.27 Make It Playful

TIPS/RESOURCES

- Have students try different introductions on quarter sheets of drafting paper. This way they can attach the one they like best to their drafts.

LESSON 6.29

Tell Me More, Tell Me More

In this lesson, students learn to start with a topic sentence and then elaborate by explaining with definitions, descriptions, or examples.

Writing Stage: Any • **Genre:** Any

INTRODUCE

Tell students that informational writers use definitions, descriptions, and examples to explain information.

When a reader is learning new information, they don't always know enough about a topic to fully understand it. This is why it is important for nonfiction writers to explain things to their readers. Today we are going to learn how writers use definitions, descriptions, and examples to explain and elaborate to better inform the reader.

INSTRUCT

Demonstration

Explain the difference between a definition, a description, and an example.

Let me show you how I explain information by using a definition (which tells what something means), a description (which describes it using one or more senses), and/or examples (which name different kinds).

If I were writing about the octopus' diet, I might start with a fact or topic sentence that says, "Octopuses eat shellfish." Many of you might know what shellfish are but some of you may not, so I will explain. First, I will use a definition to say what the word *shellfish* means: "Shellfish are different kinds of fish that have their skeletons on the outside of their bodies." This might be confusing for some to understand, so I will add a description to help them see what that looks like, such as, "These fish usually have a hard body or shell." Now, if I provide my reader with examples, this will help them get a better understanding of different kinds of shellfish, such as, "Some examples are shrimp, lobsters, crabs, scallops, mussels, and clams."

Did you see how I took one simple fact and added to it so that the reader can better understand? I was able to turn one sentence about shellfish into four whole sentences that define, describe, and give examples.

I don't always need to use all three strategies. Sometimes just using a definition, description, or example on its own is enough to make the fact clearer.

ALTERNATIVE

Explain with Examples: **Using examples from mentor texts, explain how authors use definitions, descriptions, and examples.**

GUIDE

Prompt students to come up with a definition, description, and example with a shared-writing topic. Record responses on chart paper.

Let's imagine we are writing about how to eat ice cream. In this section, the word *cone* might appear. What if someone didn't know what an ice cream cone was? How could we define it?

(Allow students 1–4 minutes to turn and talk with partners. Share exemplary responses.)

Now, what does it look like or taste like?

(Allow students 1–4 minutes to turn and talk with partners. Share exemplary responses.)

Can we add examples of different kinds of cones?

(Allow students 1–4 minutes to turn and talk with partners. Share exemplary responses.)

RELEASE

Remind students of the importance of explaining information to readers.

As you continue working on your own writing, remember to be mindful of your audience. Those who are reading your writing might not have a lot of background with your topic, so you need to thoroughly explain concepts to them. You can do this by including definitions, descriptions, and/or examples.

FOR ADDITIONAL SUPPORT, TRY

6.20 Extend Your Facts
6.22 Use Your Senses
6.32 What's It Like?

TIPS/RESOURCES:

- Have students play "Guess the Object" where one partner chooses a classroom object and uses definitions, descriptions, and/or examples to help the other partner guess the correct response.

Connect Your Ideas

In this lesson, students learn to use transition words and phrases so that their writing flows.

Writing Stage: Transitional, Fluent

Genre: All-About Book, Feature Article, Literary Nonfiction, Expository Nonfiction, Research Report, Biography, Expository Essay

INTRODUCE

Tell students that the use of transitional words and phrases connect ideas.

Nonfiction writers don't just list the facts. They connect information using transitional words and phrases to show the relationship between ideas and to make their writing sound more like a spoken conversation. These words really help the reader follow the writer's train of thought.

INSTRUCT

Explain with Examples

Present an anchor chart with transitional words and phrases. Give an example of how a writer might use each one.

There are many different words that writers choose from to show how ideas are connected. *(Display chart of terms.)*

Addition To give an idea and then add more to it, use words, such as: *In addition, Furthermore, Additionally,* and *Also.* For example, I might say: "Octopuses mostly eat shellfish, such as crabs, shrimp, and lobster. *In addition*, they also eat larger prey like sharks."

Comparison To compare things that are similar, use words, such as: *Similarly, Comparatively, In comparison, Likewise, and Along with.* For example, I might say: "Octopuses use their beaks to break into the shells of their prey. They then use their saliva to paralyze their prey. *Similar* to some snakes, they have saliva that is venomous and deadly."

Contrast To show how things are different or opposite, use words, such as: *Unlike, In contrast, Differing from, However,* and *On the one hand … On the other hand.* For example, I might say: "Octopuses have 9 brains. *Unlike* other animals, they have a central brain and a brain in each arm."

Summary To draw a conclusion for a big idea, use words, such as: *In conclusion, In summary, Altogether,* and *In short.* For example, I might say: "Octopuses can camouflage to match their surroundings. From their funnels, they can also shoot ink to ward off predators or water to get away quickly. They can even squeeze into tight places. *Altogether*, they have many ways to hide and escape."

Time To show time order, use words, such as: *First, First and foremost, Second, Next, Then, After that, Following that, Finally, Soon after, Last,* and *Last but not least.* Here is an example: "*First*, octopuses lay thousands of eggs. *Then,* they string them up in their dens. *After that*, they care for the eggs by spraying them clean with water. *Finally*, after five months, the eggs hatch and thousands of baby octopuses swim out to sea."

 |

GUIDE

Using a shared-writing experience, provide students with a few sentences to connect.

Let's see if we can think of the relationship between these sentences and what transition words might work.

"The octopus stretches its arms along the ocean floor to feel for food. When the octopus finds a crab, it pounces on it. The octopus squirts poison into the crab. The crab becomes paralyzed."

What kinds of transition words would work here?

(Allow students 1–4 minutes to turn and talk with partners. Share exemplary responses.)

RELEASE

Remind students that transition words show relationships between ideas.

So when you are drafting and revising your own writing, remember that it's important to link ideas together. This not only helps show relationships between information and ideas, but it also makes your writing flow better and sound more like conversation.

FOR ADDITIONAL SUPPORT, TRY

6.38 So What?

TIPS/RESOURCES

- Provide students with a list of transitional words to keep in their drafting folders as a reference.

*See sample chart, "Transition Progression," on page 357.

LESSON 6.31

Bring It to Life

In this lesson, students learn to use imagery rather than a dictionary definition to describe.

Writing Stage: Fluent

Genre: All-About Book, Feature Article, Literary Nonfiction, Expository Nonfiction, Research Report, Biography, Expository Essay

INTRODUCE

Tell students that the use of imagery can bring nonfiction topics to life.

In order to help readers understand nonfiction, it can be helpful to define things using imagery rather than dictionary definitions. This helps the reader make a picture in their minds. It makes the information clearer and more concrete.

INSTRUCT

Explain with Examples

Explain to students the various techniques that a writer uses to create imagery.

Let me explain how writers use imagery. First and foremost, imagery can be created using any of the five senses: sight, taste, sound, touch, and smell. Writers sometimes use just one of the senses or a combination of senses. When writers use imagery, they often use vivid and descriptive language such as precise verbs and adjectives to describe. Additionally, writers might also include comparisons such as metaphors and similes. These help the readers make a connection to something that is familiar to them when trying to picture or learn something new. The use of imagery helps a reader evoke their own senses so that they can experience the idea or topic being described.

Let's look at the difference between a dictionary definition versus one with imagery. If I were writing about a shark's fins, I would probably use definitions to help readers understand the different kinds of fins. For example, "A dorsal fin is an unpaired fin on the back of a shark, fish, or whale."

If you were first learning about sharks, you might be able to picture it well in your mind.

Let me try defining the dorsal fin with imagery. For example,

> "A dorsal fin is a triangular-shaped fin on the back of the shark that is mostly flat on either side. Its coloring is solid and matches the color of the shark's back. The dorsal fin is fixed and does not move as it helps keep the shark upright so that it doesn't roll over while swimming. It also helps with sudden turns."

 |

GUIDE

Ask students to notice and name the different techniques used in the example.

Which definition helps you create a clearer image in your mind? Which senses did this definition evoke? What techniques do you notice that I used here?

(Allow students 1–4 minutes to turn and talk with partners. Share exemplary responses such as, "The second one has language to help you visualize.")

RELEASE

Explain to students why they might consider imagery in their own writing.

Remember, it is easy to look up a term and paraphrase its definition for your reader. However, you have to ask yourself, "Will my reader understand this well? Will they be able to picture it?" If not, consider bringing it to life with imagery that evokes the senses, makes comparisons, and uses precise and vivid language.

FOR ADDITIONAL SUPPORT, TRY

6.22 Use Your Senses

6.32 What's It Like?

6.44 On a Side Note ...

TIPS/RESOURCES:

- Gather examples of literary nonfiction for read-alouds and text study.
- Provide students with a variety of objects to describe using their senses, comparisons, and precise language.

What's It Like?

In this lesson, students learn to use comparing and contrasting to make the information in their writing clearer.

Writing Stage: Transitional, Fluent
Genre: All-About Book, Feature Article, Literary Nonfiction, Expository Nonfiction, Research Report, Biography, Expository Essay

INTRODUCE

Tell students that one way to revise their drafts is to use comparisons and contrasts to clarify meaning.

You may have heard of a simile from a teacher while reading or writing poetry. Comparisons work in poetry because they create a strong image in your mind. There are times when informational writers need to do the same thing for their readers. Today I want to teach you that we can use comparisons in our informational writing to give our readers a better picture of our topic.

INSTRUCT

Demonstration

Model for students how to help readers visualize by either comparing or contrasting a detail from the topic to something the reader likely knows.

Watch me as I read this part of my draft. I'm looking to see where there is an idea, a fact, or a concept where a comparison would improve the reader's understanding.

> *Sharks' Bodies*
>
> "Sharks don't have bones, rather their spines are made of bendable cartilage. Cartilage is the stuff that your nose and ears are made of."

Maybe I can compare how cartilage bends or moves to a straw. I could add, "It bends but is light and keeps its shape like a plastic straw. This allows the shark to move quickly and stay afloat."

Let's keep going.

> "Because a shark is always moving, it's skin is tough. Some sharks, like the great white, have powerful tails that help them move quickly through the water."

Many people may think of fish as slimy, but sharks aren't slimy like most fish. Therefore, I can make a contrast. I can write: "Because a shark is always moving, it's skin has to be tough to protect it from injury. It doesn't have scales, and it isn't slimy like its fish relatives." I can also make a comparison, "A shark's skin feels rough and gritty like wet sandpaper."

ALTERNATIVE

Explain with Examples: **Show examples of comparison and discuss why an author used it in a particular place and the desired effect on the reader.**

 |

GUIDE

Prompt students to try the strategy on a different part of your text.

Let's look at this part together. See if you can help me think of some comparisons or contrasts that will help my reader.

"Some sharks have incredibly sharp teeth. They have rows and rows of teeth, one behind the other. If they lose a tooth, another one growing behind it moves forward to take its place."

Take a minute to turn and talk: What comparisons or contrasts would make this clearer, or more vivid, in the reader's mind?

(Allow students 1–4 minutes to turn and talk with partners. Share exemplary responses.)

RELEASE

Remind students to try adding comparisons when an image in the reader's mind would help them understand the topic.

As you revise today, pay attention to details or facts where the reader may need a little more help to understand. Try using both comparisons and contrasts to make it clear for your reader so you can teach them more!

FOR ADDITIONAL SUPPORT, TRY

6.16 Everything Counts in Exact Amounts
6.18 What Does That Mean?
6.20 Extend Your Facts
6.22 Use Your Senses

TIPS/RESOURCES

- Chart some common similes and encourage students to add to them from books they read.
- Use poetry as a mentor text for creating strong images.
- Give students increased practice with this strategy in shared writing.
- Use examples from nonfiction mentor texts.

What Are Your Stats?

In this lesson, students learn to use statistics and exact numbers to give precise information and make a better argument.

Writing Stage: Transitional, Fluent
Genre: All-About Book, Feature Article, Literary Nonfiction, Expository Nonfiction, Research Report, Biography, Expository Essay

INTRODUCE

Tell students that one way to revise is to use statistics and exact numbers.

I remember this one gum commercial from when I was a kid: "4 out of 5 dentists recommend this product for their patients." That's only 80 percent, which seems kind of *meh*, but it was still memorable. Today we're going to think about numbers and statistics as a way to add an air of authority to our work.

INSTRUCT

Demonstration

Model how to add statistics and exact numbers to your writing. Be sure to name where the best places are to do this work.

Watch how I look for places where I use generalities such as *many*, *most*, or *some*.

Here's a part of my piece on Title IX, where I'm writing about the U.S. Women's Soccer team suing for equal pay. I want to highlight that almost 50 years later this problem still exists.

> "Even though the men's soccer team has a far worse record than the women's team, they still earn considerably more than their female counterparts."

What statistic, or exact numbers, do you think I could use here? *(Give students a minute or so to think with a partner.)*

I'm hearing it would be useful to have a comparison of female and male earnings. I have an article here that I could use. It reports: "U.S. Soccer awarded the men's team a $5.375 million performance bonus after losing in round 16 of the 2014 World Cup. It awarded the women $1.725 million for winning the 2015 World Cup."[1]

This information connects with what I want to highlight. I can write:

> "Even though the men's soccer team has a far worse record than the women's team, they still earn considerably more than their female counterparts. For example, according to the *Washington Post*, the men's team was given a '$5.375 million performance bonus after losing in round 16 of the 2014 World Cup,' while the women's team was given '$1.725 million for winning the 2015 World Cup.'"

ALTERNATIVE

Explain with Examples: **Show students a mentor text(s) where the author uses a variety of numbers and statistics. Discuss the merits and drawbacks for each.**

GUIDE

Prompt students to apply the strategy to a section of their own writing.

Take out your drafts and find a section you want to look at with a partner. Read it and talk through what kind of information you might add. Look for places where you use general terms such as *more, less, many, some*, or *a lot*. Make a note of where you need information and jot the kinds of sources where you might find it.

(Allow students 1–4 minutes to turn and talk with partners and jot plans for quick research. Share exemplary responses.)

RELEASE

Remind students about the value of using data.

As you're working on your draft today, pay attention to places where your reader might have questions about exact numbers or statistics. Notice where your phrasing is vague, or you speak in generalities, and give it some heft.

FOR ADDITIONAL SUPPORT, TRY

6.15 Be Specific
6.16 Everything Counts in Exact Amounts
6.22 Use Your Senses
6.34 Lean or Extreme

TIPS/RESOURCES

- Name specific search engines for students.
- Show students how to make a quick poll or survey, in person or using digital tools.
- Do a quick demonstration on search terms as a mid-workshop interruption.

[1] Clark, L. (2019, June 5) *USWNT fights for equal pay as it fights to defend World Cup title.* Washington Post. Retrieved from Newsela: https://newsela.com/read/USWNT-equal-pay/id/52606/?collection_id=339&search_id=4246853e-6285-41aa-9ae8-ceff73809e89

LESSON 6.34

Lean or Extreme

In this lesson, students learn to use extreme language or exaggeration to drive home a point.

Writing Stage: Transitional, Fluent
Genre: All-About Book, Feature Article, Literary Nonfiction, Expository Nonfiction, Research Report, Biography, Expository Essay

INTRODUCE

Tell students one way to highlight a point is to use exaggeration.

As informational writers, we work to give our readers as much information as we can. In doing so, we consider the language we use. We can choose words that will have an impact on our reader. As we revise, we can use extreme language or exaggeration to get our point across.

INSTRUCT

Demonstration

Model for students how to think through choices about using extreme language or exaggeration by connecting them to the purpose of a piece.

Watch me as I revise my piece to impact my reader.

Emergent / Transitional *(Display these sentences.)* "Pit bulls are good dogs. Some people think they are scary. Most pit bulls are loving and smart."

I could exaggerate this. I could change it to say: "Pit bulls are incredible dogs! Some people who believe stereotypes think they are scary. I know pit bulls are so loving (they give kisses all the time!) and very smart. They love learning tricks!"

Do you see how I added the words and phrases "incredible" and "all the time" so that I could make sure to be very positive about pit bulls? And for the people who don't like pit bulls, I tried to make it sound like they are thinking about stereotypes.

Fluent Here's my draft about pit bulls. I want people to think that it's wrong to make assumptions about them. *(Display writing.)*

> "People assume pit bulls are more aggressive than other dog breeds. That assumption has led to problems. For example, some states have anti-pit bull legislation that makes owning pit bulls illegal. In states where pit bulls are allowed, landlords can discriminate by not allowing pit bulls in apartments. This makes it difficult for pit bull owners to find housing."

Here's how I could add some extreme language to describe the discrimination. I might use words like *needless*, *pointless*, or even *uncalled for*. Maybe I want to exaggerate the problem by saying, "It is impossible for pit bull owners to find housing."

ALTERNATIVE

Inquiry: **Using mentor texts, have students investigate the kinds of extreme language or exaggeration writers use and their effects.**

GUIDE

Prompt students to use extreme language or exaggeration on a shared text.

(Adjust as needed to accommodate different writing stages.) Let's look at this informational piece we've been working on about our school. Here we're giving the reader information about the playground and we want them to think how amazing it is:

"Our playground is big. It has three climbers. It even has a rock-climbing wall. There are swings and a few kinds of slides." How can we use exaggeration to improve this?

(Allow students 1–4 minutes to turn and talk with partners. Share exemplary responses.)

RELEASE

Remind students to apply the strategy as they revise.

As you revise today, be sure to think about what you want your reader to believe as you think of adjectives or phrases that exaggerate or emphasize what you are trying to say.

FOR ADDITIONAL SUPPORT, TRY

6.15 Be Specific
6.16 Everything Counts in Exact Amounts
6.32 What's It Like?
6.35 Your Opinion Counts
6.37 Tell It Like It Is

TIPS/RESOURCES

- Use word lists or word walls for extreme language.
- Connect exaggeration to purpose so that students are not exaggerating randomly.
- Consider putting students in partnerships to help each other.

Your Opinion Counts

In this lesson, students learn to include thoughts, ideas, opinions, or reflections to show how their thinking has grown or changed.

Writing Stage: Transitional, Fluent
Genre: All-About Book, Feature Article, Literary Nonfiction, Expository Nonfiction, Research Report, Biography, Expository Essay

INTRODUCE

Tell students one way to revise is to include opinions and reflections.

Authors of informational texts have choices regarding ideas they choose to add to their writing, including opinions and reflections. Showing our thinking can call attention to ideas we think are important. Today, think about how you can include your beliefs in your writing.

INSTRUCT

Demonstration

Model how to add your opinions judiciously for greater impact.

Watch me as I look back at my piece to find where I want my reader to really think. I could pick the introduction to set up the thinking with a particular lens. I could look at the conclusion to leave my reader with a final thought, reflection, or call to action. I can also look in between for any parts that really wowed me.*

I found a place in my draft on Title XI where I think I might try this:

> "Even though the men's soccer team has a far worse record than the women's team, they still earn considerably more than their female counterparts. For example, according to the *Washington Post*, the men's team was given a '$5.375 million performance bonus after losing in round 16 of the 2014 World Cup,' while the women's team was given '$1.725 million for winning the 2015 World Cup.'"

In my mind, that's crazy! They were given that much for losing—losing! How much more of a bonus were they given for winning? So I could begin to rewrite this part to add my thoughts:

> "Even though the men's soccer team has a far worse record than the women's team, they still earn considerably more than their female counterparts. How much more? According to the *Washington Post*, the men's team was given a '$5.375 million performance bonus after losing in round 16 of the 2014 World Cup,' while the women's team was given '$1.725 million for winning the 2015 World Cup.' That's more than three times as much, and for losing!"

ALTERNATIVE

***Inquiry:* Reading mentor texts, ask students to identify places where authors include their opinions.**

 |

GUIDE

Prompt students to use the strategy on another part of your draft.

Let's look at this next part: "Soccer isn't the only sport where there are discrepancies in pay. According to Adelphi University, in 2019, the average WNBA salary was $75,181 compared to $8,321,937 in the NBA. And the top male athlete in 2019, Lionel Messi, earned $127 million compared to Serena Williams' $29.2 million."

What reflections could I add to this to support my reader's understanding of Title IX?

(Allow students 1–4 minutes to turn and talk with partners. Share exemplary responses. Add those changes to the draft.)

RELEASE

Remind students to try the strategy, thinking specifically of places where they want to have an impact on their reader.

As you revise today, pay attention to places where you want your reader to be affected by the information you are giving them. Adding your reflections and opinions allows your reader to share the "Ah-ha!" moments you had while researching your topic.

FOR ADDITIONAL SUPPORT, TRY

6.26 Invite Your Reader

6.28 New Beginnings

6.29 Tell Me More, Tell Me More

6.36 Something to Think About

TIPS/RESOURCES

- Use multiple examples from mentor texts to help students recognize when and how authors include their opinions in different types of informational texts.

*See sample chart, "Where Should I Add My Opinion?," on page 358.

Something to Think About

In this lesson, students learn to ask the reader a question so that they take a moment to consider the information.

Writing Stage: Any • **Genre:** Any

INTRODUCE

Tell students they can revise by asking the reader purposeful questions.

You know how when you first meet someone, you tend to ask each other questions? We do that as a way to connect. As writers, we can use questions in a similar manner. Today I want to teach you how to look for places in your writing where planting a question would be effective.

INSTRUCT

Demonstration

Model for students how to ask questions in order to hook or engage the reader.

Watch me as I think about where I might add some questions for my readers.

Emergent / Transitional Let's look at the beginning of my book about transportation. I could connect to experiences by asking: "Have you ever been in a car, zooming along with the wind blowing in the window?" Or if I want them to think about my bigger topic, I could ask: "What are some ways people go from place to place? Do you like to go fast or take your time?" I might have to add: "This book will teach you all of the ways people get around."

There might be other spots where I want to add a question. This page is about buses. I could ask: "Have you ever been on a bus?" Or, maybe make it a guessing game: "What kind of transportation is big, carries a lot of people, is sometimes yellow, and makes a lot of stops?" See how I made it like a riddle?

Fluent I'm going to look for places in my draft about transportation where I want to hook my readers—maybe in the introduction or at the start of a subsection—or get them to think more deeply.

Here I'm writing about how choosing to ride a bus could decrease your carbon footprint: "Buses and trains are the most environmentally friendly form of travel with 0.17 lbs. of carbon emission per passenger mile versus 1.83 per passenger mile." I could start by asking: "What form of transportation is the most environmentally friendly?" I could also have the reader reflect by asking: "What would it mean for CO^2 levels if more Americans chose to ride buses?"

ALTERNATIVE

Explain with Examples: **Use mentor texts to give examples of ways that questions are used to engage and inform the reader.**

 |

GUIDE

Prompt students to try the strategy with a partner in the next part of your draft.

Let's look at the next part. What questions could we add? Remember, questions can prompt readers to think about their experiences, think more deeply about the topic, or nudge them to take action.

Emergent / Transitional Here's what I wrote about how there are different kinds of bikes—with 1, 2 and 3 wheels, bikes with motors, and tandem bikes. I wrote about how you can do wheelies and tricks on BMX bikes, and even commuter bikes that fold up and fit in your backpack!

Fluent Here I'm writing about the impact that choosing to ride a bike a short distance, as opposed to driving, has on the world around us: "It cuts down on emissions, but also lessens congestion on roadways which increases safety for pedestrians. Less congestion on roads also reduces the need for increased roadway capacity, thus preserving unpaved land."

(Allow students 1–4 minutes to talk with partners. Share exemplary responses and add the changes.)

RELEASE

Remind students that asking questions of the reader can strengthen their writing.

When you revise today, look to see where you can ask questions to engage your reader. This can both build interest and create opportunities for them to think more deeply about the information you're sharing.

FOR ADDITIONAL SUPPORT, TRY

6.17 Watch Out!
6.35 Your Opinion Counts
6.38 So What?
6.39 I Don't Know What Else to Say!

TIPS/RESOURCES

- If students struggle, have them react to facts. Do they feel shock? Amazement? Fear? Those emotions can connect to questions: Can you believe _____? Have you ever thought _____? Who knew _____?

LESSON 6.37

Tell It Like It Is

In this lesson, students learn to include information that pertains to the good, the bad, and the ugly of the topic.

Writing Stage: Transitional, Fluent

Genre: All-About Book, Feature Article, Literary Nonfiction, Expository Nonfiction, Research Report, Biography, Expository Essay

INTRODUCE

Tell students that one way to revise is to add negative and positive aspects of their topics.

Social media apps get a lot of criticism because users "curate" what they share about their lives. That means they can exaggerate what really happened—like when someone posts a selfie with perfect lighting. They probably deleted 500 other selfies first. It's not the complete picture! Good informational writing gives a full picture. Today I want to teach you to include information that pertains to the good, the bad, and the ugly of our topics.

INSTRUCT

Demonstration

Model for students how to research and incorporate negative information into their writing.

Watch me as I apply this strategy to my Title IX draft.

I've given information about why Title IX is good. Most of the information I've read is about how it has benefited women and society. So the first thing I know I need to do is to see if I can find more "cons" to balance my piece. From a quick search, I learned that while Title IX increased women's participation in sports, it did not address or compel funding of those programs. In most schools, the money is spent on men's sports. Some schools got rid of entire sports programs rather than ensure equal allocation of funds! Many schools did the right thing in creating women's teams but gave all the coaching positions to men!

Now that I know this information, I have to decide how to put it into my draft. I could weave it into the draft sentence by sentence using phrases such as *on the other hand,* or *unfortunately.* Or I could give it its own section or paragraph. Then it might begin like this:

> "Although Title IX has played a pivotal role in moving toward gender equity, it has created some problems as well. For example, while Title IX increased women's participation in sports by creating more programs, it didn't do anything to fund those programs."

If I were to weave it into the existing draft, it might sound like this:

> "Title IX ended the discriminatory practice of unequal spending of federal funds, and sports programs in colleges had to provide more opportunities for women. However, just because schools were mandated to spend funds equally, didn't mean that translated to equality."

ALTERNATIVE

Explain with Examples: **Using an array of mentor texts, show students where writers have included negative information in their writing.**

 |

GUIDE

Prompt students to make a plan for how to use this strategy.

Now think about what you might need to do to include the good, the bad, or the ugly into your writing. Make a plan for how you're going to do that.

(Allow students 1–4 minutes to turn and talk with partners. Share exemplary responses.)

RELEASE

Remind students that the good, the bad, and the ugly of a topic give readers a fuller understanding.

Now that you have a plan, you're going to spend time putting that plan into action. Keep in mind that, for me, most of the information was how Title IX was beneficial, so I had to look for the not-so-great parts. If you are writing about a topic that's not so great, then your research might be on the better aspects of your topic.

FOR ADDITIONAL SUPPORT, TRY

6.39 I Don't Know What Else to Say!

6.41 Not Everyone Agrees

6.46 I Didn't Even Think of That

6.48 Look Through a New Lens

TIPS/RESOURCES

- Create an exit ticket where students draft a plan first. This supports accountability for teachers and students.

So What?

In this lesson, students learn to support facts and ideas they share with reasons, vivid examples, and anecdotes.

Writing Stage: Transitional, Fluent

Genre: How-To Book, All-About Book, Feature Article, Literary Nonfiction, Expository Nonfiction, Research Report, Biography, Expository Essay

INTRODUCE

Tell students one way to revise is to back up their information with reasons, examples, and anecdotes.

Have you ever shared something interesting only to be met with, "So what?!" While obnoxious, this response may mean that you have not convinced the listener why your finding matters. As writers, sometimes our first drafts can be met with a "So what?" reaction by peers. Use this response to revise! Today I want to teach you some techniques for compelling your readers.

INSTRUCT

Demonstration

Model for students how to support information using reasons, examples, and anecdotes.

Watch me as I look to see where I might add some supporting facts—reasons, examples, or anecdotes. Notice how I use phrases including *For example, One time, This is important because,* or *In addition.*

In this section, I am writing about an octopus' intelligence. I write, "The octopus has a complex nervous system—they're basically full of neurons. Two-thirds of their bodies contain neurons. Neurons are nerve cells that transmit information."

I ask myself: "So what? Who cares about neurons? Why did I include this fact?"

If I use the phrase *One time*, I could tell the story about how I saw an octopus in the aquarium working on an enrichment toy that it figured out how to unscrew, which took the food out, and then put the lid back on. I could include that octopuses get bored and stressed in environments where they aren't challenged. I could also give an example from the film, *My Octopus Teacher*, where the octopus learns to recognize the filmmaker Craig Foster and uses shells to protect herself. These are both examples of how the octopus uses a complex system of neurons to learn.

Did you notice how I used these examples and anecdotes to add more to my information and show why the facts are worthwhile?

GUIDE

Prompt students to assist you in revising a text by adding reasons, examples, and anecdotes.

Let's look at this piece we've been working on together about our school. This is the section about our auditorium. We wrote, "The auditorium is a special place in our school. It's big and beautiful with long, red curtains in front of the stage. It holds about 500 people."

Let's ask: "So what? Who cares about the auditorium?" Can we add reasons why it's important to our school?

(Allow students 1–4 minutes to turn and talk with partners. Share exemplary responses.)

See how asking, "So what?" gave us so much more to say?

RELEASE

Remind students that this technique can help them add information and spice up their work.

As you write today, ask yourself, "So what?" and even, "Who cares?" Push yourself to add reasons why your information is important to the reader. That way, not only will your reader learn more, they will take the importance of your topic to heart.

FOR ADDITIONAL SUPPORT, TRY

6.15 Be Specific
6.16 Everything Counts in Exact Amounts
6.20 Extend Your Facts
6.21 Say More

TIPS/RESOURCES

- Chart sentence frames or transitional phrases for adding reasons, examples, and anecdotes, such as: *Because*, *For example*, and *One time.*

LESSON 6.39

I Don't Know What Else to Say!

In this lesson, students learn to ask questions to help fill in gaps of information.

Writing Stage: Transitional, Fluent
Genre: All-About Book, Feature Article, Literary Nonfiction, Expository Nonfiction, Research Report, Biography, Expository Essay

INTRODUCE

Tell students they can revise their writing by asking questions for additional information.

I remember when I was in school, I would work hard on a draft and think, "I'm done!" Then I'd show my piece to my teacher, who would read it and come up with a million questions related to information I hadn't addressed. So today I want to teach you that you can ask these questions while drafting to help you fill in gaps.

INSTRUCT

Demonstration

Model for students how to ask questions in order to fill in informational gaps in their writing without straying too far from the main idea.

Watch me as I use this strategy. First, I'm going to go sentence by sentence to see where I can fill in information. Some of the questions, or interrogative words, I'm going to use as prompts are: *Who? What? When? Where? Why?* (the 5 Ws) and *How?* (the H). I can also add: *Do? Can? Which? Whose?* (*Chart question words.*)

(Display a section from your own writing.) Here's a section on the legislative branch: "The legislative branch of government, which includes Congress, is primarily responsible for creating laws."

I could ask, "Who makes up Congress?" I know the answer to that: "The House of Representatives and the Senate." I could ask, "How do people become members of Congress? How many members of Congress are there?" If I ask why we have them, that's answered in the larger piece: "We have three branches of government to create a system of checks and balances." So I don't need to ask that question here. I'm will jot some notes on the side and keep going.

Here's the next part of what I wrote: "Congress also can declare war and confirm or deny presidential appointments." Here I could ask, "How do they confirm or deny appointments?" I know! They vote.

Another way I can try this strategy is to read a chunk of text and see what questions remain at the end of a section or page.

ALTERNATIVE

Guided Practice: **Have students ask questions and work together to answer them on a shared piece of text.**

GUIDE

Prompt students to use questions to gather more information.

Let's try this together. I'm going to read the next part of my piece to you, and I want you to see what questions you have to help me fill in any gaps in my writing.

"The president leads the country. The president is the head of state, head of the federal government, and commander-in-chief of the armed forces. Presidents serve four-year terms and are limited to serving two terms. Presidents sign bills into law and have the power to veto bills."

(Allow students 1–4 minutes to turn and talk with partners. Share exemplary responses.)

RELEASE

Remind students that when they are asking questions, the purpose is to add to their readers' understanding.

Either on your own or with a partner, be sure to ask yourself if each question will add more to your main idea. It is important that your answers don't take you on a tangent. After you add to your writing, reread it to make sure it all still fits together and feels cohesive.

FOR ADDITIONAL SUPPORT, TRY

6.21 Say More
6.23 Do They Fit?
6.25 Check It Together
6.29 Tell Me More, Tell Me More

TIPS/RESOURCES

- Decide how you want the lesson to go: partnerships, individual work, or both.
- If students need help weaving answers into paragraphs, stop and show them during a midworkshop interruption, or as a follow-up lesson.

What Do the Experts Say?

In this lesson, students learn to include quotes from experts or critics in the field in order to give their nonfiction pieces journalistic heft.

Writing Stage: Fluent
Genre: Feature Article, Literary Nonfiction, Expository Nonfiction, Research Report, Biography, Expository Essay

INTRODUCE

Tell students that they can add to their drafts by including information from experts.

Journalists often go to experts in the field when putting together a story. That's because experts have a depth of knowledge that makes them trustworthy sources. Today I want to teach you how writers include information from experts or critics in the field in order to sound more well-versed and convincing.

INSTRUCT

Demonstration

Model for students how to incorporate quotes from experts that support the information on the page.

Watch me as I find places in my draft where I could use an expert opinion.

Here's a section about the aye-aye, a kind of Malagasy lemur: "The aye-aye is an extremely rare lemur. It is in its own family of lemurs and seems to be able to live in a wide variety of environments, including both the rain forest and deciduous forests. Unfortunately, they are endangered. The aye-aye has large ears that enable it to hear grubs moving in trees. Aye-ayes have long, thin, spidery fingers that they use to draw grubs out from the holes they gnaw in trees."

First, I ask myself, "Why might I benefit from an expert here?"

Going back to my sources, I think I read something about lemur fingers. I know there are some lemur experts at the Duke Lemur Center. I could probably do an online search for the Center, or on someone who works there, and see if they have any articles or are quoted anywhere.

Here's an article that quotes an expert. If I'm going to add that quote, I need to let my reader know who the expert is and what about her history or experience makes her an expert. For example, I found information from an expert named Cathy Williams, a lemur veterinarian. I could write, "According to Cathy Williams, the lead veterinarian at the Duke University Lemur Center, a world leader in lemur study and care, of all of the lemurs, the aye-aye is 'the most curious and inquisitive.'"[1]

ALTERNATIVE

Explain with Examples: **Using mentor texts, show students examples of expert voices woven into informational texts.**

 |

GUIDE

Prompt students to try the strategy on the next part of a text using a quote you provide.

Another expert says that the aye-aye has "the largest brains of any lemur relative to their body mass."[2] The expert is Dr. Adam Hartstone-Rose and according to the article, he is a lemur expert from North Carolina State University.

Turn and talk to your partner about three things:

1. Is this quote useful?
2. Do I have enough information on the expert to introduce him with authority?
3. How I might use the quote in my draft?

(Allow students 1–4 minutes to turn and talk with partners. Share exemplary responses.)

RELEASE

Remind students to add some expert quotes.

When you go off to write today, look through your draft to find places where you could use expert information. Then make sure you have biographical information to introduce your expert in a way that conveys their authority. This will help you elaborate and apply the quote effectively.

FOR ADDITIONAL SUPPORT, TRY

6.41 Not Everyone Agrees
6.42 Back It Up!
5.19 Ask an Expert

TIPS/RESOURCES

- Help students define *expert* so they choose valid sources.
- Make a chart that outlines the steps of this lesson: What can I use an expert for? Who is the expert? etc.
- Make a chart of transitional phrases: *According to ..., In the words of ...*, etc.

[1] Jazynka, K. (2018, September 10) *Helping endangered lemurs hang on.* Washington Post. Retrieved from Newsela. https://newsela.com/read/elem-helping-endangered-lemurs/id/45836/?collection_id=339&search_id=9f3777e1-078b-46dd-baf2-79a84fc60336

[2] *These creepy lemurs are the only six-fingered primates on Earth.* (2019, November 6) Washington Post. Retrieved from Newsela. https://newsela.com/read/six-fingered-primate/id/2000000856/?collection_id=339&search_id=60c7d4f4-35a7-45da-b07b-1cdb49f2b930

LESSON 6.41

Not Everyone Agrees

In this lesson, students learn to include opposing viewpoints or information to provide the reader with a more complete picture of the topic.

Writing Stage: Fluent

Genre: Feature Article, Literary Nonfiction, Expository Nonfiction, Research Report, Biography, Expository Essay

INTRODUCE

Tell students that one way to revise is to add opposing information.

Writers of informational texts make choices about the facts they include. Often these facts align with the author's point of view. However, as authors, it is important to provide a variety of perspectives to help our reader get the full picture of a topic. Today I want to teach you how to include opposing information or viewpoints in your writing pieces.

INSTRUCT

Demonstration

Model for students how to add an opposing viewpoint, while being sure to maintain focus on the main idea.

Watch me as I look at my draft on hurricanes. My point of view is that climate change is real and that the data overwhelmingly supports this. However, some people might say that storms in the past killed more people. I need to address that. So to strengthen my argument, I will include information that might provide an alternative explanation for why past storms were so devastating.

For example, I can add a section about the Great Galveston Storm in 1900. This storm destroyed more than 3,600 buildings and killed anywhere from 6,000 to 12,000 people. It hit Texas on September 8, 1900, as a Category 4, with wind gusts reaching higher than 135 mph. I could add, "This storm was deadlier than Maria, a stronger Category 5, which recently hit Puerto Rico killing at least 5,000."

I need to explain why this past storm did so much damage compared to more recent storms that were bigger and stronger. I will emphasize that poor communication—not the level of the storm—is what made the Galveston Storm so deadly. Storms today are stronger and more frequent. Back then it was the lack of technology and communication that caused such devastation.

So even while adding opposing viewpoints and new information, I keep my purpose in mind. I connect it back to my main idea.

ALTERNATIVE

***Inquiry:* Using a mentor text, investigate how authors include contradictory ideas and use signaling language.**

 |

GUIDE

Prompt students to try the strategy on another part of the draft, or in a shared demonstration piece.

Now it's your turn. Let's look at this draft we've been working on about sharks. Initially I left out the information about sharks killing humans because the numbers aren't that significant. However, I think it is important to address this misconception head on. Those facts are: "There were 64 unprovoked attacks and 41 provoked attacks (when people bothered, poked, or got too close to sharks), five of which were fatal, in 2019. Of the fatal attacks, two were unprovoked. This is in keeping with the average of four fatal attacks per year."

How can I add the information about sharks killing humans in a way that won't detract from my main idea?

(Allow students 1–4 minutes to turn and talk with partners. Share exemplary responses.)

RELEASE

Remind students that adding contradictory information can reinforce the main idea.

When you revise today, think about places where maybe you left out information that didn't fit because it contradicts your ideas. If you don't know about an opposing idea, search to see if people have other ideas about your topic and try to add them like we did today.

FOR ADDITIONAL SUPPORT, TRY

6.36 Something to Think About
6.37 Tell It Like It Is
6.38 So What?

TIPS/RESOURCES

- Create a chart of sentence starters for contradictory information, such as: *Unlike* _____, *On the other hand* _____, *Some experts believe* _____, *While* _____, or *Rather than* _____.

Back It Up!

In this lesson, students learn to decide when to quote directly and when to paraphrase so their pieces strike a balance between research and their own ideas.

Writing Stage: Fluent
Genre: Feature Article, Expository Nonfiction, Research Report, Biography, Expository Essay

INTRODUCE

Tell students that writers make decisions about what to quote and what to paraphrase.

As a nonfiction writer, sometimes you encounter sentences and passages that capture ideas so beautifully that it seems silly to try to paraphrase them. Other times, it is quite easy to put information you've read into your own words. Today I want to teach you how to think through this decision.

INSTRUCT

Guided Practice

Using a shared demonstration text, revise together, deciding when to use direct quotes and when to paraphrase.

Let's try this together by looking at a section I want to add to my draft about rats. Our first job is to decide whether to quote or paraphrase.

I'm trying to give people information so that they don't just think of rats as disgusting vermin. This part is about rat relationships—how rats care for other rats—from the book *Oh, Rats!* by Albert Marrin. As we read, notice any parts of the text that are particularly powerful or well written:

> "In most animal species, the weak and the sick are usually killed or left to die. For example, should a shark get hurt, other sharks, smelling its blood, will eat it instantly. Rats are unusual because family members show 'pity' to the unfortunate. Finding a family member with its tail caught in a trap, they may bite through the tail to free its owner. Sometimes able-bodied rats lead blind rats. Families may feed crippled members all their lives."[1]

Now turn and talk to your partner: Is there a part of this that seems particularly powerful and worth quoting? *(Give students time to talk.)*

I hear you saying that this part makes sense for me to quote because it is so well written:

> "Rats are unusual because family members show 'pity' to the unfortunate." And, "Families may feed crippled members all their lives."

The rest I'm hearing I should paraphrase. To do that, I read it, cover it, retell it, and then write it. Take a minute to do this with your partner. *(Give students time to talk. Share out exemplary responses.)*

ALTERNATIVE

Demonstration: **Model for students how you decide what information to paraphrase and what to quote. Talk through your choices.**

 |

GUIDE

Provide another paragraph for students to quote or paraphrase.

Now you try it with this part:

"Rats are highly intelligent and have good memories. Should one eat poisoned bait and die, the rest of its family group will avoid similar bait in the future. Moreover, the first rat to find unfamiliar food may become suspicious and leave it alone. 'If a few animals of the pack pass the food without eating any,' a researcher notes, 'no other pack member will eat any either.'"

(Allow students 1–4 minutes to turn and talk with partners. Share exemplary responses. Discuss the merits of one choice over the other.)

RELEASE

Highlight the difference between paraphrasing and plagiarizing.

Today, make thoughtful choices about what you want to paraphrase and what you want to quote. Remember to paraphrase without plagiarism we have to do more than change a few words around. It might help you to read, cover, retell, then write.

FOR ADDITIONAL SUPPORT, TRY

6.40 What Do the Experts Say?

TIPS/RESOURCES

- Give partnerships a way to jot notes during the lesson.
- Don't dwell on the mechanics of quoting.
- For long quotes, model how to pare quotations down using ellipses.
- Chart steps for paraphrasing as a reminder.

[1] Marrin, A. (2006) *Oh, Rats! The Story of Rats and People.* Dutton Juvenile.

How Can I Help You?

In this lesson, students learn to consider if the reader needs visuals to help them understand the information or to provide additional details that the words don't say.

Writing Stage: Transitional, Fluent
Genre: All-About Book, Feature Article, Literary Nonfiction, Expository Nonfiction, Research Report, Biography, Expository Essay

INTRODUCE

Tell students they will determine the kind of visuals they could use to support their information.

One of the ways authors try to engage and educate their readers is through the use of visuals. Writers use graphs, charts, maps, pictures, photographs, cutouts, cross sections, and diagrams, along with captions and callout boxes to explain features and to teach readers more. Today we're going to work with partners to see what kind of visuals we can add to our drafts.

INSTRUCT

Explain with Examples

Show students various visuals with their features and functions. Discuss how each visual adds to or supports the information on the page.

I've gathered some mentor texts so that we can explore the kinds of visuals we can add, what they're called, and what they do.

(List visuals that will resonate with your students. Below is some language to give you ideas.)

Here is a map that shows where pit bulls are and aren't allowed due to breed discrimination. If the writer had to write out the information, she'd have to list each state! This allows her to give a lot of information succinctly.

Here the writer chose a cross section. See how it looks like someone just took a knife and sliced across? It can be used to show what's inside of something. In this case, it's the layers of a leaf. In writing, it's hard to accurately describe how things work in layers.

This writer chose to use a cut-away. Similar to a cross section, it shows the insides of something, but just a part—a little slice. The cut-away can also show a close-up of something, such as under the hood of a car, that focuses on the engine.

(Continue noticing different types of visuals and what they do to clarify information.)

Do you see how some information lends itself to one kind of visual more than another?

ALTERNATIVE

Inquiry: **Have students look at various visuals and discuss the question: What does this do for the reader? For the information?**

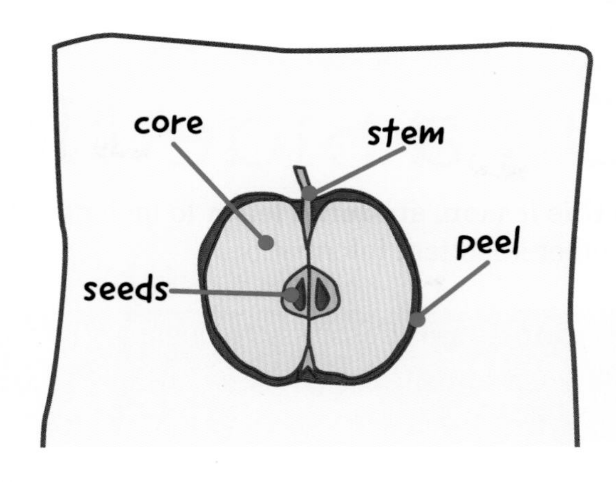

GUIDE

Prompt partners to discuss and give advice on what kind of visuals are needed.

I need everyone here to act as my writing partner. Let's look at this piece we've been working on about our school. Here's the section about the playground. You can see I've written about what we have on our playground. Look at our list of visuals. Think about what I want to do—teach you about all of the things on our playground. Turn and talk. What visual would help teach my reader more?

(Allow students 1–4 minutes to turn and talk with partners. Share exemplary responses.)

RELEASE

Remind students to focus not only on which visual to use, but why it is useful.

As you go off to work today, you're going to give your partner advice about what visuals you think will work best in their writing. You can go page by page, or section by section, taking turns. When you finish, work to add those visuals to your piece if you agree with your partner's assessment. You can also add some ideas of your own!

FOR ADDITIONAL SUPPORT, TRY

6.44 On a Side Note ...

TIPS/RESOURCES

- Offer the opportunity for students to work alone if they prefer.
- Allow students to look at mentor texts for ideas and inspiration.

LESSON 6.44

On a Side Note ...

In this lesson, students learn to include sidebars for fun facts, definitions, quizzes, or other important information.

Writing Stage: Transitional, Fluent
Genre: All-About Book, Feature Article, Literary Nonfiction, Expository Nonfiction, Research Report, Biography, Expository Essay

INTRODUCE

Tell students that sidebars are a fun way to include information that may not fit in the body text.

Nonfiction writers often use sidebars to include clarifying, interesting, important, or playful information that may not fit in the body text. Sidebars can be used for fun facts, definitions, or other important information. To add a bit of playfulness, sidebars can come in the form of jokes, riddles, or question and answer games related to the topic.

INSTRUCT

Demonstration

Model how you might include a variety of sidebars in your own writing.

Let me show you how I can inform and engage my reader with sidebars. I am going to try it with my writing about "The History of Ice Cream."

(Display writing and show students how you plan to include sidebars.)

I am going to consider places where I can either include a sidebar about interesting or important information that didn't fit within the paragraphs of that section or places that I can engage the reader in a playful way.

In my introduction, I talk about how ice cream is a popular treat all around the world. I will include a fun fact as a sidebar that shows just how popular it is. I will draw a callout box and write: "Did you know that 9 out of 10 consumers have purchased ice cream in the last 6 months!"

Later, when I talk about different ice cream flavors, I will include a bar graph that shows the top 5 flavors: *chocolate (14%), vanilla (13%), butter pecan (11%), mint chip (8%),* and *cookies and cream (8).*

When I write about places that you can buy ice cream, one of the places I named was a *creamery*. Since most people don't know that word, I will include a callout box in the sidebar with a definition: "A *creamery* is a place that sells ice cream or other milk products."

In the section where I teach how to make ice cream at home, I will include a riddle. I will write the answer upside down so the reader has time to think before reading it: "Where can you learn to make ice cream?" (In sundae school.)

ALTERNATIVE

***Explain with Examples:* Show mentor texts that represent a variety of sidebar examples. Explain why the author included the information.**

UIDE

sk students to help you come up with a sidebar r another part of your book.

o you think you can help me come up with nother sidebar?

n this section, I talk about when people ypically eat ice cream—as a dessert, a snack, sweet treat, or to cool off on a hot day. Can you hink of a warning or important information I should nclude here?

Allow students 1–4 minutes to talk with partners. hare exemplary responses. Add one to your writing.)

RELEASE

Remind students that sidebars are a way to provide additional information to engage readers.

So as you are drafting and revising your work, whenever you have additional information—definitions, riddles, or quizzes—that do not fit within the body of your text, you can include it in a sidebar as a way to inform and engage your readers.

FOR ADDITIONAL SUPPORT, TRY

6.6 Text Features Enhance Understanding

TIPS/RESOURCES

- Remind students to look back at their planning notes to find additional facts.
- Have students look for opportunities to define content-specific vocabulary in sidebars.

Top 5 Flavors
Chocolate (14%)
Vanilla (13%)
Butter Pecan (11%)
Mint Chip (8%)
Cookies and Cream (8%)

LESSON 6.45

Give Me a Sign

In this lesson, students learn to include headings and subheadings that organize their writing and orient the reader.

Writing Stage: Transitional, Fluent

Genre: All-About Book, Feature Article, Literary Nonfiction, Expository Nonfiction, Research Report, Biography, Expository Essay

INTRODUCE

Tell students that headings and subheadings help organize information.

Nonfiction writers often organize their writing with headings and subheadings because it makes their writing easier to read. Headings and subheadings also help readers understand the main idea in each section and quickly locate specific information.

INSTRUCT

Demonstration

Model for students how you add headings and subheadings into your writing to chunk and organize it.

Watch me as I organize my writing using headings and subheadings. *(Use a prepared writing piece to which you can add headings and subheadings.)*

In my draft, "The History of Ice Cream," I cover a lot of information. Reading this from cover to cover without any breaks may be a bit exhausting. More importantly, the whole piece isn't just about the history; it has other sections as well. I am going to include some headings and subheadings to break it up into readable chunks.

In this first section, I talk about the first known references to ice cream in 2000 BC. I discuss various references to ice cream throughout the world over the past 4,000 years. I think I will put a bold heading up on top that says, "The Origins of Ice Cream." A bit further down the page, I talk about the origins of ice cream in the United States. This won't need a new heading because it still goes with the heading I already have. However, I could use a subheading "Ice Cream in America."

In the next section, I discuss how it used to be made and how it is made today. I will use the heading, "Making Ice Cream." But since I want my reader to know the difference between the past and present, I am going to use subheadings that read "Past" and "Present" above each part.

This next section is mostly about the different forms of ice cream. I am going to call this section, "Ice Cream Many Ways." In the paragraphs that follow, I will use subheadings to categorize the different forms: "Cups," "Cones," "Sundaes," and "Sandwiches."

ALTERNATIVE

Explain with Examples: **Use a mentor text with headings and subheadings to show how the author uses them to organize information.**

GUIDE

Ask students to help you come up with a heading and subheading for the next section of your writing.

Can you help me with this next part? In the next section, I write about all the different things you can put on ice cream. Can you think of a heading or subheading I can use?

(Read aloud a few paragraphs about toppings. Allow students 1–4 minutes to turn and talk with partners. Share exemplary responses.)

RELEASE

Encourage students to try headings and subheadings to help organize their own writing.

So as you continue to write and revise, you may want to use headings and subheadings to organize your writing. This helps readers because you are breaking up the information, identifying the main ideas, and supporting their ability to find information fast.

FOR ADDITIONAL SUPPORT, TRY

5.5 The Notorious TOC

TIPS/RESOURCES

- Have students lean on the table of contents for headings.
- Remind students that headings are often sufficient; subheadings aren't always necessary; some texts don't use either.

LESSON 6.46

I Didn't Even Think of That

In this lesson, students learn to include additional "chapters" or sections for the topic, such as an embedded "How-To," "Fun Facts," or "Different Kinds" section.

Writing Stage: Any

Genre: All-About Book, Feature Article, Literary Nonfiction, Expository Nonfiction, Research Report, Biography, Expository Essay

INTRODUCE

Tell students that they can elaborate by adding new sections to their writing.

Nonfiction writers often embed interesting facts about a topic within a chapter or section. Some popular ones are: "How-To," "Fun Facts," and "Different Kinds."

INSTRUCT

Demonstration

Using your own example, show students how you add a variety of sections to your writing to engage your reader.

Sometimes there are things that I might want to add to my writing that don't necessarily fit into paragraph form. When that's the case, I might include a section that is a visual list my readers can peruse for interest. *(Write or display the examples below.)*

For example, in my section on the different forms of ice cream, I include information about ice cream sundaes. I write that sundaes usually involve multiple scoops as well as toppings. In that section, it wouldn't make sense for me to list all the different kinds of popular sundaes. Instead, I can make a grid or list that uses pictures and descriptions rather than writing it in paragraph form. I can include: Classic Hot Fudge, Banana Split, Brownie, Turtle, Crème de Menthe, and Peanut Butter Chocolate.

Another section I may want to include is a "How to Make Ice Cream" section. I will teach the reader a simple recipe for making ice cream at home. Just like my other section, I can use boxes with pictures and words for each step. I can start with a "Things You Need" square and draw and label: sugar, light cream, vanilla, measuring cup, measuring spoons, blender, and a small plastic pan. Then, step-by-step, I will teach the reader how to make ice cream using the ingredients.

I might also include a "Fun Facts" section with interesting information that doesn't fit into any of my other sections. Again, using pictures and words inside of boxes, I can include facts like, "The world's tallest ice cream cone was 9 feet tall!" Or "It takes 50 licks to finish a single-scoop cone."

ALTERNATIVE

Explain with Examples: **Using mentor texts with engaging sections, show students a variety of examples.**

GUIDE

Ask students to consider adding another section to their own writing.

Now think about your own topics. Is there any additional information that you would want to include in a fun and engaging section for your readers? Share with your partner.

(Allow students 1–4 minutes to turn and talk with partners. Share exemplary responses.)

RELEASE

Remind students to turn to mentors for ideas for additional sections that might engage their readers.

So as you continue writing and revising your own work, remember that you can add interesting information in a variety of sections. You can try one of the three we talked about today, or you can look through mentor texts for more ideas!

FOR ADDITIONAL SUPPORT, TRY

5.13 Learn from a Mentor

6.6 Text Features Enhance Understanding

TIPS/RESOURCES

- Remind students that they do not need to include all or any of these sections; they should consider what might be relevant for their topic and audience.

LESSON 6.47

Try On a New Structure

In this lesson, students learn to consider text structure when revising, including description, compare/contrast, cause/effect, and more.

Writing Stage: Transitional, Fluent

Genre: All-About Book, Feature Article, Literary Nonfiction, Expository Nonfiction, Research Report, Biography, Expository Essay

INTRODUCE

Tell students another way to add or make changes is by considering text structures.

One way nonfiction writers convey information is through text structure. Text structures help you consider how you are going to organize and present information. Today we are going to use text structure to help us write and revise.

INSTRUCT

Explain with Examples

Give students a definition of each structure. Talk through a few examples with your own writing.

The most common structures in nonfiction text are:

Description defines or describes different attributes, characteristics, and features of something.

Compare / Contrast shows what is the same or different between two or more similar topics.

Cause / Effect identifies the relationship between why something happens and what causes it to happen.

Problem / Solution shows when there is a problem and how the problem gets solved.

Life Cycle organizes the stages of life in order from birth to adulthood. It shows how the life form changes in each stage.

Narrative tells a story about a topic from beginning to end.

Procedural provides step-by-step instructions to complete a task.

Each section or "chapter" in a nonfiction text can have its own structure depending on what you are trying to teach. Deciding on a structure before you write can help you shape how you present the information. If you reread a section and it feels weak, changing its structure may help you improve it.

For example, in my writing about airplanes, my section where I describe different airplanes will be too long and boring if I simply write this as a list. Instead, I could use a compare and contrast structure to describe how planes differ in size, shape, use, and type.

ALTERNATIVE

Demonstration: **Using a prepared draft, rewrite a section of your topic by changing the structure. Explain your rationale for the change.**

GUIDE

Ask students to help you decide on a text structure for another section of your own writing.

Help me consider a structure for the turbulence section of my airplane piece.

Should I use **description** to explain what turbulence is and the characteristics of a plane ride getting shaky and rumbly when turbulence occurs? Should I use **cause and effect** to describe what is happening to the weather conditions in the sky that cause turbulence? Should I consider **problem and solution** where I describe how a pilot changes altitude to avoid turbulence and smooth out the ride?

Which do you think might be best and why?

(Allow students 1–4 minutes to turn and talk with partners. Share exemplary responses. Choose an idea to apply to your writing.)

RELEASE

Remind students that text structures impact the presentation of ideas.

So as you continue working on your drafts, remember that it is important to think about the text structure you will use. It will help you make decisions on how you want to convey and present information about your topic.

FOR ADDITIONAL SUPPORT, TRY

4.5 What's Your Angle?
4.9 Who's Your Audience?
5.12 Build Me Up

TIPS/RESOURCES

- Use a shared-reading experience to discuss the different structures that the author(s) use(s).
- Provide students with a description of different text structures to keep as a resource.

LESSON 6.48

Look Through a New Lens

In this lesson, students learn to revise with a more sophisticated lens. Options include: geography or place; background and historical time lines; famous examples or record breakers; and more.

Writing Stage: Fluent
Genre: Feature Article, Literary Nonfiction, Expository Nonfiction, Research Report, Biography, Expository Essay

INTRODUCE

Tell students that one way to revise a draft is going back with a specific lens.

Writers constantly reread their writing, tweaking it and making changes so that it makes sense, flows, and includes enough detail. Sometimes writers look back with a specific lens—looking for opportunities to add and include specific information to fill in gaps for the reader.

INSTRUCT

Explain with Examples

Name and explain the different lenses you might use in your revision. Give examples of details you could include.

Watch me as I use some common lenses and think about whether this information is useful in my writing about airplanes.

Geography and Place considers information related to places. I might include information about where the first plane was invented, the first flight was flown, or the world's busiest airports.

Background and Historical Time Lines emphasizes the background and history of airplanes. I can include information about what the first airplane looked like and how it evolved over time.

Famous Examples or Record Breakers helps me focus on different milestones in airplane travel. For example, I can include information on the first woman to fly or the first fighter jet pilots.

Breakthroughs or Game-Changers highlights advances in the field of aeronautics, such as the first plane to break the sound barrier, the longest haul flight, or the largest plane ever invented.

Discoveries and Inventions allows me to focus on significant inventions, like the jet engine or scientific discoveries that made flying possible.

Hidden Gems and Unsung Heroes highlights people or things that went unnoticed or didn't receive the credit they deserved. Perhaps, I can include information about "behind the scenes" people who make air travel safe or inventors whose contributions were overlooked.

Do you see how looking through each of these lenses gives me so many more details that I can include in my writing?

ALTERNATIVE

Guided Practice: **On a shared text, try using different lenses as you revise together.**

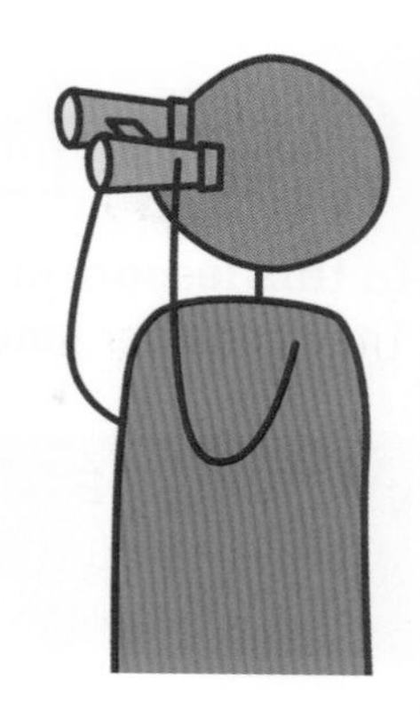

GUIDE

Ask students to consider a lens that they might try for revision.

Take a moment to consider which revision lenses might work for your writing. What are some details you think you can add to your writing?

(Allow students 1–4 minutes to turn and talk with partners. Share exemplary responses.)

RELEASE

Encourage students to revise using a variety of lenses.

Remember that sometimes you can make simple revisions to make sure your writing makes sense, flows, and includes enough detail. You can also make more substantial revisions by looking for opportunities to include information that fills in knowledge gaps your reader might have. You can create a lens of your own.

FOR ADDITIONAL SUPPORT, TRY

6.39 I Don't Know What Else to Say!

TIPS/RESOURCES

- Create an anchor chart or provide students with a copy of the different lenses with definitions and examples.
- Have partners work to help one another use the lenses in each other's writing to generate ideas.

Get in Line

In this lesson, students learn to reread and evaluate the order of sections or chapters in their work. They consider natural order, moving from general to specific information, or sequencing.

Writing Stage: Fluent
Genre: Feature Article, Literary Nonfiction, Expository Nonfiction, Research Report, Biography, Expository Essay

INTRODUCE

Tell students that one way to revise is to consider reorganizing sections.

Nonfiction writers ensure that the information they present to their readers follows a logical order. They consider large scale revisions that reorder their information by looking across the whole draft and moving sections around.

INSTRUCT

Explain with Examples

Use a shared example to explain to students how you would order information from general to specific.

First, I want the more general information to come at the beginning of my writing and the more specific information to follow. For example, if I were writing a book about "The Planets," I would make sure my general information about the Milky Way galaxy, the stars, and the planets come first. Then I would go into my specific information about each planet.

Next I want to consider the logical order or sequence of my sections. A logical order for sections might follow time order, size order, or alphabetic order.

For my sections on the planets, I might put them in order based on distance from the sun, size, temperature, or the date they were discovered. It really all depends on what my book is mostly about. If my angle is about temperature or size, then ordering them in that way would make the most sense. If my book is about discoveries in astronomy, then I would consider putting them in the order in which they were discovered. If my book is about general information about the planets, then it makes most sense to order them in the way they exist in the natural world—Mercury, Venus, Earth, Mars, Jupiter, Saturn, Uranus, Neptune, and dwarf planet, Pluto.

If I have written my sections on individual sheets of paper, I can simply reorder the pages. If I have more than one section on a sheet, I will have to cut all my sections apart and then tape them back together in the correct order.

 |

GUIDE

Ask students to help you decide on an order for a topic. Provide section and heading ideas to scaffold the strategy.

Will you help me order my book on "The Life Cycle of the Frog"? *(Have the headings below written out.)* The sections are: Froglets, Eggs, Habitats, Tadpoles, Conclusion, Frogs vs. Toads, Amphibians, Tadpole with Legs, Adult Frogs, and an Introduction.

Which is the more general information that we would start with? *(Give students 1–2 minutes to turn and talk. Reorder the sections based on responses.)* It sounds like you mostly agree that we would start with the Introduction, followed by "Amphibians," "Frogs vs. Toads," and "Habitats."

Which would be a logical order for the remaining sections? *(Allow students 1–4 minutes to turn and talk with partners. Share exemplary responses. Reorder the remaining sections.)* You've all agreed that the most logical order might be time and how they grow: Eggs, Tadpoles, Tadpoles with Legs, Froglets, Adult Frogs, Conclusion.

RELEASE

Remind students to review the order of their sections to make sure it seems logical.

So as you finalize your drafts, remember some bigger revision moves are to ensure that the order of your sections makes sense for the reader to understand your work. Start with general information before moving into more specific details. Then make sure the specific information follows a logical order and sequence.

FOR ADDITIONAL SUPPORT, TRY

6.23 Do They Fit?

6.24 Out of Order

TIPS/RESOURCES:

- Study the table of contents in mentor texts to discuss why the ordering of sections makes sense for the topic.
- Remind students to check for smooth transitions by rereading the last sentence of one section and the first sentence of the next section.

Revise Reasons and Order

In this lesson, students learn to draft or revise their essays so they start and end with their strongest reasons.

Writing Stage: Fluent • **Genre:** Expository Essay

INTRODUCE

Tell students that today they will organize their reasons, placing the weakest in the middle and the strongest first or last.

Whenever we write essays, we want to make them as persuasive as possible. If you are like me, you notice that some of your reasons seem more substantial than others. Perhaps one reason has tons of information that supports your idea, while another reason might just have one or two facts. Today we are going to learn to switch up the order of our reasons so that we tuck the weakest one in the middle and begin and end our essay with the strongest ideas.

INSTRUCT

Demonstration

Show students how you think about your reasons and organize them.

Watch me as I organize the reasons in my essay, "Speedy Sharks."

The main idea is that sharks are fast swimmers. I have three key supportive details: they are made out of cartilage, not bones; they are shaped like airplanes; and their tail shapes propel them powerfully through the water. All three reasons support my idea. Now let me examine each reason to see which should be first, second, and last.

Reason 1 "Sharks don't have any bones and their skeleton systems are made of cartilage and muscle." This reason is strong because it impacts the weight and flexibility of the shark's body. But I don't have much more information on this.

Reason 2 "Sharks are shaped like airplanes, making their bodies aerodynamic. The shape of their body makes them fast swimmers." This reason feels pretty strong. If you compare the body of a shark and the shape of an airplane, you can easily see the similarities. I think that this one should be either my first or last reason.

Reason 3 "The shape of the shark's tail is in the shape of a crescent. This unique shape allows the shark to glide through the water at considerable speeds." This reason is interesting, and I have a lot of details. I think this should be my first reason.

So now I have a new order for my reasons:

Reason 1: The shape of the shark's tail is in the shape of a crescent.

Reason 2: Sharks don't have any bones and their skeleton systems are made of cartilage and muscle.

Reason 3: Sharks are shaped like airplanes, making their bodies aerodynamic.

I thought about which reasons felt stronger and changed the order, placing the strongest ones first and last and the weakest one in the middle.

 |

GUIDE

Ask students to evaluate which reasons are stronger or weaker to determine the best order.

Let's have you give it a try.

Let's consider a shared idea: recess is healthy and fun. Some reasons to support this are: we can hang out with friends, we participate in physical activity, and we get to go outside and get fresh air. Which of these reasons feels strong? Weak?

(Allow students 1–4 minutes to turn and talk with partners. Share exemplary responses.)

RELEASE

Remind students to consider revising the order of their reasons.

Today, think about the details that you have from the strongest to the weakest. Consider how you will revise the order by placing the strongest reasons first or last and the weakest in the middle.

FOR ADDITIONAL SUPPORT, TRY

6.35 Your Opinion Counts

6.37 Tell It Like It Is

6.38 So What?

6.41 Not Everyone Agrees

TIPS/RESOURCES

- Use a shared topic or an idea that doesn't require research and have students think about reasons and the strength of each one.

LESSON 6.51

Wrap It Up

In this lesson, students learn to write a conclusion that summarizes their key points and leaves the reader with an idea, feeling, or call to action.

Writing Stage: Fluent
Genre: Feature Article, Literary Nonfiction, Expository Nonfiction, Research Report, Biography, Expository Essay

INTRODUCE

Tell students that they will focus on a conclusion that summarizes their key details and provides a sense of closure.

As writers, we work hard to make sure our writing is full of information that is clear and engaging to our readers. One thing that we can't forget about is the importance of a strong ending. We don't want to stop suddenly and leave the reader hanging or feeling incomplete. Instead, we need to write a conclusion that summarizes our key points and leaves the reader with an idea, feeling, or even a call to action.

INSTRUCT

Demonstration

Show students how you consider different ways to conclude your piece. Think aloud about the key points you will include as well as how you consider a final idea.

Let me show you how I think about a conclusion for my piece about the octopus. My main points are the octopus has unique features, it's highly intelligent, and it plays an important role in the ocean's ecosystem. So I will want to summarize these three main points in my conclusion. I also want to consider circling back to my introduction. (*Quickly read aloud your introduction.*) In my introduction, I mentioned how the octopus can solve problems, so I will be sure to include something about it being an intelligent animal. Lastly, I need to consider how I want to leave my reader ... with an idea, a feeling, or a call to action. An idea or feeling would just be a statement that connects to what I think and feel about the octopus. A call to action would be where I am asking the reader to help affect change. Since my piece isn't about saving or protecting the octopus, I don't think a call to action is going to be part of my conclusion. Perhaps my conclusion goes:

"The octopus is an incredible animal to learn about. It has many unique features that are unlike any other animal in the world. In the vast oceans, the octopus plays a crucial role in keeping the ecosystem balanced. The octopus is a fascinating animal. As you learn more about the octopus, you develop a whole new appreciation for this bottom feeder."

Do you see how I wrote a conclusion by circling back to my introduction and summarizing my key points?

ALTERNATIVE

Explain with Examples: **Using mentor texts, show students examples of how authors craft conclusions.**

GUIDE

Prompt students to summarize their key points and then finish with a final feeling or call to action.

Now to help you do this, let's follow a simple process.* Reread your introduction. You should be able to say it in a simple way. Then think about how you will leave your reader—with an idea, a feeling, or a call to action?

(Allow students 1–4 minutes to turn and talk with partners. Share exemplary responses of different types of conclusions you overheard.)

RELEASE

Remind students that it's important to wrap up their writing and give the reader a sense of closure.

Today, as you write, think about your conclusion. How will you wrap it up? Try out a few ways until it feels just right. Remember, you want to summarize your key points and also leave your reader with an idea, feeling, or a call to action so that they have closure.

FOR ADDITIONAL SUPPORT, TRY

6.11 Say Hello and Goodbye
6.14 What's Your POV?
6.28 New Beginnings

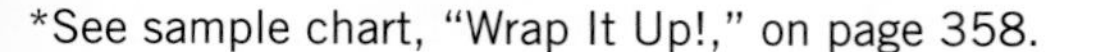

TIPS/RESOURCES

- Create an anchor chart that outlines a process for writing a conclusion.*
- Using shared writing, craft a conclusion together as a class.

*See sample chart, "Wrap It Up!," on page 358.

Everything Will Flow

In this lesson, students learn to read their writing out loud to see if it mimics the sound of conversation. They will focus on the length of their sentences and how their sentences begin.

Writing Stage: Fluent
Genre: Feature Article, Literary Nonfiction, Expository Nonfiction, Research Report, Biography, Expository Essay

INTRODUCE

Tell students that they are going to learn to listen for rhythm and flow in their writing.

When we read fiction stories, we use a storytelling voice—using different intonation and expression to match what's happening in the story. When we read informational texts, our voice takes on the tone of an expert or a teaching voice. We want it to sound like natural conversation and flow. We can do this by reading our writing out loud, listening for the rhythm created by varied sentence beginnings and lengths.

INSTRUCT

Demonstration

Show students how to vary the beginnings and lengths of sentences in order to create rhythm and flow.

Watch me as I read my writing, paying close attention to my sentence beginnings and lengths. I want to make sure that my sentences start in different ways, just like they do in a real conversation. I also want to make sure that my sentences have varied lengths—some short and also some longer. Here I have my writing about the octopus:

> "The octopus is an interesting creature. The octopus is an animal that lives in the sea. The octopus is a smart animal. It can solve problems. The octopus is able to camouflage."

I am going to stop here because I can already hear something. "The octopus is," The octopus is." Did you hear it? I started almost every sentence the same way! I also felt like my writing sounded abrupt. All my sentences were short, simple sentences. I think I need to go back and revise the beginning of my sentences and change some of their lengths. Perhaps it can go like this:

> "The octopus is an interesting creature that lives in the sea. Not only is the octopus a smart animal, but it can also problem solve. The octopus camouflages with rocks, coral, shells, and other things in the ocean to hide from its predators."

Do you see how I read my writing aloud and listened for rhythm and flow? To improve it, I combined some sentences and varied my beginnings.

 |

GUIDE

Prompt students to read their writing out loud and discuss possible changes with a partner.

Now it's your turn. Read aloud your writing to yourself and think about how it sounds. Does it have rhythm and flow? Does it sound like natural conversation? Or is it abrupt and disconnected? *(Give students 1–2 minutes to read their writing.)*

Now consider how you will change your sentences to give it a better flow. Share your ideas with your partner.

(Allow students 1–4 minutes to turn and talk with partners. Share exemplary responses.)

RELEASE

Remind students to listen for a conversational tone in their writing.

Today we focused on how our writing sounds to the reader. We can make changes so that our writing sounds like natural conversation. As you write today, consider the changes you and your partner shared and how you can make some of those revisions to your writing.

FOR ADDITIONAL SUPPORT, TRY

2.21 Rhythm Is Gonna Get You
6.27 Make It Playful
6.30 Connect Your Ideas
6.32 What's It Like?

TIPS/RESOURCES:

- Keep changes visible so students can compare work before and after.
- Go line by line to show how you think through the changes for students who need more support.

LESSON 6.53

Make It Pop

In this lesson, students learn to look for words they might want to make "pop" by bolding, using capitals, or applying playful fonts.

Writing Stage: Any • **Genre:** Any

INTRODUCE

Tell students that they will consider different ways to make parts of their writing stand out.

Think about when you're reading a nonfiction text. One of the features that usually pops out is how the author uses visual elements to get the reader's attention. Writers use bold words, all caps, and playful fonts to alert the reader to important words and phrases. Our eyes are drawn to these words because they look different than the rest of the words on that page. Today we will look at words we want to accentuate in our writing.

INSTRUCT

Demonstration

Show students how you consider different words to highlight. Explain how these highlights enhance the look and meaning of your writing.

Watch me as I think of ways I can make some words and phrases pop out.

Here in my writing, I wrote about the different types of octopuses. There is the common octopus, the dwarf, and the giant octopus. It might make sense for me to bold each type so that it stands out more to the reader. *(Quickly go over the words with a bold pen.)*

Let me take a look at a different part of my writing. Here I wrote about how the octopus has a funnel. The funnel allows the octopus to jet away fast to escape danger. The word *funnel* might be a word that I need to define in the glossary because it's a content-specific word, so it would make sense for me to make it a bold word, too. Also, on this page I have a picture with a caption that says: "The octopus jets away to escape it's enemy. Watch it go. ... Swoosh!" I think I can use some font play to give it more presence. The word *jets* would look better if it was in all caps so it emphasizes how quickly the octopus moves. I also want to play with the word *swoosh*. Since I am using onomatopoeia, it would be fun to make the word squiggly and the letters swinging upwards.

Do you see how I thought about how I can make my writing pop? I thought about the words I want to highlight to get the reader's attention so they know the meaning of content-specific words. I also used font play to make certain words attract the reader's eye.

ALTERNATIVE

Explain with Examples: **Use a mentor text that shows the different use of bold words, capitals, and playful fonts.**

 |

GUIDE

Ask students to help you come up with ideas to make your writing come alive.

Now you are going to help me think about what else I can make pop in my writing. The next part is about how the octopus hunts for food. I wrote:

> "The octopus is a skillful hunter. It uses its tentacles to reach out and grab its prey. The suction cups on each tentacle grab hold of it so it can't escape. Then it pierces the prey with venom, paralyzing it and leaving it no chance but to succumb to the hungry octopus."

Which words should I emphasize?

(Allow students 1–4 minutes to turn and talk with partners. Share exemplary responses.)

RELEASE

Remind students to think about which words they can highlight.

Today we focused on how to make our writing pop. We discussed the importance of signaling to the reader content-specific words or phrases that carry special meaning for explaining the topic. As you write, think about how you can make your words pop to highlight important content-specific words and to get the reader's attention.

FOR ADDITIONAL SUPPORT, TRY

6.4 Label It
6.15 Be Specific
6.18 What Does That Mean?

TIPS/RESOURCES

- Prior to this lesson, students should know the content-specific words they will include in their writing.
- Create an anchor chart with different types of fonts.

Weigh It Out

In this lesson, students learn to look at the parts of their writing to weigh them for volume and depth.

Writing Stage: Transitional, Fluent
Genre: All-About Book, Feature Article, Literary Nonfiction, Expository Nonfiction, Research Report, Biography, Expository Essay

INTRODUCE

Tell students that today they will weigh parts of their writing for volume and depth.

Nonfiction writers have to make sure that their writing comes across as balanced. We don't want one part of our writing to be long and strong while other parts are short and weak. We need to think about the weight we give to different parts of our writing and make some adjustments to balance it out. We can remove parts that seem weak or develop some sections more.

INSTRUCT

Explain with Examples

Show students how you look at your writing and make changes by developing or removing ideas.

Let me explain how to look at your writing and weigh out the different sections while considering volume and depth. *Volume* is referring to how much I wrote. *Depth* refers to the quality of the information in my writing, or how powerful it sounds.

Here I have a section on how the octopus hunts for food. *(Display the writing for students.)*

"The octopus is a skillful hunter. It eats shrimp, clams, lobster, and other crustaceans. It uses its tentacles to reach out and grab its prey. The suction cups on each tentacle hold on to the prey until it's ready to eat. Then it pierces its prey with venom, paralyzing it and leaving it no chance."

This part has volume because there are five sentences about how the octopus hunts. This part also has depth because I go into detail describing what the octopus eats and how it captures its prey. Now let me compare it to another section.

"The octopus is able to camouflage and blend in with all the different ocean life. This helps it hide from its predators. The octopus also has a funnel that helps it escape. It can go fast."

This has far less volume and depth. Perhaps I can add a few more details. I think I should also remove the last sentence because it feels weak. A revision might sound like this:

"The octopus is able to camouflage and blend in with all the different ocean life. It can turn blue to match coral or quickly appear to be as still as a rock at the bottom of the ocean floor. This skill helps it hide from its predators and protects it from being eaten. The octopus also has a funnel that helps it escape. The funnel swooshes water out, which allows the octopus to jet away quickly from its enemy."

GUIDE

Ask students to help you make changes to a part of your writing.

Can you help me with this next part?

> "The octopus goes to her den to lay thousands of eggs. She weaves them together into strands so they are hanging in the den. The eggs are tiny. Once the babies hatch, the female octopus dies."

How do you think this section compares to my other sections? *(Allow students 1–4 minutes to turn and talk with partners. Share exemplary responses.)*

I heard some of you say that I should develop this section. You said the sentence, "The eggs are tiny," should be removed because it is weak. Some of you said that it would be interesting to know why the female octopus dies after the eggs hatch.

RELEASE

Remind students to think about how to keep balance in their writing.

Today we focused on how to weigh out the different parts of our writing so we have balance in volume and depth. As you write today, consider the parts of your writing that you can develop more or the parts you may need to remove.

FOR ADDITIONAL SUPPORT, TRY

6.39 I Don't Know What Else to Say!

6.50 Revise Reasons and Order

6.51 Wrap It Up

TIPS/RESOURCES

- Have students work in partnerships to examine balance.
- Revise sample student writing or a shared-writing piece.

LESSON 6.55

Revising the TOC (Table of Contents)

In this lesson, students learn that once they have settled on the final version of their writing, they can revise the table of contents to reflect new, removed, or reordered sections.

Writing Stage: Transitional, Fluent
Genre: All-About Book, Literary Nonfiction, Expository Nonfiction, Research Report, Biography

INTRODUCE

Tell students that today they will revise the table of contents to be accurate and reflect the changes they made to their writing.

Now that we are nearing the end for writing this informational piece, it is important we look back at our table of contents and make sure it's accurate and reflects all of our revisions. We might have a different order than we originally planned, or we might have new sections to include. We may have also removed some sections that were not developed. Revising our table of contents helps our reader know what to expect and where to find specific information.

INSTRUCT

Demonstration

Show students how you revise your TOC by looking at your writing to make sure the order is correct and accurate.

Watch me as I look through my writing and compare it to my original table of contents, thinking about the sections that I might have added or removed. Then I will revise my table of contents accordingly.

Here is my original table of contents. *(Show students your original table of contents and make the changes as you go.)* The chapters I have are: "What Are Sharks?"; "What Do Sharks Eat?"; "Different Kinds of Sharks"; and "Cool Facts About Sharks."

Now let me look through my writing and cross-check it with my table of contents to see if the chapters and the order are still the same. The first part I have here is my introduction. I think that took the place of the first chapter I have listed as "What Are Sharks?" I will change that on my table of contents. My second section is called "Different Kinds of Sharks," so I need to change the order on my table of contents because I had that listed third, and now it's second. My fourth section is called "Sharks Here, There, Everywhere," which I didn't have listed on my table of contents because it is a new section I developed. I will add it now.

Do you see how I am revising my table of contents? I am looking at my writing and comparing the order of my sections. I am also looking for new sections I added or ones that I eliminated. As I go through this process, I make the changes to my table of contents to reflect my actual writing.

GUIDE

Prompt students to think about the revisions they will need to make to the table of contents. Have them share with a partner.

Now it's your turn. I am going to give you a few minutes to start this process and have the opportunity to talk through it with your partner. Start by looking at your original table of contents and comparing it to your writing. What changes do you notice? Is the order different? Are there new sections? Did you eliminate any parts? Take a few minutes to turn and talk with your partner.

(Allow students 1–4 minutes to turn and talk with partners. Share exemplary responses.)

RELEASE

Remind students the importance of revising the table of contents based on the final version of their writing.

Today we talked about the importance of the table of contents being accurate and reflective of the final version of our writing. We want to ensure that our reader has a clear picture of what's inside our writing so they can preview and locate information easily. We can revise our table of contents to reflect new, removed, or reordered sections.

FOR ADDITIONAL SUPPORT, TRY

5.5 The Notorious TOC
6.24 Out of Order
6.25 Check It Together
6.47 Try On a New Structure
6.54 Weigh It Out

TIPS/RESOURCES

- Study the table of contents from mentor texts to convey the importance of organization and clarity.
- Have students come up with catchy phrasing for the chapter titles.

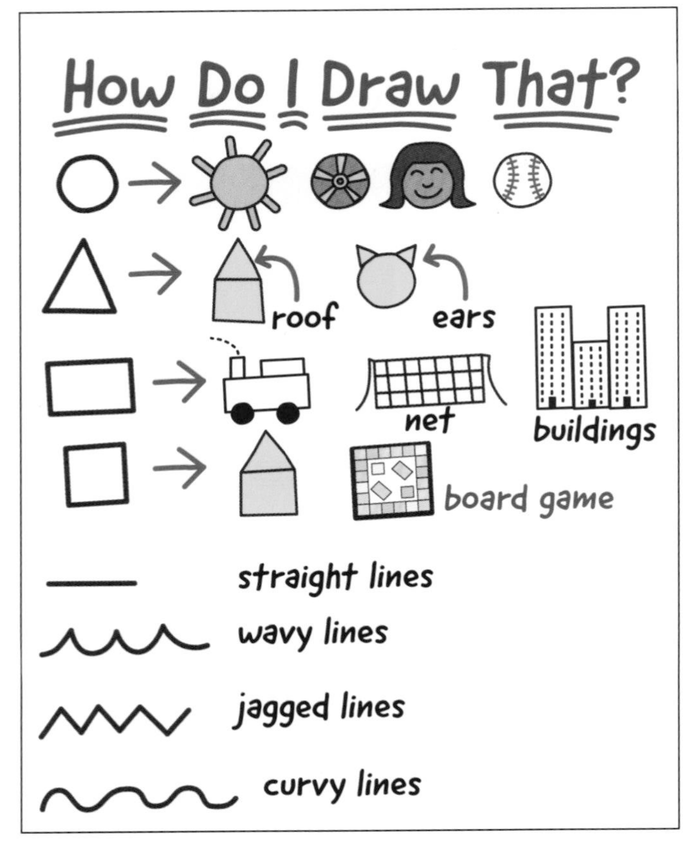

Lesson 6.2 How Do I Draw That?

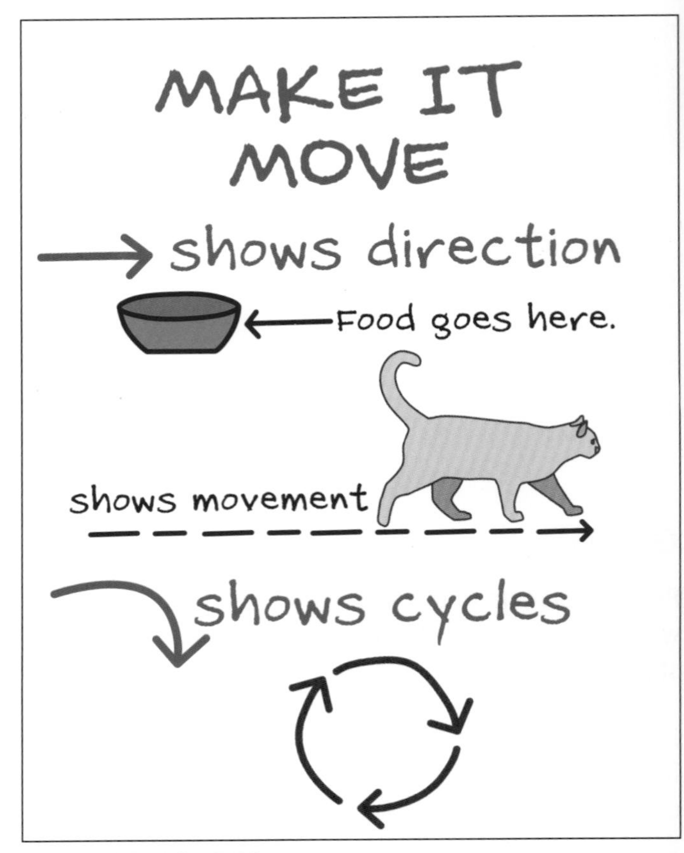

Lesson 6.5 Make It Move

What's Your Point Of View?

Third Person:
- sound like an expert
  —"Dogs can be big."

Second Person:
- talk to the reader
  —"Your dog can be big."

First Person:
- speak from experience
  —"I know dogs can be big."

How do you want your writing to sound?

Lesson 6.14 What's Your POV?

 |

Lesson 6.21 Say More

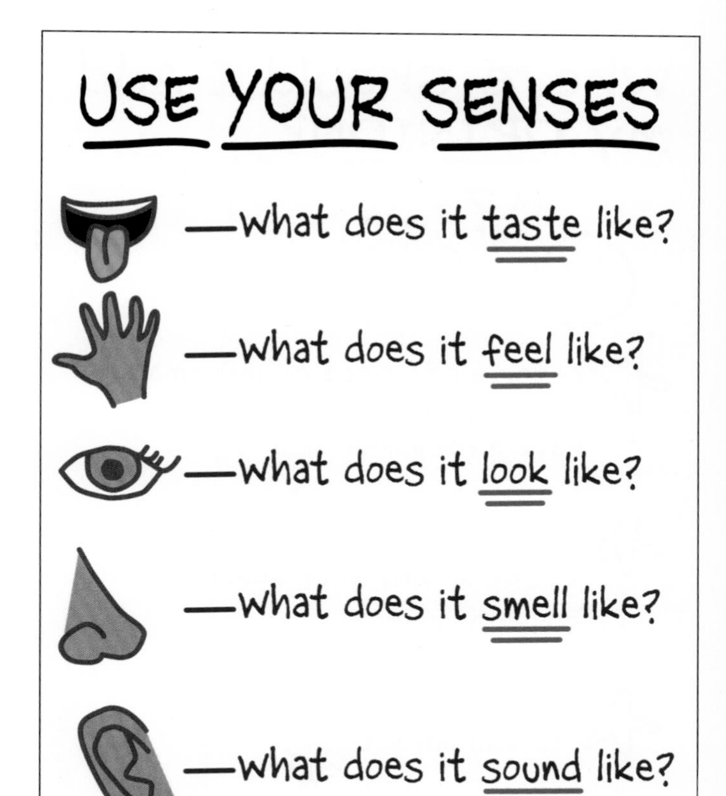

Lesson 6.22 Use Your Senses

Lesson 6.30 Connect Your Ideas

Where should I Add my OPINION?

- After a key piece of information where your reader should have a response!
- In the beginning of a piece to set up why your reader should care.
- At the end of the piece to add impact.

Lesson 6.35 Your Opinion Counts

1. Reread your introduction
2. Restate it, simply
3. Add... feeling
   idea
   call to action

Lesson 6.51 Wrap It Up

Edit & Proofread

The series of lessons in this section contain strategies to fix errors in conventions. Editing can happen while a student is in the midst of drafting or at the completion of the writing piece. Proofreading, similar to editing, involves one last check before going to publication. The lessons:

- include correcting errors in spelling, punctuation, capitalization, and spacing; and
- teach writers how to independently use editing checklists and proofreading marks when correcting their own or someone else's writing.

Descriptors for Editing and Proofreading

Emergent Writers	Fluent Writers
• Use class-made editing checklists to proofread work independently and in partnerships.	• Use checklists as tools for both accountability and as a reminder to edit closely.
• Make the process visible by using a different color pen to edit.	• Make the process visible by using a different color pen to edit.
• Cross out misspelled words and use a word wall to make corrections.	• Lean on digital tools to correct errors.
• Check for sentence capitalization and end punctuation.	• Rely on peers to edit collaboratively or with fresh eyes.

At-a-Glance Guide

Edit & Proofread

Title		Lesson
7.1	**Do You Hear Me? Do You See Me?**	Reread to hear more sounds and add them to words.
7.2	**Read the Room**	Use resources in the room to check spelling, such as word walls, concept charts, anchor charts, environmental print, and books.
7.3	**Put an End to It**	Check for end punctuation.
7.4	**Stand Up Tall**	Check for correct capitalization.
7.5	**Watch What You Say**	Check quotations for correct punctuation.
7.6	**Putting Paragraphs to Work**	Edit paragraphs for clarity and organization.
7.7	**Look It Up**	Check the spelling of topic-specific words.
7.8	**Just Right Sentences**	Edit for fragments and run-on sentences.
7.9	**Check Yourself!**	Use a checklist—either independently or with a partner.

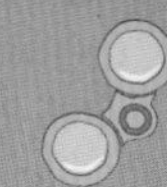

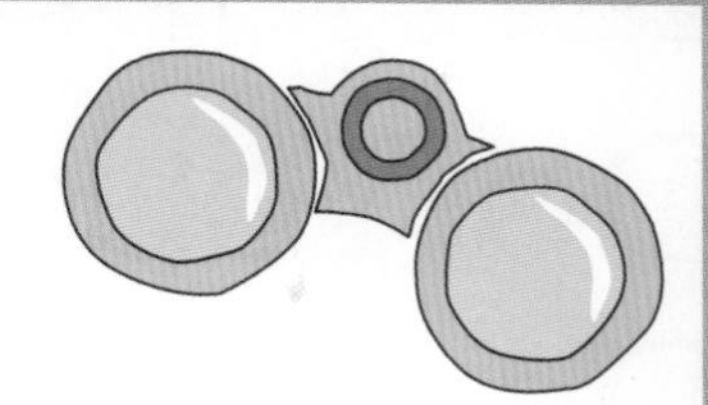

Writing Stage	Genre	
Emergent Transitional	List Pattern	How-To All-About
Emergent Transitional	List Pattern	How-To All-About
Emergent Transitional	List Pattern	How-To All-About
Any	Any	
Transitional Fluent	Feature Article Literary Nonfiction Expository Nonfiction Research Report	Biography Expository Essay
Transitional Fluent	Feature Article Literary Nonfiction Expository Nonfiction Research Report	Biography Expository Essay
Any	Any	
Transitional Fluent	All-About Feature Article Literary Nonfiction Expository Nonfiction	Research Report Biography Expository Essay
Any	Any	

Do You Hear Me? Do You See Me?

In this lesson, students learn to reread in order to hear more sounds to add to their words.

Writing Stage: Emergent, Transitional • **Genre:** List, Pattern, How-To Book, All-About Book

INTRODUCE

Tell students that writers check their spelling to make sure their writing is readable.

One of the main things writers look for are words that are misspelled. Why? Because we want our readers to be able to read every word we've written. Today I am going to show you a way to check your spelling.

INSTRUCT

Demonstration

Model how you sound out words and check for missing sounds. Use phonetic and approximated spellings based on spelling rules students have previously learned.

We are going to look to make sure that all the letters we hear are in the words. First, we'll say the word out loud, then point under each letter as we read it back, looking and listening for the sounds. If we notice that a letter is missing, then we insert the letter using a caret or by crossing out the old spelling and rewriting the new spelling above.

(Display writing with spelling errors.) Here I have a piece of writing about trucks with labels and sentences. Watch me as I check the spelling in the labels.

Here is a picture of a bulldozer *(written bulzr).* Let me first say the word out loud and clearly, *b u l l d o z e r.* Next, I am going to point under each of the letters to read back what I wrote while looking for the letters and listening for the sounds. *(As you point and read, note the missing letters.)* I can see and hear *b-u-l-z-r.* I am missing some sounds in the middle. I don't see the **/d/ /ō/**. I think I need to add two letters, **d** and **o**. I will cross out the word with a single line and rewrite it above. *(Rewrite the word, showing students how you combine the existing and new letters to spell the word phonetically.)*

Next is a picture of a dump truck (*written dmp tuk*). I'll say the first word out loud, *d u m p.* I'll say it again as I point under the letters and look and listen for the sounds. As I read this back, I can see and hear "*d-m-p.*" I am missing a sound in the middle, **/u/**. I think I need to add the letter **u**. Since I need just one letter, I will insert the letter **u** with a caret. Now I can try it with *truck.* Let me say it out loud, *t r u c k.* Let me point and read it back **/t/ /u/ /k/**. This is missing something, **/tr/**, that sounds like the beginning of the word *tree.* It needs to have a **tr** at the beginning. Let me add the letter **r** and read the rest of the word **/u/ /k/**. Wait a second. This sounds right but I know **/uck/** is a word family, like in the word *duck.* So *truck* probably ends like *duck. (Put a line through the old spelling and rewrite the word by combining word parts.)*

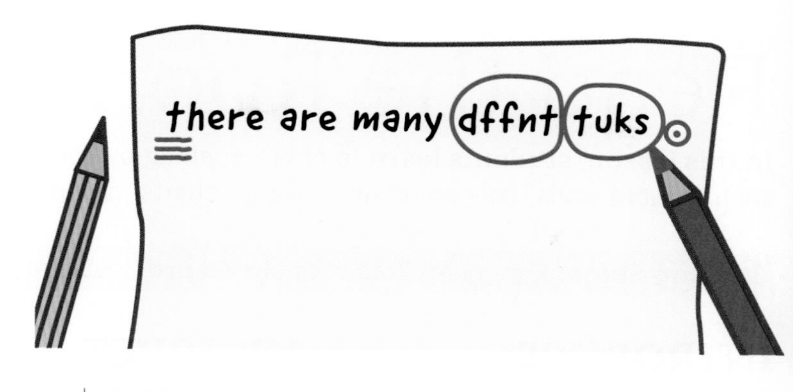

GUIDE

Ask students to help you correct spelling errors in your sentences as you look for missing letters and sounds.

Will you help me with these next sentences? Here I have written, "There are many different trucks." (*written "There are many dffnt tuks."*).

(Repeat the process, asking students to help you correct each word.)

RELEASE

Remind students that editing and proofreading are important for making their writing clear.

Remember that whenever you finish up your writing, it is important to double check the spelling to make sure others can read it. It is even more important to triple check and proofread if it is a piece of writing you plan to publish and share with the world.

FOR ADDITIONAL SUPPORT, TRY

2.3 Stretch It Out

2.6 Clap It Out, Then Sound It Out

2.7 That Sounds Like ...

TIPS/RESOURCES

- Have partners take turns placing one piece of writing between them to check for spelling errors.

LESSON 7.2

Read the Room

In this lesson, students learn to check spelling by using resources in the room, such as word walls, concept charts, anchor charts, and more.

Writing Stage: Emergent, Transitional • **Genre:** List, Pattern, How-To Book, All-About Book

INTRODUCE

Tell students that they can use the room to make sure words are spelled correctly.

One way writers edit their work is by checking the spelling of words. When we are drafting, we might forget some letters in our words. The good news is we have many resources in the classroom we can use to find the correct spelling, including word walls, concept charts, anchor charts, environmental print, and books.

INSTRUCT

Inquiry

Ask partners to observe their surroundings and locate the places that will help them find words.

When we come to a word in our writing we are unsure about how to spell, we might be able to locate the word in our room. If so, we can either bring our writing to the word or bring the word to our seat. Then we cross-check, letter by letter, to make it match. If we need to make any changes, we cross out the word and rewrite it.

Let's think about the places where we can find words in our classroom. Take a minute to talk with your partner about where we can look to find help with spelling. *(Give students 1–2 minutes to come up with ideas. Chart their responses.)*

You are all so observant! We can find words in many places:

- Word Wall – helps us spell sight words
- Color Chart – helps us spell color words
- Number Chart – helps us spell number words
- Name Chart – helps us spell our classmates' names
- Shape Chart – helps us spell names of shapes
- Calendar & Weather Board – helps us spell days, months, seasons, and weather words
- Anchor Charts – help us spell lots of different words
- Classroom Signs and Labels – help us spell classroom objects and places in the room
- Books – help us spell many words from the titles and pages

ALTERNATIVE

Demonstration: **Using your own writing with errors, show students how you check your spelling by cross-checking with words in your environment.**

November

Sunday	Monday	Tuesday	Wednesday	Thursday	Friday	saturday
		1	2	3	4	5
6	7	8	9	10	11	12
13	14	15	16	17	18	19

GUIDE

Ask students to help you proofread your writing by locating words in the room, cross-checking letter by letter, and making corrections.

(Display an enlarged piece of writing with spelling errors.)

Here I have a piece of writing about trucks. Will you help me check my spelling? This first page is about fire trucks. It says, "Hear is the rad fir tuk." *(Here is the red fire truck.)* Let's check the words we can find around the room. The first word is *here*. Where can I find it? Yes! It's on the word wall. Please point to the word *here*. Will someone go stand next to the word and read it letter by letter so that I can cross-check it? Uh-oh. I must fix it. Let me cross it out and rewrite it above. (*Repeat with* is, the, *and* red.)

Now I am wondering if we can find the word *fire* in the classroom. Where could that word be found? That's right! I bet the word on the fire alarm that begins with the letter ***f*** is *fire*! Let's cross-check it letter by letter. Will someone go read it to me?

Lastly, can anyone think of where we might find the word *truck*? I think we have a book with that title! *(Get a book with the correct word. Repeat the steps of cross-checking and correcting.)*

RELEASE

Remind students that editing and proofreading are important for making writing readable.

Remember that whenever you finish up your writing, it is important to double check and edit the spelling. It is even more important to triple check and proofread if it is a piece of writing you plan to publish and share with the world.

FOR ADDITIONAL SUPPORT, TRY

1.21 Be Resourceful!

1.22 Partners Are Resources, Too

TIPS/RESOURCES

- Provide students with small copies of word walls and concept charts.
- Allow students to use the environment in partnerships to help one another edit their work.

Put an End to It

In this lesson, students learn to check their writing for end punctuation.

Writing Stage: Emergent, Transitional • **Genre:** List, Pattern, How-To Book*, All-About Book*

INTRODUCE

Tell students that writers edit to make sure their end punctuation is correct.

Writers edit and proofread their writing to make sure it will be readable to others. One way we do this is by checking for end punctuation. End marks show that a thought is finished. They also show the reader how to read a sentence. Since end marks can be periods, question marks, or exclamation points, the reader knows to either keep his voice flat, raise it up, or say it with excitement.

INSTRUCT

Guided Practice

Using a displayed pattern book, identify whether the sentence has end punctuation and if it's correct.

Let's try it. When we are writing books that have one sentence per page, we can ask: "Is this a telling sentence, an asking sentence, or a shout-it-out sentence?" Let's try it with my pattern book about food. *(Display a piece of writing, one sentence per page, with missing or incorrect punctuation. Read and edit together.)*

Let's read: "What do you like to eat, little dog"
Let's check: Is there an end mark? No.
Let's ask: Is this a telling, asking, or a shout-it-out sentence?

That's right. It's an asking sentence, so I will add a question mark at the end.

Let's read: "I like to eat bones"
Let's check: Is there an end mark? No.
Let's ask: Is this a telling, asking, or a shout-it-out sentence?

That's right. It's a telling sentence, so I will add a period at the end.

Let's read: "What do you like to eat, little boy."
Let's check: Is there an end mark? Yes.
Let's ask: Is this a telling, asking, or a shout-it-out sentence?

That's right. It's an asking sentence, so I will have to change the period to a question mark.

**For How-To Books, use steps as examples. For All-About Books, rely on the example in the Guide section.*

ALTERNATIVE

Demonstration: **Using your own writing, model how you edit by identifying whether the sentence has end punctuation and if it's correct.**

 |

GUIDE

Using a displayed page of a book with multiple sentences missing punctuation, identify where and what end punctuation would fit.

Now let's try a trickier one with many sentences on a page.

Let's read: "Animals eat different kinds of foods monkeys like bananas lions like meat dogs like bones and cats like fish. What kind of food do you like to eat I love ice cream."

Let's check: Are there end marks? Well, there is one. But when I read it aloud, it sounds jumbled.

Let's reread the first three words: "Animals eat different." Is that a complete thought? No. Let's try four words: "Animals eat different kinds." Nope. Let's try five words: "Animals eat different kinds of." No, no no. Let's try six words: "Animals eat different kinds of food." That could work! Let's see if seven words work: "Animals eat different kinds of food monkeys." No! I think "Animals eat different kinds of food" sounds right. Is it a telling, asking, or shout-it-out kind of sentence? Yes, it's a telling sentence. Let's use a period there.

(Repeat the process for the other sentences.)

RELEASE

Remind students that appropriate end marks make their writing readable.

Remember that whenever you finish up your writing, it is important to double check and edit the punctuation to make sure it is clear to others. It is even more important to triple check and proofread if it is a piece of writing you plan to publish and share with the world.

FOR ADDITIONAL SUPPORT, TRY

2.10 Stand Tall, Stand Proud

2.11 Give Them a Break

7.4 Stand Up Tall

TIPS/RESOURCES

- Incorporate interactive editing for five minutes daily or weekly.

Stand Up Tall

In this lesson, students learn to edit their writing by checking for correct capitalization.

Writing Stage: Any • **Genre:** Any

INTRODUCE

Tell students that today they will learn to edit their writing by checking for capitals.

As we edit our writing, we need to make sure we are using correct capitalization.* We know that the first letter in the first word of a sentence needs to be capitalized. We also want to make sure that we are using a capital letter for the word *I*. And finally, we want to check all proper nouns—names of specific people, places, and things.

INSTRUCT

Demonstration

Show students how you check your writing for correct capitalization. Explain the process and then model with your own text or a piece of shared writing.

(Display a writing piece with mistakes in capitalization.)

Watch me as I look through my writing, one sentence at a time, and check for proper capitalization. I can't just look for everything at once. I have to hunt for each thing separately—as if playing a game of "I Spy." First, I am going to check the first letter in the first word to make sure I used a capital letter. I will then make sure the letters that follow are all lowercase. Next, I will play a little "I Spy" for capital *I*. Anytime *I* stands alone, I must make sure it is capitalized. Then, before I move on to the next sentence, I will check to see if I have any proper nouns, which are names of specific people, places, or things. If I forgot a capital letter, I can simply change the lowercase letter to a capital letter by crossing it out and writing it correctly above. Once I complete that process for one sentence, I move on to the next sentence and repeat.

(Repeat this process a few times with appropriate examples as time permits.)

Did you notice how I thoroughly checked my writing for capitals? Do you see how I didn't rush through but instead, read one sentence at a time and made sure the first letter in the first word of each sentence was a capital? Then I checked for correct capitalization for the letter *I*. And finally, I edited for any proper nouns. After I checked one sentence, I went on to the next one, then the next.

ALTERNATIVE

Guided Practice: **Display a piece of writing with errors in capitalization. Work together to make the appropriate changes, discussing why those changes are necessary.**

 |

GUIDE

Prompt students to look at the next part of your writing and find the letters that need to be capitalized.

Do you think you can help me with the next few sentences? As we do this, we will follow the same process that I just showed you. We are going to read one sentence at a time. First, we will look at the first letter in the first word and check that it's a capital. Then we will check to make sure I used proper capitalization for the word *I*. And finally, we will edit for proper nouns. We will fix any errors and make the appropriate changes.

(Display sample writing with capitalization errors throughout. Chorally, read each sentence one by one and triple check—once for the first letter in the sentence, once for I, and once for proper nouns. Invite a student up to make each change when you notice an error.)

RELEASE

Remind students to check their writing for proper capitalization.

Today we focused on how to edit our writing for proper capitalization. As you check your writing, remember to keep in mind the process we followed—reading one sentence at a time to check for capitals. First, check the first letter in the sentence. Then spy for capital *I*. And finally, check for proper nouns—the names of specific people, places, or things. We want to make sure that we are using capital letters correctly so that our writing is readable.

FOR ADDITIONAL SUPPORT, TRY

2.10 Stand Tall, Stand Proud

7.3 Put an End to It

7.9 Check Yourself!

TIPS/RESOURCES

- Create a capitalization chart.
- Using dry-erase boards, have students write sentences with correct capitalization.
- Reinforce capitalization in interactive writing.

*See sample chart, "Stand Up Tall," on page 380.

Watch What You Say

In this lesson, students learn to edit their writing by checking quotations for correct punctuation.

Writing Stage: Transitional, Fluent
Genre: Feature Article, Literary Nonfiction, Expository Nonfiction, Research Report, Biography, Expository Essay

INTRODUCE

Tell students that today they are going to edit their writing by checking quotations for correct punctuation.

As we write, we want to make sure that we are using proper punctuation with quotation marks. Quotation marks are used when you are referencing information from another source. When you quote someone, you need to make sure that you are using their exact language. This helps the reader know that it's someone else's words or idea and not your own.

INSTRUCT

Demonstration

Show students how you check your writing to make sure you used quotation marks correctly.

Watch me as I check my writing. Quotation marks always come in pairs to "hug" the sentence—one at the beginning of the quote and one at the end. Commas and periods always go inside quotation marks but colons, semicolons, and dashes go on the outside. Question and exclamation marks have their own rules. The easiest way for us to think about this is to ask: "Does the punctuation go with the quote, or does it complete the rest of the sentence?" If the quote itself has a question or exclamation mark, then you put it inside the quote. If the quote is embedded in a sentence that is either interrogative or exclamatory, then it goes outside of the quotation mark.

I am going to check and see if a quote in my writing is punctuated properly. *(Display quote with mistakes.)*

> In the book, *Sharks*, by Seymour Simon, he says: "Sharks have killed fewer people in the United States in the past one hundred years than are killed in automobile accidents over a single holiday weekend.

Here I have quotation marks before the second word, sharks, (not the title of the book), so that is correct. Uh-oh! I think I am missing quotation marks at the end. They always come in pairs. But where does the period go? Periods and commas go inside quotation marks. Let me add the quotation mark and keep the period inside. *(Quickly make the changes and reread the sentence.)* Now, that's better!

ALTERNATIVE

Explain with Examples: **Show students how authors use quotation marks correctly giving examples of the different types of punctuation involved.**

 |

GUIDE

Prompt students to edit prewritten sentences that have intentional errors in punctuation.

You and your partner are going to edit a sentence to make sure that the quotation in it is punctuated correctly:

> In the book *Surprising Sharks*, Nicola Davies teaches us that, "sharks' senses are fine-tuned, ready for the tiniest hint that might mean food![1]

What is missing? Yes, a quotation mark at the end. Does the exclamation mark go inside or outside the quotation mark? How can you know?

(Prompt students to turn and talk as they work together to correct the punctuation. Repeat the process with 3–4 sentences with intentional missing punctuation.)

RELEASE

Remind students to check for proper placement of punctuation when quoting a source.

Remember, we always use pairs of quotation marks to "hug" the text we are quoting. Also, recall the rules—commas and periods always go inside quotation marks, but colons, semicolons, and dashes go on the outside. Question marks and exclamation marks have their own rules depending on the sentence. Keep these in mind today and whenever you are quoting someone in your writing.

FOR ADDITIONAL SUPPORT, TRY

2.12 Who Said That?
6.40 What Do the Experts Say?
7.5 Watch What You Say
7.8 Just Right Sentences

TIPS/RESOURCES

- Make an anchor chart with quotation rules.
- Display a labeled exemplary quote.

[1] Davies, N. (2005). *Surprising Sharks.* Candlewick.

*See sample chart, "Check Those Quotes!," on page 380.

LESSON 7.6

Putting Paragraphs to Work

In this lesson, students learn to organize paragraphs by rereading them and thinking about which sentences they need to break up or combine.

Writing Stage: Transitional, Fluent
Genre: Feature Article, Literary Nonfiction, Expository Nonfiction, Research Report, Biography, Expository Essay

INTRODUCE

Tell students that they will learn how to combine or separate paragraphs.

Think about how much faster you can find things when they're organized. Imagine you're getting dressed and you open up your pants drawer and find a sock! Good chance this might slow you down or confuse you. Well, the same thing can happen to our readers if our writing is disorganized. Today we are going to learn to edit our paragraphs for clarity and organization.

INSTRUCT

Demonstration

Show students how you read and reorganize sentences to make clearer paragraphs.

Watch me read my writing to see if my paragraphs are organized in a way where all the information fits together. *(Display your writing.)*

> "The octopus can hide and escape from its predators in many ways. It can camouflage against any surface because it can change colors. It can also hide beneath a mound of shells by quickly using its tentacles to flip shells around its body. Since the octopus has no bones, it can even squeeze into small places to hide. The octopus can also shoot water out of its funnel to zoom fast through the water so it can escape its predator. The octopus is skillful at hiding and escaping."

Everything seems to go together with hiding and escaping so far. Let me keep on reading.

> "The octopus is a very intelligent animal. It can sense danger and know when to use its secret weapons quickly and effectively to get away! The octopus can trick its predators by squirting out ink that can blind the predator or cause it to attack the ink cloud instead of the octopus. It is smart in the way it can hide and escape from its predators."

As I read this, I notice that the second paragraph goes with hiding and escaping, but it is too much to put together as one big paragraph. Perhaps I can make one paragraph about hiding and the other about escaping. Let's rework it.

ALTERNATIVE

Inquiry: **Display a mentor text and discuss paragraphing choices. Why might the author have decided to put things together or separate them?**

GUIDE

Ask students to help you reorganize your paragraphs.

Can you help me figure this out? If I want to make the first paragraph about hiding and the second about escaping, which sentences may need to move? See if you and your partner can come up with a suggestion.

(Allow students 1–4 minutes to turn and talk with partners. Share exemplary responses.)

I heard that the sentence about the octopus shooting water from its funnel makes the most sense in paragraph two. Should we put it before or after the sentence about the ink? *(Allow students to call out responses.)* Perhaps after the sentence about the ink since it shoots the ink, then gets away.

Now let's look at our topic and closing sentences to make them match the content of each paragraph.

(Allow students 1–4 minutes to turn and talk. Share exemplary responses and revise. For example, "The Octopus is skilled at hiding." And, "They are smart in how they escape from predators.")

RELEASE

Remind students how to edit their paragraphs for clarity.

Today we focused our thinking around paragraphs—making sure they are clear and organized. We can do this by reading them to see if any paragraphs need to be separated or combined.

FOR ADDITIONAL SUPPORT, TRY

2.20 Put It in a Paragraph

6.29 Tell Me More, Tell Me More

TIPS/RESOURCES

- Have students work with a partner to edit their paragraphs.
- Give students a few opportunities to practice combining and separating paragraphs.

Look It Up

In this lesson, students learn to check the spelling of topic-specific words.

Writing Stage: Any • **Genre:** Any

INTRODUCE

Tell students they can use tools to check the spelling of key words related to their topics.

One thing we want to be sure about when we're editing our work is that all of the words associated with our topic are spelled correctly. One way to do that is to look them up in a dictionary or in other books about the topic.

INSTRUCT

Demonstration

Model how to check your spelling using physical or online dictionaries and/or books about or related to the topic.

I know that we're using our knowledge of spelling patterns and our word wall words as ways to check our work. But when I'm writing a book about a topic, not only do I want to teach you about it—I want to spell all the words related to it correctly! Let me show you with my own work.

Here's my piece on gardening and how plants grow. This part has text, but it also has labels and subheadings. Notice how I check through all of the parts.

In this text box, I'm not really sure how to spell *minerals*. I feel sure that I have the beginning sounds correct, *m-i-n*, so I can look the rest up in a dictionary. *(Model looking through a dictionary.)*

M-I-N-E-R-A-L-S. That's right. The dictionary also gives a pronunciation guide which is helpful for readers. I could include that in my information book. *MIN-er-als*. You stress the *MIN*, so I have that in caps, and I broke it up to show the syllables. *(Display written pronunciation of the word.)*

Now I'm going to look at this other diagram of a plant. Uh-oh! Looks like I wrote *p-e-D-a-l-s* instead of *p-e-T-a-l-s*. I'm glad I checked that! *Pedals* is a word so it doesn't get flagged by a spell-check. It's just the wrong word for my book. So I'll make that change. I don't think I need a pronunciation guide here.

Do you see how I looked closely to make sure that I used the right words, and that they're spelled correctly? I also thought about how I could add a pronunciation guide for some of the key words.

ALTERNATIVE

Guided Practice: **Work with students to use related books and materials to check the spelling of topic-specific words.**

 |

GUIDE

Prompt students to try the strategy using a shared text. Provide a variety of tools for students to try.

Let's try this together. We'll check the words that are related to my topic and make note of any changes. *(Display the sentence below. Provide students with tools to check spelling.)*

> "Plants grow using photosinthesis. That is when plants take water from the soil and carben dioxide from the air to make shugar out of it that they use to grow."

(Allow 1–4 minutes for students to turn and talk with partners. You may choose to have partnerships come up and make changes to the text.)

RELEASE

Remind students to look up topic-specific words as they edit.

As you edit today, be sure to check the specific words related to your topic. Be sure to check all parts of your writing, including titles, headings and subheadings, labels, and text features, even glossaries. We want to make sure we look like authorities on our topic, and one way to do that is to be sure words are spelled correctly.

FOR ADDITIONAL SUPPORT, TRY

7.1 Do You Hear Me? Do You See Me?

7.2 Read the Room

TIPS/RESOURCES

- Have multiple spelling resources available (dictionaries, laptops, etc.).
- Tuck in a brief explanation of how dictionaries work, if needed.

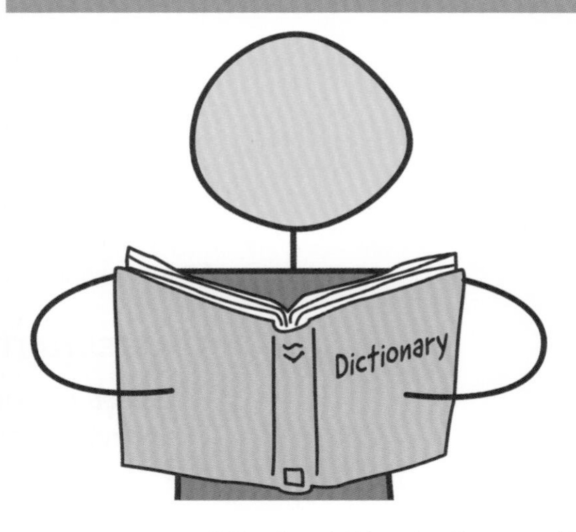

Just Right Sentences

In this lesson, students learn to edit for fragments and run-ons to make sure each sentence is a complete thought.

Writing Stage: Transitional, Fluent

Genre: All-About Book, Feature Article, Literary Nonfiction, Expository, Nonfiction, Research Report, Biography, Expository Essay

INTRODUCE

Tell students it is important to check for fragments and run-on sentences in their writing.

Just because something starts with a capital letter and ends with a period, question mark, or exclamation mark doesn't mean it's a sentence. When we're editing, we need to make sure that our sentences are complete thoughts.

INSTRUCT

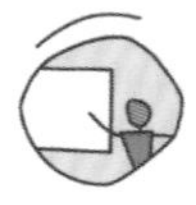

Demonstration

Model for students how to define and identify fragments. Provide a process for correcting these mistakes.

First, I go sentence by sentence and ask myself: Does this sentence have a subject and a verb? Is this a complete thought? If not, I make it into a sentence that has both parts.

If it passes the fragment test, I check to see if it's a run-on. A run-on sentence isn't just a long sentence. It is a sentence that has two independent clauses put together without the use of either a coordinating conjunction or proper punctuation. If I find a run-on sentence, I will need to decide which way to go. I can add the correct punctuation, or I can break it into two sentences.

I'm going to do this with my draft about science fiction writer, N.K. Jemisin:

> "N.K. Jemisin is a best-selling science fiction writer, she is the first author to win three Best Novel Hugo awards in a row, she won a Nebula award, two Locus awards, and she won a MacArthur Genius Fellowship, she was a counselor, educator, and editor before becoming a full-time writer."

Whoa. I'm out of breath just reading it aloud! Let's see if it's a run-on. The first part, "N.K. Jemisin is a *New York Times* best-selling science fiction writer" could be its own sentence—it has a subject and a verb. I could just start the next sentence with a capital **S** in *she*, but I need to make sure it makes sense. I could make the next part its own sentence, too. So now it reads: "She is the first author to win three Best Novel Hugo awards in a row." (*Continue modeling with other sentences.*)

ALTERNATIVE

Guided Practice: **Coach students on the use of the strategy through a shared text.**

GUIDE

Prompt partners to try the strategy on a shared piece of writing.

Look through this part of my draft about Octavia Butler, another science fiction writer. Do any sentences need to be corrected? *(Display text with mistakes below.)*

> "Like N.K. Jemisin, Octavia Butler won Hugo and Nebula awards for her science fiction, she also was the recipient of a MacArthur 'Genius' Fellowship. Kindred, published in 1979. This was her bestselling book, she was well known for both her Patternist and Parable book series."

(Allow 1–4 minutes for students to turn and talk with partners. Share exemplary responses.)

RELEASE

Remind students to check their work for incorrect sentences.

Today, when you go off to write, reread each of your sentences checking for fragments and run-ons. This way you can make sure your reader is able to read your text smoothly. It will also help you come across like the experts you are!

FOR ADDITIONAL SUPPORT, TRY

2.13 Keep 'Em Separated
2.14 Give Them Room to Breathe
2.21 Rhythm Is Gonna Get You
2.22 Conjunction Connection

*See sample chart, "Fragment/Run-On Flowchart," on page 380.

TIPS/RESOURCES

- Note that some very short and very long sentences are appropriate to convey a message.

LESSON 7.9

Check Yourself!

In this lesson, students learn to use a checklist—either by themselves or with a partner—to proofread.

Writing Stage: Any • **Genre:** Any

INTRODUCE

Tell students they will learn to use a checklist to edit their work.

Have you noticed how people make shopping or to-do lists and check off the items as they go along? Checklists are a great way for us to make sure we've done everything—whether we're using one to go food shopping or to check our writing to get ready for publication. We focus on one part of the list at a time and check our writing against it to make sure that we've accomplished all we needed to. We can even give our writing checklist to a friend so they can look at it with fresh eyes.

INSTRUCT

Demonstration

Model how to check your writing using a checklist.

Here's my checklist. I know that I've done these things, so I can say yes to all of them, and then I'm done, right? Easy! Nooooo!!! That's not how you use a checklist! I have to go through each part. So I'll start at the top. The first thing on my checklist is about end punctuation. I have to read through to make sure that I have end punctuation, that it's in the right places, and that my sentences are complete and not fragments. It's not as simple as just looking for periods. This reminds me that I can have a variety of end punctuation, so I might want to change some based on the tone I want to create.

(Demonstrate how to read through your piece, talking about end punctuation, and making changes to satisfy the checklist.)

Now I can check this off my checklist and move on to the next item.

ALTERNATIVE

Guided Practice: **Coach students through using a checklist on a shared piece.**

GUIDE

Prompt students to use the checklist on a shared piece of writing.

Let's look at the next part of our checklist. What are we looking for? Capitalization! Can you quickly tell your partner what we need to look for if we're checking for capitalization?

(Give students 1 minute to turn and talk. Share exemplary responses.)

Now take a minute to look through this next piece, and we'll talk about what changes need to be made in order to check this item off our checklist.

(Allow 1–4 minutes for students to turn and talk with partners. Share exemplary responses. You can invite partners to make the changes on the piece itself, or print copies for partners to make changes.)

RELEASE

Remind students to use the checklist as they edit with a partner.

Today, as you make your way through this checklist, take your time. Have your partner go through the checklist as well. Sometimes it's a good idea to have someone use fresh eyes to look at writing. They will catch anything you might have missed.

FOR ADDITIONAL SUPPORT, TRY

6.25 Check It Together

TIPS/RESOURCES:

- To prevent rushing, have students use tally marks for each time they notice a convention, rather than checking "yes" to a category.

*See sample chart, "Editing Checklist," on page 380.

Lesson 7.4 Stand Up Tall

Quotes "hug" the sentence or phrase.

In the book, *Sharks*, by Seymour Simon, he writes: "Sharks have killed fewer people in the United States in the past one hundred years than are killed in automobile accidents over a single holiday weekend."

, . commas and periods go INSIDE the quotes

In the book, *Sharks*, by Seymour Simon, he writes: "Sharks have killed fewer people in the United States in the past one hundred years than are killed in automobile accidents over a single holiday weekend."

Lesson 7.5 Watch What You Say

Lesson 7.8 Just Right Sentences

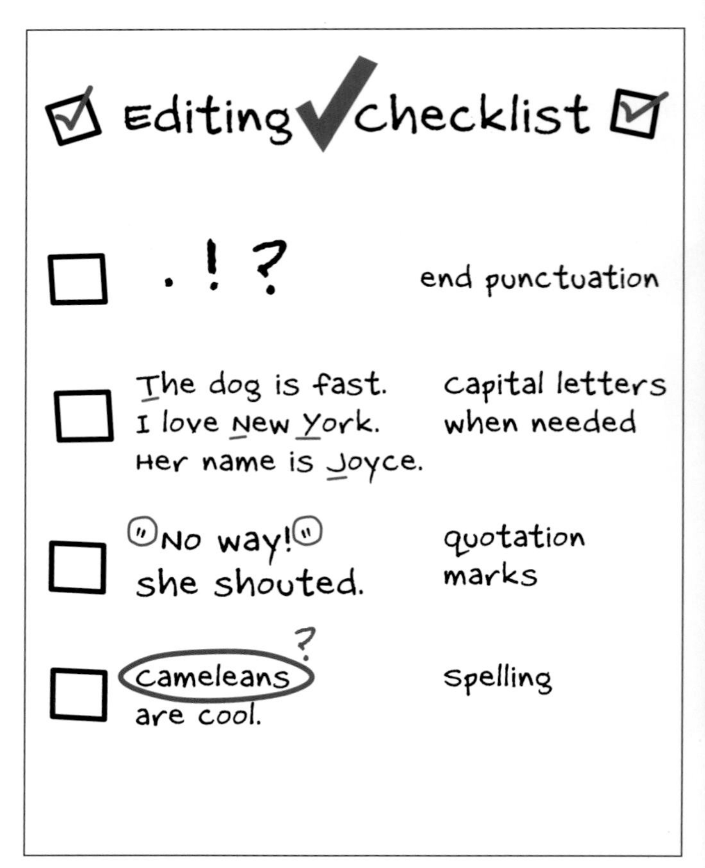

Lesson 7.9 Check Yourself!

 |

Present & Reflect

The series of lessons in this section contain suggestions for students to publish and present their writing to others. The lessons:

- include different publishing features a writer might include; and
- are typically used at the end of the unit.

Descriptors for Presenting and Reflecting

Emergent Writers	Fluent Writers
• Select one of the many written pieces from their folders to publish. • Add color detail to their illustrations. • Incorporate additional publishing features (e.g., covers, titles, etc.). • Celebrate their writing by sharing and reading aloud with others. • Reflect on their growth as writers.	• Recopy their writing to make sure it is legible and includes all revisions and editing corrections.* • Add illustrations and publishing features (e.g., titles, dedications, etc.). • Celebrate their writing by sharing and reading aloud with others. • Reflect on their growth as writers.

* While independent students in the upper grades will typically recopy or electronically produce their writing, we do not include such lessons for emergent or primary grade students.

At-a-Glance Guide

Present & Reflect

Title		Lesson
8.1	**Pick and Choose**	Select one book from the folder that elicits pride and engages an audience.
8.2	**2B Real**	Add feature elements that are colorful, realistic, and engaging.
8.3	**Lay It Out**	Consider a layout for the picture book or article sections.
8.4	**Give Credit Where Credit Is Due**	Add a reference page that lists all the sources.
8.5	**Help Your Reader Learn More**	Add a "For More Information" section.
8.6	**Text Features That Organize**	Zoom in on ways to better organize writing.
8.7	**Publishing Features That Entice**	Create catchy publishing features.
8.8	**Reach Your Audience**	Celebrate with a book or "expert fair."
8.9	**Present at a "Conference"**	Create a poster or slide show that summarizes the research.
8.10	**Compliments and Questions**	Give specific compliments and questions to fellow writers.
8.11	**Reflect on Your Journey**	Reflect on learning growth and set new goals.
8.12	**Help Others Set Goals**	Provide and accept feedback for "glows" and "grows."

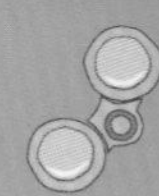

Writing Stage	Genre	
Emergent Transitional	List Pattern	How-To All-About
Any	Any	
Transitional Fluent	How-To All-About Feature Article Literary Nonfiction	Expository Nonfiction Research Report Biography
Fluent	Feature Article Literary Nonfiction Expository Nonfiction	Research Report Biography Expository Essay
Transitional Fluent	All-About Feature Article Literary Nonfiction Expository Nonfiction	Research Report Biography Expository Essay
Any	How-To All-About Feature Article Literary Nonfiction	Expository Nonfiction Research Report Biography Expository Essay
Any	Any	
Any	Any	
Fluent	Feature Article Literary Nonfiction	Expository Nonfiction Research Report
Any	Any	
Any	Any	
Any	Any	

Pick and Choose

In this lesson, students learn to prepare to publish by selecting one book from their own folder. They consider which writing makes them proud and engages their audience.

Writing Stage: Emergent, Transitional • **Genre:** List, Pattern, How-To Book, All-About Book

INTRODUCE

Tell students that they will use guiding questions to help them determine which piece to publish.

We are coming to the point in our writing process where we need to decide which book we will choose to publish. We have all been working hard, which is evident in all the booklets you have in your folders. With all these choices, it's important that we spend some time thinking about this decision carefully. We should consider which one we are the most proud of, which is the most clear, and which one our audience would appreciate.

INSTRUCT

Demonstration

Show students how you choose a piece of writing to publish by considering how it makes you feel, how much it says, and how the audience may respond to it.

Watch me as I go through my writing folder and use the questions on this chart to help me remember what I should consider while I make this important decision. *(Display an anchor chart with guiding questions and refer to it repeatedly while you make a selection. Use these questions: Is this my best writing? Does it say the most about my topic? Am I proud of this work?)*

Here I have my writing about transportation. Is this my best writing? Well, I remember working hard on this, but I don't think it's my best. I don't remember putting my best effort into it, so let me see what else I have in my folder. Here I have a piece on cats. I remember working hard on this one because I love cats, but let me see what other questions I should consider. *(Refer to anchor chart.)* Does it say the most about my topic? Well, now that I think about it, I only wrote a little on each page, where I know I wrote so much more in some of my other booklets. So maybe this isn't the best choice. Let's see what else I have. Here is one about the beach. I recall working quite hard on this one. There is also a lot of writing on each page. Am I proud of this work? I am very proud because I know I used a lot of details in the pictures and words of this booklet. In fact, I had so much to say that I even added extra pages. This is definitely my best writing, the one where I said the most and feel most proud of.

Do you see how I chose a booklet to publish? I made sure to ask myself these questions to help me decide.

 |

GUIDE

Prompt students to think about the booklets they have in their folders and use the questions to guide their thinking on which one to choose.

Let's start this work together. Choose one booklet from your folder. Let's read the guiding questions on our chart so you remember what to ask yourself. *(Read the anchor chart together.)* Explain to your partner whether you think the piece you are holding is your best writing, one where you say the most about your topic, and the one which you are most proud of.

(Allow 1–4 minutes for students to turn and talk with partners. Share exemplary responses.)

RELEASE

Remind students to carefully choose the piece they will publish.

Today you will choose the writing that you are going to publish. Remember that you want to be thoughtful in your selection so that you can feel proud of what you put out into the world, while also exciting your audience for what they will learn. As you go through each booklet in your folder, use the guiding questions to help you decide which reflects your best work, has the most to say about your topic, and makes you feel most proud.

FOR ADDITIONAL SUPPORT, TRY

4.1 Chatterbox

4.3 Stay Connected

TIPS/RESOURCES

- Create a class chart that lists the topic each student has chosen to publish.

2B Real

In this lesson, students learn to make realistic illustrations, find photographs that show appropriate detail, locate multimedia to put into their presentations, and/or use digital tools to create charts or graphs.

Writing Stage: Any • **Genre:** Any

INTRODUCE

Tell students that they will consider adding publishing features to their writing.

As we prepare for publishing, we need to think about how to ensure that our writing will be engaging. We know as readers that a text really grabs hold of us when the visuals are colorful, realistic, and informative. Today we will consider the use of life-like illustrations, photographs, multimedia elements, and digital charts or graphs.

INSTRUCT

Explain with Examples

Explain each feature and give an example of how it might work with your topic. You may choose to use a mentor text.

Let me explain to you some of the different options.

Create Realistic Illustrations with Color and Details Informational texts often include illustrations that are bold and colorful and that include the tiniest of details. The colors that are used tend to be realistic so that they match how they appear in the real world. Or they can be bold, more colorful versions of real world colors. Including details will help it look lifelike and give the reader more information. For instance, in my writing about the octopus, I could make a realistic illustration of an octopus. I could also include details such as the eyes, beak, and eight arms with rows of suction cups on each arm.

Find Photographs Nothing beats a real-life photograph that shows intricate details of your topic. Perhaps there's something about your topic that is a bit tricky to illustrate, such as the rows and rows of shark teeth. I would want my reader to see how sharp the teeth are and how there are several rows going back into the shark's mouth, which is difficult to draw accurately. In that instance, a photograph could be a wise choice to include as a publishing feature.

Locate Video/Multimedia Another option is to include a video clip in the presentation that highlights key aspects of the topic. Video clips are great tools that not only engage the audience but also bring the topic to life. For example, I could have a video showing how the octopus has the ability to squirt ink out of its funnel to trick its enemy. I can find a video clip of that and add it to my presentation.

Use Digital Tools Digital tools can be used to make charts, maps, graphs, and other features that you can add to your published piece. Sometimes, drawing these things can be hard and quite unrealistic, but using a digital tool can help the information look clean and clear. For example, in my writing about sharks, I have a part about the sharks that live in different areas of the world. With a digital tool, I can create a map that highlights the different species in each ocean.

 |

GUIDE

Prompt students to consider and discuss what they might include in their writing.

Think about your writing and what you want to bring to life. Maybe you'll revisit, revise, or create a new, detailed illustration. Perhaps you might consider including a real photograph. Or if you're working on a presentation, perhaps you can find and include a video clip. And last, consider using digital tools to make a clear visual for your readers.

(Allow 1–4 minutes for students to turn and talk with partners. Share exemplary responses.)

RELEASE

Remind students how they can bring their writing to life.

Today we focused on some features that can make our writing interesting, clear, and informative. These features include: illustrations, photographs, videos, and digital tools. As you prepare to publish today, consider how you'll make your writing come alive!

FOR ADDITIONAL SUPPORT, TRY

6.6 Text Features Enhance Understanding

6.43 How Can I Help You?

TIPS/RESOURCES

- Create a chart that lists each visual publishing feature. Include an example and an explanation for easy reference.

Lay It Out

In this lesson, students learn to consider a layout for their picture books or article sections. They will play with pictures, text placement, highlighting techniques, and more.

Writing Stage: Transitional, Fluent

Genre: How-To Book, All-About Book, Feature Article, Literary Nonfiction, Expository Nonfiction, Research Report, Biography

INTRODUCE

Tell students that today they will consider the layout for their writing.

Sometimes the way something looks and appears is what makes it appealing to someone. Oftentimes, we peek inside a book and decide if it "looks" interesting. As writers, we need to think about how we are making our writing appealing. We can do this by considering the layout of our writing. The layout refers to text and illustration placement across one or two pages. Today we will consider the layout of our writing and play with different ideas and options to see what works best as we prepare to publish our piece.

INSTRUCT

Demonstration

Show students how you consider various layout and design options for your writing, including text placement, background color, use of images, and single versus two-page spreads.

Watch me as I think about the layout for my writing. *(Have a prepared demonstration piece of writing that you can cut apart and manipulate.)*

Here I have my writing about the octopus. I have certain sections with headings and plenty of illustrations and features, but perhaps I can make it a little more engaging for readers by thinking of the layout. For instance, the first section is my introduction. I think it would fit best on a single page since I don't have too much information in this part. Maybe I could cut out this section header, put a box around it, and go over it with a big, bold, blue marker. Then I can place my introduction right underneath it so my text placement will go from top to bottom. It would probably be visually pleasing if I made the background a bluish color to match the colors in the ocean. For this next section on different types of octopuses, I think a two-page spread would work best. So maybe this information can go left to right across the two pages. There is a huge range in sizes for octopuses, and if I lay it out across a two-page spread I'll have more space. It will also be easier for the reader to see the drastic contrast in sizes. I also think that cutting out my section heading and using a blue background like I did for my introduction would work well throughout my book.

Let me show you what my writing looks like now with some of the changes to the layout. *(Show students the new layout.)*

Do you see how I thought about the layout of my writing? Did you notice how I thought about how I could engage the reader and present my information in the most clear, organized, and interesting way?

 |

GUIDE

Prompt students to consider the layout of their writing and how to make it more appealing to the reader.

Now it's your turn to give it a try. Take out your writing and think about how it currently looks. Ask yourself: Can it be more engaging? How so? Can I play around with the text and images to make things pop? Should I add a background color? Should certain sections fit on one page or span across a two-page spread?

(Allow 1–4 minutes for students to turn and talk with partners. Share exemplary responses.)

RELEASE

Remind students of the importance of considering the layout for their writing.

Today we focused on the layout of our writing. We considered different options to present our writing in a way that is appealing to the reader. We want readers to see our writing and say, "Ohhh, look at that book. That looks interesting!" We can appeal to readers by thinking of our layout options and page spreads, making highlighted headings pop out, and using background colors. Let's lay it out!

FOR ADDITIONAL SUPPORT, TRY

8.6 Text Features That Organize
8.7 Publishing Features that Entice

TIPS/RESOURCES

- Have your writing prepared in advance.
- Decide what tools and how creative students can get in this lesson—gather glue, scissors, construction paper/ scrapbook paper, markers, etc.
- Have some mentor texts handy for students to study various layouts.

Give Credit Where Credit Is Due

In this lesson, students learn how to add a reference page that lists all the sources they used, including the title, author, publisher, and date of publication.

Writing Stage: Fluent
Genre: Feature Article, Literary Nonfiction, Expository Nonfiction, Research Report, Biography, Expository Essay

INTRODUCE

Tell students that today they will make a reference page to list the sources they used in their writing.

We have been working on our informational pieces of writing—gathering information, collecting facts and ideas, researching specific things about our topic, and putting it all together. As writers, one of the things that you have to be cautious of is making sure you give credit to an original source. It might be citing where you found a fact or giving the author credit for an idea of theirs that you're including in your own writing. To do this, you'll need to make a reference page that includes the sources you used with the title, author, publisher, and date of publication. This shows the reader where you found your information and gives the reader another place to look if they want to learn more about the topic.

INSTRUCT

Explain With Examples

Show students the reference page you made. Explain why each source needed to be cited.

Let me show you how I created my reference page to give the proper credit.

For my piece about sharks, I used a lot of different resources. For instance, I relied very heavily on the book, *Sharks*, by Seymour Simon for some basic background information about sharks. I also used some of the ideas and surprising facts in *Surprising Sharks,* by Nicola Davies. So on my reference page, I will include both of these titles, authors, and publishing information. I also used some websites to help me gather facts to support my idea that sharks are strong swimmers. I will include those websites on my reference page as well. Here is what my reference page looks like. *(Display reference page.)* I can find this important information inside the books that I used—on the cover and in the front matter on the copyright page.

Do you see how I thought about the different sources I used for my writing? Then I listed them all on a reference page to give credit to the original sources. This allows the reader to see where I got some of my facts and ideas ,and also gives them a way to read up more on the topic.

GUIDE

Prompt students to think and share with their partners the sources they need to include on their reference pages.

Think about the sources you used that helped you create this piece of writing. Who do you need to give credit to? Turn and talk with your partner to discuss the sources you think should be credited on your reference page.

(Allow 1–4 minutes for students to turn and talk with partners. Share exemplary responses.)

RELEASE

Remind students about the importance of having a reference page.

Today we talked about the very important work of giving credit to the original sources we use in our writing. When we write an informational piece, oftentimes we gather information from books, articles, and websites. We need to make sure that we create a reference page that reflects the original sources so that we aren't accidentally "stealing" an author's idea or taking information from a website and pretending like it's our own.

FOR ADDITIONAL SUPPORT, TRY

5.17 The Best Laid Plans
5.20 Writers Take Note
6.40 What Do the Experts Say?
6.42 Back It Up!

TIPS/RESOURCES

- Have your reference page premade.
- Have other reference pages to show as examples.

Help Your Reader Learn More

In this lesson, students learn to add a "For More Information" section so that readers can research the subject further, if interested.

Writing Stage: Transitional, Fluent
Genre: All-About Book, Feature Article, Literary Nonfiction, Expository Nonfiction, Research Report, Biography, Expository Essay

INTRODUCE

Tell students that nonfiction writers sometimes provide additional resources for their readers.

Nonfiction writers hope that the information they teach will not only make their readers smarter but also curious to learn more. Since writers can't include *everything* there is to know about any given topic, they sometimes direct their readers to places where they can find additional information. These resources can include: books, websites, apps, magazines, television programs or channels, places to visit, and organizations to join.

INSTRUCT

Demonstration

Model how you search for appropriate resources to add at the end of your writing.

One kind of publishing feature that we can include in our writing is a "For More Information" section.

I'm going to include a "For More Information" page at the end of my writing about the Solar System. Now I have to think about my audience. If my readers are children, I cannot send them to places for adults because they won't understand the information. The information also has to match my topic. So if my book is mostly about the planets, readers don't need books about galaxies, stars, etc. Lastly, I don't want to send my readers to places they likely know about. Now that I have narrowed it down, I might want to limit it to the top 5–10 things.

(Begin a "For More Information" page. As you locate a resource, add it to your list.)

First, I will look through our classroom or school library for some books. I know that the books will be kid-friendly. *(Have a collection of books handy and model how you select an appropriate title.)* Perhaps I will include this book, *The Planets,* by Gail Gibbons. It is about my topic, it is kid-friendly, and it has interesting information.

Next, I can search for websites. *(Do a quick web search.)* I will type "space websites for kids" in the search bar. It looks like NASA and National Geographic both have websites for kids. I trust those sources because NASA is part of the government and National Geographic is a reputable publisher. Let's click and see if they are any good. If so, we can include these websites.

I can also check the app store on my tablet or phone device for interesting resources. *(Search for apps.)* Let's see which have the highest rating and are free. Here in the app store, there is a review for "Star Walk Kids." Let's read it and see if it's worthwhile. It says great things and it's for kids 4+.

 |

GUIDE

Ask students to help you include additional resources to your piece.

Let's do another search for "space magazines for kids." Let's read the descriptions and take a look to see if any are worth adding to our list. *Astronomy for Kids* looks interesting—what do you think? I have another idea! Let's think about local places to visit or possible clubs at our school or in our community that readers can join to learn more about planets.

(Allow 1–4 minutes for students to turn and talk with partners. Share exemplary responses.)

RELEASE

Remind students to consider a "For More Information" page for their topics.

So, readers, one publishing feature you might include in your writing is a "For More Information" page. It won't be relevant for all topics, but if it is, you should consider adding one.

FOR ADDITIONAL SUPPORT, TRY

8.4 Give Credit Where Credit Is Due
8.7 Publishing Features That Entice

TIPS/RESOURCES

- If technology isn't available, consider limiting resources to just books and periodicals.
- Ask the school media or technology specialist to help.

LESSON 8.6

Text Features That Organize

In this lesson, students learn to zoom in on ways to organize their writing, including a table of contents, subheadings, visuals, glossaries, and indexes.

Writing Stage: Any

Genre: How-To Book, All-About Book, Feature Article, Literary Nonfiction Expository Nonfiction, Research Report, Biography, Expository Essay

INTRODUCE

Tell students that text features organize the information and help readers better understand.

Nonfiction writers often use text features to help their readers understand information. They use some text features to organize information and other features to enhance the reader's understanding of the information.

INSTRUCT

Explain with Examples

Using a variety of mentor texts, explain the purpose of different text features that aid the reader. Explain to students that there is no need to overuse text features if their writing doesn't warrant them.

It is important to remember that not all information books use text features. And some may only use a few. Writers only include what will help the reader focus and better understand the concepts and ideas.

Text features that organize include:

Table of Contents If the book or article has many sections or chapters, it helps set the reader up for the kind of information they will learn about a topic. It also helps readers locate a specific section quickly.

Headings These give the reader an idea of what each section is about. Consider using headings if your chapters or sections have different categories of information. Otherwise, your chapter title will be enough.

Subheadings If the information underneath the heading needs to be divided into more sections, then consider using subheadings. These break information down further for readers.

Index Use this to help your reader jump to specific information in a book beyond just the chapters, such as ideas, concepts, and details.

Text features that enhance understanding include:

Visuals These give readers a picture in their minds, through diagrams with labels, photos with captions, charts, and graphs. Readers get a better sense of details and learn more than what the words alone say.

Glossaries A glossary helps define words and concepts that are specific to the topic and that the reader may not know. If you have a lot of topic words, create a glossary as a reference. If you only have a few words, consider using a callout box or embedding the definition in a sentence.

Do you see how text features are tools to help the reader?

GUIDE

Ask students to consult with a partner about text features that need to be added or removed from their writing.

Take a moment to look at which text features you have already included as you prepare to publish. Should you add or remove any?

(Allow 1–4 minutes for students to turn and talk with partners. Share exemplary responses.)

RELEASE

Remind students to be mindful of their text features as they prepare to publish.

As you prepare to publish, remember that text features are there to help guide your readers. Decide which ones will be most useful for them to help locate and understand your information clearly.

FOR ADDITIONAL SUPPORT, TRY

6.43 How Can I Help You?

6.45 Give Me a Sign

6.55 Revising The TOC

TIPS/RESOURCES

- Display an anchor chart that has examples of the different text features.*
- Compare and contrast books on the same topic that use different text features.

*See sample chart, "Text Features," on page 408.

LESSON 8.7

Publishing Features That Entice

In this lesson, students learn to create publishing features that include catchy titles, cover illustrations, author bios, and more.

Writing Stage: Any • **Genre:** Any

INTRODUCE

Tell students that writers include a number of publishing features to entice the reader.

Authors often include different publishing features that entice, excite, and inform their readers. They try to make the writing jump off the shelf and into a reader's hands with a compelling cover and sharply written text in the front and end matter.

INSTRUCT

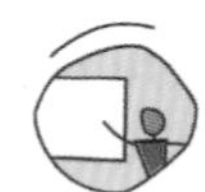

Demonstration

Model how you create different publishing features for your own writing, including a title, cover art, bio, synopsis, and dedication.

Let me show you. I am going to publish my piece, "The Planets."

Title I could just call this piece "The Planets," but I am not sure it will excite a reader. Perhaps a catchier title like "Journey to the Planets" will get my reader wondering what it would be like to go to each planet.

Cover Art Drawing a picture of a planet feels flat. Perhaps my cover would better match if I drew the planets small and far away with a spaceship heading in that direction and a person inside. That would give the readers the feeling that they themselves were the ones in the spaceship.

Author Bio Sometimes an author's bio can convince a reader to pick up a book because it shows that they are knowledgeable. My bio can't just say how old I am, where I live, etc. Instead, it has to show why I am an expert at planets. Perhaps it can read, "Mr. L is a third-grade teacher in New York. His favorite subject to teach is science, especially astronomy. He has been fascinated with the night sky since he was a young boy."

Synopsis Creating a little blurb can get a reader interested in reading a piece. I could write, "This book is about the different planets." However, that doesn't seem exciting. Perhaps instead I can write, "Journey into the unknown! This book will take you through space as you travel to each of the planets. Learn what life would be like if you were given the chance to live in these mysterious places." Wouldn't you be more interested in reading this now?

Dedication Lastly, writers include dedications that honor someone or a group of people. It can be someone who inspires them or someone they are grateful for. I can write, "This book is dedicated to Mom and Dad for buying me my first telescope."

 |

GUIDE

Prompt students to consider publishing features for their writing.

I want you to think about the publishing features you plan to include for your writing. What ideas do you have so far for your topic? Which one do you think you will begin with?

(Allow 1–4 minutes for students to turn and talk with partners. Share exemplary responses.)

RELEASE

Remind students that the right publishing features draw a reader's eye.

So, writers, or should I say publishers, as you go off to prepare to publish your writing, remember that the features you include help entice your reader to make them want to read your work. Be mindful of how you create your title, cover art, bio, synopsis, and dedications so that your work jumps off the shelf.

FOR ADDITIONAL SUPPORT, TRY

8.2 2B Real

TIPS/RESOURCES

- Create an anchor chart with different publishing features.
- Give students collections of texts for them to study and discuss different features and effects on the reader.

Reach Your Audience

In this lesson, students learn to celebrate with an "expert fair" where they read and answer questions for fans about their process, knowledge, and experience.

Writing Stage: Any • **Genre:** Any

INTRODUCE

Tell students that authors celebrate their hard work by having a book launch or celebration.

In order to celebrate their accomplishments and generate excitement about their projects, writers will have a book launch or celebration. This may include receptions, book tours, or special visits to bookstores so that writers can meet their audience, autograph copies of their work, and answer questions from fans.

INSTRUCT

Explain with Examples

Explain to students how you will celebrate their work.

(Select the celebration most appropriate and feasible for your class.)

Roundtable During this type of celebration, we will sit with a group of students at a table and take turns presenting our writing. We explain what our writing is mostly about and we read all or part of our writing. Once we read, we go around and allow a compliment and question from each tablemate.

Partner Reading We can celebrate with a partner reading where we share our entire piece with our writing partner. We then hear compliments and questions from our partner. We also thank our partners for their ongoing support and the specific ways that they helped us make our writing the best it could be.

Buddy Celebration We will buddy up and present our work with a student from another class. We read our entire piece and allow for compliments and questions from our buddy.

Museum Share In a museum share, we lay our pieces on our desks, and the class circulates and looks at everyone's work. We can leave questions or compliments on comment cards for the pieces we read.

Expert Fair In an expert fair, we line up the tables around the room. We each take our place behind the table with our writing in front of us. We invite guests to come. We explain our topic and show parts of our book. We allow for compliments and questions.

Guest Reception During a guest reception, we invite caretakers or school building guests into the classroom where we read and share our work with them. Then we answer their questions.

Ceremonial Share During a ceremonial share, we will each get called up, one-by-one, to present the title of our book to the entire class. Everyone applauds as our books are placed into the classroom library or up on a bulletin board for all to see. We can then read each other's work at different times of the day.

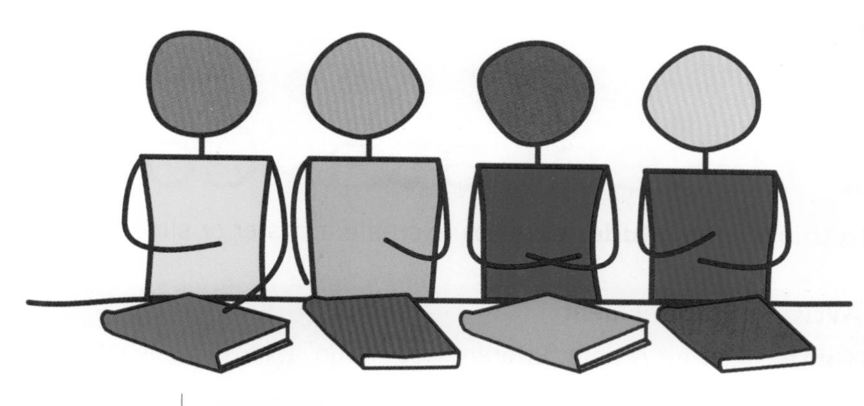

GUIDE

Explain the expectations of the presenter and audience. Have students practice in partnerships.

As we prepare to celebrate, it is important to know the jobs of the presenter and the audience. Turn and face your partner with your writing in your hands. Decide which partner will present first.

The presenter holds up their writing so that it is visible to the audience. The presenter looks at the attendee(s), specifically at their eyes, when speaking. The presenter speaks in a tall, clear, slow voice. We can start by saying, "My name is _____, and the title of my piece is _____. It is about _____. Let me show you the most interesting part _____." *(Allow students to practice.)*

The attendee has the job of keeping a calm body and looking interested. Look at the presenter's eyes or at their book. It is important to hold your questions until there's a pause or the presentation is finished. Give a specific compliment, using the phrase, "I like the way you _____." *(Allow students to practice.)*

RELEASE

Remind students of the importance of good etiquette when presenting at or attending a celebration.

So, presenters and attendees, remember that when you go to celebrate today, use proper etiquette. Be curious toward one another's ideas and questions when speaking and listening.

FOR ADDITIONAL SUPPORT, TRY

8.10 Compliments and Questions

TIPS/RESOURCES

- Brainstorm a list of possible compliments and questions.
- Watch a video of a presentation and ask students to comment on the behaviors they see.

Present at a "Conference"

In this lesson, students learn to create a poster or slide show to present their work.

Writing Stage: Fluent
Genre: Feature Article, Literary Nonfiction, Expository Nonfiction, Research Report

INTRODUCE

Tell students they can present their writing to others by creating a poster or slide show with an accompanying "talk."

There are many professions where people are asked to present their ideas at conferences—professors, doctors, and teachers, to name a few. Typically, instead of reading a paper aloud, they create a poster or digital slide show and talk about the major points. They add graphics that help engage their audience and illuminate their findings as well. To prepare for publication, we're going to pretend that we're getting ready for a conference—turning our writing into presentations by distilling our ideas into key points and finding images to support our work.

INSTRUCT

Demonstration

Model for students how to distill your final piece of writing into a poster or key slides to support your talking points.

Let's look at this section from my piece about architecture. First, I will identify the key points. In this part, I'm writing about the Classical Style of architecture. It was developed by the ancient Greeks and Romans. Greeks built temples in rectangular shapes with porticos, or porches, supported by columns. Romans built with giant arches, making huge public spaces such as amphitheaters, the most famous being the Coliseum. Maybe I'll come up with the key points and then think about a catchy title. So the important styles the Greeks developed were the Doric, Ionic, and Corinthian columns, which are identified by their capital—how they are designed at the top. So far, I could say:

Classical Greek and Roman Architecture

Greeks
- Temples
- Portico

Styles:
- Doric
- Ionic
- Corinthian

Romans
- Arches
- Amphitheaters (Coliseum)

I might add pictures of the columns, temples, and the Coliseum. Then I will practice summarizing the information to sound like talking.

ALTERNATIVE

Guided Practice: **Try this strategy with students by asking: How can we take the information in this section and put it on a poster or slide? What images might we add?**

GUIDE

Ask students to help you with the next section of your poster or slide show.

Let's look at the next part of my writing. What key points would you add to a poster or put on a slide? Would you add any visuals? (*Display the next section of your writing. Give students time to brainstorm and quickly sketch ideas for a poster or slideshow.*) Once you have come up with your ideas, think about what you would say if you were presenting.

(Allow 1–4 minutes for students to turn and talk with partners. Share exemplary responses.)

RELEASE

Remind students that when presenting, they want to summarize key ideas.

When you go off to prepare for publishing today, look at your writing in "chunks" that could be sections or paragraphs. Take the big ideas in those parts and create a poster or slides. Then create a presentation and rehearse it so that you're ready to talk with your peers when we publish.

FOR ADDITIONAL SUPPORT, TRY

8.2 2B Real

8.3 Lay It Out

TIPS/RESOURCES:

- Present models of professional posters or slides.
- Show videos of lectures so that students can see the difference between what's on the slide and what the person speaking says.

Compliments and Questions

In this lesson, students learn to give specific compliments to their fellow writers and ask questions about both their processes and their topics.

Writing Stage: Any • **Genre:** Any

INTRODUCE

Tell students that active listeners give feedback when they hear someone present their work.

When we listen to someone present their work, it is important to respond with feedback. Feedback includes compliments and questions for the presenter.

INSTRUCT

Explain with Examples

Explain to students that feedback involves different ways to compliment a writer and ask questions about their topics and their process.

As we all know, writing and publishing requires a lot of time and hard work, so we want to compliment writers for the things they did well. A good compliment must be specific. We cannot just say, "I like your writing." Instead, we name exactly what we think the writer did particularly well.

We can compliment their ideas by saying: "I really like your topic." "I like your title." Or "I like your angle, or what you said about the topic."

We can compliment how they organized their writing by saying: "I really like the chapters or subtopics that you included." Or "I like the order in which you put the information together."

We can compliment how they developed their writing and used details by saying: "I really like the details you included. They really helped me understand." Or "I like the way you said a lot about each fact/idea."

We can compliment their style and craft by saying: "I like the way you used visuals. Your pictures are well done." Or "I like the way you used a table of contents (headings, glossaries, fun facts, sidebars, etc.)."

We can compliment their presentation: "You were very clear when you shared your ideas." Or "You speak really well when you present."

A good, active listener also asks different kinds of questions that show they were paying attention. We can ask questions about the topic if we want to learn more about something. Questions begin with: *who, what, when, where, why, how, does,* and *did*.

We can also ask questions about their writing. These usually begin with the phrases: "How did you _____?" "What did you _____?" "When did you _____?" "Why did you _____?" or "Where did you _____?"

GUIDE

Read an excerpt from your own writing to elicit compliments and questions.

Let's try it. You will all be my audience. I am going to show and read you a snippet or chapter of my writing. You and your partner will think of a compliment you can give me for my ideas, organization, development, craft, and presentation. Then we will follow up with some questions.

(Read a piece of your writing. Ask the students generate compliments for each category.)

RELEASE

Remind students that active listeners give specific compliments and questions.

As you go off and present your published pieces to one another in our celebration today, be active listeners by paying attention to what the speaker is saying, looking closely at their work, and thinking about what specifically impressed you and what you wondered about.

FOR ADDITIONAL SUPPORT, TRY

8.9 Present at a "Conference"

TIPS/RESOURCES

- At the end of the celebration, fishbowl a partnership that did particularly good work.

*See sample chart, "Compliments and Questions," on page 408.

LESSON 8.11

Reflect on Your Journey

In this lesson, students learn to reflect on how they've grown as a writer and set new goals.

Writing Stage: Any • **Genre:** Any

INTRODUCE

Tell students reflecting on our work is a way to set goals and grow.

Reflecting on our experience is part of being human. We look back, we learn, we set goals, and we move forward. We do this after so many experiences, it only makes sense to do this in writing as well. In fact, there's tons of research about how pausing to reflect is the way people learn. So today we're going to pause and reflect on what we've learned about ourselves as writers in order to both celebrate our accomplishments and set goals for future writing.

INSTRUCT

Demonstration

Model for students how you read your writing to acknowledge your growth and to set goals.

I've created a series of prompts to help us reflect.*

- What did you learn about: The genre? Structure? Elaboration? Conventions? The writing process? Volume and stamina? Yourself as a writer?

- What's an example of your best work? What did it take to achieve that?

- What's an area where you'd like to improve and why?

Let me show you what some of this reflection and goal-setting work might look like. I put a self-stick note on the part in my writing that I think reflects my best work. (*Display work.*) And this is what I wrote about it:

> "I think this part where I really elaborate shows some of my best work. I did this by making sure to balance facts with ideas, descriptions, and even comparisons to help my facts come to life. One area I'd like to improve in is stamina. I notice in my notebook, some entries are focused and long; others are short and scattered. I'd like to get better at making use of my time every day."

Do you see how I had a specific part of my writing that I liked and reflected on what I did to make it that way? Then I set a goal for myself based on something I noticed in my folder/notebook.

GUIDE

Ask students to choose one prompt to discuss with a partner.

Let's try one of these prompts together. Take a minute and talk to your partner.

(*Provide a prompt for students to discuss. Allow 1–4 minutes for students to turn and talk with partners. Share exemplary responses.*)

RELEASE

Remind students that reflecting on past work is the way we grow in writing and in life.

Today, when you go back to reflect on your writing, really think about how you've grown and what you've learned to do. Then consider what goal you might set for yourself or your next writing piece.

FOR ADDITIONAL SUPPORT, TRY

8.10 Compliments and Questions

8.12 Help Others Set Goals

TIPS/RESOURCES:

- For emergent writers, connect prompts to specific tools or charts in the classroom.
- Support students by asking them to highlight places in their writing that correspond to a particular prompt.

*See sample chart, "Reflection Questions," on page 408.

Help Others Set Goals

In this lesson, students learn to reflect in partnerships by providing each other with feedback for "glows" and "grows."

Writing Stage: Any • **Genre:** Any

INTRODUCE

Tell students partners can help them celebrate and set goals by sharing "glows" and "grows."

Writing partners can serve as teachers to us. They can give us compliments, or glowing admiration of our work. They can also give us ideas for how we can grow, or push ourselves, as writers.

INSTRUCT

Demonstration

Model for students how to be a helpful partner by sharing positive feedback, as well as a tip for improvement.

Watch me as I look at this piece of writing from my partner, and how I imagine the feedback I'm going to give my partner. First, I'm going to give them a compliment, or a "glow." I'm going to make sure it's both positive and specific. I could say, "I love how you said more about your topic. You tried to give your reader a lot of facts. Like here, you said that an octopus is a cephalopod. And here you said that an octopus has eight tentacles. You're really teaching your reader a lot!" Now I have to find a specific thing they could do to make their writing better. I might say, "You can also teach by adding labels to your drawings. Like, I know you know the parts of the octopus—you have them in your writing. It would also teach your reader to have a drawing and then label that drawing."

Did you see how I thought about something good that they were doing, and I found examples to share with my partner? Then I thought about something that I think they could add to make their writing even clearer.

 |

GUIDE

Prompt students to be your writing partner by asking them to work through "glows" and "grows" using a piece of projected text.

Now it's your turn to try. Look at this other piece of text. Turn to your partner and work to find as many glows and grows as you can. Remember, when you're sharing a "grow," be careful and kind in your language.

(Allow 1–4 minutes for students to turn and talk with partners. Share exemplary responses.)

RELEASE

Remind students that writers, and people, grow when they have support, as well as clear and kind feedback.

When you go off to work today, share your writing with your partner. Take turns giving your partner honest, but kind, feedback. Be sure to consider adopting your partner's "grow" as a goal for yourself.

FOR ADDITIONAL SUPPORT, TRY

8.10 Compliments and Questions

8.11 Reflect on Your Journey

TIPS/RESOURCES

- Chart examples of "glows" and "grows" in different categories (topics, structure, elaboration, conventions, taking risks).
- For accountability, transitional and fluent writers can give their feedback on paper.

*See sample chart, "Glow and Grow," on page 408.

Lesson 8.6 Text Features

I like how you used details here when you said a whale's skin was smooth like an egg.
I love how you organized your ideas in a sequence. It helped me learn more!
I like how you added so many visuals. Your drawings brought your facts to life.

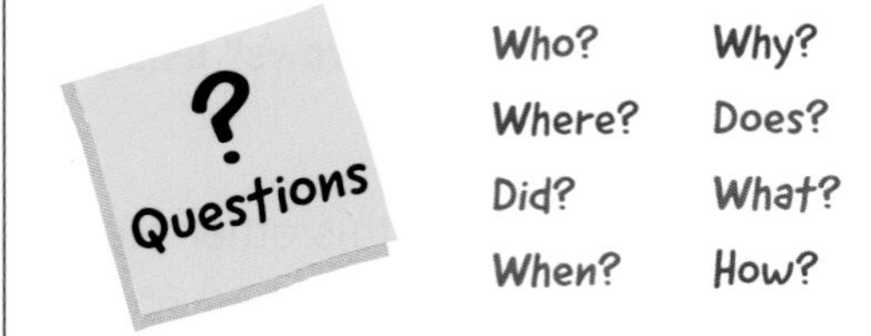

Why did you include this map?
What is the most important thing about electric cars?
Does your book have a glossary?
When did you become interested in Spain?

Lesson 8.10 Compliments and Questions

Reflection Questions

Take a moment to reflect on your work in this unit. Answer the questions honestly and provide evidence for your ideas—either in the writing itself or by attaching relevant work.

1. What did you learn about the genre? If you've written this genre before, what aspects of it are clearer to you now, or how has your understanding changed?
2. We spent a significant amount of time working on elaboration. What strategies worked best for you and why? Which didn't work, or which did you use less and why?
3. What did you learn about yourself as a writer?
4. Please copy/paste an example of your best work in this unit. Why are you particularly proud of it? What did it take for you to achieve this?
5. What's a goal you can set for yourself in our next unit of study? It could be a process goal (generating ideas, revision), a habits goal (volume, using time), or a quality of writing goal (word choice, structure).

Lesson 8.11 Reflect on Your Journey

GLOW	GROW
I love how you used examples and comparisons to bring your facts to life.	You could bring in 5 senses to add more specific details to your facts, too.
I love how you made your pictures and words match.	You could add more labels to teach your reader even more.
I love that you have vocabulary words in bold, and there's a glossary.	You could add text features—drawings or photographs—to help your words come to life.
I love how you have an "about the author" page!	You could add a "fun facts" page.

Lesson 8.12 Help Others Set Goals

 |

Appendices

Sample Units & Planning Template

Emergent Writers
List and Label Books

Time Frame: 5 Weeks

GOALS:

- Generate topics of personal expertise.
- Structure and organize writing with main idea and details.
- Use letters and letter sounds to spell phonetically.
- Use environmental print for writing words.
- Use conventions of spacing and punctuation to form simple sentences.
- Collaborate with peers to strengthen writing.

IMMERSION: (3–5 DAYS)

- **Read-Aloud Titles:**
  - *Exactly the Opposite* by Tana Hoben
  - *My First Library: Boxset of 10 Board Books for Kids*
  - *Freight Train* by Donald Crews
  - *National Geographic Readers: Go, Cub!* by Susan B. Neuman
- **Shared-Writing Topics:**
  - Our Class Alphabet Book
  - What We Learn at School
  - A Healthy Lunch
- **Interactive Writing Activities:**
  - Isolating beginning and ending sounds
  - Writing CVC words
  - Using words in the class environment
  - Capitalization, spacing, periods
- **Anchor Charts:** Brainstorming Topic Possibilities
  - 1.11 Just Get Started
  - 2.5 Say It, Hear It, Write It, Read It, Repeat
  - 6.2 How Do I Draw That?
  - 8.2 2B Real
  - 8.12 Help Others Set Goals

Weekly Focus: Getting Started With Simple Label Books

Day 1	Day 2	Day 3	Day 4	Day 5
1.11 Just Get Started *Think about a topic by talking, touching, drawing, and writing.*	**6.1 Pictures Can Teach** *Draft each page of the book by drawing a picture to show big ideas.*	**6.4 Label It** *Use labels in drawings.*	**3.1 I Spy with My Little Eye** *Use the space around you to get ideas.*	**6.2 How Do I Draw That?** *Draw ideas by using basic shapes and lines.*

Weekly Focus: Writing More Organized Books with Details

Day 6	Day 7	Day 8	Day 9	Day 10
5.1 How Will It Go? *Plan how a book can be organized using various text structures.*	**6.3 Put It Under a Microscope** *Show details by zooming in and drawing an object large.*	**2.1 Who's On First?** *Stretch out words by listening for the beginning sound.*	**2.2 First and Last** *Stretch out words by listening for the beginning and ending sounds.*	**6.7 Make It Match** *Write words to match the picture in each part of the book.*

Weekly Focus: Spotlight on Conventions

Day 11	Day 12	Day 13	Day 14	Day 15
6.8 From Labels to Sentences *Use the words:* The, my, a, an, our, this, *along with describing words to create simple sentences.*	**2.3 Stretch It Out** *Stretch out words by saying them slowly, listening for beginning, medial, and ending sounds.*	**2.9 Give Them Some Space** *Record a word, read it back, and place a spacer before writing the next word.*	**2.5 Say It, Hear It, Write It, Read It, Repeat** *Stretch out longer words with a specific process.*	**2.11 Give Them a Break** *Use end marks correctly by first saying and writing a sentence.*

Weekly Focus: Writing with Partners and Mentors

Day 16	Day 17	Day 18	Day 19	Day 20
1.22 Partners Are Resources, Too! *Partners can be helpful to generate ideas and gather feedback.*	**1.9 Talk It Out** *Talk with a partner to share information on a topic.*	**1.6 Borrow Ideas from Others** *Look through other books for inspiration.*	**1.17 Be a Copycat** *Study a mentor text for content, structure, and craft.*	**8.12 Help Others Set Goals** *Help students set goals for their writing.*

Weekly Focus: Proofreading and Publishing

Day 21	Day 22	Day 23	Day 24	Day 25
8.1 Pick and Choose *Select one book to publish that gives a sense of pride and appeals to the audience.*	**7.2 Read the Room** *Use resources in the room to check spelling.*	**7.3 Put an End to It** *Check for end punctuation.*	**8.2 2B Real** *Create realistic illustrations and other visual media.*	**8.8 Reach Your Audience** *Celebrate with a book or expert fair.*

Transitional Writers
All-About Books

Time Frame: 5 Weeks

GOALS:

- Generate ideas based on experience, expertise, and interest.
- Write topic sentences with supporting details.
- Elaborate on facts by extending sentences and using words: *most, all, some, many.*
- Include text features, sections, and domain-specific vocabulary.
- Use previously taught spelling patterns to spell new words.
- Form compound sentences.
- Incorporate publishing features to enhance writing.

IMMERSION: (3–5 DAYS)

- **Read-Aloud Titles:**
  - *Apples* by Gail Gibbons
  - *National Geographic Readers: Penguins!* by Anne Schreiber
  - *My Soccer Book* by Gail Gibbons
  - *Our Solar System* by Seymour Simon
  - *Sharks* by Seymour Simon
- **Shared-Writing Topics:**
  - All About School
  - All About _____ Grade
  - All About _____ (topic from content area)
- **Interactive Writing Activities:**
  - Using known spelling patterns for spelling words, adding end punctuation, and writing compound sentences
- **Anchor Charts:**

Class Chart of Topics

  - 1.18 Go with the Flow
  - 3.2 Think with Your Heart
  - 6.21 Say More
  - 7.9 Check Yourself!

 |

Weekly Focus: Writers Teach About Topics They Know Really Well

Day 1	Day 2	Day 3	Day 4	Day 5
1.1 Dream a Little Dream *Make book covers to represent the different topics to write about.*	**5.2 Make a List, Check It Twice** *List information about a topic across fingers; make a page for each.*	**3.2 Think with Your Heart** *Think of things that are loved.*	**6.26 Invite Your Reader** *Create an introduction that explains why topic was chosen and why it matters.*	**1.22 Partners Are Resources, Too!** *Partners can be helpful to generate ideas.*

Weekly Focus: Writers Say More About Their Topics

Day 6	Day 7	Day 8	Day 9	Day 10
1.7 Try It On for Size *Create a table of contents to see if there is enough to say on a topic.*	**6.29 Tell Me More, Tell Me More** *Start with a topic sentence and then elaborate.*	**3.10 Flaunt Your Expertise** *Think about topics of expertise.*	**6.21 Say More** *Use the sentence starters* most, all, some, many, *and* few *to elaborate on ideas.*	**6.20 Extend Your Facts** *Start with a fact and then add a second sentence.*

Weekly Focus: Writers Include Features and Different Parts

Day 11	Day 12	Day 13	Day 14	Day 15
6.45 Give Me a Sign *Include headings and subheadings that organize the writing.*	**1.17 Be a Copycat** *Study a mentor text for content, structure, and craft.*	**6.18 What Does That Mean?** *Use domain-specific words and terms.*	**6.6 Text Features Enhance Understanding** *Use visual text features to clarify and amplify information.*	**6.46 I Didn't Even Think of That** *Consider including additional sections for the topic.*

Weekly Focus: Writers Put Conventions to Work

Day 16	Day 17	Day 18	Day 19	Day 20
2.7 That Sounds Like ... *Spell words by listening for little words or word parts.*	**2.11 Give Them a Break** *Use end marks correctly by first saying and then writing a sentence.*	**1.18 Go with the Flow** *Don't get slowed down by spelling concerns.*	**2.15 Be Descriptive** *Be more precise by using adjectives to describe nouns.*	**2.23 Come Together** *Write compound sentences that connect ideas.*

Weekly Focus: Writers Proofread and Publish

Day 21	Day 22	Day 23	Day 24	Day 25
4.3 Stay Connected *Choose an idea that is cared about the most.*	**7.1 Do You Hear Me? Do You See Me?** *Reread to hear more sounds and add them to words.*	**7.9 Check Yourself!** *Use a checklist, independently or with a partner.*	**8.7 Publishing Features That Entice** *Create publishing features to entice readers.*	**8.8 Reach Your Audience** *Celebrate with a book or expert fair.*

Fluent Writers
Feature Article

Time Frame: 5 Weeks

GOALS:

- Generate topics of expertise and interest.
- Use nonfiction structures that best support the information.
- Consider audience when gathering information.
- Elaborate.
- Develop an informational voice with word choice and punctuation.

IMMERSION: (3–5 DAYS)

- **Read-Aloud Titles:**

Selections from periodicals with feature articles such as:
  - *Ranger Rick, Muse*
  - *Studies Weekly*
  - *Sports Illustrated Kids*
- **Shared-Writing Topics:**
  - Our School
  - Our School Nurse (or spotlight a teacher)
  - Something from Social Studies or Science (Ecosystems, What is Matter?)
- **Interactive Writing Activities:**
  - Creating compound and complex sentences
  - Using conjunctions
  - Playing with punctuation: commas, dashes, colons, and semicolons
- **Anchor Charts:** Brainstorming Topic Possibilities
  - Mentor Chart (see Lesson 1.17 for ideas)
  - 2.20 Put It in a Paragraph
  - 3.13 A Bit of Advice
  - 5.12 Build Me Up
  - 6.14 What's Your POV?
  - 7.8 Just Right Sentences
  - 7.9 Check Yourself!
  - 8.11 Reflect on Your Journey

 |

Weekly Focus: Generate Ideas with Mentors in Mind

Day 1	Day 2	Day 3	Day 4	Day 5
3.10 Flaunt Your Expertise *Think about topics of expertise.*	**3.12 Get Schooled** *Generate ideas by thinking of myriad topics learned in school.*	**3.13 A Bit of Advice** *Generate ideas by thinking about a problem.*	**2.20 Put It in a Paragraph** *Write in correct paragraph form.*	**1.7 Try It On for Size** *Create a table of contents to see if there is enough to say on a topic.*

Weekly Focus: Organize Considering Audience

Day 6	Day 7	Day 8	Day 9	Day 10
4.3 Stay Connected *Choose an idea that you care about the most.*	**4.5 What's Your Angle?** *Develop an angle for a writing piece.*	**5.12 Build Me Up** *Try out different text structures for writing.*	**5.13 Learn from a Mentor** *Consider additional sections by studying mentor texts.*	**4.9 Who's Your Audience?** *Consider the audience to develop ideas.*

Weekly Focus: Structure and Elaborate

Day 11	Day 12	Day 13	Day 14	Day 15
5.18 5Ws (and 1H} *Ask questions to research more: Who? What? When? Where? Why? How?*	**5.24 Grow Your Word Banks** *Create a word bank of domain-specific vocabulary.*	**6.14 What's Your POV?** *Consider the point of view to connect with an audience.*	**6.20 Extend Your Facts** *Start with a fact and then add a second sentence.*	**2.13 Keep 'Em Separated** *Separate descriptors of three or more with commas.*

Weekly Focus: Revise for an Audience

Day 16	Day 17	Day 18	Day 19	Day 20
6.47 Try On a New Structure *Consider text structure when revising.*	**6.42 Back It Up!** *Decide when to directly quote and when to paraphrase.*	**6.15 Be Specific** *Use precise language for nouns and action words.*	**6.31 Bring It to Life** *Use imagery rather than a dictionary definition to describe.*	**2.21 Rhythm Is Gonna Get You** *Create voice and rhythm by varying sentence lengths and beginnings.*

Weekly Focus: Proofread and Publish

Day 21	Day 22	Day 23	Day 24	Day 25
7.8 Just Right Sentences *Edit for fragments and run-on sentences.*	**7.9 Check Yourself!** *Use a checklist independently or with a partner.*	**8.3 Lay It Out** *Consider a layout for the picture book or article sections.*	**8.7 Publishing Features That Entice** *Create publishing features to entice readers.*	**8.11 Reflect on Your Journey** *Reflect on learning growth and set new goals.*

Unit Planning Template

Unit:

Time Frame:

GOALS:

-
-
-
-

IMMERSION: (3–5 DAYS)

- *Read-Aloud Titles:*
- *Shared-Writing Topics:*
- *Interactive Writing Activities:*
- *Anchor Charts:*

Weekly Focus:				
Day 1	Day 2	Day 3	Day 4	Day 5
Weekly Focus:				
Day 6	Day 7	Day 8	Day 9	Day 10
Weekly Focus:				
Day 11	Day 12	Day 13	Day 14	Day 15
Weekly Focus:				
Day 16	Day 17	Day 18	Day 19	Day 20
Weekly Focus:				
Day 21	Day 22	Day 23	Day 24	Day 25

 |